2010

PROMISE ME THE DAWN

PROMISE ME, the DAWN

Amanda MacLean

MULTNOMAH BOOKS
SISTERS, OREGON

Also by Amanda MacLean
Westward
Stonehaven
Everlasting
Gift of Love (A Christmas Joy)

PROMISE ME THE DAWN
published by Palisades
a part of the Questar publishing family

© 1996 by Amanda MacLean

International Standard Book Number: 0-88070-955-3

Cover illustration by Bill James
Cover designed by Kevin Keller
Calligraphy by Bill McConaughy, Portland, Oregon
Edited by Paul Hawley

The Holy Bible, New International Version (NIV) © 1973, 1984
by International Bible Society, used by permission of
Zondervan Publishing House.

The New King James Version (NKJV) © 1984 by Thomas Nelson, Inc.

Printed in the United States of America

For information:
QUESTAR PUBLISHERS, INC.
POST OFFICE BOX 1720
SISTERS, OREGON 97759

96 97 98 99 00 01 02 — 10 9 8 7 6 5 4 3 2 1

THE PROMISE

1906

Weeping may endure for a night,
But joy comes in the morning.

PSALM 30:5, NKJV

1

San Francisco

MOLLY QUINN UNLATCHED THE FRONT GATE and paused to look up at the imposing Nob Hill Victorian. Letting out a small sigh, she squinted, tilting down the wide brim of her straw hat against the bright spring sun. The house would fit into her plans nicely, she decided, assessing the gingerbread-trimmed porch, the dormer windows on the second floor, the ornate cupola on top.

Molly moved onto the cobbled pathway leading to the house. An English garden, growing recklessly in well-planned disarray, bloomed profusely on either side of the walk. Black-eyed Susans, wild roses, irises, and tiger lilies shot up here and there, their colors a splash of brilliance against the alabaster white of the house. The perfume of the blossoms, the wild and cheerful look of the garden, made Molly momentarily homesick for England.

She blinked away the threat of tears, straightened her back, and made her way across the stone walkway to the front stairs. She took them in a few quick steps, then rang the bell at the side of the heavy oak-and-glass entry door.

While she awaited the butler, Molly smoothed her long pale-blue-and-white striped skirt and fluffed the leg-o'-mutton sleeves on the matching jacket. Then, peering at her reflection in the glass, she licked her fingers and smoothed a few stray wisps of hair and adjusted the froth of silk flowers atop her hat's brim.

As usual, it had slipped distressingly cockeyed on her mass of dark curls. Letting out an impatient sigh, she yanked out the hat pin and prepared to re-anchor it. Still frowning at her reflection, she held the headpiece with one hand and worked the pin into her hair with the other.

Suddenly, Molly's reflection disappeared. She let out a small gasp and felt her cheeks color as she lifted her eyes. Through the glass, several inches above the place where her own image had been moments earlier, a young man stared back at her. Trying to look more composed than she felt, Molly gave him what she hoped was a confident smile as he opened the door.

"May I help you?" the man inquired pleasantly enough, though one eyebrow was raised in amusement.

Molly breathed a sigh of relief. At least he was only the butler, albeit the most handsome she'd ever laid eyes on. In a heartbeat, Molly took in everything about him, from his chiseled jaw to the cleft in his chin, from his swept-back auburn hair to his gray eyes, the color of the sky just before first light. And his voice. Though he'd spoken only a few words, it had the unmistakable tone of British aristocracy. A perfect touch for the ideal servant. Though she wondered why he would go to such lengths to please his Yankee employer. "You are...?" He left the question hanging.

"I'm here to inquire about the position," Molly finally said.

"The position?" He looked confused, though his gaze never left hers.

She nodded briskly. "Your people are looking for a domestic," she reminded him in case he'd forgotten.

"Of course," he finally said. "Please, come in." He opened the door wider. "I'm sorry," he said as he stepped back for Molly to enter. "We...ah...we were expecting someone...ah... quite different. The agency sent over a courier yesterday to tell us you were coming."

Molly swallowed hard. She hadn't come from any agency. She'd seen the position advertised in this morning's *Herald.* She quickly weighed the outcome of telling him so. "Well, in any case," she said finally, "here I am." She continued through the doorway, holding her skirt up daintily as she stepped across the threshold.

"Miss...ah...Miss?"

"Miss Quinn." Molly met his gaze evenly, though she noticed his still held a hint of merriment. She figured it had to do with her foolish primping moments earlier. "Miss Molly Quinn," she murmured, lifting her chin to add a touch of grace and sophistication.

"We thought the agency was sending a Mrs. Waldemar, an older woman. You can understand my confusion."

"Mrs. Waldemar? Oh, dear." Molly widened her eyes. "I don't know the details," she went on hurriedly. "But I gather she was suddenly indisposed." Then she found herself on the verge of giggling, so she bit her lip and frowned. Her sweet mother had always said she could tell when Molly had spun a yarn by the nervous giggle in her voice. Molly hoped it didn't show now. She gave the man a curt, professional nod.

Zachary MacAlister gazed at the young woman as she turned to face him in the entry. He had never seen anyone quite so charming.

At first impression, everything about Molly Quinn seemed delicate: her heart-shaped face and porcelain complexion, the tendriled curls at her forehead, the soft and cultured cadence of her voice.

She was petite; the top of her head barely reached his shoulder. But the fiery determination shining through her demeanor, an irrepressible spirit, made her seem almost statuesque. Not to mention irresistible. He'd been aware of that the moment he saw her adjust her hat and smile at her reflection in the window.

Now her hat, its brim as wide as her shoulders, tilted upward until her emerald eyes, regarding him calmly, appeared from under the mound of pale pink silk roses. Her eyes shimmered with light and life, and long, thick lashes rimmed them like kohl.

Already he hoped the Forresters would hire this Miss Molly Quinn. Though he wondered why the agency had sent over someone of such diminutive stature. He had specifically asked for a strong, robust woman.

Zach gave Molly an encouraging smile. "Please follow me," he said at last. "I'll take you to meet Mrs. Forrester. It is she who will be conducting the interview."

Molly nodded and stepped to Zach's side as they moved down the long carpeted hallway toward the parlor.

"You do understand about Mrs. Forrester?" Zach started to open the highly polished double oak doors leading to the parlor.

Before his hand reached the brass door handle, Molly stopped him abruptly, lightly touching the back of his hand. "Understand?"

"Surely the agency told you?"

She paled noticeably. "Told me…?"

"That she can be a rather difficult woman."

12

Molly tilted her head. "Difficult?"

He laughed. "A tyrant really. Perhaps they didn't want to scare you off by mentioning it."

"I've worked in difficult circumstances before. Not much frightens me." Just looking into this spirited young woman's face, somehow Zach knew this must be true.

"She can be quite demanding for someone so diminutive."

"And that is no problem either."

"They must have told you about the fetching."

She narrowed her eyes. "Fetching?"

"And lifting."

Molly hesitated briefly. "Ah, yes," she finally said, though for the first time Zach noticed a tentativeness about her demeanor—as if she really didn't know.

"Because of her condition."

"Of course," Molly said, with another of the quick nods he'd noticed earlier.

"Break a leg." He smiled and held the door open for Molly to enter.

Molly glanced up at him, a small frown creasing her forehead.

"An old theater term," Zach explained with a quick laugh as he followed her into the room. "It means that I wish you good luck for your performance."

"My performance..." Molly repeated softly. The young butler didn't know how correct he was. "Yes. Yes, of course," she murmured. "Thank you." Then she moved with him toward a small figure seated across the ornately furnished room. This was the tyrant?

"Gwennie…?" The young man's voice was gentle. Molly was puzzled. Though she had no experience working as a domestic, she certainly knew better than to address an employer on such familiar terms. "Gwennie, this is Miss Molly Quinn, sent over by the agency."

Molly's eyes adjusted to the dim light. A white-haired woman sat in a high-backed silk brocade chair near the parlor stove. Her legs rested on a matching footstool, a fringed lap robe covering them. Molly suddenly understood what the butler had earlier alluded to: the elderly woman was an invalid.

"Thank you," Mrs. Forrester said to the young man. "Now, leave us please. I would like to speak to Miss Quinn alone, if you don't mind."

"Of course. I thought you might." He moved a ladder-back chair next to the older woman, then nodded for Molly to be seated. "And do you want me to ask Kingsley to join you?" He paused briefly, looking at Mrs. Forrester before heading to the door.

"It's not Kingsley the young lady will be caring for, now is it?" Mrs. Forrester countered. "I think we'll just let him fuss with his roses. I'll send for him later, after I've made my decision."

Molly figured Kingsley was either Mr. Forrester, or the gardener. Though why the gardener would take part in her interview was beyond her comprehension.

"Come closer, Miss Quinn," the woman said after a moment's scrutiny. "My eyes aren't what they used to be."

"Yes, ma'am." Molly scooted her chair toward Mrs. Forrester as the older woman stared into her face. Now that Molly had grown accustomed to the dim light, she could see her pale blue eyes.

"I dare say you don't look a bit like what I ordered," the older woman finally pronounced, her surprisingly strong voice—with its hint of cultured English roots—not matching her frail frame. Then she glanced down at her legs. "'Tis difficult," she sighed deeply. "These are not much good anymore. Rheumatic soreness made them useless a long time ago." Again, she peered into Molly's face. "I am unable to walk. I am unable to fetch the things I need."

"You need someone to be your arms and legs."

"And I can no longer read. Weak eyes, my doctor says."

"So you also need someone to read to you."

The older woman nodded appreciatively. "You are familiar with the classics?"

"Yes, ma'am."

"Good. But from the looks of it, you might not be up to the other. You do appear a bit peaked, I dare say."

Molly sat up straighter in the chair and lifted her chin. "I'm strong, Mrs. Forrester. Whatever the job requires, I can do."

Mrs. Forrester regarded her thoughtfully. "Before we get to your references, Miss Quinn, tell me about yourself—besides the fact that you are a new arrival."

Startled, Molly gave her a quizzical glance.

"Your accent, dear. 'Tis as rich and thick as clotted cream. I would say you've been here less than a week." She settled back in her chair, seeming pleased at her speculation.

Molly drew in a deep breath. She had a feeling she'd met her match and might as well tell the truth. At least most of it. "I arrived a week ago Saturday," she said. "And being here—"

Mrs. Forrester interrupted. "Is the last place you thought you would ever find yourself?"

Molly smiled. "Yes. How did you know?"

"Acute powers of observation, dear. And the rest?"

"Actually, I came to join a relative, to become his business partner. But when I got here I found that he had become..." Molly faltered. Letters from Winston Carlisle-Jones, her favorite cousin, had convinced her to travel to America, land of golden opportunity, and join him in a scheme that would make their whole family rich. Molly's extended family had collected the needed funds for her journey. They had also gotten together quite a fat sum and deposited it in a London bank to be wired to San Francisco immediately upon her instruction. All their hopes and dreams rested on hers and Winny's investments.

But how could she tell her prospective employer what she'd discovered about Winny after she arrived? No, that secret was best kept to herself, at least for now. She sighed again. "I arrived only to find he'd become...quite indisposed," she finally added.

Mrs. Forrester nodded slowly. "So, I suppose that you found yourself without a place to stay, as well as without funds to return home."

Molly let out a long sigh. "Yes," she said simply. She was indeed too proud to wire home for the money that was only to be spent for investment purposes. "What you've supposed is the truth."

"And your references?"

"I'm sure you've guessed by now that there are none."

A gentle smile crossed Mrs. Forrester's wrinkled face. She nodded. "Yes, I had. And you've never worked as a domestic servant before, have you?"

Molly shook her head.

"Or as a companion?"

"No."

"You have no experience?"

Without answering, Molly stood to go. "I'm sorry I took your time unnecessarily, Mrs. Forrester."

"Dear, sit down." She gestured to the chair. "As far as I am concerned, we've only begun the interview. Now, as I said before, tell me about yourself."

Molly told the older woman about her large family of aunts and uncles, her brothers and sisters back home in the countryside near London, her ailing mother and hard-working father. She related stories of a happy childhood in a bustling houseful of people.

Molly even found herself telling Mrs. Forrester about the depression years of the 1890s, when there had not been enough food on the table for all to eat. And how her father worked three jobs at once, as a schoolmaster, a store clerk, and, during the worst of it, as a street cleaner. Her father had educated her well, from the sciences and classics to the rudiments of business and enterprise.

He had also encouraged her willingness to tackle hard work. Though Molly didn't say so to Mrs. Forrester, he had instilled in her the desire to create big dreams, telling her that they would provide the foundation for successful endeavors later on. And he had admonished her to do whatever was necessary to see that those dreams became reality.

"He taught me that one does what one has to do," Molly concluded, squaring her shoulders. "That's why, with or without experience or references, I know I can do the job you require. I would be privileged to work for you, Mrs. Forrester."

Mrs. Forrester seemed to ignore her last comment. Instead, she scrutinized Molly with pale, watery eyes. "It seems you love your family very much. It must be terribly difficult to be so far away from home." She paused, and for a moment only the loud

17

ticking of the clock on the mantel could be heard echoing in the silent room. "Why did you come to America, Miss Quinn?"

Molly took a deep breath. "It's a land where one may find opportunity to get on in the world. In terms of business success, particularly." She smiled softly. "At least that's what I've heard."

"You're ambitious." It was a statement, not a question. The older woman looked pleased. "So you don't plan to make a career of domestic help?"

"No." Molly hated to say so, knowing that in this case her honesty might cost her a job she desperately needed.

Mrs. Forrester laughed heartily. "I thought not. And all the better. But I do want to know—if your financial circumstances improve, will you then be returning to England?"

Until now, Molly hadn't even dared ask herself that question. But staring into the face of the woman in front of her, she suddenly knew the answer. And surprisingly, she realized that she had known from the moment she'd stepped onto the wharf at San Francisco Bay. "No. Of that you can be assured. This is my new home."

Mrs. Forrester took Molly's hands in her thin, frail fingers. "Dear, you've found employment—and a home—for as long as you like. I do need you to be here twenty-four hours a day. Your room will be right down the hall so that you can hear me call."

Molly squeezed the frail hands warmly. "Oh, thank you, Mrs. Forrester. You'll not be sorry. I promise."

"Now tell me where you're staying. I'll have Zachary send for your things."

"Zachary? The butler I met earlier?" The image of the handsome man flashed before her.

For a moment, Mrs. Forrester looked confused, then a smile crept over her withered face, and she began to chuckle. "Zachary? Our butler?" She laughed softly again. "Dear, dear, let me tell you all about our Zach. His is a splendid story. He's quite the—" A soft rap at the door interrupted Mrs. Forrester's words. "Come in," she called out pleasantly.

The young man Molly had assumed was the butler opened the door. A muscular and scowling gray-haired woman stood beside him. Without a glance in Molly's direction, he spoke directly to Mrs. Forrester. "Mrs. Waldemar from the agency is here. It seems she was the one intended for the interview, not Miss Quinn. In fact, Gwennie, according to Mrs. Waldemar, the agency knows nothing about a Miss Molly Quinn." His words were clipped. Mrs. Waldemar narrowed her eyes at Molly.

"Mrs. Waldemar is quite mistaken," Mrs. Forrester said calmly. "I have just found the perfect candidate for the position."

Zachary cut her off. "Gwennie, you're making a mistake."

Still seated, Mrs. Forrester leaned forward, drawing her shoulders up as tall as she could. "Maybe you didn't hear me, Zachary. I have just hired Miss Quinn. I am quite pleased with my choice." She smiled at Molly, then moved her calm gaze to the deflated Mrs. Waldemar. "I'm sorry. The position is taken. You might check down the street. I hear the Thorntons are looking for help. But I suggest you remove your sour look before applying. That alone will jolly well help you more than any references you might have."

Mrs. Waldemar sputtered a reply, then turned and fled from the room.

"If you don't mind," Zachary said to Molly, his voice cold as he strode toward the two women, "I would like to speak to my aunt in private."

"Your...aunt?" Molly stammered, feeling her face flush.

Zach arched a brow, but the withering look he gave her was not filled with amusement this time. "Yes, my aunt. My great-aunt, to be exact."

"But you led me to believe that you were hired help."

"I led *you?*" He spat out the words angrily. "What was all this folderol you gave me about the agency and poor Mrs. Waldemar being suddenly indisposed?"

"You didn't stop me when I referred to 'your people.'"

"You could just as easily have meant my relatives, but that's beside the point. Back to Mrs. Waldemar—"

Molly interrupted. "Relatives? How was I to know you were related to the owners of the house?" She gave him back his withering look. "Furthermore, you led me to believe that this gentle woman was a tyrant."

"He said that?" Mrs. Forrester laughed with hearty delight. "Children, children, children..." she said, to no one in particular. "I've made a wonderful choice. You remind me of Kingsley and me when first we met. I've not had such fun in years."

2

MOLLY STOOD BEHIND GWEN FORRESTER, who was seated before the dressing table mirror. Smiling at the older woman's reflection, Molly gently brushed out her waist-long white tresses.

"That's eighty-nine, dear—eleven to go."

Molly nodded. One hundred strokes each night. And Mrs. Forrester carefully counted every one. Next she would lay out the soft cloth ribbons for Molly to tie the curls. After a week, it had already become a ritual. As had the morning brushing and braiding and winding into a stylish twist at the nape of Gwen's neck.

"One hundred. Splendid, dear, as usual. I've not once felt you yank or pull. Now, for the curls. You wind, and I'll hand you the ties."

Molly parted a strand of the thinning hair, held it taut, then rolled it over her fingers. In a moment, it was tied in a neat bow. She repeated the process until Mrs. Forrester's entire head was covered in silver curls and rag ribbons. Molly couldn't help smiling at the image in the mirror. Mrs. Forrester's small, wrinkled face was nearly lost under the mass of curls.

The older woman patted her hair, looking pleased. "Molly, dear, whatever did I do without you?"

Molly helped the frail woman into her nearby wheelchair and steered it toward her bedroom. Kingsley Forrester had designed the chair—a stylish Queen Anne with two wheels from a bicycle and two from a child's wagon—for his wife while tinkering in his workshop. He'd been so pleased with the results that he quickly made two more, one for each floor of the mansion.

For the past several months, Gwen Forrester told Molly, her husband had been working on a device to hoist her, chair and all, from floor to floor. He'd knocked out walls to create a center shaft for the elevator. Hired workers joined him each day from dawn to dusk, creating a cacophony of drilling, pounding, and sawing that carried throughout the house.

"Dear?" Mrs. Forrester asked, as Molly lifted her into bed. "Would you mind terribly if I asked you to read longer tonight? Kingsley probably won't be upstairs for hours, and I'm feeling a tad restless."

"Is something wrong, Mrs. Forrester?"

"No, dear. It's just the weather. Too warm for this time of year. And still. For days now it seems we've had not a whisper of breeze. 'Tis the sort of thing that sets my heart to fluttering."

Still alarmed, Molly touched her fingertips to the older woman's forehead to check for fever. But her skin felt cool to the touch. "Maybe it would help to raise the windows."

"I believe it would. Do that, then run down to Kingsley's library and choose a volume of Shakespeare. I shall await your return with something racy in hand—perhaps *A Midsummer Night's Dream*."

Molly smiled. "I'll see what I can find."

"I do so enjoy the soothing sound of your voice. Which reminds me, I don't know how I'll make it through tomorrow without you. I realize I gave you the day off. But I shall miss your reading."

"Then I'll plan to be back here by your bedtime." Molly squeezed Mrs. Forrester's hand affectionately. "I enjoy our reading time, too."

Mrs. Forrester's wrinkled face broke into a smile. She patted her curls. "I feel better already. Go downstairs, now, dear. Return these," she gestured to a stack of books on the bedside table, "and see if you can find that Shakespeare volume."

Carrying the load of heavy books in her arms, Molly hurried from the bedroom toward the spiral staircase at the end of the hall. Lost in thought about being able at last to see her roguish cousin Winny the following day, she rounded a corner of the hallway.

At that moment, Zach strode toward his aunt's room, planning to find out why she'd given her new companion a day off on a Tuesday, the very day she was needed most. Gwen's doctor always called on Tuesday mornings, and her friends from the Ladies Temperance League called for tea in the afternoon. Tomorrow was also the day that he'd planned to head to the wharf to see about buying a fishing vessel advertised in the *Herald*.

Grumbling to himself about Miss Quinn's coming absence and the hardship it would cause for the family, he rounded the corner at full tilt.

Miss Quinn gasped audibly and jumped backward—just a heartbeat before the collision. "Sir!" Books flew upward, then landed with dull thuds as they hit the floor.

Zach glared at the young woman for a moment before stooping to pick them up.

"At least you could say you're sorry." She drew her lips into a straight line as he stacked the books in her arms one at a time.

"I dare say, you're too impatient, Miss Quinn. Not to mention that you assume I'll be rude without giving me the proper time to prove otherwise." He placed the last book atop her stack as he spoke. "I was about to say, 'I'm truly sorry,' but I wanted to undo the damage first. That's all."

Her lips softened into a smile, and he couldn't help noticing that they were the color of roses.

"No harm done, sir." She lifted her skirts and started down the stairs.

"Miss Quinn," he began. "I wanted to speak to you about tomorrow."

Turning, she looked up at him, holding the books in one hand, the banister with the other. "Yes?"

Something about her heart-shaped face as she regarded him—the flicker of something angelic in her expression—made Zach catch his breath. He paused, then swallowed hard. "Nothing, Miss Quinn." Zach wondered why his voice was suddenly husky. "Nothing at all."

He hurried to his aunt's room to bid her goodnight, and to volunteer to help at tea so that Miss Quinn could have her day off.

"Nonsense, dear," Gwen said a few minutes later, patting Zach's hand. "You go ahead with your plans. I have Cook Liu to help out in the kitchen and Kingsley close by, too. We'll get along just fine."

"Would you really tell me, Gwennie?" Zach laughed. "I have the feeling you'd never let on you needed us if I, or Kingsley, or even your new little Miss Quinn, said we had other places to be."

"You told Miss Quinn that I'm a tyrant, Zach. If I'm as soft as you described, I'm not much of a despot." She smiled lovingly up at him.

"You're a beloved tyrant, Gwennie. Much beloved."

He bent to kiss his aunt's withered cheek, then turned to leave.

Molly stood just inside the doorway. He let out a sigh, realizing that she had probably heard most of the conversation.

Their eyes met. And the room fell silent as they regarded each other. Again, Zach marveled at her expression. It was as if this young woman could see his soul—yet it wasn't in judgment. Quite the opposite. She seemed to be considering him with a sense of wonder. Or perhaps discovery.

For an instant, or maybe an eternity—Zach didn't know which—neither of them spoke. He finally moved toward her, his gaze locked on hers, then simply nodded as he passed through the doorway. He didn't trust his voice to speak.

For a few moments the only sound that could be heard was Gwen Forrester's soft chuckle. As Molly walked to her bedside, the older woman murmured, "Dear, dear, this is a frolic." She laughed softly again. "Child, sit down. It's time I told you all about Zachary MacAlister and his family."

Molly pulled her chair closer, wondering at the quickening of her pulse. "I'd like that," she said.

"Zach's from a titled family. His father is Stewart MacAlister, the Duke of Sommerset, with a large estate in Kent."

Molly was stunned. "I've heard the name, though I know nothing of the family itself." She considered the implications. "That means your nephew must also be a duke. That is, if he's the eldest son."

25

"No, he'll not inherit the title, nor any of the lands. There are three brothers in line ahead of him." Mrs. Forrester shook her head slowly. "There are other, rather tragic circumstances regarding his family. I'll not go into them now. But the part of his story Kingsley and I understand very well is that of missing the inheritance by order of birth."

Molly waited for her to go on.

"My father was the younger son of a duke. Ironically, Zachary's grandfather was my father's older brother, the one who inherited the title and lands. The original family was from Scotland. Charles MacAlister received the estate as a reward from King George II for helping defeat Bonnie Prince Charley in the eighteenth century. But then, I am going on, aren't I?" She laughed. "Well, anyway. Back to this century. Even if things had been different a generation back, as a woman, I wouldn't have inherited title or lands, anyway."

"Is that why you left England for America?"

The older woman chuckled. "Perhaps. But mostly I came for love."

"How long have you been here?"

"Dear, dear, many years now." She shook her head slowly. "Kingsley caught gold fever back in the fifties. I was younger than you, and desperately in love. I would have followed my man to the ends of the earth. As it was, the Mother Lode was almost that." She laughed softly. "Oh, the tales I could tell about that part of our lives. I wanted riches and stability, and Kingsley wanted wild adventure."

Her pale eyes softened with the memories. "We didn't strike gold in the fields, but we certainly found the adventure Kingsley craved. Then—I must say, at my instigation—we opened a store catering to the miners. Right in downtown

26

Columbia. Then we opened other stores in Sacramento, then San Francisco and San Jose.

"About that time, I found myself with child, so I said to my Kingsley, 'We need to live in a city, raise our children where schools and shops and friends are abundant.'" She chuckled. "So we moved here, to San Francisco. The original house was small, one story. Modest by anybody's standards.

"Then it was destroyed by an earthquake."

Molly looked at her sharply. "Earthquake?"

"Oh, yes, dear. We have them quite often, you know." Reacting to Molly's expression, she smiled gently. "But we'll save that part of the story for another time."

Molly nodded, and Gwen hurried on as if anxious to get past some frightening memory. "Anyway, after the big quake, Kingsley came up with the plans to build this place." She looked proud as her gaze moved across the room. "He said it would be the finest in all San Francisco. And he was right. It still is. There might be some bigger nowadays, but back then, all the rest seemed to shrink in comparison."

"Where are your children now?"

"I only had the one child live past age five." Her eyes filled with tears, and a frail hand moved above her heart. "My other babies are buried out back." She smiled softly. "And the one who lived—Lawton—lives in Sacramento. We've turned over our entire business to him. Everything's in his name. Kingsley no longer wanted the encumbrances—lock, stock, and barrel, as they say in this country. And Lawton has worked hard to earn it."

"And your nephew?" Molly couldn't help asking. "How long has he been here?"

Mrs. Forrester regarded Molly intently. "Zach's been with us

27

just six months. Though he won't be here much longer. Already he's traveled up and down the coast looking for a place to start his fishing business. Last he said, he's chosen Monterey. And I've no doubt that he'll do it. He's got an independent streak. Doesn't want help from us, his family, or anyone.

"Even if he'd been the Duke's eldest son, I dare say he would have turned his back on title and wealth. Zach means to live simply, as far away from material riches as possible." She shook her head slowly, still watching Molly. "At least that's his plan," she added solemnly. "His mother's written me that whatever that young man sets out to do, there's no stopping him. He's a stubborn one, that boy. Dear, dear, he is just like me."

The next morning, Molly awoke at dawn, stretched, and moved to the window of her small room, looking out over the waking city. Again, the air was balmy and clear. Not a whisper of a breeze, she noticed, just as Mrs. Forrester had observed the night before. And quiet. Eerily quiet. No early morning music of chirruping birds, chattering squirrels, or yipping dogs nosing about.

But then, Molly knew only London with its clamor and bustle. Maybe San Francisco was a different, more subdued city. She'd heard that fog often shrouded the place, though she'd seen little trace of it since her arrival. A heavy mist would be welcome, she decided. Perhaps its familiarity would help her shake this strange sense of foreboding.

A shiver spidered down her spine. Molly turned from the window and hurriedly dressed in a long, slightly flared skirt and full-sleeved shirtwaist, anxious to be on her way to visit Winny.

Squinting into the dressing table mirror, she pinned her

long hair into a high twist, then adjusted her straw hat atop the loose curls. Finally satisfied with the results, she made her way down the stairs to the front door, not intending to join the others for breakfast.

But as she moved past the dining room door, Kingsley Forrester called to her.

"Molly, dear, do come in and join me." He was sitting alone at the linen-covered table. Nearby windows overlooked his rose garden. Above the table hung an ornate crystal chandelier, polished to gleaming. The early morning sun struck it to perfection, showering the room with prisms of light—and their shadows, she noticed.

Molly smiled. How could she resist? Both Kingsley Forrester and his elegant breakfast room beckoned her.

"Cook Liu has made popovers, and we've some fig preserves that my Gwennie put up last summer. Please, come, sit down." He patted a chair near him, then shouted toward the kitchen, "Liu, get this little lady some coffee. And hurry! It's too early to be without for long."

Molly smiled up at the tall white-haired gentleman as he stood and pulled out her chair. She had never known anyone his age with quite as much energy. He was agile and talkative, in fact, a splendid conversationalist on just about any subject. Each day, he rose at dawn, cheerfully looking forward to working on a new wheelchair design, or overseeing some new phase of the elevator construction, puttering in his greenhouse, or pruning his roses.

Cook Liu, a seemingly ageless Chinese man, brought in the silver coffee server and filled the delicate cup at Molly's place setting.

"'Tis an early hour to be up and about," Kingsley Forrester

said, with a smile. And Molly thought—as she had dozens of times since her arrival—how much she enjoyed hearing the faint cadence of her mother country in his voice. "Off for a jolly day of sightseeing in the city?"

Molly reached for her coffee, considering her answer. But before she could lift her cup to her lips—or speak—a low rumble erupted from the depths of the earth. It was followed by a quick jolt. A few seconds of silence. And then another shudder.

Molly set down her cup with a clatter. She grabbed the table to keep her balance. But it moved with her. Above the table, the chandelier jingled and danced.

It was over in seconds, but Molly's heart pounded rapidly for a few minutes longer.

Across from Molly, Mr. Forrester laughed nervously. "Your first earthquake, dear? What did you think of it?" His voice was light, but Molly noticed his skin's pallor. He stood and reached to halt the chandelier's gentle swaying.

"Yes," Molly breathed. "My first."

"I'm sure Gwennie slept right through it. This little shaker was nothing. We have them from time to time. These we don't worry about. It's the others…" He paused as Cook Liu refilled his coffee cup.

Molly let out a shaky breath.

He laughed again. "Back in sixty-five was the worst in recent memory. We had just finished building our first house at this location. Hadn't even moved in yet. It was a good thing. That quake threw the little house right off its foundation." He shook his head slowly and took a sip of coffee. "Just picked it up like a toy and tossed it a few feet to one side."

Molly shivered, considering such violent strength coming out of the earth.

Mr. Forrester reached for her hand and patted it gently. "You'll get used to our little shakers, dear. They're part of life in California." He smiled at her over the rim of his cup. "Now, where were we before the earthquake interrupted us? Ah, yes. Now just what calls you away so early in the morning?"

"I've got a relative in the city. A cousin. I plan to pay him a visit today." Molly spread fig preserves onto a hot popover, noticing that her hands had finally stopped trembling. "He— my cousin Winny—was to meet my ship when I arrived, but he didn't show up. I did find out, however, that he'd met with dire circumstances that detained him."

"Dire circumstances?"

"Yes." Again, Molly wondered how much she should say about Winny. Knowledge of his whereabouts could lead to her dismissal, and she needed her job too desperately to take any chances. "He'd gotten himself into a dreadful state," she said simply.

Mr. Forrester regarded her solemnly, then changed the subject. After a few minutes, she excused herself and headed out the door.

As she walked along the cobbled street in the bright sunshine, Molly thought about the long and difficult day ahead. She had planned it down to the minutest detail. First, she would catch the Nob Hill cable car, take it to the waterfront district, then board a ferry for Sausalito on the north shore of the bay. Once there, she planned to hire a carriage to take her the rest of the way to Winston Carlisle-Jones's last-known residence.

A few minutes later, she stepped onto the cable car and found a seat halfway back. The bell jingled as they began moving down the hill. Molly sighed deeply. Yes, this was going to be a most difficult day. Cousin Winny had a lot of explaining to do. What she'd been told by his former employer wasn't something a person could easily explain.

"I don't trust her." Zachary had joined his uncle at the breakfast table. Though the older man had finished eating, he lingered over a cup of coffee and the morning paper.

"I disagree." Kingsley Forrester set aside the *Herald* and gave Zach his full attention. "Miss Quinn has given us no reason to be unhappy with her work. In fact, Gwennie could not be happier."

Zach took a sip of coffee. "She lied about being sent by the agency."

"Miss Quinn wanted the job. Gwennie said she was desperate. This morning she alluded to having found her cousin—her only contact here—in some unfortunate state when she arrived. She is young. Alone. That must have been difficult. I admire her for having the gumption to seek work like this."

"You do know she has never held any position before this? That she had no references?"

"Of course. Gwennie told me as much. That's what I meant. Miss Quinn has spirit."

Zach shook his head slowly. "I don't know, Kingsley. There's something about her. Something secretive..."

Kingsley chuckled. "I can see why that might bother you. Or maybe I should say, interest you."

"What do you mean?" Zach felt himself color.

He raised an eyebrow and chuckled again. "You do know what they say, don't you?"

Zach pushed his chair away from the table, crossing his long legs at the ankles. He knew one of his uncle's lighthearted hom-

32

ilies would follow. "No, what?"

"There's nothing quite so attractive—or more lethal to the heart, mind, and spirit—as a woman of mystery. Especially a comely woman such as Miss Quinn."

Zach laughed heartily. "And who, may I ask, is 'they'?"

"You're looking at him, son." He grinned.

"You're experienced in these matters?"

"After fifty-eight years of marriage, my Gwennie's still a mystery to me." The deep creases in Kingsley's face softened. "She's the most splendid, mysterious woman in the world."

Then Kingsley leaned toward Zach, his expression serious. "Let our Miss Quinn have her secrets, son. I'm sure she'll tell us anything we need to know in her own good time. Let me emphasize, if we *need* to know." He paused. "Trust her, Zach."

The younger man nodded. His uncle was probably right. He should at least trust the young woman until she proved him wrong.

Minutes later, Zach strode down the street toward the cable car station to board a car for the waterfront district. His appointment was set for noon. He had plenty of time. Besides, the boatyard—within a stone's throw of the Ferry Building—wouldn't be difficult to find.

3

MOLLY REACHED THE FERRY BUILDING at the waterfront and took her place in line at the ticket window. Finding that the next boat to Sausalito was scheduled for an hour and a half later, she decided to take a short walk around the waterfront district.

The sun was high as she stepped onto the wharf. She breathed in the smells of the salt water and sea and listened to the music of the gulls in flight. A breeze off the water gently lifted the curls that had slipped down on her forehead.

Fishermen and dockhands called to each other, and shopkeepers looked up and nodded as she passed. A few fat seals tumbled and splashed and barked from underneath the wharf, and the deeper grunt of a sea lion echoed from behind a docked vessel. Pelicans glided overhead, touched down on fishing boats to scavenge for scraps of bait, then swooped into the air again, their booty hanging awkwardly in their bills.

Molly strolled to the end of the long wharf. A cloak of mist lay offshore, soft and familiar, reminding her of home. Ferries churned by, laden with San Franciscans, young and old. As snatches of conversation drifted across the water, she could make out the distinct sounds of Chinese, French, and German, a thick Irish brogue, the familiar tones of the British and

Australians. The claims of the San Franciscans must be true, she concluded. San Francisco, the crown jewel of California, was not only the largest city west of the Mississippi, it was also the most cosmopolitan. No matter how much she missed England, this place seemed wildly exciting, containing the best of everything the world had to offer, from its people to its splendid beauty.

She let out a satisfied sigh and smiled, gazing up at the sky-line. San Francisco's hills were covered with some of the finest examples of modern architecture that could be found. The lofty dome of the Spreckles Morning Call building gleamed in the morning sun. In the nearby financial district, row upon row of skyscrapers with their ornate façades spoke of the city's wealth and seemingly indestructible vitality.

Farther up the hill, Molly could make out the elegant Palace Hotel, where news accounts reported Enrico Caruso would stay during his visit in April. The hotel's fame was widespread, attracting royalty and leading businessmen, artists, and politi-cians from around the world. She'd heard that its famous guests had included Napoleon Bonaparte, J. P. Morgan, Oscar Wilde, and Teddy Roosevelt. Long before she left London, Molly had heard of its palatial rooms and gardens and attention to guest comfort and safety, even down to its newly installed fire sprin-klers.

For a long time, she gazed at the city, now shimmering in the sun under a brilliant blue sky. Then suddenly, the sun slid behind the gathering fog, and the skyline disappeared, almost as if swallowed by a dark and heavy gloom.

Molly shuddered and quickly looked away, glancing back at the tower clock on the Ferry Building. It was nearly time to catch the Sausalito ferry. Within minutes, she was hurrying across the building's polished marble floors to the boarding area.

Zach stepped off the trolley car in the center of the waterfront district. The Ferry Building was directly in front of him, the shipyard just beyond. Checking his pocket watch, he then strolled toward the shipyard and his waiting appointment. He glanced at the passengers milling about the deck of the ferry as he passed by. Then he stopped and squinted into the crowd.

There was no mistaking the petite Molly Quinn with her dark hair and straw hat. She was moving toward the railing at the bow, looking north across the water.

Zach hurriedly read the ferry schedule outside the building, checked his watch again. It was 11:30, and this obviously was the ferry to Sausalito.

Sausalito? He'd been in San Francisco only six months, but it was long enough to know why most people traveled across the bay to Sausalito. Without hesitation or a second thought about the appointment he was going to miss, Zach strode into the building, tossed the ticket agent a coin, and demanded a ticket.

As he sprinted through the Ferry Building doorway, the gangplank was lifting slowly. He waved and shouted for the dockhands to hold it down. Moments later, he raced across the wooden planks. It lifted again, and the ferry pulled away from the dock.

Zach slipped into the crowd, noticing as he did so that Molly was still looking out over the bow and hadn't seen him board.

The bay was choppy, and by the time the ferry was halfway

to Sausalito, the fog had settled in, bringing with it a bone-chilling dampness to the air. In the distance, a foghorn cried its mournful tones.

Zach stayed in the rear of the ferry. To assuage his guilt, he told himself that he was following Molly for the good of the family. He simply wanted to see firsthand the "dire circumstances" that had befallen her relative. If his suspicions were correct about Molly's destination—and her cousin's residence—Kingsley and Gwennie had been far too trusting. And it was up to Zach to see that no harm befell them.

Nearly an hour after leaving the dock at San Francisco, Molly stepped again onto solid ground in the small fishing village of Sausalito. She had no time to waste looking at the sights in this charming town. Not as many motorcars were on the streets as in San Francisco. She hailed a horse-drawn carriage and told the cabbie her destination.

"It's about ten miles from here," he told her. "You sure you want to go...alone?"

Molly nodded and stepped into the carriage as he held open the door.

The cabbie shrugged. "Okay by me, Miss. You *do* know what you're doin', right?" He squinted into her face.

"I've no doubt about it," she said. "But I'll want you to wait for me when we get there."

"I'll have to charge you for the time."

"All right. I won't be long."

The cabbie climbed to the driver's seat and flicked his whip over the horse's back. The vehicle lurched forward. As they moved away from the bay, the heavy fog receded and she could see the rolling hills of the countryside. The spring rains had colored the grasses pale green, and live oaks dotted the hillsides, surrounded by wildflowers of purple and gold. The beauty was incongruous with her destination.

The carriage swayed as it rounded the hilly curves. Molly held onto her wide-brimmed hat, feeling it had fallen off to one side. She anchored it again with the hat pin, wishing she had a mirror.

Then she sighed, wondering why she'd bothered. Her destination certainly didn't require perfection of dress or coif.

The cabbie suddenly halted the horse. "There it is," he called down to her. "Take a look out yonder. It's quite a sight!"

Molly peered through the carriage window. Across the valley, through the fog, she could barely make out the shapes of the long, low-profiled buildings. But one stood out from the others. It was unmistakable. The guard tower.

Molly nibbled at her bottom lip. "So this is it," she whispered to herself. "This is San Quentin."

In another vehicle a few miles back, Zach asked the driver to halt. "I realize I just told you to follow the carriage ahead, but I'm curious. Is this the way to the prison?"

The man laughed coarsely and spat at the ground. "There's only one reason folks take this road."

"San Quentin?"

The cabbie laughed again. "That's right, San Quentin. Home of murderers, thieves, and downright crazy-boned mean critters."

"You're sure nothing else is down this road?"

"Sure as I'm sittin' here."

Zach drew in a deep breath. His suspicions had been confirmed.

"Only ones travelin' out here are criminals or their kin." He grunted a laugh. "The latter's probably the category of your missy up ahead."

Zach's voice was harsher than he intended when he spoke. "You can turn around now."

"Wha—?"

"I said turn around. Take me back to the Ferry Building."

"Huh," he snorted, nodding his head as if calculating a lower fare. "Whatever you say."

The cabbie abruptly turned the vehicle toward Sausalito. As it rattled along and later, on the trip back across the bay, Zach tryed to sort out his feelings.

What exactly had he discovered? That Miss Quinn was related to a criminal? It was probably through no fault of her own. She'd arrived from London to find her cousin in "dire circumstances," as she called it.

On the other hand, they knew nothing about Miss Quinn, her background, or her family. Only what she had told them.

What if there was more to it than that? She was ambitious. Even his aunt had confided that much about her conversation with Miss Quinn. But how ambitious? More than one young woman had come to America in search of riches, preying on the elderly and infirm to realize their dreams. Perhaps her 'cousin' (if he was even that) had chosen Kingsley and Gwennie Forrester and made the arrangements for Miss Quinn to arrive just at their moment of need.

But Molly? He pictured her angelic face, her eyes sparkling with emerald light, her smile that caused his heart to skip each time he saw it. And just breathing her name—Molly—made him think of rushing brooks and whispering breezes. *Molly*.

But could this same young woman be capable of crime? Zach squinted into the darkening late-afternoon sky. Something inside him cried out against any thought of it.

There was only one wise solution. He needed to protect Kingsley and Gwennie, but he also needed to be careful of making false accusations. As the ferry glided across the bay, Zach considered his choices. By the time it docked in San Francisco, he had decided what he would do.

First he would wire his father in Kent, asking him to make inquiries into Molly Quinn's family, particularly the relative housed in San Quentin. Then he would simply watch the young woman very carefully, making sure she did nothing that would bring harm to his aunt and uncle.

He didn't want them to be worried while he awaited word from the duke. So he would say nothing of the matter until he had some facts in hand.

"So it's true, then? You are guilty?" Molly stared at her cousin through the wire barrier that separated them. A guard stood nearby, listening to every word. Molly fought to keep her tears from spilling down her cheeks. "How could you, Winny?" Her voice was little more than a whisper. She reached for his fingers through the wire.

Her cousin's freckled face seemed paler than she'd ever seen it. He brushed his bright red hair from his forehead, then nodded. "I never thought it would turn out like this, Molly. I didn't." His voice wavered. This young man sounded nothing like the carefree, lively cousin she'd so esteemed in London. He'd had dreams of getting on in the world, "climbing to the top of the heap," he'd always said.

"You mean you didn't think you'd get caught?" There was a big difference, and Molly hoped that wasn't what he meant.

He didn't answer, and Molly saw a touch of defiance in the angle of his head.

"Why did you do it, Win? You wrote that things were going jolly well. You said if I'd join you, we'd make investments through your company, better the whole family."

"It was a lie. And I didn't want to face you with the truth. I was working as a flunky, a common bookkeeper. Not investing other people's money, the way I said. Not working my way to the top. I wanted the family to think I'd finally made something of myself, that I was getting on famously, so I wrote all those lies."

"But you asked me to join you. Surely you knew I'd find out the truth when I got here."

"I never thought you'd come, Molly. I didn't think you could afford it. I had no idea that all our family and friends would pitch in and send you."

"So, you tried to get rich fast."

He nodded, not meeting her eyes.

"To impress me, and the others."

Winny shrugged slightly, still not looking up. "I started making deposits to fictitious accounts, then withdrew those funds to invest. Made a lot of money for a while. I paid back all of what I initially borrowed. Then I got greedy. I borrowed a larger amount, invested again. That's when I lost nearly all of it. My employer got suspicious. Made inquiries..." His voice trailed off, and he let out a long sigh. "Of course, everything's gone now. Including my job. I can't even go home again." He laughed bitterly.

Molly squeezed his hand. "You haven't hurt anyone but yourself. I can't say our family will understand, but it's for you to tell them about your muddle, not me."

"But surely you will sail back to England." His voice faltered. "Soon, I would suppose. And the family will want to know why you've returned so suddenly. You'll have to tell them."

She shook her head. "I've decided to stay. I've taken employment."

"You have, now?"

"Yes, I'm a companion to an older woman up on Nob Hill. It's quite a splendid place to be." She smiled. "At least temporarily."

"I'm glad you'll be here, Molly. Just knowing you're nearby makes me not quite so lonely." His expression seemed to soften.

"I want to go through with our plans, Winny. And I'll need your help."

"Investments?"

"Yes. The family paid my passage here for a purpose. I intend to see it through."

Winny smiled. "So, our enterprise shall continue after all. 'Tis music I'm hearing now, dear Molly."

She was glad to see his mood lighten. He seemed more like the Winny of her childhood. "We don't need to move fast. You were in a hurry. And as you said, you got greedy. We'll take our time, study our options. Will you help me?" She paused, her gaze locked on his. "And our investments will be completely legal."

Then, for the first time since she arrived, a wide smile split Winny's pale face. "Legal?" He raised an eyebrow, then laughed at his own joke. "Actually, I'm not sure there's much I can do from in here, legal or otherwise."

She leaned forward, earnestly. "We'll work together, Winny. You tell me what I need to investigate. I'll get the numbers, the information. You study everything I bring you. We'll calculate our every move very carefully. When we're ready, I'll send for the money."

"It is still in London?"

"Ready to be wired. I'll just need to say when."

Winny grinned again.

"Though I dearly love my position with the Forresters, I didn't come to America to work as a companion for the rest of my life."

He threw back his head and laughed. "That's my cousin Molly."

Nearby, the prison guard stared at them blankly, seeming to listen to every word.

Zach paced the floor of his room, awaiting Molly's return. It was dusk and a heavy fog blanketed the ground.

On his way back from the waterfront district, he'd taken the trolley downtown and wired his father in London to make inquiries about the Quinn family. He'd even asked the duke to investigate any connection Molly Quinn might have with San Quentin. Of course, discovering the answers to his questions could take weeks.

Now, as he waited for Molly, he wondered at the wisdom of keeping the information from Kingsley and Gwennie. Truth was, he felt a bit sheepish for having followed Molly. After all, as Kingsley had earlier told him, a young woman is entitled to her secrets.

He pulled back the lace curtain and stared into the fog.

Kingsley was probably right. But when those secrets involved a visit to San Quentin, that was quite another matter.

Down the street a small, shadowy figure made her way toward the house. As she drew closer and into the soft glow of the streetlight, Zach could see Molly's proud and unmistakable carriage as she strolled purposefully toward the gate. He couldn't help smiling. She might be petite, but the way she tilted her chin upward and gazed at the house, a resolute expression gracing her face, there seemed to be an inner strength, even courage, within her.

Could this beautiful young woman be wrapped up in some illegal doings? It didn't seem possible. But what if he was wrong? After all, he felt responsible for his elderly aunt and uncle's well-being. And she—someone they knew very little about—was living under the same roof.

As he watched Molly unlatch the gate and step toward the house, he suddenly had an idea. If he could befriend the young woman, win her confidence, then perhaps he could find out firsthand about her dealings. By the time his father wired him the results of his investigation, Zach would have conducted his own.

Zach removed his jacket, slung it over the oak coat valet, then pulled from his wardrobe a change of clothes for supper. Meals taken at the Forresters' were relatively formal affairs, though never stuffy. Not with Gwen and Kingsley's lively leading of the conversation.

But it wasn't just supper that made Zach anticipate a pleasant evening ahead. No, tonight he planned to find a time to speak with Miss Quinn. Alone. It would be the first step in winning her trust.

And it wouldn't be an unpleasant task. He smiled, pulling on his shirt. Not in the least.

4

MOLLY FINISHED READING the passage in which Theseus, Duke of Athens, was about to marry Hippolyta, the Amazon queen, then closed the worn leatherbound book.

Mrs. Forrester smiled with satisfaction and patted Molly's hand. "Well done, dear. Well done. You read as though you were an actress on stage. Your voice, your inflections. Even the voice you use for Puck is hugely realistic." She sighed contentedly. "I'm so looking forward to Hermia and Lysander. With your bent toward acting the parts, their trip into the woods is going to be a treat. But I'm too weary to keep my eyes open a moment longer. You go now, dear, and I'll see you in the morning."

Molly tucked the covers under Mrs. Forrester's chin. "Please call if you need me. I plan to walk a bit in the garden. After that, I'll be back in my room straightaway."

Mrs. Forrester raised an eyebrow. "You take your time, dear. It's a wonderful night for a stroll. And there's no place like Kingsley's rose garden. It's just this side of heaven."

Molly, resisting an urge to kiss Mrs. Forrester's withered cheek, quietly laid the book on the bedside table and put out the lamp. Within minutes, she had slipped on her coat and made her way downstairs, through the library, to the French doors that led to the garden.

She stepped down the wide concrete stairs and onto the path leading to the rose garden. The fog had cleared somewhat, and a soft half-moon glowed through the branches of the tall junipers that lined the gravel pathway.

Molly drew in a deep breath. The air was fresh and pleasant, almost balmy in its dampness. The fragrance of woodsmoke drifted toward her from one of the large Victorian's many chimneys, intermingling with the scent of roses.

A mockingbird trilled from one of the junipers, paused, then sang again. It was answered by another bird on the far side of the garden. Around them crickets chirped. Now and then, the cheerful croaking of frogs from a distant pond carried toward her on the breeze.

She passed an ornate marble fountain, feeling its spray and enjoying the sounds of the flowing water as it dripped down tiers of seashell-shaped bowls.

A moment later, Molly came into a small clearing. Soft lamplight fell on the roses. Two small wrought-iron and wood-slatted benches graced one end of the garden, and Molly happily settled onto one, pulling her cloak tighter against the chill.

"Good evening, Miss Quinn." A deep voice interrupted her reverie.

Molly turned. Zach MacAlister entered the clearing and lolled against the iron lampstand, a thoughtful expression on his face, his jacket held carelessly over one shoulder. Molly briefly wondered if he'd followed her, then dismissed the thought. The son of a duke, the nephew of her employer, would have no reason to trail after her on a nighttime stroll.

"Mr. MacAlister," she murmured, still looking up at him in surprise.

Zach's eyes smiled into hers as he walked nearer. "Gwen's sleeping?"

Molly nodded and returned his smile. "She drifted off after she'd had her fill of *A Midsummer Night's Dream*."

"She does enjoy her Shakespeare. What a delight for Gwen that you can read it with the 'inflection'—as she says—that she so enjoys."

Molly nodded toward the opposite bench. "Would you care to sit down, Mr. MacAlister?"

"Only if you'll call me Zach." He settled his lanky frame onto the bench.

"Then you must call me Molly. 'Miss Quinn' always reminds me of my maiden aunt." She laughed softly.

"All right, Molly."

For a moment, neither spoke. Molly gently touched a rose on a nearby bush, lifting it to her face to drink in the fragrance. "It is lovely out here," she said, after a moment. "A sanctuary from the world. I think a person could forget all her woes after a few minutes in such a garden."

"Surely you don't speak of yourself, Molly."

She laughed softly. "Don't we all have our share, Zach?"

"Ah, but you're answering a question with a question."

"If Socrates can, it follows that I can as well."

He laughed appreciatively. "Touché, dear Molly. Touché."

"Mrs. Forrester tells me you've come to America to seek high adventure." Molly enjoyed watching the handsome man across from her, the way he swiped back his auburn hair, the way his gray eyes reflected the soft glow of the lamplight, the way he settled back against the ridiculously small and fancy settee, nearly overpowering it with his physical presence.

"Adventure?" He chuckled, crossing his ankles and laying

an arm along the back of the bench seat. "I suppose that's one way of looking at it." Then his expression turned serious. "Actually, I came here to simplify my life." He frowned as if wondering whether to tell her more. "You see, my family is rather complicated...." His voice trailed off. Frowning, he didn't go on.

Molly suddenly felt sad for him. "You didn't want to spend life in the manor?"

He looked surprised. "That's part of it. How did you know?"

She smiled gently. "Mrs. Forrester told me."

"Ah, yes. She does like to tell tales. What else did she say?"

"Only that you're planning life on the high seas."

"Not quite the high seas, I suppose. I just want a small vessel for fishing, only large enough to make a living. I've always loved the ocean. Sailing has long been a passion, even before I left home."

"Why here? England, it would seem, offers opportunities just as grand."

"Years ago, I read a book called *Two Years Before the Mast* by Richard Henry Dana. Though he wrote it in 1841, Dana describes the California coast in a way that captured my heart and mind. Even before I arrived, I knew it was to be my home. Especially after I visited Monterey Bay, just south of here. There's no more beautiful place on earth."

Zach's expression softened, and for a few moments, he seemed lost in thought. Then he again met her gaze and laughed lightly, almost as if embarrassed to be caught spinning daydreams. She smiled, and he went on.

"I've investigated and found that there's a good market for fishing out of Monterey. Part of a growing canning industry. Salmon, sardines, some abalone. That sort of thing."

"It sounds like an empire in the making."

His brows furrowed into a frown. "What do you mean? I have no intention—"

Molly interrupted him with a small chuckle, surprised at his reaction. "Don't worry," she said. "I'm not sentencing you to a life building a fishing and canning empire. I simply meant that it might be a good investment. Good fun to captain a fishing boat, but good business to own the boat, the fleet—the entire enterprise."

"That sort of thing doesn't interest me in the least."

"It does interest me." She lifted an eyebrow coquettishly, enjoying her own dream possibilities. "Immensely."

"So you've got a bit of a business mind yourself?" His tone was light, almost teasing, but his gaze held hers with steely intensity. "And is that why Miss Molly Quinn has come to America? To build an empire of her own?"

For a moment, Molly, chin tilted upward, merely held his eyes with her own. Something behind his expression disturbed her. As if his words weren't spoken merely from idle curiosity. She shrugged and laughed again, softly. "Ah, now how could a mere house companion have such grand designs?"

"You're doing it again, Molly." His features softened. But Molly wondered whether the moonlight or the changing shadows caused by the gathering mist had caused her to imagine his piercing expression moments earlier.

"And that is?"

"The Socratic method. Answering a question with a question."

"'Tis a bad habit, I'm afraid." But she meant 'convenient' instead of 'bad.' A convenient habit that gave one time to collect one's thoughts. She smiled disarmingly. She was probably being too harsh in her judgment of Zach.

She let out a small sigh. "Actually, I've made no secret of my reasons for coming here. I intend to work my way up. It is the land of opportunity, they say. And I will put that theory to the test. Give it my all. See what comes of it." She laughed softly. "My dreams are different from yours, Zach. I wouldn't be content with a boat. I would want to command a fleet, own the canning company—the entire operation."

"Build an empire?" He cocked an eyebrow.

She nodded briskly. "If that's what results."

"Some of the results are the enjoyment of great wealth, the political and social standing—"

Molly cut him off. "The challenge, Zach. More than any of those things, I want to taste the challenge. Most women are content to stay at home raising children and sending their husbands off to work. They venture out once in a while to work with their friends in the ladies aid society, or march with the Women's Christian Temperance Union, or collect food and clothing for a settlement house. But creating a work of one's own, watching it grow, blossom, bear fruit, like a well-planted garden…that's a world open only to men. Not women."

His expression was thoughtful. "And you want a garden of your own."

"I've known it all my life, it seems." She laughed suddenly. "My cousin Winston says I'm born for it."

"Your cousin Winston?"

"Yes, my favorite cousin, Winston, though I call him Winny," she sighed, not daring to add more.

For several minutes neither spoke. Only the sounds of the crickets and frogs and the trickling fountain water could be heard from across the courtyard.

Zach's voice was quiet when he spoke again. "Yours seems a lonely dream, Molly."

"If it happens, I think I shall be too busy to be lonely." Her words were light, but as she looked at him, she felt the driving passion of her dream, the same passion that always seemed to overwhelm her when she considered it.

"Perhaps that's exactly why I don't want any part of empire building. I've seen it from the other side. And believe me, it can be lonely and sad for those around you."

She looked at him and frowned, unable to picture anyone or anything mattering more than her dream. "You may be right," she conceded, though she said it more for his sake than her own.

Zach didn't comment.

They remained in the garden for a short time longer, speaking of San Francisco, agreeing that they loved the beautiful city and its people. Molly told Zach how much she enjoyed Kingsley and Gwen and the privilege of living in their home. As they stood to move back to the house, though, she again suspected there was something more on Zachary MacAlister's mind. The hard look, the furrowed brow, the deeply thoughtful regard as she spoke, all puzzled her.

Outwardly, he remained the perfect gentleman. But behind those fathomless gray eyes, something bespoke a wariness she didn't understand.

As they entered the softly lit room, Zach's expression changed as he hailed Kingsley, smoking his pipe near the fireplace. The transformation was so immediate that Molly again wondered if her imagination was simply working overtime.

She bade both gentlemen goodnight, made her way to the main hall, and stepped onto the wide staircase, one hand on the balustrade. As she ascended, she glanced down to the open library door, sensing she was being watched.

As she suspected, Zach's gaze followed her, his expression thoughtful, as if he were trying to make up his mind about something. As their eyes met, Molly wondered at the quickening of her heart.

Two days later, Zach asked Molly to join him for a stroll down the tree-lined street. It was evening, and she gladly accepted, catching her breath in wonder—again—as he took her hand and placed it in the crook of his arm. For the longest time, his eyes held hers. Astounded—because it was the first time a man had affected her so—Molly found herself nearly speechless. She hoped the twilight covered the blush on her cheeks. But with a gentlemanly smile, Zach merely turned her toward the moonlit boulevard and began to speak of the fishing boat he was hoping to purchase. Molly took a deep breath as she walked beside him, trying to concentrate on his words instead of her madly pounding heart.

The next evening, her powers of concentration were sorely tried again.

"Do you like ragtime?" Zach asked, as they sat on a wrought iron settee in the garden. They had been covering topics from favorite books to observations of life in San Francisco compared to London. Now they'd turned the conversation to artists and composers.

A gentle mist was falling, and Zach raised an umbrella to keep off the drizzle. His very nearness distracted Molly terribly. "Ragtime?" she repeated.

"The music of Scott Joplin."

She smiled. "His music was played on board ship as we crossed."

"What did you think?"

She wondered if she should admit her liking for the daring new syncopated rhythm. Finally, she said, "Actually, I enjoy it." She smiled a bit sheepishly. "I wouldn't admit this to just anyone—and my mother would think me terribly improper if she knew—but just hearing the rhythm makes my feet take on lives of their own."

He laughed. "That would be a sight."

"And you? Do you like rag?"

He hummed a few notes, shaking his head slightly to the beat. With a laugh, Molly joined in. They made it through the toe-tapping song, then burst into laughter as they began another.

"Good show," Zach said. "But now, m'lady." He stood and bowed formally before her. "Though this isn't truly proper dancing music, may I have the honor?"

Smiling, Molly stood and took his hand. Still holding the umbrella above their heads, with his free hand Zach drew Molly closer. Then they both hummed another lively Joplin tune and began moving to the melody, kicking up their heels on the appropriate beat and laughing more than dancing.

The drizzle had now turned to a light rain, and Molly thought the sound of it only added to the rhythm of the music and her delight at finding herself in Zach's arms.

Suddenly, Zach stopped and looked down at her. For a time they stood staring at each other in the gathering dusk, the rain streaming in rivulets off the umbrella.

As Molly searched his eyes, she thought he wanted—no, needed—to tell her something. Something terribly important.

And in her own heart, she recognized growing feelings too new for words. Or was it her imagination? Just as she was trying to decide, Zach touched her cheek. A touch so light, so intimate, it almost brought tears to her eyes. But so unexpected, it caught her by surprise.

In confusion, she stepped away from him.

"I'm sorry," he said quietly. "I shouldn't have done that."

Molly touched her face where his fingers had been, but she didn't answer. "I need to look in on Mrs. Forrester now," she finally said.

He nodded, and sheltered them both with the umbrella as they walked back through the garden to the house.

Zach paused at the doorway, turning toward her again. "Molly...?" he began. "There are some questions I need to ask you." He didn't smile.

"All right," she said, suddenly feeling the terrible weight of her secret about Winny.

"Will you meet me tomorrow at the same time?"

"Here?"

He nodded, then opened the door to let her cross the threshold.

"Tomorrow's my day off, but I'll be back by early evening. I'll be here," she said softly. "In the garden."

"Winny," Molly whispered excitedly. It was the next day and her second trip to San Quentin. Her cousin sat across the barricade from her. "I've heard about a splendid business opportunity."

He rubbed his red hair and blinked. "For us?"

She nodded vigorously. "What do you know about the fishing industry?"

"Only that I get seasick and don't ever want to be near a boat."

"Be serious."

He shrugged. "It's a growing industry here in California. But I don't know if it's a worthwhile investment. The population's growing, so that's a positive element long-term. But for the short term?" He shrugged again. "I don't know."

"How about canning?"

"Canning what?"

She let out an exasperated sigh. "Fish. Canning fish, Winny."

He suddenly looked more interested. "Sardines?"

She nodded, glad to see he was finally following her. "And salmon. Albacore."

Winny grinned suddenly. "Monterey Bay."

Molly could hardly contain her excitement. "Yes, the canning industry. It's just starting. What if we invested our money in a company?"

"Do you think our family will be interested in sardines?" He wrinkled a freckled nose distastefully.

She laughed. "I've already thought of that. How about salmon? It sounds a bit more...more romantic, perhaps?"

Winny threw back his head and guffawed. "Ah, yes. Spoken like a true investment agent. Salmon canning. I like it."

"Where do I get the information we'll need?"

Winny frowned in thought. "I'll give you a couple of names, investment agents in the city. I've worked with them and know they're good at what they do. I know it sounds impossible, given where I've landed. But I've still got friends in the city. Not everyone turned their back on me."

Molly wrote down their names.

"You'll find their office in the financial district."

She nodded, her excitement building. "I'll have the information for you by next visit. In fact, I think I'll try to see them on my way home from here. After you consider the information,

I'll wire for the money, then plan a trip to Monterey, if necessary."

"If you need to go there, it's not a difficult trip. There's a regular train into Salinas. Then you can catch the Del Cortés Special to Monterey."

"The Del Cortés Special?" She hadn't heard of it.

"It's run by the Del Cortés Hotel in Monterey. It's mostly for their guests, but anyone can ride the train."

Molly smiled broadly. "Since I'm going to be an investor, maybe I'll put on some elegant airs and stay there."

Winny chuckled. "You're the last person I can imagine putting on airs, Molly. You're the genuine article."

She nodded her thanks and stood to leave.

"Moll?"

She looked down at her still-seated cousin.

"It's a solid idea. I've always said you're 'to the manor born,' even without the requisite airs. Maybe this is the beginning." He stood as the guard came to take him back to his cell.

"It's an exciting prospect." She drew in a deep breath. "And this time, it will be honest money, Win. Just ours and the family's."

Winny nodded in agreement. Then the guard roughly grabbed his arm to lead him away. Winny yanked his body free. As he stepped back, a strange grimace, almost akin to hatred, crossed his face. The expression was so brief that Molly nearly missed it.

"Winny—" She stepped to the barricade, but it was too late. The heavy door slammed behind Winny and his guard. Molly walked from the visitor's room, troubled. But by the time she settled into the carriage for her ride from San Quentin to Sausalito, she had decided the exchange had been her imagination.

She turned her thoughts back to their conversation about her plan. It seemed solid, as he had agreed, certainly well worth investigating. Bouncing along the road leading to the ferry landing, she looked across the sparkling bay, carefully considering the challenge ahead.

Monterey Bay lay just a hundred miles south, and she could almost feel the place beckoning her.

"It's all yours!" The weathered fisherman's face split into a nearly toothless grin. He folded Zach's bank draft and stuck it in his pocket. Then he handed the captain's log to Zach and shook his hand heartily.

Zach grinned.

"Give me two weeks to complete the outfitting. I'll even ride with you to Monterey, if you want me to. See you get her there in one piece."

"I'll pick up your train fare back."

"It's a deal." And the two men shook hands again.

Minutes later, Zach strode along the dock back to the trolley. He had just swung onto the back of the car heading into downtown, when he noticed Molly Quinn seated at the front of the vehicle. He was disappointed that there wasn't an empty seat near her.

It was Tuesday, her usual day off, and he supposed she'd just been to San Quentin. He was still weighing the questions about her cousin, questions he planned to ask tonight.

Since their first encounter in the garden a week ago, he had grown accustomed to their unspoken habit to meet each evening. Their time of gentle conversation and soft laughter grew dearer to him by the day, helping to put to rest most of his suspicions.

He sighed, thinking of their dance in the rain the night before. He had never beheld a woman so lovely, so fresh and unspoiled, so filled with the joy of life.

He wondered if it truly mattered that she wasn't terribly open about her family, particularly the favorite cousin she mentioned—Winny, was it? Everyone, he supposed, had their family secrets. Why should he demand that she be any different?

He remembered her passion as she spoke of her dreams. Her face always brightened with joy at the prospect of creating a work all her own, and her eyes sparkled with delight at the unlimited possibilities ahead.

The bell jingled, and the trolley lurched and groaned as it moved into town. Ahead of him Molly Quinn sat, shoulders straight, looking forward.

But he could see the gentle turn of her cheek, the swirl of her dark hair beneath the wide brim of her hat. She wore the soft blue-striped shirt and fitted jacket, the same that he remembered from her first visit to the Forresters. He also remember how it brought out the jewel tones in her eyes. He sighed deeply, wishing he was sitting beside her. Well, he would remedy that, he decided, as soon as they changed to the Nob Hill cable car in the city.

Perhaps he should simply let his suspicions go, not even bother with the questions he'd planned to ask tonight. He'd not heard from his father, but the more he observed and spoke with Molly Quinn—befriended her, as he'd set out to do—the more certain he was that his original misgivings were unfounded. Every family had its black sheep. Perhaps hers was in San Quentin, though he couldn't imagine someone so refined and gracious had that kind of secret.

Minutes later, the trolley stopped at the downtown station.

But before Zach could make his way forward to greet Molly, she had stepped hurriedly from the car.

From the higher vantage point of the cable car, he saw Molly make her way through the crowd and up the street toward the financial district.

Slightly ashamed of himself, he quickly followed at a distance, glad the fog hadn't yet moved inland from the bay. He could easily see Molly's proud but petite figure as she made her way up the street through the jostling throng.

Finally, Molly stopped and gazed up at a sign on the skyscraper, checked a piece of paper she held in a gloved hand, then strode through the revolving glass doors.

He watched from outside as Molly spoke to a young man behind a counter, directly inside the building. A moment later, she entered the elevator. As soon as the elevator doors closed, Zach slipped into the building.

The man behind the counter looked up as Zach strode toward him.

"Can you tell me where the young lady—the one who was just here—is headed?"

"See for yourself." He nodded toward the guest register lying open on the counter.

Zach looked down the long list of names on the page until he reached the last one. "Molly Quinn," he murmured. "Visiting Bourke, Monaghan, and Marshal." Zach frowned, trying to comprehend what he was reading. "They're an investment outfit, aren't they?"

"Some say the best." The young man gave him an indifferent shrug. "And the most expensive. But then, you get what you pay for." He laughed with a bit of a superior tone and shrugged again.

Zach strode back to the center of the city, lost in thought. A young woman, unless she was of independent means, wouldn't have the financial assets to walk through the door of such a place. And if she had access to that kind of money, why was she working for Kingsley and Gwennie?

For several minutes, he wandered down the street, staring sightlessly in shop windows, trying to sort out his feelings. What exactly was Molly's business in San Quentin? What was she up to?

He couldn't escape the obvious answers. Finally, feeling hugely disappointed, saddened, and somehow betrayed by the new evidence against Molly, Zach headed back to the station to await the next cable car to Nob Hill.

5

ZACH SETTLED INTO A DOUBLE SEAT at the rear of the cable car, awaiting the ride up Nob Hill. He stared out at the milling crowd in the soft light of late afternoon.

The bell tinkled, and the small car clacked forward on its tracks, passengers fighting to grab seats. The place next to Zach was empty, and he hoped it would stay that way. He was in no mood to make idle conversation.

He simply wanted to get home as quickly as possible to speak to Gwennie and Kingsley about Miss Quinn and his suspicions. He'd waited long enough; he would recommend her immediate dismissal, he decided firmly. But even as he thought it, the image of her face crowded into his mind, that heart-shaped face that had beheld him with innocent joy as they danced in the rain the night before.

"Zach!" A lilting, happy voice broke into his gloomy thoughts.

He looked up. It was Molly, pink-cheeked and breathless, no doubt from running to catch the cable car.

"Is this seat taken?" Molly brushed back an errant tendril that had fallen across her forehead. She looked delighted to see him, her green eyes alight with pleasure.

"No, no. Of course not." He slid his arm off the back of the empty seat, wondering why his heart lurched so at the sight of her.

"Oh, my, what a day this has been!" Molly settled her small figure into the seat and brushed back the curl again, finally hooking it behind one ear as she turned to him.

"Busy shopping?" he asked, not wanting to hear her lies.

"Actually not. I've been seeing about some investments."

Zach turned toward her, surprised at her honesty. "You have?"

She nodded, seeming barely able to contain her excitement. "After you mentioned the growing fishing industry in Monterey, I decided to investigate."

"You did?"

Her eyes shone. "Yes! I did. I've got a small nest egg—not much—just a wee bit that my family wants me to invest while I'm here, so I visited a place in the financial district today to find out about it."

Zach swallowed hard, suddenly feeling very foolish and splendidly elated at the same time. "That's wonderful," he finally managed. "And what did you find out?"

"You're right, Zach. Exactly so! Now is a good time. Even a small amount such as I have can be invested in a small fishing business. It's just beginning. 'A very good time for the small investor,' the agent told me." She laughed triumphantly. "I could give you the biggest hug in the world, Zach, for putting me onto such a scheme. You're a dear!"

Zach thought his heart would never stop its thudding as he watched and listened to Molly's animated conversation, feeling her presence so near him, drinking in the scent of the lavender soap with which she must have scrubbed this morning. How could he have doubted her? He sighed deeply, regretting his earlier thoughts.

"Oh, but I do go on," she said suddenly. "It's just that I can't wait to get started."

"What are your next steps?"

"The investment firm will find the names of some small companies needing financial backing, let me know their recommendations. I may visit Monterey myself, see their operations, make my decision." She shrugged, then laughed lightly. "Of course, I don't know how soon. And I wouldn't leave Mrs. Forrester without help."

Zach was touched by her kindness and told her so.

The cable car stopped to let on a few more passengers, tinkled its bell, then lurched forward again. Molly grabbed a nearby steel post to keep her balance.

"It's a day for us both to celebrate," Zach said, suddenly wanting her to share in his good news.

"I'm sorry. I've been rattling on about myself. I've not even asked what's brought you into the city."

"Actually, I've been down at the waterfront."

"Oh, so have…" Molly began, then colored brightly as her words dropped off.

Zach paused, then went on as if he didn't notice. "I've bought my fishing boat, Molly. Just this morning."

"Zach! That's wonderful. I'm so pleased for you. But why didn't you tell me last night?"

He wanted to say that it was because he'd been so distracted by dancing with her in the rain. But instead, he simply said, "I wanted to wait to see if the seller was going to accept my offer." Then he gave her all the details, including the final painting and outfitting that the old fisherman was to complete by the end of April.

"Then you'll be on your way, sailing off to Monterey." She looked wistful.

"Yes. But it seems we may both land there."

"Well, in my case, only temporarily."

"I hope you'll find reason to visit your investment from time to time." He raised an eyebrow. "Watch it grow. Every garden needs tending, you know."

"I may have to do that." She smiled into his eyes, seeming pleased that he remembered her analogy. "Indeed, I may."

The cable car had come nearly to the end of its Nob Hill route. On either side of the street, the large Victorian mansions gleamed in the late afternoon sun. "San Francisco certainly is beautiful." Molly watched them pass by as the cable car rattled along.

"Gwennie tells me that except for some of our misty evenings, this has been a particularly mild, balmy spring. And it's only mid-April."

Molly nodded in agreement. "The bougainvillea covering the porches, the tulips bursting through the earth, even the little children in their straw hats and pinafores playing in the gardens." She sighed. "When the afternoon sun strikes Nob Hill a certain way—the way it is doing right now—it's almost like a painting, a happy moment bathed in light and captured forever in my memory. Never to be stolen away."

"You make it sound as if you don't think it will be here forever. The place will fade, but your memory won't."

She laughed. "As if that could happen. No, I was thinking that I won't be here forever."

Again, Zach noticed a wistfulness about Molly, though it seemed to suddenly pass as two little boys raced alongside the cable car, playing with their hoops and sticks. The driver shook his fist and shouted for them to move away. They did, but not before the younger child stuck out his tongue and waggled his ears at the carload of passengers. Before the cable car had rumbled from sight, the child's nanny sprinted into the street, grabbed him by the shoulder, and hauled him homeward.

Zach chuckled, then turned again to Molly. "And if you're not here in San Francisco, where might you be when 'forever' comes?"

"Mm, forever…" She sighed. "Sometimes I think it would be lovely to see that far ahead, or even into next week, for that matter." Molly shivered as the sun slipped behind the rolling fog bank, rapidly moving inland. She gazed into the darkening streets, surprised at how different they appeared in the now-gray light.

They were nearly to the end of the line. The little bell jangled merrily, breaking into her somber thoughts. Molly smiled up at Zach. "I suppose it's a good thing we can't. It would take away some of life's challenges, don't you think?"

The cable car halted with a jolt. "I agree," Zach said, as they moved toward the nearest exit.

He helped her step to the ground, then tucked her hand in the crook of his arm, and they strolled side-by-side toward the large Forrester Victorian. He unlatched the gate, and stood back to let her enter first. But before she stepped through, he hesitated.

Molly met his gaze, feeling herself almost tumble into the liquid depths of his eyes. She no longer saw in his expression the puzzling scrutiny from her first days with Mrs. Forrester. Instead, he seemed to behold her with something akin to admiration. That pleased her. But there seemed to be more than that. Affection, perhaps? And that made her heart turn somersaults. Her breath caught. She waited for Zach to speak.

"Molly," Zach began, his voice suddenly husky. "I'm very glad you've come to San Francisco. Actually, no…more than that, I'm glad you've come to this house."

She nodded. "I'm glad I've found this place." She didn't add, *and you,* though it crossed her mind. "It's become a sanctuary."

Above them, the streetlight cast a warm glow into the gathering mist. A few crickets sawed their songs from underneath the front hedge, and a spotted owl called from atop a nearby juniper.

"Were things that bad before you arrived?"

"Actually, after I arrived. It was then I found my circumstances completely altered. Nothing was as I had expected it to be."

"It must have been difficult."

She was trying to decide whether to tell him about Winny when he spoke again. His tone was soft, understanding, but his words stunned her.

"It must have to do with your trips to San Quentin," he said.

Molly stepped backward. "What?"

"I'm sorry," he said, looking stricken. "But it's all right. I've known right along."

"You've known about Winny?" She felt ready to cry. "How could you have? No one did."

"That first day, when you headed to Sausalito, I happened to be near the Ferry Building. I saw you board and decided to follow."

"You followed me?" Molly felt betrayed, her privacy violated. "All the way to San Quentin?" Her voice dropped to a ragged whisper. "How could you?" she cried. "Why did you think you needed to?"

"It was the agency. They hadn't sent you. I worried on behalf of—"

She interrupted with an indignant cry. "You didn't trust your aunt's judgment?"

"Gwennie and Kingsley are elderly. Perhaps easy prey—"

"Easy prey?" By now Molly was nearly shouting. "You thought of me as someone capable of preying on the defenseless?" She was sickened by his words.

"Oh, I've really put my foot in it, now, haven't I? Let me try to explain."

Hot tears welled and threatened to spill. Molly shook her head vehemently. "There's no need, Mr. MacAlister. I think you've explained quite enough." She moved toward the open gate.

Zach reached for her arm. His touch was strong, though gentle. It briefly stopped her from passing by him. "Please wait, Molly," he pleaded. "I'm sorry. Please forgive me."

"I suppose our walks in the moonlight, our talks in the garden," her voice trembled with anger, "our dancing in the rain were simply ploys to uncover my surreptitious activities."

He tried to speak, but Molly shook her head. "I can only imagine the questions you were going to ask me tonight." She glared at him. "Questions gauged to entrap, perhaps? Or calculated to gather more background for your case against me."

"Please, Molly." He reached for her hand.

But she pulled away and, without another word, headed for the door.

Zach didn't follow.

"Dear, whatever is the matter?" Mrs. Forrester reached for Molly's fingers and gave them a gentle squeeze. "You seem very sad tonight." Molly had just wheeled the older woman into the upstairs sitting room. A fire crackled behind a grate in the hearth, giving off a welcome warmth.

"Over there will be fine, dear heart." Mrs. Forrester nodded to a place near the floor-to-ceiling window overlooking the back courtyard.

Just as the downstairs library reflected Mr. Forrester's sophisticated yet rugged warmth, this room was completely Gwen's. It reflected the essence of her nature, from its lace curtains and vases of freshly cut flowers, to the gramophone and music collection and shelves crammed with the works of her favorite authors. The Jane Austen shelf held *Lady Susan, The Watsons, Sense and Sensibility, Pride and Prejudice, Mansfield Park, Emma,* and *Persuasion.* Another held the works of Arthur Conan Doyle, the stories of Sherlock Holmes prominently displayed. Her favorite and newest work by Doyle, the leather-bound copy of *The Hound of the Baskervilles,* lay near a reading lamp on a table by the window. Only her cherished Shakespeare would Mrs. Forrester allow to be housed in the library downstairs, mostly because she knew of her husband's fondness for reading and rereading the works.

It was a pale room, filled with soft colors, pinks and yellows and greens, nearly matching the garden beyond the courtyard below. Oversized chairs, footstools, and a single small couch were covered with a fabric of faded floral chintz. Crocheted pillows and throws, fashioned by Mrs. Forrester herself, added more touches of femininity.

A small walnut secretary stood in one corner, with a vase of roses atop a lace circle and a grouping of silver-framed family photographs below a delicately cut Venetian mirror.

The sitting room had come to be Molly's favorite in the entire house during the weeks since her arrival.

"Now," Mrs. Forrester sighed, when settled into her favorite spot, "please bring my lap robe. Yes, that one will be fine. Then,

Molly, dear, please wind the gramophone. I believe I'm in the mood for the Brandenburg."

After Molly wound the machine, Mrs. Forrester leaned back and closed her eyes. "Ahh, yes, the music is enough to transport a person straight through the gates of Glory."

Molly smiled in agreement.

After a few minutes, Mrs. Forrester fixed her gaze on Molly's face. "Move over here beside me," she commanded, nodding to a nearby chair. Her eyes were bright with concern. "What's troubling you so, dear? You've not been yourself all evening. You and Zachary barely spoke at supper, to each other or to anyone else."

Molly sank into the chair, plumping a crocheted pillow at her back. "Mrs. Forrester—" she began.

But Mrs. Forrester interrupted. "Dear child, I believe, before you say anything more, that I'd prefer having you call me Gwen."

Molly looked up in surprise.

"If we still lived in England, I would probably be as stuffy as any of them about such things. But," she let out a deep sigh, "I'm in America and I'm getting too old for formalities." She leaned toward Molly. "So, will you do an old lady a favor?"

Molly nodded and took hold of her withered hand. "I'd be honored. But you may change your mind in a moment."

"It has to do with what you're about to tell me?"

"Yes. You see, I've got a cousin named Winston Carlisle-Jones."

"A fine British name, if I do say so."

"He's English through and through, from the top of his carrot-colored head to the soles of his shoes. But he's in America now. Has been for a number of years."

Gwen's pale eyes didn't leave Molly's face. She merely nodded.

"And I told you about the dire circumstances I'd found myself in when I first arrived in San Francisco?"

Gwen nodded again, slowly.

"I came here to join Winny—that's what I've always called him. He was working at an investment firm. He'd written us all about his successes." Molly took a deep breath. "My family paid my passage, hoping that I could work with Winny, making some investments on their behalf."

"It sounds like a splendid plan."

"It was. After Winny had written of the golden opportunities in this land, I was taken with the thought of sailing here." She hesitated, not wanting to go on, but knowing she must. "But when I arrived, I found that Winny had been arrested."

"Arrested, child?"

"Yes. For embezzling money from his firm."

Gwen drew in a shaky breath. "Dear, dear. What a blow that must have been for you."

"It was. When he didn't meet my ship, I went to his office building straightaway. I was told he was no longer employed there." She swallowed hard and looked down.

"And that he'd been sent to prison?" Gwen's voice was gentle.

"Yes. I was told his new residence was San Quentin."

Gwen covered her mouth in shock.

"There was nothing to be done about it. I couldn't undo his crime. I wasn't about to wire home for money. I had to make my own way."

"And a jolly fine job you did of it, too." There was admiration in Gwen's voice. "You waltzed right over here to Nob Hill and into our hearts and lives."

Molly, giving Gwen a loving and appreciative look, sighed deeply. "Thank you for that. I wasn't sure how you'd feel about having someone in your employ whose relation is incarcerated in state prison."

"His folly had nothing to do with you, dear, or with who you are." She looked thoughtful for a moment, then added, "But why tonight? Why is this bothering you so? And what does it have to do with our Zachary? Did you tell him?"

"Actually, I had planned to keep my worries about Winny to myself. I've not even posted a letter to my family about it. It is a shameful affair, something I'm far from glad to tell."

"I can understand that. It seems it should be no one else's business."

"Zach found out."

"How could he have? You told no one."

Molly looked away. To say anything would be tattling. She couldn't bring herself to do it. "You'll have to ask him, Gwen," she finally said. "He knew about San Quentin, but none of the rest. It seems he'd begun his own investigation."

Gwen didn't press her, but reached again for Molly's hand and held it gently while they both watched the crackling fire. After a bit, she asked Molly to wind the gramophone once more, then stoke the fire.

Later, as Molly wheeled her chair back to her bedroom, Gwen announced with a worried voice that Mr. Forrester planned to try out the new elevator the following morning. "He's taking me to the ground floor in the lift. Then to the rose garden to celebrate the sunrise," she said quietly.

"That should be a grand event!" Molly smiled broadly for her sake.

"I don't like being cooped up in small places," Gwen announced. "Gives me trouble catching my breath."

"Well, how long can it take to get from one floor to the

71

next? You can probably hold your breath for longer than that," Molly said, hoping to alleviate her fears.

"It gives me the shudders simply to consider it."

"Would it help for me to come with you?"

Gwen smiled up at her. "No, child. This is something special my Kingsley has planned. He wants me all to himself." She shook her head and smiled softly. "But thank you for suggesting it."

Molly lifted Gwen into bed, fluffed her pillows, and pulled the covers under her chin. As she reached to turn down the light, Gwen caught her hand. "Dear heart," she said quietly, "Zachary is a good man, perhaps a tad cautious, even overzealous in his protectiveness."

Molly didn't want to hear anything more about the young man, but she listened politely, out of respect for Gwen.

"Give him a chance for forgiveness, Molly. Bitterness never breeds anything good."

Molly nodded.

"Do you promise?"

She smiled gently and bent to kiss Gwen's withered cheek. "Yes. I promise," she said and turned out the light.

Molly retired early. But she couldn't sleep. The air seemed too still, too heavy, too warm. She tossed off her covers, then chilling, pulled them back on again.

And her mind was awhirl, first planning her next trip to the investment firm, picking up the papers they said they'd have ready for her, then running it all by Winny, and finally taking her delightful jaunt to Monterey.

Then her thoughts turned to Zachary, not that they'd been

far from him all night. His distrust troubled her deeply. She sighed, picturing his face, the strength she saw in the cut of his jaw, the light in his eyes as he regarded her, the laughter in his voice, as if some spring of joy were hidden inside him.

That's why it hurt so much that he'd discovered her secret and, even worse, that he'd sneaked after her as if she were some despicable criminal.

Molly felt her cheeks flame in embarrassment at the mere thought of what he'd done. Never had she been so humiliated. That alone was unforgivable, she concluded. She might as well turn her thoughts elsewhere.

Only she couldn't. The image of his face, his gently smiling eyes, wouldn't leave her.

Then she heard her name whispered.

At first, she thought it was her imagination. She sat up in bed—and heard it again.

Soundlessly, she pulled on her dressing gown and slippers and went to the open window.

She couldn't help smiling. There below her, Zach stood in the starlight.

"Molly," he whispered loudly, "I must talk with you." She reached for the window, planning to close it with a determined thud, but he whispered her name again. "Molly, please. We must talk."

Molly sighed, not knowing whether to hold onto her anger or to give in to her heart.

"Can you meet me in the garden?" he whispered.

Her heart won the battle. "All right," she finally whispered back. After all, she had promised Gwen that she would give him another chance.

Moments later, she moved silently down the hallway to the

stairs, then outdoors to Kingsley's garden.

Zach waited for her by the fountain, turning as he heard the approach of her footsteps.

"Thank you for coming." His voice was subdued.

She stopped near the roses across the small courtyard. Neither of them moved. They just gazed at each other in the dim light.

"I should have come to you with my suspicions," he said finally.

"Yes, you should have."

"Is it too late?"

"For forgiveness?"

"Forgiveness," he sighed. "And…" His voice faltered.

"And what, Zach?"

For a moment he didn't speak. "Let's just start with forgiveness. Then I'll see about audibly completing my thoughts." He gave her a sheepish half-smile.

"First, I need to ask *your* forgiveness," she said, noting his surprise. "I should have told you and the Forresters about Winny."

He moved closer. "I can understand why you didn't. Just look at the way I behaved. No telling how I would have reacted, had I known from the beginning. You have nothing for which to be forgiven."

"And neither do you, Zach. I had a long talk with Gwen tonight. She tried to explain your protective love for her and Kingsley. I really can't blame you for suspecting me."

He moved closer still. "You need to know that our encounters in the garden, our evening walks, weren't planned to elicit information. Please, don't think that I was using those times for anything other than what they were."

74

She looked up at him. "And, pray, what were they?"

He smiled into her eyes. "The outward expression of something that's happening deep inside my soul, Molly."

She caught her breath. His answer stunned her.

"I can't help myself." He reached for her hand and drew her nearer.

"Oh, Zach..."

"That's what I started to ask earlier. Is it too late to start over again?"

"Start over?" Her voice was barely a whisper, and she felt herself trembling inside.

He touched her face, tracing his fingertips along her cheek to her jaw. "Something is happening to me that has never happened before." He smiled gently, and when he spoke again his voice was husky. "You've touched my heart, Molly. In a way, I feel I've known you forever. In another way, everything seems new—every breath, every step, every heartbeat. My entire world seems fresh and newborn, just since I met you." He caught both her hands in his and lifted her fingertips to his lips. His gaze never left hers.

"I understand," Molly finally said, when she thought she could trust her voice. "Because it's the same for me." She looked at him in wonder. "You're in my every waking thought—even in my dreams."

"Dreams...," he murmured, and a look of sadness crossed his face. Molly understood what had caused it. "Which dreams, Molly?"

She smiled gently and pulled her hands away, then walked slowly toward the fountain. Her back was to him when she spoke. "Those dreams that don't include the futures we have mapped out for ourselves." Then she turned toward him again. "I find myself thinking of you instead of the business I want to start, instead of weighing the investments I want to make."

"And it disturbs you."

She nodded. "My dreams of business success are my passion, Zach. They've been with me since girlhood. I don't plan to let them go."

"I wouldn't ask you to." For a moment, neither of them spoke. Then Zach said quietly, "I've never explained the reasons for my passions, Molly."

"About your dreams? About life at sea?"

He gave her another half-smile. "In a way, yes." They moved to a wrought-iron bench and settled onto it. "I won't bore you with the details, but I once knew a man who was so obsessed with increasing his holdings—of lands and possessions—that he had little time for anything else. He had no time for his family, his children, or his wife. He alienated friends. Money, or rather the making of it, became his god. Just when he thought he had it all, it no longer mattered."

Molly waited for him to continue.

"He was thrown from a horse." Zach's face was grim. "The blow to his head erased his memory. The family he once loved, then ignored, are now taking care of him...only he doesn't recognize any of us."

Molly took Zach's hand and held it between both of hers. "The man is your father?"

He nodded.

"Gwen spoke of your family. But she never mentioned your father's..." She faltered. "...illness."

"There was really no reason for her to. We no longer dwell on it."

"I'm so sorry, Zach. I truly am," Molly said.

"My father had everything—titles, land, financial holdings around the world. But he lost it all in the end. Now he can't even enjoy his material trappings. None of it was worth the price. None of it." He looked at her earnestly. "My dream is just as filled with passion as yours, Molly. But it is the exact opposite. You want to build an empire, tend it like a garden, enjoy its fruits for years to come." He shook his head sadly. "But me? I want a simple life free of those things, a simple life filled with love."

"You think 'my garden' has no room for love?"

"Yes. I've seen firsthand the destruction wrought by such a dream."

"You're wrong, Zach. I don't know what happened to your father, why he made the choices he did. But it doesn't have to be that way."

"I hope not, Molly." His voice held deep sadness. "I hope not." Neither spoke for several moments. "It's getting late," Zach finally said and helped Molly to her feet. They stood for a moment near the fountain, looking deep into each other's eyes.

Molly saw his pain—and his passion. "What will we do?" she whispered, and she knew he understood her question. Without speaking, he drew her into his arms. They held each other in the deep silence of the night, but her question went unanswered.

Back in her bed, Molly stared at the ceiling for hours, thinking of Zach and considering their conversation.

But her thoughts were interrupted by an eerie absence of sound. All the familiar night music, the crickets and owls, the rowdy mockingbirds, the rustling of leaves by the gentle bay breeze, all had fallen strangely silent.

She finally heard the downstairs floor clock chime five times. Outside, dawn was just breaking. Frowning with the knowledge that she'd not slept a wink, Molly tossed back the covers on her bed, moved toward the window, and pulled back the curtains.

In the street, a milk truck horse clopped along. And she could hear the clinking of bottles as the milkman made his deliveries, house to house. The sounds were a welcome respite from the quiet of the night.

She awaited the morning calls of the birds. Even a cat's yowl or a dog's yipping would break the quiet. But there was none.

A deep, eerie silence seemed to have settled on the city. Shivering, she pulled her dressing gown closer.

In her uneasiness, she remembered another morning a few weeks ago when she'd felt the sense of abnormal silence. The earthquake, gentle by Mr. Forrester's standards, but frightening to Molly nonetheless. She quickly dismissed the disturbing thought that the same strange quiet might be the harbinger of another quake.

Another shiver traveled down her spine. Molly turned abruptly from the window and walked across the room to her tall, wooden wardrobe. After choosing a soft floral morning dress—hoping its dainty lace and cheery design would brighten her outlook—she slipped off her gown and pulled on the wrap, tying it in a bow at her waist. Its silk lining, long ruffled folds, and full sleeves warmed her chilled limbs. She sighed, glancing into the mirror as she sat in front of her dressing table. Her long dark hair was a jumble of messy curls from her sleepless tossing and turning. She brushed it out and tied it with a ribbon at the nape of her neck.

She was just shoving her feet into her dainty house slippers, when she heard the squeak of Gwen's wheelchair as Kingsley pushed it down the long hallway. Gwen was about to receive her first ride in the lift. Molly thought about the woman's fear of small, enclosed places. It struck her that Gwen's love for Kingsley and her pride in his inventions would help her get through her first elevator ride.

Molly stood, planning to run downstairs and greet them as the elevator doors opened. She smiled to herself, thinking how much she'd grown to care for the elderly couple in the short time she'd been with them. She would enjoy congratulating Gwen on her first ride and also congratulating Kingsley on his ingenious design. Maybe she would even help Cook Liu serve them breakfast in the garden.

She had just taken her first step toward the door when it happened.

A deep rumble exploded from the earth.

In that confusing instant Molly thought something had gone wrong in the elevator. She had to get to Gwen and Kingsley!

But before she could move, the first jolt of the massive quake struck, knocking her to the floor. But it was the rumbling sound, not the shaking, that caused her heart to nearly burst with fear. She didn't notice the earth's violent upheaval until she found herself thrown across the room.

Molly covered her head with her arms and wound herself into a ball. There was screaming above the noise of the house breaking to pieces like so many matchsticks. The violent shaking still hadn't stopped when she realized the screams were her own.

CHAPTER

THE FIRST WAVE OF THE VIOLENT SHAKING finally stopped. For several minutes, smaller quakes followed. Then the earth was still again, though the tall Victorian house groaned almost as if dying. Taking a deep breath, Molly tried to stand. But her legs felt more like rubber than flesh and bones. In the dim light, she tried to assess the damage.

Her bedroom had been tossed and jerked and pitched to the point that nothing was where it belonged. The wardrobe had overturned on the spot where she had been standing, its contents strewn across the room.

Molly crawled toward her iron bed and gasped. It had lifted with such force that it had broken through the floor, and she could see the dining room below. The early morning light was just filtering through the now-glassless window frames, and she could make out the dining table, the chandelier hanging crookedly to one side.

An aftershock rumbled and shook the room again, though not as violently as the initial quake. Molly held her breath. Very carefully, she backed away from the jagged cavity where her bed rested precariously. The floor creaked beneath her weight.

She felt her way to the door. Another quake hit, and in terror she grabbed the overturned dressing table, pushing a chair out of her way. In a moment, all was silent and still again. She crawled over the wardrobe and tried to open the bedroom door, desperate to get to the hall on the other side.

The house, in the violent shaking, seemed to have lost its symmetric form. The doorjamb was cockeyed, and the door wouldn't budge. She pulled at it with all her weight, but still it wouldn't move. She rattled the crystal doorknob so hard that it broke from the door, falling into her hand.

She had to get out! She had to see to Gwen and Kingsley! She pounded frantically on the door and yelled until she thought she would go hoarse.

"Molly?" A muffled voice on the other side called to her.

"Zach?" Molly wanted to sob, so glad was she to hear his voice.

"Yes, it's me, Molly. Can you open the door from that side?"

"No. I've been trying, but it's no use. And the knob just fell off."

"I'll see if I can find something to pry it open. Hold on. I'll be right back."

Another aftershock hit, and the house shuddered. The bed teetered on the edge of the splintered crater. Molly worried her entire bedroom floor might crash into the dining room below. "Zach?" she called out. "Hurry. Oh, please hurry."

"I'm here again, Molly. Just a minute longer." His voice sounded so ordinary that it comforted her. She could hear scraping and prying around by the door hinges. "Stand back," he commanded.

She did, and the door fell through. Dropping the fire poker he'd used as a pry bar, Zachary pulled her into his arms. "Are you all right?"

The strength of his arms calmed her. She relaxed against

him for a moment, then let out a shaky breath. "I'm not hurt. How are you?"

He helped her through the doorway, still holding her close to his side. "I'm all right. It's a miracle we survived. Look around at this mess."

Molly's eyes were getting used to the darkly lit hallway. Plaster had fallen from the walls, leaving the old house's twisted wooden frame exposed.

"We've got to see about Gwen and Kingsley," she whispered, still holding onto Zach.

"I've already checked their bedroom. It's empty. I'm hoping they had already gone downstairs. Maybe they're outside, out of danger."

Molly stopped, covering her mouth with her hand. "Oh, no!"

Zach looked at her questioningly. "What is it?"

"The elevator. They were going to try it out this morning. I heard them here in the hall just before the quake. Gwen told me last night that this would be her first ride...." Her voice faltered. She thought of Gwen's fear of the contraption.

"We've got to get to them." Zach didn't let go of Molly's hand. Together, they raced toward the elevator shaft. The heavy door was closed. "Kingsley?" Zach shouted.

There was no answer.

"Kingsley? Gwennie?"

Still there was no answering call.

"Let's get downstairs. Maybe we can get to them from the bottom level." Molly spoke urgently, trying to ignore her panic. She remembered what Gwen had told her about not being able to breathe in the small elevator space. She prayed the dear woman wasn't inside.

They moved through the debris, the still-falling plaster, to the staircase. Zach held up his hand for Molly to halt. It was much lighter now, and she drew in a startled breath. The staircase had separated from the upstairs landing. It was unreachable from their position. There was no way down.

Zachary swallowed visibly. He didn't speak, but Molly could see the distress on his face. Still clinging to his hand, she squeezed it. "Maybe a window?"

He nodded. "There's a tree outside my room, just beyond a small balcony. If we can reach a branch, then we can climb down."

"Let's try."

Moments later, just as the sun began to rise, Zach climbed into the tree. He reached back to help Molly join him, grabbing her hands, helping her step onto the heavy limb. For a brief moment their eyes met, then he continued to help her climb downward. Finally, he jumped to the ground.

Molly sat on the bottommost branch, waiting until he was out of the way so she could jump. But Zach reached up, grabbed her by the waist, and hoisted her to the ground. Just being in his arms for that brief heartbeat gave her comfort.

They hurried to the front of the house. Some of the neighboring houses had collapsed with the force of the quake. Others had moved off their foundations, in some cases by ten and twelve feet, as if they'd been picked up in one place and dropped in another. Chimneys were down, bricks scattered like children's building blocks. Windows were broken, porches off kilter, roofs caved in. Sidewalks had buckled. The quake's sheer destructive power on display sickened her.

People, mostly still in their nightclothes, wandered the streets in front of their houses. She could hear the cries of those who were trapped in their houses...the wailing of those on the outside who couldn't reach their loved ones. Some dug frantically through the fallen bricks and loose boards that once comprised their walls. Alongside them, dogs whined and dug and barked.

Molly held her hand to her mouth in dismay.

"Don't look now, Molly." Zach took her arm. "We'll take it all in later. Just concentrate on finding Gwennie and Kingsley."

She nodded mutely and followed him into the house. They made their way through the rubble of the entry hall. The house still trembled with every aftershock. They passed the dining room, and Molly looked in to see her bedstead still teetering at the edge of the jagged chasm in the ceiling.

Zach met her gaze, his expression solemn. They stopped only once, at the library, where Zach hurried in to grab another fire poker to use as a pry bar.

She was just steps behind him when he reached the center of the house. Molly could make out the elevator in the dim, plaster-dusted light. The iron grate and heavy double doors were jammed shut, just as they had been upstairs.

Zach moved close and shouted. "Kingsley? Are you in there? Can you hear me?"

Molly thought she heard a weak and muffled voice. "Gwen!" she shouted. "Kingsley?" There was an answer, but Molly couldn't quite make out the words. "We'll have you out in a minute! Zach's got tools." She needed to give them hope.

Zach worked on the iron grate, shouting again into the elevator as he worked. "Hold on, now. We're almost there."

Kingsley's voice, now stronger, answered. "I'm here, son. We're all right, but please hurry."

Another quake hit, lasting longer this time. A loud crash from the dining room told Molly that her bed had fallen through. She grabbed hold of Zach unashamedly. He put an arm around her briefly and gave her a squeeze, still working the pry bar with his other hand.

"Help me, Molly," he whispered frantically. He showed her where to hold the bar, then together they leaned forward, finally forcing open the iron grate. The heavy wooden doors remained closed.

"Kingsley built this lift too well," Zach muttered, forcing the poker in the crack between the doors. There was a creak, and an opening appeared. Just inches wide, but an opening nonetheless.

"Okay. Again. Help me, Molly."

Molly put her weight with Zach's, straining to push open the doors. They parted farther.

"Dearest hearts," Gwen whispered hoarsely from one corner of the lift.

The Victorian shuddered again. Molly had the sinking feeling that it was the old house giving up. "We've got to hurry," she whispered to Zach. "I don't think there's much time."

He nodded in agreement. "You walk with Kingsley. I'll carry Gwen."

With a heavy grunt, Zach pushed the elevator doors wide enough to pass through. Gwen had been knocked from her wheelchair and lay crumpled next to Kingsley, whose leg was twisted underneath him.

"Can you walk?" Zach spoke gently, as if they had all the time in the world. He reached down to gather Gwen's light body into his arms.

Kingsley nodded and tried to stand, but couldn't. "I don't know," he said weakly. "I don't have much strength."

"I'll help you." Molly stepped into the elevator and knelt beside him. "Put your arm around my shoulder. Place your weight on the other leg. That's right. Now slowly, we'll stand together. That's right. Gently. Take your time." She swallowed hard and braced herself, feeling his dead weight pulling her down.

Zach stood outside the elevator, Gwen in his arms. "Go ahead," Molly said to him. "Get her out. Then you can come back to help me."

He gave her an agonized look. Their eyes met again in understanding. There might not be enough time for him to get back before the house fell. One more strong aftershock...She didn't want to think about it and turned her attention back to Kingsley.

He struggled again to get to his feet. Molly bit her lip and, holding him tightly, finally managed to help him stand. He leaned against her. "Maybe the wheelchair?" he suggested.

But Molly shook her head. "There's too much clutter between here and the door." She smiled softly. "We'll make it. Just hold onto me." Slowly, they began to move through the long hallway.

Kingsley's breathing was labored, and Molly wondered if he might have other injuries. "Do you need to stop and rest?"

He assured her he didn't. They kept walking toward the front door. His massive head moved side to side as he took in the destruction. "My, my," he sighed, with each room they passed. "Oh, my." But his sighs seemed to carry the weight of the world.

They passed the dining room where the iron bed had now fallen through. The crystal chandelier lay shattered on the floor. Molly was struck by the hazy sunlight streaming through the windows. It didn't seem right that the sun had risen, that life was going on as usual, when everything else had so suddenly changed.

"I do need to stop, Molly," he whispered raggedly. "Just for a moment." He rubbed his head, wincing as if in pain.

"Do you need to sit down?"

"No, dear. Just rest a moment." He closed his eyes. "I'm not sure I can make it. I want you to go on ahead."

Molly was alarmed. "I'm not going to leave you. You can make it! You must. For Gwennie. For us all."

He looked slowly around at the destruction. Valuable paintings and family pictures were twisted in their frames on the floor. Everything was covered with plaster dust, splinters of wood, and broken furniture. Tears filled his eyes. He suddenly looked very old.

"You told me that you lost everything in the last earthquake. Right on this site. You rebuilt. And the house you built was better than the first. You can do it again."

"This was my life's work. And it's gone. I don't know if I can bear it."

Molly wouldn't let him give up. "No, Kingsley." She realized that she'd called him by his given name for the first time, just moments earlier in the elevator. Suddenly, matters such as station and decorum were unimportant. Her voice was stern as she continued. "You're going to make it. You'll build again, even if I have to get out a hammer and saw and work beside you. I'm going to see to it. And I'm not one to go back on my word." They were walking toward the door again.

Kingsley let out a wheezing sound much like a short cough. He grinned at her, and Molly realized it was a laugh. "I would wager you're not," he said.

They had almost made it to the front porch, when it struck. Another aftershock. Stronger than any of the others.

Molly knew that the old house was about to collapse.

Kingsley knew it too. He grabbed Molly into his arms as if to protect her, holding her close as the house shuddered violently one last time and crashed around them.

Then all was dark and silent.

Zach dug frantically with his bare hands, pulling, ripping boards and debris from the pile of rubble. Dust filled the air, clouding his vision. Neighbors ran from across the street and joined him, frantically trying to reach Kingsley and Molly before they suffocated.

He heard a moan, then another. It was Kingsley! He lifted a heavy beam, then another. Finally, he reached Kingsley. Beneath him lay Molly's crumpled figure.

She was so still, so pale. Zach's heart stopped.

Kingsley gave him a weak smile as Zach pulled him out, then gently laid him on a blanket where Gwennie waited.

Zach turned back to Molly. A stab of grief sliced into his heart. How could she still be alive?

He bent over her and felt the soft moisture of her breath against his cheek. Carefully, he brushed off the plaster and dust. He touched her face, but she didn't open her eyes.

"Molly," he whispered. "My precious Molly." He lifted her into his arms and struggled to his feet, holding her close. Tears streamed unashamedly down his face as he carried her away from what had once been the elegant Victorian. "God, help her," he breathed. "Help us all."

7

Carmel-by-the-Sea

DEVON O'ROURKE STRETCHED HIS ARMS and yawned as he stepped outside his artist's studio. He leaned against the door-jamb, absently rubbed his sand-colored hair, and stretched again before walking onto the porch, a worn and rickety plat-form supported by tall posts atop a steep hillside. It was just before dawn, and a pale light had begun to crown the forested hills beyond the Carmel Valley.

Devon moved to the waist-high railing, rested his arms on it, and breathed in the early morning scents carrying toward him on the ocean breezes—the nearby pines, still damp from their blanket of nighttime mist; the mixture of baking bread from his neighbor Mary Rose's kitchen; and the spring fragrance of her garden and small orchard at the rear of her cottage.

And of course, there was the sea breeze itself. Hinting of salt and sand and water creatures, its scent was bold and fresh. Devon rejoiced in it, as he did nearly every morning, feeling wonderfully alive and thankful that God had given him such a day.

If he faced southwest, he had a sweeping panorama of the sea, just beginning to hint at the peacock color it would later become. But Devon locked his gaze on the silver horizon, where dawn's pastels would soon overcome the darkness.

For some time, Devon had carried on a detailed study of light. Sometimes he felt obsessed by his attention to it, often spending hours observing its dappled play on dancing wind-blown leaves, or its warmth shining through a cottage window, or its powerful streaming through a fissure in dark storm clouds.

Then at his easel, Devon would experiment, mixing colors on his palette until they resembled the light he'd seen. Mostly he used white with slight touches of yellow, red, and blue, depending on the light's source.

Devon watched every change on the horizon. He was lost in thought, mentally mixing colors on his palette, when he heard the sound of quick footsteps below him.

The sun had nearly risen now, and Devon could make out Mary Rose's slight figure as she opened her back gate and made her way up the trail from her cottage. She carried a tray with a pitcher of coffee, a couple of thick pottery cups, and a plate of what he knew was still-warm bread from her oven.

Often in the early morning, while little Jesse slept and as she listened for his waking calls, Mary Rose joined him in their "morning room," as she laughingly called his porch. And they would enjoy a bit of a sunrise breakfast—the bread, some peach preserves from her orchard, steaming coffee, and sweet conversation.

When she reached the small wooden bridge between their properties, Mary Rose looked up and smiled.

The sight of her made Devon's heart skip. Even in the pale dawn light, he could make out her blond curls, still mussed from sleep, the graceful way she carried herself as she walked toward him in her long ruffled morning coat. As the sky turned brighter, he knew he would see her wide, sea-green eyes and the dusting of freckles across the bridge of her nose, a sight that never failed to stir something deep inside him.

Carl Sheffield, Mary Rose's husband, had been one of Devon's closest friends. After his death two years earlier, Devon had watched over Mary Rose and her infant son for his friend's sake, helping her with the cottage. He soon found, however, that Mary Rose was a strong and resilient young woman. She appreciated Devon's kindness, but she made it very clear that she valued her independence.

Though she needed him less and less over time, their friendship deepened. Mary Rose took joy in Devon's art, just as he took joy in her "living artistry," as he called it—her beautiful gardens filled with herbs, flowers, and vegetables, planted in patches along a rock-lined pathway; her warm and delightful little cottage, filled with sunlight and splashes of color, as bright and resplendent as her gardens.

When Mary Rose reached the foot of the studio stairs, Devon raced down them two at a time, then carried her tray up to the porch.

Two weathered chairs and a small wicker table were tucked in one corner. Mary Rose smoothed a well-worn blue cloth with white checks across the table, and Devon set down the tray.

"It's a beautiful day," Mary Rose murmured, settling into one of the chairs. A squirrel scampered from a pine and jumped onto the porch. Mary Rose tossed it a piece of bread crust, smiling as it sat on its haunches and nibbled the morsel.

"I'm glad the rains have passed. I've got some wild irises to put in today." She poured coffee in Devon's cup and handed it to him.

Devon, sitting beside her, took a sip of the steaming liquid. As usual, both chairs faced the ocean, a distance down the pine-forested slope. They were close enough to enjoy the sounds of the breaking waves, yet high enough on their lofty perch to see the stretch of rocky coast for miles in either direction.

Mary Rose had just begun slicing the bread, when she looked up at Devon, a combination of curiosity and fear in her clear eyes. "What—?" she began.

A low rumble growled from inside the earth. Then a rocking motion began. Devon's tools clattered and jangled inside the studio. The landing creaked and groaned and shuddered violently, threatening to detach from the old building.

"Earthquake!" Devon shouted, grabbing hold of her.

"The baby!" Mary Rose cried. They both tried to stand. But the quake, seeming to hit in waves, prevented it.

Then it stopped as abruptly as it had begun. An unnatural quiet followed. For one instant, then two. Nothing.

Standing at last, they took a few short steps to the stairs, Mary Rose clinging to Devon's arm.

Suddenly, another deep rumble erupted from the earth. The shaking began again, this time stronger, seeming as if it would never stop.

Then the earth was still.

Mary Rose and Devon looked at each other, stunned. For a moment, neither spoke as they waited to see if it was really over.

"Jesse! We've got to get to him. Hurry, Dev. Oh, please hurry!" she sobbed, heading for the stairs, nearly stumbling in her haste. Devon ran behind her, down the path, over the bridge, and into the cottage yard.

Moments later they raced through the kitchen and into the

great room. Jumbled clutter lay all around them—books off shelves, furniture turned on its side. Dishes and pans were strewn everywhere, though amazingly, few looked broken.

They hurried to the nursery door. Not a sound carried from the little room. No crying. No calling out for his mommy. Nothing but silence.

Devon held his breath, fearing the worst. Mary Rose looked up at him white-faced.

"Jesse," she whispered, pushing open the door. "Jesse."

She moved through the doorway. Devon was just a step behind her. The room was strewn with books, toys Devon had made for the little boy, rag dolls fashioned by Mary Rose. The tiny trundle bed had tipped, its mattress flipped up to one side.

At first, there was no sign of Jesse, with his rosy cheeks and ready smile. Then in the corner, at the far side of the room, a little head popped up from a nest of blankets and pillows.

"Big noise!" He smiled, his eyes opening wide. "Big, big boom."

Devon let out a long sigh, realizing he'd almost feared to breathe since the quake started.

"Yes, Jesse," Mary Rose said, visibly swallowing back her tears. "It was." She made her way across the room to her son, and Devon could tell she was struggling to keep from crying. "Jesse boy," she whispered, drawing the child into her arms.

For the longest time, the two stood together in the center of the nursery, Mary Rose holding Jesse close to her heart.

Another small shuddering quake hit, and Mary Rose reached out for Devon to join them. The room was still shaking as Devon stretched his arms around them both. After a few minutes of quiet, the windows rattled again, and Devon tightened his hold. Then it passed, and all was still again.

Devon let his arms down and started to back away from Mary Rose and Jesse. But Mary Rose looked up at him. "Dev, why don't you pray for us now? Pray that we'll get through this." Her voice still trembled.

His arms slipped around her and the baby again. "Father in heaven," he prayed. "Thank you for your loving care, for protecting us just now. You've said you'll be with us always, and we feel your presence, right now, in this place. Your arms are around us.

"You created this earth. You know what happens in its depths. Though we are frightened, the world and everything in it is in your hands. We tremble in terror, though your mighty angels stand guard around us."

"Angels 'round us," repeated Jesse, his little face frowning in serious concentration, his eyes squeezed shut.

"Be with us, Father. May we rejoice in you, glad that we belong to the God of the Universe who is the same—today, yesterday, and tomorrow. Whose faithfulness never falters. Make us a blessing, Lord, to those around us…and may we reflect your deep compassion to all we meet today."

"…us a blessing, Lord," Jesse whispered softly, his tone matching Devon's, though he couldn't say his rs.

Devon gave the little boy a squeeze.

Another small quake shuddered across the earth's surface. Devon held the little family tighter and continued praying. "May we be aware of your presence whatever befalls us today."

The newly risen sun was now streaming through the nursery's single window, and outside a mockingbird warbled its morning song. It was answered by its mate from a nearby pine. Sparrows and finches joined in, singing and twittering at a bird feeder Mary Rose had built.

A gentle sea breeze picked up, lifting the lace curtains at the small window and rustling the peach tree just outside.

"A-men!" Jesse suddenly shouted, then opened his wide eyes and smiled triumphantly. "Big, big noise!" he said, looking around the nursery. "And a big, big messy place, Mommy!"

"Amen to that, Jesse boy. Amen." Mary Rose laughed softly. "We'd better get started."

For the rest of the morning, Mary Rose and Devon cleaned up the clutter. Jesse played contentedly beside them, chattering happily with each aftershock. The smaller quakes continued from time to time, though lessening in intensity.

Mary Rose was surprised that more of her dishes hadn't broken. The quake had mostly toppled things off shelves, but caused little real damage. By early afternoon, the cottage was back to normal, furniture in place, kitchen swept clean of pottery chips and glass shards.

Mary Rose emptied the dustpan outside the back door, hooked a stray curl behind an ear, then stepped back into the kitchen. "Shall we start all over again with our toast and coffee?" She smiled up at Devon, suddenly feeling famished. "Now that we can get to the stove."

"You and Jesse go ahead. I think I'd better be getting to the studio to take care of the mess there." She walked with him to the door, and he hung the broom on its hook outside.

"I'll be up to help you as soon as I've fed Jesse."

"You said something about planting wild irises today. I can handle the cleanup. It's mostly paints and brushes and easels and the like." His gaze held hers, tenderly. "It might be good for you to do some gardening once Jesse's down for his nap."

She was touched that Devon knew how much it meant to her. "I'd forgotten about the irises," she said, with a small frown. "I would like to get to them, but only if you're sure you don't want a hand at cleanup. You've done so much down here."

"I'll holler over the railing if I get into a jam," he laughed and gave her hand a squeeze. Then he strode to the gate, through the pear, peach, and cherry orchard beside the house, across the bridge, and up the steep pathway that led to his studio.

Mary Rose watched Devon go, wondering about her growing affection for him, yet acutely aware of her loyalties to Carl, her dead husband, the man whom she'd loved since childhood. After a moment, she let out a deep sigh and turned back to the house to feed Jesse and tuck him into his trundle for a nap.

The sun, warming her shoulders, was at a slant, on its sliding descent into the ocean, when Mary Rose knelt and pushed her spade into the dark rich soil. She'd planned the placement of the wild irises weeks before they were due to bloom, just behind a river-rock border on the upper terrace. And she'd watched those places on the slopes above the valley where she knew the lacy purple-and-lavender blossoms would first push through the earth.

Everything about Mary Rose's garden delighted her. Just as Devon planned the minutest detail of a painting's composition—the colors on his palette, the depth of texture, broad strokes or fine—Mary Rose planned and planted her own compositions.

Each stone-bordered terrace was like a separate room, almost an extension of the cottage, with colors and patterns of light ever changing. Closest to the cottage, and the shade it provided, was her herb garden. She grew rosemary, sweet basil, and thyme, and in a small clay pot in one corner, she was coaxing a bay tree to thrive.

Farther up the slope and along the winding path, her plots of fruits and vegetables brought her unceasing joy. The mild climate of Carmel-by-the-Sea caused her carrots, squash, China peas, lettuce, beans, sweet corn, tomatoes, and musk melons to grow in riotous color and lush profusion year-round.

At the very top of her garden's slope, near the brook that separated her land from Devon's, Mary Rose had planted a small olive tree among the pines that bordered the place. In the shade of the trees, she had planted ferns and bleeding hearts, with their lacy fronds and tiny crimson blossoms. And it was in a sunny patch of land, to one side of the ferns, that she now worked the soil, planting the wild irises, a curving border in front of a profusion of lilac bushes.

Mary Rose gently lifted one of the iris bulbs, placed it in the earth, then tamped the soil around it. She repeated the process until all the young plants were in place.

Satisfied, she stood, brushed her hands on her long-skirted coverall, and moved to a small rough-hewn redwood bench that Devon had fashioned for her. She settled onto the bench and smiled, pleased with the fragile beauty of the flowers, now dancing in the breeze. Behind her, the brook bubbled noisily along its fern-lined banks. Breathing in the sweet perfume of the lilacs, just ready to burst into bloom, she closed her eyes and whispered a prayer of thanksgiving.

It was a sacred place, more so than anywhere else in the garden. It was here that Mary Rose came to pray each morning and evening. She even thought of it as her prayer garden and imagined that her Savior awaited her arrival when she came. She spoke to him as her friend, as if he sat beside her on the bench or knelt beside her on the soil as she planted and weeded and mulched the garden. Mary Rose sometimes laughed with him about Jesse's latest antics, cried with him in her loneliness, sang with him as she worked, little songs of worship and love that she made up as she went.

It was also here that Mary Rose had shed bitter tears and had cried out to God in anguish when Carl died, feeling her heart would break with the pain of her loss. Her husband had been her best friend, confidant, soul mate. She didn't think she could go on without him.

But she had. God had been faithful and compassionate, his presence very real.

Now it was more than two years later, and something inside Mary Rose was awakening, as if it were a seed that had once seemed dead in the winter ground and was now reaching up into the spring sunlight.

The deep affection she held for Devon alarmed her. She suspected he was falling in love with her, though ever the gentleman, he had never made inappropriate advances or so much as hinted about his feelings. But lately his eyes revealed a deep compassion. Her heart responded, even leapt with joy, at the mere thought of him.

But it frightened her. How could she let go of Carl? How could she be unfaithful to his memory?

"Father, I can't do it," she breathed, looking heavenward. "Not yet. I'm scared to death. Help me with my feelings. I know I can't mourn Carl forever. Yet I can't let go of him."

She felt the warmth of tears behind her eyes. "Today, when Devon held Jesse and me after the earthquake, I kept thinking it should be Carl's arms around us, protecting us, praying for us."

She sniffled. "But I couldn't remember him any longer. I couldn't remember how it felt to be in his arms."

In the branches of the olive tree, a sparrow twittered and sang. A jay squawked and chattered. High above, the call of a hawk carried on the wind. And beyond the garden, in the forest of pines, a squirrel scampered from one tree to the next.

"And then, Lord, I was suddenly glad that Devon was there. It's flesh and blood that I need, not memories." She sniffled again. "But still, I can't let go." She buried her face in her hands, not moving for several minutes. "And I don't know if I ever can!"

Finally, from the cottage a small voice called out, "Mommy! I wanta get up." Mary Rose gathered up her gardening tools and hurried toward her son.

From his porch, Devon watched Mary Rose as she stood to return to the cottage. Though she'd never said, he knew that the place where she planted her irises was sacred ground.

She moved into a patch of sunlight. And as the sun touched her hair it took on the color of liquid gold, dazzling him even from this distance. Watching her in that setting, with its profusion of color and dappled sunlight, made him think that it was a scene from an Impressionist painting. A Monet, perhaps? A Degas?

Devon suddenly smiled. Why not paint Mary Rose? He wasn't a student of Impressionism. Its popularity had been declining, at least in Europe, for a decade. Besides, his work didn't fit into any popular category. He was simply O'Rourke, painter of light, and he would paint Mary Rose holding Jesse as only he could.

His gaze fell again on the sunlit garden. *Yes!* He wanted to shout it to the heavens, so glad was he for the inspiration.

And while he worked, he'd be able to gaze into those clear eyes of hers with their beautiful depths. He would capture on canvas the light they held. He would paint her bathed in the shimmering, pastel light of her garden.

A portrait of light.

He would tell Mary Rose first thing in the morning.

8

"THE NEWS OUT OF SAN FRANCISCO isn't good." Devon sipped his coffee, looking at Mary Rose. The sun was just rising, casting streaks of light across the worn planks of the studio porch.

"What have you heard?" Mary Rose drew in a deep breath, pausing as she spread preserves on a slice of bread.

"Apparently, the quake occurred practically beneath the city. They've had a lot of damage, much more than here."

"I was so frightened yesterday. And I'm sure what we experienced was nothing to compare with what the San Franciscans must have felt." She shuddered just thinking of it. "It must have been terrible."

"And it's getting worse. Sterling rode over from Monterey late last night and stopped by on his way home. At this point, there's still telegraph service out of San Francisco, but they're not sure for how much longer."

Mary Rose tilted her head, watching him intently. Sterling was an eccentric novelist who lived up the hill just beyond the studio. He traveled into Monterey more often than some of the other artists and writers in Carmel and often acted as their "window to the world."

"You mean it could get worse?" Though she couldn't imagine anything worse than the already devastating quake. "Aftershocks?"

"Fires. After the quake, people didn't know there were gas leaks. They lit fires for cooking and such. There were explosions." Devon's voice dropped sadly. "Fire is spreading throughout the city, and there's nothing anyone can do to stop it."

Mary Rose shook her head.

Devon set down his cup. "The water mains broke in the primary quake. There's no water pressure for the fire department to fight the fires."

"What are they going to do?"

"Sterling said they're talking about dynamiting some areas of the city, to get rid of the fuel, I suppose, so that the fires will stop at those points."

Mary Rose drew her hand to her mouth, trying to comprehend the tragic losses. "I can't imagine such destruction. It is, or was, one of the most beautiful cities in the world."

"Even the fire department was considered the best in the country."

"I think about the terror I felt trying to get to Jesse. Think about the mothers and fathers in the middle of the worst of it trying to get to their children or other loved ones. Oh, Dev…" She looked at him sadly. "There must be many who died or were injured. I wonder if the hospitals were damaged."

"I don't know. Sterling didn't mention it."

"They need our prayers. And I wonder if we can send food or clothing? Or blankets, baby clothes, nappies? Think of all the things they may need."

Devon nodded. "I'll try to get as much information as I can."

They spoke for several minutes about collecting necessities

for the San Franciscans and how the items could be transported. Mary Rose said she'd stop by the mission, speak with Father Gabriel, and see what they could do to help.

"Now," Devon said expectantly. "On a lighter note, I have something I want to talk with you about." He raised an eyebrow.

"And that is?"

Devon leaned back in his chair, took another sip of coffee, and watched her, a curious light in his eyes.

Mary Rose felt her heart catch. More often now, she noticed his powerful shoulders and neck, his strong jaw, his hair the color of wet sand, his eyes alive with curiosity, warmth, and feeling. She sighed deeply, thinking she would never tire of looking into those eyes, touching that face. Then she caught herself, suddenly embarrassed. How could she dwell on such an intimate thought? She swallowed hard, noticing Devon's tender expression as he regarded her.

"What is it you want to talk about?"

"I saw you working in your garden yesterday. The light was just right, the colors perfect. It occurred to me that I should paint you there."

Mary Rose smiled and tilted her head. For a moment she didn't know how to respond.

"You and Jesse together. I would like to place you in the upper garden, near the lilacs and wild irises."

She was touched. "It's a lovely thought. But I don't know how I could possibly keep Jesse still enough for you to do a sketch, let alone an entire oil."

"I've already thought of that. I would do a series of quick sketches, different poses. That way Jesse can get down and run between sketches. We could, of course, stretch the sittings out over several days. Then, when I begin the painting, I would do the same thing."

Mary Rose nibbled on her lower lip as she thought about it. "I think it's a splendid idea," she finally said, then smiled. "When do you want to start?"

"This afternoon."

"That soon? What shall we wear? I don't have clothes elegant enough. I've made some things for Jesse that will work, but I—"

Devon interrupted her. "I don't want you in anything elegant, Mary Rose. Even your gardening clothes would work beautifully. This isn't a painting for hats or frills of any kind. I want an inner light to shine through—from you, from Jesse, from your garden."

She nodded, understanding, but wondering at his husky tone. "I don't know about the gardening coverall. But I'll find something appropriate." Then she frowned. "Are you sure you want to stop your work on the lighthouse?" He'd been nearly obsessed with finishing his most recent painting. She couldn't imagine him dropping it to start another.

He grinned. "I put on the final touches last night."

"You did?"

"After Sterling stopped by, I couldn't sleep, unable to shake the awfulness of his news about San Francisco. I decided to work for a while, to try to get my mind off the tragedy." He stopped and poured both of them more coffee, took a sip, and set down his cup. "I found that the darkness emanating from the earthquake and its aftermath somehow transferred itself onto the canvas. The lighthouse took on new meaning. All at once the mix of color and hue seemed superfluous." He frowned. "As if the real light would be there anyway, no matter what I did. I just needed to get out of the way."

Mary Rose nodded slowly. "May I see it?"

"I was hoping you'd ask." Standing, Devon led the way into the studio, through the small room that served as his kitchen, and into a long, narrow room. It was filled with easels and stacks of canvases, paints, palettes, open sketchpads, charcoals, and tubes of oils. Splotches of paint covered the floor. The room smelled wonderfully of paints and rubbing compound.

At the far end of the room, a huge canvas rested against a massive easel. Lighted by a west-facing window, it dominated the room.

Mary Rose moved closer. It was the lighthouse. Devon had worked for months on it, but she hadn't seen it since its earliest stages.

She caught her breath in awe. Everything on the canvas was done in the shades of darkness—lavender, gray, black, and navy—except for the light emanating from the lighthouse itself. And for that he'd created a soft, almost shimmering gold.

"Watch this." Devon stepped to the window and pulled the drapes.

The lighthouse torch seemed to dim with the changing light. He opened the curtains a few inches, and the torch grew brighter. She looked up at him in wonder, then back to the painting. It seemed as if the light had an inner glow all its own. As if Devon and his oils had nothing to do with it.

She studied the painting in silence, feeling the sudden warmth of tears behind her eyes. She was overwhelmed by Devon's gift. Taking a deep breath, she looked up at him. He watched her expectantly.

"You've done it," she said reverently. "You've captured light. Real light. Its warmth. Its brilliance. Its glow." She looked back at the painting. "It's different than any of the others you've painted, Devon. It's inanimate, yet it's alive. I can't explain it. But I see it. It's there. It's really there!" Her voice was filled with delight for him.

His smile widened. For a moment, Mary Rose thought he might grab her into a bear hug and whirl her about the room. She could see the merriment and pride and raw joy in the depths of his eyes. "Maybe this one at last will make a difference."

Devon knew what she referred to. He'd been struggling to make his first big sale. For the longest time, he painted the rugged California coast, its crashing waves, its powerful beauty. And he'd sold a few of his works, mostly to tourists at the Del Cortés Hotel, though not for much more than it took to keep him supplied with canvases and paints.

Mary Rose was still staring at him, as if she saw something in him she'd not noticed before.

Devon's attention turned from the lighthouse. Regarding the young woman before him, Devon was almost overwhelmed by emotions long buried. Mary Rose, her friendship, her under-standing were more important than anything having to do with his art. More important than life itself.

"Mary Rose," he began, wanting to tell her how he felt but knowing the time wasn't yet right. He drew in a shaky breath. "There's so much—"

She interrupted as if sensing what he might say. "You know, Devon, don't you, what you're becoming known as in the colony?" She laughed lightly.

He shook his head. "No, I've not heard any rumors."

"A painter of light."

He liked the title.

"In fact, I ran into Xavier at the milk stand one day last

week. He said that in Carmel-by-the-Sea, the O'Rourke name is becoming synonymous with light."

"Xavier always has been one for overstatement." Devon grinned, delighted anyway.

"Dev, why don't we take the lighthouse to the Del Cortés? Perhaps they would hang it in the lounge."

"And put a price tag on it?"

She nodded, a twinkle in her eye. "A very high price tag on this one, Dev. Don't sell yourself short."

"Let's make a day of it. We'll take Jesse, have a picnic on the beach, spend some time in Monterey watching the fishing boats."

"After the last time we did that, Jesse chattered about the pelicans for weeks. Even pretended to fly like one. That was his favorite part of the trip. He'll be delighted when I tell him we're going again."

"But before we go, I want to do some preliminary sketches of the two of you in the garden."

"Do you still want to begin today?"

"I can't think of anything I'd like better." He gazed at her thoughtfully for a moment. "I think the garden light is best in late afternoon. That's when I saw you there yesterday."

She gathered up the breakfast things, loading them onto the tray. "Just after Jesse's nap. Then maybe he'll cooperate and stay on my lap long enough to capture him on paper." She folded the blue-checked cloth and placed it atop their stacked plates.

Devon, carrying the tray, escorted her down the rickety stairs to the path leading across the bridge. "Until we meet in the garden," he said formally, with a quick bow.

Mary Rose grinned as she took the tray from him, her face alight with tender affection. "Ah, sweet knight," she said, with a quick curtsy. "Enjoy my presence now. Before long, I'll be as famous as the Mona Lisa and daren't speak to my friends." She laughed. "But then, if you're as famous as Leonardo da Vinci, perhaps you won't be speaking to your friends."

Devon suddenly took hold of her hand and pressed her fingers to his lips. "I can think of nothing more sorrowful, fair maiden, than the thought of never again hearing the sound of your voice."

She regarded him solemnly for a moment before smiling again. "Until the garden, then," she said, slowly withdrawing her hand, her eyes never leaving his. Then she was off down the path.

They met in the garden at 3:30. Devon thought the light couldn't have been more perfect. He moved the redwood bench so that Mary Rose was seated in front of the lilacs and irises. Behind her bloomed a profusion of roses in pink, silver, and cream.

Mary Rose wore a princess-style gown in varying shades of pale blue. It had an underblouse of netting that rose high on her delicate, long neck. The garment itself, though simple in design, was made of silk and fell in soft folds around her feet when she sat.

"You look beautiful," Devon managed, as he set up his easel.

She pulled Jesse onto her lap. Impressed with the newness of the game, he sat still, staring at Devon with wide eyes. Mary Rose had dressed him in a shirtwaist suit with short pants, matching leggings, and a small blue tie at his neck.

Pools of late afternoon sunlight filled the garden. Around them the birds warbled and sang, squirrels jumped and barked and twittered. And Devon, standing at the easel, sketched furiously, capturing one expression after another.

"Now, a smile," he would coax, as he began a new sketch. Then, "More serious, please just for a moment. Wonderful. Perfect."

Jesse tired of the game after a bit and wriggled out of his mother's arms.

"Let him go. I can get back to him later," Devon murmured absently, his gaze never leaving Mary Rose. "Tilt your face toward the sunlight. That's good." And he added a few lines here, a touch of shading there.

Mary Rose drew in a deep breath and stretched her arms.

"Are you tired?" Devon was sorry he hadn't noticed how long he'd kept her there.

She smiled gently. "I'm fine, Dev. Really." Beside her, Jesse played contentedly with a miniature rocking horse that Devon had carved for him weeks earlier. The little boy chattered to the horse as if it could hear him. Then he rocked it on the ground, making horse sounds as if the animal were having the grandest time ever.

Mary Rose's eyes smiled into Devon's above the little boy's blond head. It struck him as the kind of intimate exchange that would occur between a child's parents. And it touched him that she had included him in such a way.

Jesse, still lost in play, rocked the little horse. Devon sketched the top of Jesse's head with its wisps of curly hair, his round little cheek, his tiny nose and dimpled hand.

As he worked, Devon thought about the awesome responsibility it would be to raise such a child. How could he just step in and take Carl's place? His feelings for Mary Rose were not frivolous. His care for her, and for her child, already ran deep. Too deep for words.

Yet how could a nearly starving artist provide the care that this young family needed? Devon barely made enough to take care of himself. How could he think of providing for a family, giving this baby everything he needed from now until adulthood? It was a frightening thought.

Devon continued sketching, though he noticed that now he'd added more shadows. He thought about the trips he often made up and down the coast, the days he spent painting lighthouses such as the one at Point Piños. Or traveling to missions around the state, sometimes spending weeks capturing the perfect light. Or the seaside cottages he'd found along the coast where he'd spent days studying the light emanating from their small, shuttered windows.

Would it be fair to subject a family to that kind of physical absence? He knew the answer was no.

"The light is fading," he said quietly to Mary Rose. "I think it's time to go in. I'm sorry I kept you so long." He put away his pastels and folded the easel.

Mary Rose watched Devon. Something had happened moments earlier, some dark thought, perhaps some hidden anxiety, had suddenly plagued him. She had seen the transformation on his face as he sketched her son. It was as if Devon had lost hope or lost hold of some precious dream. A desperate sadness had overtaken him. She wondered what it could be. Did it have something to do with Jesse, or with her?

She considered the slope of Devon's shoulders as he put away his artist's tools. She fought the urge to go to him, look into his eyes, and tell him that whatever it was, she was there for him. They would see it through together.

Together? Perhaps that was the lost dream he'd realized just moments earlier.

They'd walked to the edge of something beautiful. A bridge was there for them to cross, a bridge across all those things that kept them apart. But, she wondered, was either of them ready, or willing, to take those steps?

Was it fear she saw just now in Devon's eyes? Or was it her own reflecting back through his?

Mary Rose shivered in the fading sun and called to Jesse. After a quick goodbye to Devon, she carried her son back to the cottage, aware that the artist stood silently, watching her go.

CHAPTER

9

THE FOLLOWING DAY, Devon still was not himself. Mary Rose had taken breakfast up to the porch as usual, and he'd been cordial, even friendly. But the joy they usually took in each other's presence had strangely disappeared. He watched her thoughtfully, and there was still affection in his face, but something had changed within him.

He was putting an emotional distance between them. Mary Rose felt it as clearly as the difference between standing in the sunlight or in the shade.

Walking along the path to the cottage, she thought of his cavalier words the day before—that he could think of nothing more sorrowful than never again hearing the sound of her voice. Now, twenty-four hours later, it was as if he'd decided to do just that.

Mary Rose reached the brook between their houses. She hesitated. It was still early, and she knew Jesse would still be sleeping soundly. Suddenly, she decided that she wouldn't cross the bridge. Decisively, she set down the breakfast tray near a clump of manzanita and turned, practically running in her haste to return to the studio.

She sprinted up the stairs and banged on the door.

A few moments later, a puzzled Devon opened it. "Mary Rose..." He frowned in surprise.

"We must talk," she said evenly.

He raised his eyebrows, almost as if he didn't know what she was talking about. "Do you want to come in?"

She shook her head and took a deep breath. "Would you mind walking down to the bridge with me? Jesse's due to wake soon, and I want to be sure I hear him."

Devon joined her on the porch, then together they walked on the path toward her cottage.

After a moment, they stood near the small bridge. Devon leaned against the railing. She stood across from him. "This sounds serious," he said, his eyes narrowing.

"It is." Mary Rose swallowed hard.

"Go on, then."

"This is difficult for me."

He waited and seemed to clench his jaw a bit.

"I treasure your friendship," she finally got out.

"And I yours, Mary Rose. You know that."

"Then what's happened?"

He blinked. "What do you mean?"

"Something happened yesterday when you were sketching Jesse. I saw it in your face."

Devon looked away as if unable to meet her eyes. For a moment he didn't speak. Finally, his gaze again locked on hers. "I don't know if I'm ready to tell you, if it's the right time."

"You must tell me, Devon. I can't bear it if you don't."

He sighed deeply, raggedly. "I'm wrestling with my feelings for you, Mary Rose." His voice was husky. "Yet, I'm not good for you...our love can't be. I won't let it be."

Mary Rose didn't interrupt, but she thought her heart would

break as she listened to his words. He reached for her hand and squeezed it as if he acutely understood her feelings.

"I care for you deeply, Mary Rose. More deeply than life itself. When I'm near you my heart seems ready to burst with joy. I love looking into your eyes, your beautiful sea-green eyes." He smiled gently. "Everything about you is perfect." He regarded her for a moment quietly, frowning slightly. "Don't you see what's happened?"

She shook her head slowly.

"I've fallen in love with you, Mary Rose." His eyes seemed to caress her face. "And it's not something I take lightly. I want to spend the rest of my life with you, and with Jesse."

Still, Mary Rose didn't speak.

"But as I was sketching Jesse yesterday, I realized what a responsibility it would be to raise him. It was as if I were looking at myself for the first time in years. Who I am. What I have to offer."

"I don't understand," she whispered.

"Mary Rose, I saw my life as an artist, a poor artist, and I suddenly realized that I can offer you and Jesse nothing. Look at me." He gestured toward the studio. "Even if you were to have me, I can't give you anything that a husband needs to give his family."

"Except love," she said quietly. But he didn't answer.

After a moment, Mary Rose took a deep breath. "Dev, I understand fear. I've got a bushelful of my own. I'm not going to tell you you're wrong. But I think you need to know where I stand in all this."

He nodded, looking sheepish. He brushed his sand-colored hair from his forehead. "I'm sorry. I've been speaking from the depths of my heart, so wrapped up in my own fears and anxieties, I've not even asked how you feel."

"When Carl died I didn't want to live. Jesse was my only reason for going on. Carl had been my life, my love, since I was just a little girl. I never expected to love again." She bit her lip. "Until lately."

Devon nodded, his gaze never wavering from hers.

"Suddenly, I can't wait to be with you. I find myself thinking about you all the time when we're apart. Sometimes when I see the way light falls on a rose petal as it lifts in the breeze, I want you to share the moment with me. Or when a hawk glides on the wind, or the look of the ocean turning gold and lavender in the sunset." She swallowed hard. Her voice was a whisper when she continued. "Every joy, large and small, I want to share with you."

His expression told her that he understood. "Yesterday morning you saw the lighthouse and spoke about the way I captured the light. I felt the same way. You knew exactly what I meant, as if you'd been standing beside me. No, not beside me. It was almost as if you'd been in my heart as I worked. As if you were a part of me."

Mary Rose blinked back her tears. "We can't lose that, Dev. I'm scared, too. Sometimes I think I can never let go of Carl and the memory of our years together. To begin life with someone else, to love again...without letting him go..." Her voice faltered. "I...I wouldn't do that to you." She could see the pain in his eyes. He understood.

For a moment neither spoke. Then Mary Rose sighed deeply. "Where do we go from here?"

Devon reached out and took her hand. For a moment, he gazed into her face, his expression speaking of his deep affection. Then slowly, he pulled her closer. He gently touched her cheek, then trailed his fingers to the dusting of freckles across the bridge of her nose. Cupping his hands beneath her chin, he lifted her face slightly.

Then his lips touched hers. "I love you, Mary Rose." His voice was low and hoarse. He kissed her again.

Mary Rose thought her heart would pound through her ribs. The tender warmth of his lips on hers, the very nearness of him, felt so right. As if she'd somehow come home. She stepped back slightly, her eyes wide as she beheld him. Her fingertips covered her lips, almost as if in awe of what had just happened between them.

Then she reached up and traced across his forehead and down his cheek to his jaw with her fingertips. Devon closed his eyes and drew in a deep and ragged breath.

"I love you," she breathed. "I don't know where we'll go from here. All I know is that I love you."

He caught her hand and pressed her palm to his lips, watching her solemnly. "I can't go through the rest of my life without you, Mary Rose. And I'm agonizing over what to do about it."

"Material things don't matter to me, Dev. I know you've said it's important to you, that you want to provide for Jesse and me. But Carl left us with the cottage. It's paid for and—"

He interrupted her, his voice gruff. "You'd be supporting me. I would never allow it."

Then Mary Rose suddenly smiled. "What about the light-house?"

He narrowed his eyes. "The painting?"

"Yes." She nodded vigorously. "What if it sells for your asking price?"

"It would be a miracle." He didn't sound convinced.

She smiled into his eyes. "Maybe that's how God will provide for us."

He considered her words. "If the lighthouse sells at the Del Cortés, it would make a difference. Perhaps others will follow." There was hope in his voice. "But what about your fears, Mary Rose? Selling the painting may get rid of mine, but what about yours? What about Carl?"

Mary Rose tried to picture her husband, but she had a difficult time of it. She looked into Devon's eyes, feeling drawn into their crystal depths. Suddenly, she couldn't remember the color of Carl's eyes. She traced her fingers along Devon's jaw line, and she couldn't remember the shape of Carl's face.

She sighed deeply, knowing perhaps for the first time that as she awoke to her love for Devon, Carl's image seemed to be disappearing. She thought of the painting. Since Carl's death, she'd come through two years of darkness, and now love—as bright as any torchlight—was calling her home. It was time to bury Carl's memory and look to a future of light and laughter and hope.

"Perfect love casts out fear," she finally whispered, almost as if to herself. "Somehow, my fears don't seem as overwhelming as they did even a short time ago." She gave him a tremulous smile. "I'm willing to try to move beyond them, if you are."

Devon gathered her into his arms once more. For a moment they stood together, their arms wrapped around each other. "I think we need to take that painting to Monterey," Devon said softly, his cheek resting on her head.

"You need to title it before we go," Mary Rose murmured against his shoulder.

"Do you have something in mind?"

She nodded.

"And that would be?" He moved back slightly to better see her face.

"Hope."

"Hope?" He smiled into her eyes. "It's perfect," he said. "Perfect."

A few days later, Devon hitched an old gray to a wagon he had borrowed from Sterling. He loaded the carefully wrapped painting into the back, and Mary Rose climbed up onto the driver's bench. As soon as she was settled, Devon lifted Jesse up into her outreached arms, then scrambled up to take the reins beside them.

The gray moved forward, turning onto deep-rutted Ocean Avenue to the center of town, comprised of a few shops and several modest residences. In front of a small business about halfway down the avenue, Devon halted the wagon. He grinned at Mary Rose as Xavier bounded out the front door, his graying goatee neatly trimmed, his ever-present beret jauntily atop his head.

"Frame's ready!" he exclaimed, with his usual exuberance. As did many of the artists in Carmel, he supplemented his meager income with other work. Custom framing was a much more lucrative business than selling his watercolors. His eye for artistic composition made his services as a framer even more in demand.

Devon helped him unload the painting and carry it into his shop. Minutes later, the job was complete, and they loaded the heavy framed canvas into the wagon.

The ride passed pleasantly, with Jesse exclaiming and chattering about every bird and rock he saw along the way. An hour later, Devon halted the horse, and they looked down the cliffs at Monterey Bay. The Del Cortés Hotel basked in the bright sunlight on the opposite side of the crescent-shaped bay.

Devon flicked the reins, and the gray lumbered forward again. Just before noon, they pulled up the long, winding drive to the hotel entrance. Mary Rose stayed with the wagon while Devon went in to speak with the hotel proprietor.

Moments later, he reappeared, a dignified, graying man at his side.

"Mary Rose," he said. "This is Oliver Duckworth, manager of the hotel. He's willing to take a look at the painting."

Mary Rose nodded her greeting and watched expectantly as Duckworth examined the *Hope*.

"Yes," the manager finally murmured. "I think this will be fitting over the fireplace. If you agree on the placement, of course."

"I'd like to see the light in the room, if you don't mind." Devon glanced at Mary Rose, and she nodded her agreement.

The two men hefted the canvas out of the rear of the wagon. Mary Rose was holding Jesse, as they all walked through the wide entrance of the hotel.

Duckworth led them through the lobby to the center of the hotel. A massive stone fireplace stood at the far end of the room, flanked by floor-to-ceiling windows. Dark wood beams, cathedral-like in the high ceiling, together with a polished oak floor created the perfect setting for the work.

Duckworth pointed above the fireplace. "I'd say that would be the place," he said, scrutinizing the wall. "Your painting is massive, powerful. It needs space and light."

It seemed the man understood something about art.

"I agree," Devon said. They carried the *Hope* closer to the place where it would be hung.

"And what was the price you wanted to place on it?"

Devon told him, and the man raised a cautious eyebrow. "I don't think you understand. It's here on consignment. That means that the hotel will receive fifty percent of the selling price. For you to get your asking price, we have to double the sale amount."

"I realize that," Devon said evenly. "My asking price is firm."

"No one's sold a work for even a quarter that around here. Not to diminish your work." He frowned. "Please, don't get me wrong. I believe the piece is magnificent. It's just that I don't think any piece of art can command such an exorbitant amount."

"If you'd rather not take the chance—" Devon started to pick up the canvas.

"No, no. Wait." Duckworth seemed to study the painting for a bit. "Let's hang it. Let me take another look at it once it's in place. Perhaps we can make a compromise. An agreement we're both comfortable with." He called for two hotel employees to bring a ladder.

Several minutes later, the painting was in place. The dark stones, the soaring cathedral ceiling, the dark frame around the painting, all blended into the background. At the forefront was the lighthouse, its torch glowing as if from the light of a thousand candles.

For a moment no one uttered a sound. Even Duckworth seemed at a loss for words. Finally he spoke. There was awe in his voice. "We'll keep your asking price, Mr. O'Rourke. And even at that, the buyer is getting a bargain for such a masterpiece." He frowned, squinting as he studied it. "There's something about the light."

Mary Rose, holding Jesse, smiled into Devon's eyes. He nodded and mouthed the words, "Our hope."

"Our hope," Jesse chirruped, without the r, and laid his head on his mother's shoulder.

After Devon signed the consignment papers, Duckworth escorted the three back to their wagon. Several carriages filled with people pulled up to the hotel. Weary, worn, and subdued, the young and the old filed from the vehicles. Some carried small suitcases or satchels. Most carried nothing.

"There's a mass exodus out of San Francisco," Duckworth explained solemnly. "The first trainload arrived this morning. We've heard thousands are pouring out of the city. Of course, we can only put up a few hundred. Tent cities are already springing up all over the area. For some reason, Monterey's been deemed a safe haven."

A young mother caught Mary Rose's sympathetic glance. She hugged her infant close and shivered visibly.

Mary Rose moved toward her. "Is there anything we can do?"

She shook her head. "Just pray for those unable to get out." Her voice was soft. "The devastation, the fires." The young woman's eyes filled with tears. "So many hurt and dying. Just pray for us all." The woman's husband drew near and cradled his wife with his arm. They walked together into the hotel.

CHAPTER

10

San Francisco

WHEN MOLLY AWOKE, she was in Zach's arms. Supporting her head with one hand, he gave her a sip of water with the other. Until he told her, she remembered nothing of being dug out of the Victorian's rubble.

Her first thoughts were of Kingsley. "Did he make it?" she whispered. Zach's worn face reflected his worry and concern.

"Yes, he'll be fine. His leg was wrenched badly when he fell in the elevator. It's amazing he wasn't hurt worse."

"And Gwen?"

He smiled. "She's amazing. Up and about. She's even found an old, discarded chair to wheel about in."

Squinting in the dim light of the tent, Molly looked around, confused. "Where are we?" She was lying on a cot.

"We're in a camp they've set up for those who lost everything."

Everything? She tried to comprehend, then suddenly remembered. "The house. I remember it…falling on us."

Zach nodded.

"How long have I been asleep?" She touched her head and winced. She ached all over. "This a hospital of sorts?"

Zach grinned. "One question at a time. You've been out since

122

yesterday morning, about twenty-four hours now. And yes, this is a makeshift hospital. Though not much of one. They've sent one nurse to care for hundreds of people. I'm just glad I was able to get you into a tent last night. Out of the cold."

Molly closed her eyes. "It's pretty awful, isn't it?"

"Yes."

"Do you have any idea how the rest of the city fared?"

"There's destruction everywhere. And not much communication, to the outside world or within the city. I heard that the telegraph office was operating until this morning." His voice dropped.

Molly's eyes opened, and she searched his face. "What happened this morning? Another quake?"

"Fires. They began yesterday, Molly. They're spreading fast."

"I don't understand."

"People started fires, for cooking, for warmth, not realizing that there were natural gas leaks in their homes. In some cases, electric wires sparked. The gas ignited. Within minutes, the fires exploded into firestorms. Nearly the whole city is in flames."

"The whole city?" Molly tried to sit up, but her neck hurt too badly. She winced again, and Zach supported her shoulders as she settled back onto the pillow.

"As soon as you're able, I'll take you outside to see for yourself. There's no way I can explain the devastation."

"What about the fire department? I read that they're the best equipped in the state."

"Most of the water mains broke in the quake. The fire department, even with all their fancy equipment, is helpless. They can only stand by and watch the firestorms take everything in their paths."

Molly drew in a shaky breath. "Are we safe?"

Zach looked at her intently, then nodded. "Yes," he finally said. "We are for now, Molly. When you feel ready, I'll take you to the top of the hill, to look out at the city." He gave a short and ironic laugh. "At what used to be the city."

"The fires?"

He nodded. "It's an image you won't forget for the rest of your life. It's as if the entire city is in flames."

Molly tried to take it all in. "How about the other parts of town? Was the damage as severe as what happened on Nob Hill?"

"Worse. Chinatown went down with the quake, then burned to the ground. The waterfront district survived the shaking, but it didn't really matter. The fires destroyed it within hours. The financial district is nearly gone. Some of the other districts are burning right now, from Portsmouth Square to Market Street. North Beach..."

He shook his head sadly. "Hundreds of homes and businesses are already in ashes. The plan, last I heard, was to attempt to stop the fire by detonating the buildings before the fire reaches them. I guess they figure they're destroying the fire's fuel."

Molly looked up at Zach incredulously. "Who made the decision to set off the explosives?" In light of the devastation that had already befallen San Francisco, she couldn't imagine that man-made destruction could help stop the fires. It saddened her to imagine the magnificent buildings in the financial district reduced to piles of rubble. She shook her head slowly at the enormity of it all.

"The army's come in to bring order, from arresting looters to blowing up buildings. A general by the name of Freddie Funston is in charge. He's a hero from the Spanish-American

War." Zach suddenly grinned. "I've heard they call him Fearless Funston behind his back. Short redheaded man. I hear he's quite a bully."

"But he's the one who's decided to detonate the city?" Molly didn't see the humor in Zach's description of the hero. "What if he's wrong?" For a moment, neither spoke. Molly frowned, listening to the muffled sounds of explosives. "What if it doesn't help?"

"Then they'll burn anyway, so I guess he figures it doesn't matter." His eyes no longer held the look of amusement. "The explosions started early this morning, but I've noticed they're getting closer."

They spoke for a few minutes about Kingsley and Gwen, then after giving her another sip of water, Zach left the tent to check on the couple. Soon after, a stout nurse examined Molly and pronounced that she could leave the infirmary tent by evening.

Molly pushed aside the cot's single blanket and swung her feet to the ground. Her head ached terribly, and she blinked in pain. Then, taking a deep breath, she stood. Her legs wobbled, and the nurse quickly stepped to her side so that Molly could lean against her.

Molly looked down at her morning dress, the one she had slipped on just before the earthquake. It was now virtually her sole possession—a soiled and tattered, limply flowing gown with foolish ruffles and cheery print that she would probably need to wear for days. Twenty-four hours ago, she thought it would brighten her morning. Now, she looked down at the impractical dress, and struck by the irony, began to chuckle.

The nurse tilted her head in worry, then placed her hand on Molly's forehead.

"No, I don't have a fever," Molly said, still laughing softly. "It's just that I was recalling I came to America to make my fortune." She glanced down at her wrap, shaking her head slowly. "And now I've got less than I arrived with. This silly dress is all I've got to my name."

"Most folks are in the same boat. They've only got the clothes on their backs," the big woman said with a shrug.

"I suppose that's true."

"Many've lost more than houses and clothes and fortunes. They've lost loved ones." Her forehead creased in a sad frown. "And, of course, there are all those who died."

Molly was sorry she'd laughed. She was fortunate to have come through it all alive. Kingsley and Gwen had both made it. And Zach. She remembered his worried look of relief when she first opened her eyes here in the tent and saw him kneeling beside her. In a way, the three of them—Gwen, Kingsley, and Zach—were closer than family, and they'd all made it through the quake. She only hoped that Winny was safe as well.

She settled down onto the edge of the cot, her head still throbbing. The nurse gently settled her against the pillows.

"Everybody's equal now," the big nurse said, matter-of-factly, as she covered Molly with the blanket. "You'll see later when you go out to stand in the food lines. Domestics right next to society ladies, street cleaners next to bankers. Nobody had time to save anything. I hear folks from Sacramento and Monterey are sending clothing, bedding, and food for us. But until then, you'll see most folks still wandering around in their nightclothes, the same as they were wearing when the quake hit."

Molly nodded and closed her eyes.

"You just don't worry about having only a dress to your name." The nurse filled Molly's water glass and set it near the cot. "Little missy, you're going to be just fine. For now, I just want you to rest and get over that nasty knock on your head."

Molly, smiling drowsily at these comforting words, drifted into a dreamless sleep before the nurse had even stepped from the tent. She didn't wake until late afternoon. The first thing she noticed when she opened her eyes was the loving concern on Zach's face as he bent over her. The second thing was the acrid smell of smoke that permeated the air.

She blinked, feeling the sting of it in her eyes.

"Molly?" Zach spoke calmly, though she could hear the concern in his voice. "How are you feeling? Your head, is it better?"

She nodded. The pain had lessened a great deal. "Yes," she whispered. "I...I think I might be able to get up now." She touched her temple. The knot was still tender, but she could bear it.

"Do you think you can walk?"

"I feel stronger. I'm sure I can," she said. Then, noticing there was something else he wasn't saying, she frowned. "We've got to leave, don't we? That's why you're asking."

"The fires are getting too close. The whole camp has been ordered to move."

She sat up and nodded again. "I'll be all right. But how about Kingsley and Gwen?"

"They've gone on to the new site. I was able to get them in an ambulance. They'll lay claim to two more tents for us, save them until we get there."

Molly smiled up at Zach as she struggled to her feet. "You're a prince," she murmured.

He grinned back at her. "That's not what you said just a couple of nights ago."

"That was a whole lifetime ago, Zach. So much has changed.

I don't even feel like the same person."

"Nor do I," he said, as she leaned against him for support. They moved to the tent opening. "You know, don't you, Molly, that you nearly gave your life to save Kingsley?" He reached for the tent flap. "He's been telling everyone how you kept him going. He says you've volunteered to help him rebuild the Victorian, hammer and nails in hand." He laughed softly. "Now, that's something I'd like to see."

"I did no more than you did, Zach. You helped us all without any thought for your own safety."

Before they moved through the tent opening, Zach's gaze met hers. His expression was tender. "When those you care about are in danger," he said, "you give no thought to your own well-being. You see their faces in your heart and mind, not your own."

Then they stepped outside the tent.

The air was gray with smoke and soot. Molly found it difficult to breathe. Zach placed his arm around her shoulders, and Molly slid her arm around his waist for support as they moved through the throngs of people.

"We've got a ways to go," Zach said, steering her around a family trying to get their brood together to move on. "We've been told that we can move to a park a few miles out of the city. A tent city is being set up now. It will hold maybe three hundred tents. But I'm afraid it's first come, first served."

Molly nodded. "So we need to hurry."

"Only if you can, Molly. I know this will be a difficult walk for you. I tried to get another ambulance to wait."

"It's all right. Really, Zach. I'll be able to make it." She stopped suddenly and looked up at him. His chiseled jaw was smudged with soot, his clothes rumpled. He pulled her closer, and she relaxed against his powerful arm that was supporting, guiding, and moving her through the crowd. They made their way to the street and started slowly up the hill, joining the steady stream of refugees from the quake and the fires.

Molly noticed the differences in their faces. Some chatted excitedly, almost as if on a holiday. Children seemed especially unaware of the destruction around them, playing along the way, calling out to each other as they skipped along. Some had salvaged toys—a rag doll, hoops and sticks, a wagon filled with broken mementos.

Others moved along slowly as if in shock from the ordeal. Not speaking, they stared blindly ahead, trudging along as if tomorrow would never come.

Darkness had fallen by the time Molly and Zach finally reached the new campsite, a park near a forest of pines. True to their word, Kingsley and Gwen had saved two tents for them near their own. Lavatories had been set up nearby, and barrels of water for drinking and washing were already being distributed at one end of the park.

As soon as Kingsley saw them, he stood and, favoring his sore leg, limped toward Molly, his arms open wide.

"Molly," he said, gathering her into a fatherly embrace. "We're so happy to see you."

Gwen wheeled her chair over to the two of them and reached for Molly's hand. "Dearest child," she said, "we would have lost my Kingsley if you hadn't kept him moving to the doorway. If you hadn't made it to the porch..." Her voice faltered.

Molly squeezed her hand, then bent down and kissed

Gwen's cheek. "We're all alive and well, nothing is more important than that."

"Sit here beside me. You look too weary to take another step." Gwen patted the side of a cot that someone had pulled outside the tent for seating. Another cot had been placed at right angles to make an improvised sitting room, a touch of civilized warmth in the midst of chaos, Molly supposed. She gratefully settled onto the cot nearest Gwen. Zach and Kingsley sat on the other.

Gwen reached for her hand again. For several minutes no one spoke. The older woman seemed to draw strength from Molly's presence. Around them people milled about, situating themselves in their tents, going to and from the lavatory or to the wagon for their water rations. Earlier, word had spread that food rations would be handed out within the hour and wagonloads of clothing and blankets would arrive from outlying cities for distribution by morning.

"I don't know what we'll do now," Gwen mused quietly, looking at the unsettled crowd. "We can't stay here forever, you know. But we have no home. No place to go."

"I've thought about it," Zach said, looking from Kingsley, back to Gwen. "I can find transportation to take you to your son's in Sacramento...." He hesitated, watching the older man's expression. "That is, if you want to go."

"Son, we can't ask you to do that. It's a long trip. We don't know what we'll find between here and there." Kingsley frowned and shook his head. "I just don't know...."

Gwen spoke up, her voice strong. "Maybe Zachary's right, Kingsley. It's a good plan. And I think we should start out tomorrow."

Tomorrow? Molly's heart caught. She didn't want them to

leave, not any of them. But she kept silent. Their well-being was more important than her feelings of abandonment.

"Now, Gwennie..." Kingsley sat forward, his brow creased in solemn thought. He absently rubbed his sore leg. "Truth is, I've a mind not to go. I love our son, and it would be nice to visit the family. But I don't want to live with him. If we leave San Francisco now, I wonder if we'll ever return."

Gwen nodded. "Surely you're not thinking we ought to stay...in the middle of all this chaos. Where will we live, Kingsley?"

"We still own our land. No one can take that away from us." Kingsley gave a brisk nod to all of them, looking as if the decision had been made.

"But everything we owned was tied up in that house, dear. And what little savings we had has burned right along with the financial district. How can we rebuild?"

"I'll get a loan."

Gwen's voice was weaker now. She sighed heavily. "You know, dear, that I've no mind for finances. But I do know that you have nothing to borrow against." She frowned. "No coll... oh, dear. What's it called again?"

"Collateral, dear," Kingsley interjected patiently.

"Yes, that's the word. Dear, you need to remember that no one, not even your oldest banking friends, will allow you to borrow."

"We still have our income from the business. There may not be anything to secure the loan, but I can make payments." He lifted his chin proudly. "I've never been late repaying what I owed. That's got to account for something."

Gwen nodded. Molly could see worry etching her face, love for her husband, yet concern for their future.

Kingsley coughed as a smoky breeze drifted across the

campsite. He cleared his throat. "I want to rebuild, Gwennie. I've thought about it all day. We'll build a smaller house. What do we need with a house big enough to house half of San Francisco? We'll build something small and charming. Just room enough for us, and maybe Cook Liu, if he comes back."

Gwen smiled gently. "Your mind is fixed?"

Her husband nodded. "I want to do it. It may be the last chance I have to create another lovely home for my bride."

"With a rose garden in back?"

Kingsley nodded, his loving gaze meeting Gwen's.

She sighed, though not unhappily. "How can I say no to you, my darling?"

"Then you'll agree, you'll not be too uncomfortable while we work on it?"

Gwen settled back into the wheelchair. It creaked as she moved. "You need to tell me first where your lovely bride will be housed during this reconstruction."

"I figured that if Zach will help, and of course, Molly's already volunteered," he winked in Molly's direction, "we'll put up a temporary shelter. Something comfortable, though not elaborate...with a lavatory and kitchen, of course."

"No elevator?"

Kingsley laughed softly. "No elevator."

"All right, then, dearest. I'll agree."

He stood and walked over to Gwen and gave her a kiss.

"But I still worry, Kingsley, about finding the money."

"If we can't, then we'll consider going to Sacramento," Kingsley said, his voice sad. "We'll live with the children, finish out our years with our boy." His expression was solemn as he said the words.

Molly, still holding Gwen's hand, gave it a squeeze. At the

same time, her mind was awhirl with possibilities.

Zach left to see about their water rations, and Kingsley and Gwen spoke about finally being able to have a bath of sorts. But Molly wasn't listening.

Instead, she began planning her next visit to San Quentin. She would, of course, need to see when the ferries would resume their hourly run across the bay.

Once she could speak to Winston face-to-face, she planned to ask him what he knew about the banking business.

Loans without collateral. She considered the possibilities. Many San Franciscans were probably in the same position in which Kingsley found himself—solid income, willing to pay high interest, but no one to borrow from. Where might that leave someone willing to make the loans?

She smiled and turned back to Gwen and Kingsley. "The first thing we need to find for you," she said to Gwen, "is a hairbrush. It's time we got back to those hundred strokes each night."

"Ah, yes, dear heart," Gwen agreed with a long sigh. "That is at the top of my list. Maybe someone will send some brushes and combs with the clothing." She patted her hair. "Dear, dear, child, how I've missed you. You think of everything."

11

LATER THAT SAME NIGHT, after Kingsley and Gwen were settled into their tent, Zach asked Molly to walk with him to the top of the hill where they could look out over the city.

Molly felt better than she had in hours, refreshed by her small ration of food and a quick but soapy sponge bath. Best of all, the headache had nearly disappeared. As she stepped from her tent, though, she looked down at her morning dress, thinking of all she'd been through since slipping it on before the quake. Its ruffles hung limp and lifeless around her ankles. Its cheerful colors had faded to pastel grays from soil, smoke, and ashes. Well, tomorrow, she thought, with a small sigh. The promised clothing would arrive by wagon. And she planned to be at the head of the line to gather needed items for Gwennie and herself.

Zach waited for her just outside the tent. He smiled appreciatively as she walked toward him. She thought it a wonder, considering her disheveled state.

A full moon had risen above the pines. The smoke and ashes created an unearthly brown mist. The acrid smell of the fires, even from the distance of several miles, made it hard for Molly to breathe.

Zach cupped his hand beneath her elbow, helping her along the narrow pathway. When they arrived at the clearing, they walked to the edge.

Molly gasped. It was her first look at the burning city at night. She brought her hands to her face and held them there. For a moment, she was unable to speak. Zach stood silently near her.

Below them, the flames leapt skyward, a macabre dance of flickering orange, yellow, red, and blue light. It seemed that the entire city—Market Street near the waterfront, all of downtown, Chinatown, Jackson Square, everything that had made up the beautiful, enchanting, cosmopolitan place—was caught in the horrible dance.

Sadness, deeper than anything Molly had ever before known, overcame her. Quick tears filled her eyes, but she was unable to move her gaze away from the sight.

"Oh, Zach," she breathed, not trusting her voice to go on.

Zach put his arm around her shoulders and gathered her close. As had been evident in the same gesture earlier in the day, he seemed to offer her some of his own strength and warmth. Maybe to let her know she wasn't alone. Maybe to let her know he felt as she did. Or perhaps all three.

She slipped her arm around his waist, and when he pulled her closer, she felt enveloped in his tender and powerful care. Side by side they stood, silently watching the fire.

"It seems like the end of the world...," she began, but again, her voice faltered.

Zach nodded, his eyes still on the licking flames. "But it isn't, Molly. If ever a people could be known for their resilience, it's San Franciscans. You were still sleeping yesterday after the quake and didn't see the activity." He turned to her, a slight smile on his face.

"Do you know that people were on their way to work three hours after the earthquake? Men in suits and ties were walking to the financial district."

He shook his head appreciatively. "The cable car tracks had buckled so the cars weren't running, but that didn't stop them. Off to work they went, almost as if nothing had happened." He chuckled. "I heard this morning that some banker downtown, before he evacuated because his building was about to be detonated, left a sign on his door. Guess what it said."

Molly shook her head. "I can't imagine."

"Closed for Extensive Remodeling."

She finally laughed. "What spirit!"

"People throughout the country may be predicting San Francisco's demise, but not the San Franciscans themselves. They're a spunky, eccentric bunch. It will take more than an earthquake for this city to give up."

Molly again turned toward the fire. "It's still a desperate time. Terribly frightening."

"Are you thinking of returning to England?"

"No. I'll not go back. And you?" In the glow of the fires, the moonlight shining down on them, she could clearly see the strength in his expression, the compassion in his gaze.

Zach touched her face with the backs of his fingers. So lightly, so tenderly. Then his fingertips brushed under her chin, and he lifted her face. Gently, ever so gently, he covered her lips with his. The kiss was almost reverent.

He pulled back slightly and looked into her eyes. "Molly," he whispered, his voice husky. But he said no more.

Molly drew in a shaky breath, feeling her legs about to buckle beneath her. "Maybe we should sit down," she suggested, her face still tilted upward as she considered him.

He grinned, seeming as stunned by the kiss as she was. "A good idea." They settled onto a low stone wall that ringed the clearing. They faced each other, the glow of the fires behind them.

"You didn't give me an answer, Zach."

He smiled again and reached for her hand, brought it to his lips, and kissed her fingertips. "I think I forgot the question."

Molly found it difficult to concentrate. She swallowed hard. "How about you? Are you going to return to England now?"

"No. I'm not sure what's happened to the boat I told you about the other night. If it survived this, I'm still planning to head to Monterey and go into business there." He regarded her solemnly for a moment. "I won't know until I find the fisherman I bought it from."

"You've said Monterey is the most beautiful place on earth."

"Even the word 'beautiful' is inadequate." The strain of the past hours seemed to disappear from his face. "I'd love to show it to you someday."

"Tell me about it."

Zach gathered her closer, his arm wrapped snugly around her shoulders. "There's a place I want you to see, Molly. It's in the pines, much like these, on a cliff rising from the ocean. The beach is rugged and rocky, in some places covered with sea lions and seals. The sound of their barking and splashing carries up the slopes. The sea gulls cry out as they swoop and dive."

She snuggled closer, enjoying the warmth of Zach's arm around her. The smell of the burning city, the slight shudder of aftershocks, the muffled explosions, all seemed far away as she settled against him. "Tell me more," she said.

"At dawn, when the light is perfect, the ocean seems to glow with a color that defies description." He rested his cheek on her

137

head, and Molly felt cherished and safe.

"Close your eyes now and shut out the fire and the smoke," he murmured. "I'm going to tell you about a secret place. Someday you'll go there and you can tell me if I described it properly."

She looked up at him and gave him a small smile. But Zach's expression was serious. "All right," she sighed, as she shut her eyes. "Don't leave anything out."

"You can only get to this secret place by climbing from the beach, though it's not as daunting as it sounds. You see, if you know where to look, there's a natural rocky staircase just so a person can climb to the top of the sea cliff."

"How will I find it?" Her eyes were still closed.

He chuckled. "You will need a guide, of course."

"Of course."

"Once you climb to the top, you can look out at Monterey Bay to the north and to a thick and verdant pine-and-cypress-forested hillside to the south. Carmel-by-the-Sea is on the other side of the small peninsula."

"The artists' colony?"

He nodded.

"It sounds beautiful." She let out a contented sigh, picturing it.

"But that's not what makes it unique."

She waited for him to go on, feeling strangely calmed by the deep resonance of his voice.

"On certain days at first light when the sun slants across the water, something of a phenomenon occurs. I've never seen it anywhere else. It happens only in the spring."

"It has to do with the perfect light you mentioned earlier?"

"It's as if God sprinkled millions of diamonds, sapphires,

and rubies across the top of the ocean. And as the waves break, the sunlight streams through them, and they appear to be turquoise and jade."

Eyes still closed, Molly tried to picture such a place. It sounded magical, something from a child's fairy tale her grandmother might have read to her long ago. The danger and chaos surrounding them now seemed far removed from such a place.

"And will you build a castle there? It sounds like a splendid place for one."

He laughed softly. "I've thought the same thing. Perhaps not a castle, though. I've seen enough of life from within a manor. But a home? Yes. At the top of the cliff."

"And the family inside could look out at the sea, waiting for the dawn, watching for the sparkling jewels."

Zach nodded slowly, his cheek again resting lightly on her head. "Yes," he said simply. "They could."

Then he pulled away, and they sat looking at each other. After a moment, Zach spoke again. "I want to take you there someday."

She smiled. "I'll decide if you've described it properly."

His expression was now serious. Molly could see his eyes clearly in the hazy moonlight. "After all that's happened, are you still planning to follow your dreams, Molly?"

"I'm as determined as ever. I suppose there's a bit of the same spirit in me that you've described about the San Franciscans." She stared down at the smoking, fiery ruins of the city. "I want to help San Francisco rebuild. I don't know how I'll manage it, but I do know I'll give it my best effort."

"It?"

"The effort, you mean? I suppose I mean building a business." She shrugged.

"Tending your garden?"

Molly could see a sadness in his expression as he faced her. "Yes, planting and tending my garden."

"Our worlds seem so far apart."

"You'll be living in Monterey and taking your boat out on the open seas."

Zach sighed deeply and reached for her hand. "And you'll be here in San Francisco, creating an investment empire and rebuilding the city, becoming the toast of the town."

She laughed. "That's quite a prediction."

"But will you be happy?"

Molly considered him solemnly. "I suppose so," she whispered. "It's what I've always wanted to do."

"Your plans don't seem to include time for anyone else."

She looked up at him thoughtfully, considering his words, though she didn't respond to them. Instead, she asked, "What about your dreams, Zach? Will you be happy?"

He squeezed her fingers, looking down at her hands. Then he lifted them to his lips and kissed her fingertips. "I'll miss you terribly, Molly."

She swallowed hard and nodded in agreement. "You're not leaving soon, are you?"

"No. I plan to help the Forresters get settled into their temporary shelter. Then I'll be on my way down the coast." He regarded her for a moment in silence.

"Perhaps you'll be in San Francisco from time to time," she offered.

He gave her a half-smile. "Or you'll be in Monterey. You did mention investing in the fishing business there."

"We'll see each other again, Zach. We won't be that distant."

"Once a year, twice, perhaps?" He laughed softly, his voice

holding a touch of irony. He looked out at the red glow of the flames devouring the city below them. Then he turned abruptly back to Molly, his expression intense. "What if you loved someone so much that you wanted to be near them, now and forever? Would love make a difference in your plans, Molly?"

Molly looked up at him, her eyes widening. "Love?"

"Hypothetically. At what price do you give up your dream?"

She drew in a deep breath. "There is no price tag on it, Zach. It's just something I have to do. I can't do or be otherwise." She paused. "I can't give up my plans any more than you can give up yours."

He looked away from her, and his voice dropped huskily when he continued. "Love is in the equation, you know." It almost seemed that he was speaking to himself.

"Zach?"

He turned to gaze into her eyes. This time, she lifted his hands to her lips. "I've come to..." Her voice was barely more than a whisper. But she couldn't go on. How could she tell him she loved him too, then turn and walk away—walk away to follow a dream in which he had no role? She wouldn't do that to him.

"Promise me something, Molly," he said, after a few minutes.

"Anything."

His lingering gaze caressed her face. "Will you someday go with me to the sea cliff?"

"Yes."

"At dawn?"

She nodded. "I'll be there." It was a lighthearted promise, spoken by survivors of a cataclysmic event, but the invitation was also somehow dearer than any other words he could have uttered. Perhaps because the promise was something to hold onto as they moved separately into an uncertain future. "I'll meet you there three years from the day of the earthquake," she added.

He laughed softly. "Three years seems about right, for us both." He didn't explain why.

"Our promise," she repeated, smiling into his eyes. "Ours alone."

After a moment, Zach took Molly's hand and helped her stand. His expression was tender. "I'll miss you, Molly. More than life itself, I'll miss you."

Before she could speak, Zach drew her closer. He kissed her eyelids, the tip of her nose, her forehead—then, a heartbeat later, his mouth covered hers. This time his lips met hers with unbridled passion.

On her tiptoes, Molly circled her arms around Zach's neck, running her fingers through his hair, feeling its silken thickness, feeling their hearts beating almost as one.

"Oh, Molly," he murmured into her hair. "My sweet Molly, how can I bear it? I feel we've just now discovered something far too precious to let go."

Molly pulled away slightly. She touched his face gently, letting her fingers trace the side of his jaw, wanting to memorize everything about his chiseled features. Then she nestled again into his arms.

For several minutes, they stood clinging to each other, a blood-like glow in the skies behind them, a smoky haze of moonlight hovering over them.

Molly looked again into the depths of his eyes. It was as if she had stepped from some frightening shadow of the unknown into a pool of sunlight.

But as they walked along the path leading back to camp,

fresh pain filled her heart. How could she leave this man? How could she let go of her love for him? Was any dream worth the cost?

Tears filled her eyes. Zach gazed at her quizzically as she brushed them away. "It must be the smoke," she murmured.

She clutched his hand as they walked, suddenly feeling she wanted never to let go.

CHAPTER

12

THAT NIGHT, LONG AFTER MOLLY HAD RETIRED to her tent and the camp had quieted, Zach lay sleepless on his cot. Molly Quinn filled his every thought. It seemed that there had always been a place in his heart awaiting her arrival. He hadn't known who she would be, or what she would be like, but when Molly Quinn entered his life, she was an exact fit. He thought he'd known it from the time she arrived at the Forresters'.

He remembered how she'd straightened her hat and fluffed her hair, primping at her reflection in the door's darkened glass, not realizing that he stood on the other side watching her. He'd never seen such an enchanting creature, from the top of her flower-covered straw hat to the tips of her buttoned shoes. He'd seen from the beginning that her petite figure belied her fierce independence.

How did one describe Molly Quinn? Invincible? Undauntable? He chuckled to himself. Maybe there was no describing such a creature.

Zach wasn't a particularly religious man, though he did believe in the God of nature and universal sovereignty. He had to wonder if God had brought him and Molly together as part of some grand design, or if the two of them, pursuing opposite dreams, were part of some divine comedy.

Years ago, his grandmother, who claimed that God was her dearest friend, would hold him on her lap and read to him from the Bible. Odd that he should think of her words now. But the words had been coming back to him, even comforting him, during the worst of the quake and its aftermath. He couldn't remember it all, but just snatches of what she'd read to him so long ago:

Fear not...I have called thee by name and thou art mine. When thou passest through the waters, I will be with thee. And through the rivers...they shall not overflow thee. When thou walkest through the fire, thou shalt not be burned, neither shall the flame kindle upon thee....

I have loved thee. Fear not...I am with thee.

The God who spoke those words didn't appear to be callous, one who would stage a divine comedy. No, this God said: *I have loved thee. Fear not...I am with thee.*

Again, Zach's thoughts turned to Molly and to their future. Could this same God bring them through the cataclysm of the present, through the desert land that stretched before them, only to bring rivers of life and love to them later?

He considered the loneliness he so often felt. Was it Molly alone who could fill that loneliness?

Or was it God? And if it was, how would he ever know him in such an intimate way?

Zach finally drifted to sleep, almost feeling the rhythm of his grandmother's rocking chair, her frail arms holding him with a fierce love, telling the little boy he used to be that he belonged to her precious Lord.

The following morning, horse-drawn wagons filled with clothing and supplies headed up the broken streets toward camp.

Even before sunup, people shouted that they could see the slow-moving vehicles pulling toward the distribution area.

The place became a hubbub of activity. Children laughed and played as if waiting for Christmas morning. Young and old, rich and poor milled about, speaking of the latest news from the city. In the distance, the smoke still billowed from the fires, and the explosions continued without interruption. But mostly, people turned their backs to the reminders of destruction and concentrated on food and clothing.

Zach and Molly, taking it upon themselves to gather items for the Forresters, lined up in the already forming queue.

"I'm going to head into town later," Zach told her, as they moved slowly toward the lead wagon. "See if I can find some mode of transportation."

"A horse?" She smiled, picturing Zach riding it back like some Western cowboy.

He laughed. "I'm thinking more in terms of a bicycle."

"I heard someone say that some of the cable cars will be running by the end of the week," Molly said, shaking her head in disbelief. "You're right about San Franciscans, the way they're bouncing back."

"I still think it's a good idea for us to have a bicycle at our disposal. Not all the cars will be running for a while. We'll need to get around town to see about building materials for Gwennie and Kingsley."

"I want to help, Zach. I'm not afraid of hard work."

He smiled appreciatively. "Do you feel up to going into town with me?"

She nodded. "Yes. I'm sure it's going to be a shock. But I want to see for myself the destruction, the fires."

Minutes later, they took their turn at the clothing wagon.

Zach picked out warm clothing for himself and Kingsley while Molly dug into the piles of mismatched clothing, rummaging through until she'd found several warm wraps for Gwennie. Finding something to fit her own tiny size proved to be more of a challenge.

Finally, she smiled at Zach. "Here's the perfect ensemble!" She held up bicycling bloomers, leggings, and a matching sailor-collared jacket. It was navy blue, trimmed in gray. She handed the treasure to Zach, who grinned at her delight.

Digging into the pile again, she came up with a couple of gored flannel skirts, slightly worn, and two ladies' outing jackets. Nothing matched, but they would have to do. At least, she thought with a sigh, they were clean.

She put them on top of the pile already in Zach's arms, then went to a different wagon for shoes. She had to guess at Gwennie's size, and finding something small enough for herself was practically impossible. She finally settled on some nondescript slipper-like shoes, suspicious they were made for gymnasium use.

After picking up their rations for breakfast, eating with the Forresters, then helping Gwen wash and change clothes, Molly prepared for the trip into the city.

In her tent, Molly washed her hair over a basin of water, then scrubbed herself clean as best she could. She stepped into the bicycling bloomers and grinned as she looked down at herself. Secretly, she'd wanted such a costume since they first came into vogue a few years earlier. But at home in England, such outfits were considered risqué, and she hadn't had time since arriving in San Francisco to give it much thought.

Until now. She felt like dancing a small jig. Even the leggings and silly little shoes fit. It felt wonderful to be out of the ragged morning dress. And when she considered the morning stretching before her, she let out a small sigh. She would be in Zach's company. There was no other place on earth she'd rather be.

She stepped outside the tent. Zach stood watching her, scrubbed clean and dressed in his newly acquired clothes. She decided immediately that no matter what Zachary MacAlister might wear, he was still very much the titled son of a duke. He looked magnificent, standing in the sunlight, his face bright with gladness to see her.

"I'm ready," she said, moving toward him.

Gwen looked up, her wrinkled face breaking into a wreath of smiles. "Dear, dear, I wish you'd gotten me a costume like that, Molly. It would suit me much better than what I'm wearing." She looked down at the frilly morning wrap Molly had brought her from the wagon.

"I'll grab you one off the next wagon, Gwennie," Molly said, with a laugh. She twirled before Gwen, her arms out, then stopped and gave the older woman a warm hug. "I promise—sailor collar and all."

A few minutes later, Molly and Zach walked from the camp onto the street leading into the city.

"It's going to take us a couple of hours to get there, Molly. If you get tired and need to rest, we'll stop. You'll tell me?" He raised a handsome brow.

"Of course. But my head feels almost normal today. I'm sure I'll be fine."

They picked their way along the buckled, debris-strewn street, heading toward the fire still raging in the distance. Every block they passed held evidence of houses lost, piles of wood and bricks, and sometimes fallen trees.

Molly was impressed by the number of people already working to clear their property. She and Zach stopped a few times to ask families how they were doing. Everyone was eager to talk, to tell of their experiences. Many said they were getting ready to rebuild. More than one mentioned that they thought the greatest difficulty would be getting a loan without security.

But she said nothing to Zach of her plan to contact Winny for advice and to wire England at once for her family's funds.

By midmorning, they'd reached the outskirts of the financial district, only to find hundreds of people standing in groups by the barricades that denied them access to the inner city. The army had posted guards ordered to fire at anyone who tried to pass. The towering flames, now only blocks away, licked the gray skies.

An older man at the rear of the crowd warned Zach that Fearless Freddie had ordered the drafting of all men, young and old, into service to help with the detonating, guarding, arresting of looters, and street cleanup. "I'd not get any closer to the action," the man said. "Not unless you want to be grabbed off the street."

Molly and Zach backed away from the place. Smoke billowed hundreds of feet upward, and its acrid smell filled the air. "I've seen enough," she said, as Zach took her arm and guided her back up the hill a short distance.

"You rest here. I'm going to go back and inquire about where to get bicycles." He helped her settle onto a cockeyed bench leaning against a pile of rubble.

Molly was too tired to argue. Her head was now throbbing again. She nodded. "Be careful, Zach. You heard what Funston is doing."

"I will, Molly. Just stay here and wait."

She closed her eyes, resting them briefly. But it was impossible to relax, the explosions were too close. She could feel the earth tremble as each building detonated.

Minutes passed, and she began to worry about Zach. What if Funston had pulled him off the street, pressed him into service? What would she do without him? She kept her eyes closed, determined to rest for the walk, or bicycle ride, back to their camp.

Around her, people walked about the street, voicing their fears. She heard more than one say that San Francisco's earthquake and fires signaled God's wrath. An older man spoke of Mount Vesuvius erupting just before the quake. A woman said she'd heard Chicago was now at the bottom of Lake Michigan and that Manhattan Island had sunk. "The entire West Coast is aflame," a younger voice cried. "It's the end of the world!"

Molly pushed their voices and fears from her mind, but the explosions grew even closer, louder, and still Zach hadn't returned. Another deafening explosion shook the earth. Molly felt her heart quicken. Swallowing hard, she tried to push her worries about Zach from her mind.

Remembering how she'd been calmed by the beautiful, secret place by the sea, she forced her thoughts back to Zach's words of the night before. She tried to picture it now. Every detail—the jeweled water, the barking seals. She smiled at the thought.

Then her heart froze. Zach! What if he didn't meet her? What if he *couldn't* meet her? She pictured herself alone at the place and felt a prick of hot tears behind her eyes.

Where was he? What if something had happened? She stood, shading her eyes against the red glare of the fire, scanning the crowds of sightseers. But he was nowhere in sight.

Weakly she settled back onto the bench. What was happening to her? She had always taken pride in her common sense, independence, and courage. Here she was, acting like a sniveling, clinging, hothouse flower. This was not the Molly Quinn who'd traveled the seas to America to become a woman of means.

Another explosion rattled the ground, but Molly, lips pressed together, forced the anxieties for herself, for Zach, from her mind.

"Molly!" Zach finally called to her from up the street. He came to her holding the handlebars of two bicycles, one on either side.

"What's wrong?" He looked into her face. "You're pale. What's happened?"

Molly couldn't explain. She shook her head and took a deep breath. She tried not to think how his tender, quizzical gaze made her knees weak. "I…I was worried," she managed. "I thought maybe Fearless Freddie had gotten you." She laughed shakily.

Zach dropped the bicycles and gave her a quick hug.

"I…I think I'm skittish…everything is in upheaval." She meant her inner world as much as the physical world around them.

"Things will be getting better soon," he said, misunderstanding. "I've heard that some of the fires are actually starting to die out. People are moving back into their houses. All of this," he gestured toward the fire and smoke and soldiers, "will disappear. We'll all be back to normal soon."

He reached down and pulled the bicycles to standing. Both were a bit rusted and dented.

"You got one for me?"

Zach grinned as Molly tried out the handlebar bell. "Have you biked before?"

She shook her head. "I think you'll have to teach me."

"'Twill be an honor, m'lady." Still smiling amiably, he gave her a quick, chivalrous bow. "But I suggest we find some level ground, preferably without buckles and cracks."

"Which may be hard to find in San Francisco right now."

"Actually, not so difficult as you might think. The bicycle shop owner just told me that he heard the army's already repaired some of the streets. And they're already laying new track for the trolleys. A few of the cars will be ready to run again by the end of the week."

Molly followed Zach, pushing her bicycle up the street on the long trek back to camp. They had climbed a mile or two out of the city when Zach spotted a smooth and level cross street.

The small Victorian houses flanking the wide tree-lined avenue seemed miraculously untouched by the quake. A few toppled chimneys and several broken windows were the only evidence. Molly was surprised to see families going about their chores—a gray-haired woman tending her garden, a boy walking his dog, a maid hanging out wash—almost as if nothing had happened. It was a lovely place. The fires and billowing smoke seemed far away.

Several people called greetings as the two prepared for the lesson. As Molly planted one leg on either side of the bike's frame, Zach propped his bicycle against a nearby elm. Turning back to her, he explained the rudiments of balance and speed, then held the back wheel steady as she climbed onto the seat.

"Ready?"

She nodded.

"All right. Nice and easy. Slowly...slowly." And the bike began to move forward. He walked alongside Molly as she pressed down on the pedals, fighting to keep the vehicle upright.

She giggled nervously as they made their way down the street, picking up speed. "Don't you dare let go," she tossed over her shoulder. She felt precariously unbalanced.

"Steady now," Zach said calmly. "You've almost got it. Don't go too fast."

The front wheel wobbled and the handlebar twisted. She straightened both, beginning to feel a heady exhilaration. "I've got it. I think I've got it!"

"A little faster then."

"Are you still holding on?"

"I'm here," Zach called to her.

The wheels were turning faster, and Molly could feel the breeze cooling her face, lifting the hair off the back of her neck. She had never felt such a sensation of movement. It was altogether lovely.

"Okay. Put on the brakes now," Zach instructed.

Molly braked the pedals as he had shown her, and the bike stopped. Her smile widened as she hopped to the ground.

"Ready to try it alone?"

She sighed nervously.

"I'll hold on for a bit. Then, once you're rolling, I'll let go."

She swallowed hard and nodded again as she straddled the bicycle.

"Steady now. Here we go."

Hopping on the seat, she worked the pedals again, harder, faster, concentrating on keeping her balance. "Let go, I'm ready!" she called over her shoulder. Zach did as she instructed, and picking up speed, Molly sailed along the street. The feeling was frightening. And it was rollicking fun!

She laughed out loud, so wondrous was the experience. She turned at the end of the block and shouted joyfully as she headed back to Zach. "I'm flying, Zach. Absolutely flying!" She laughed again and rang the handlebar bell.

As she approached the place where Zach stood grinning at her, Molly pressed the pedals backward and came to a halt beside him.

Zach watched Molly, her cheeks bright pink from her exhilarating ride, her mass of dark curls streaming behind. The wild beauty he saw in her porcelain face at that moment made his heart catch. Her emerald eyes shimmered with joy, perhaps more pronounced now because of the contrast with the recent sadness and fear he'd seen in them.

She stood before him in the dappled sunlight filtered through a canopy of elm leaves.

"I'll never forget this day as long as I live," she said breathlessly.

"Neither will I, Molly."

Within weeks he would be leaving her, but he would always carry the memory of her look of joyous abandon. He already knew that there wouldn't be a moment she would leave his heart while he was away from her.

He wondered if she would miss him as desperately as he would long to be with her.

"You're a quick learner, Molly Quinn," he finally said. "Not to mention brave, courageous, and stalwart. San Franciscans don't realize what a force they've got among them." He paused, not wanting to let go of this moment in the sunlight. "If you take to your investment schemes as quickly as you took to this..." His voice fell off and he gave her a half smile. "I have a feeling your dreams may just come true."

She looked up as if surprised at his words. "I don't know if that's a compliment or a condemnation."

"Perhaps a little of both, depending on which of your dreams gives you the desires of your heart."

Molly didn't answer, but turned her attention back to the bicycle, preparing to mount again. He followed suit, and after a moment, they began slowly biking back toward the street that would lead them up the hill and into camp.

Within the hour, they were in sight of the dozens of tents that made up their temporary home. Though they had pushed their bikes up the hill instead of riding, their conversation had languished. Molly seemed lost in thought.

"Molly?"

She turned to him expectantly.

"This is no good, you know."

"What do you mean?"

"After last night...today, being with you. I don't know if I can leave. I don't know if I want to leave."

For a moment that seemed to stretch into eternity, Molly stared at him. He couldn't read her expression.

Finally she sighed. "Our lives are about to take different courses, Zach. We're different, you and I. We want different things out of life. Nothing can change that." She studied him again, her expression unreadable. For the first time, though, in her emerald eyes, he saw a glint of the businesswoman. Something in her gaze told him she would not change her mind about her future. Not for him. Not for love.

They wheeled their bikes across the compound to the place where Kingsley and Gwen awaited them. The stiff set of Molly's shoulders told Zach that something had altered between them. He wondered if she feared her own vulnerability, her own feelings, if she allowed herself to love him.

Or maybe, he decided, the love of her dream was greater than anything she felt for him.

At that moment, a new thought occurred to him. Would he ever be willing to stand second to Molly's ambitions?

He thought not, and something chilled in his own heart.

CHAPTER

13

THE ASHES FROM THE FIRE were barely cold when the cleanup began. Some of the heavy stone, brick, and mortar chunks were loaded onto ore carts brought in on temporary rail lines routed into the heart of the destroyed area, but most of the debris was hauled away by horses pulling drays. The work was so taxing that thousands of the horses died, creating a parade of wagons carrying them from the city to be burned. Much of the debris was dumped in the bay, but when that was filled in, the rest was towed in barges outside the twin peninsulas known as the Golden Gate and dumped into the ocean.

By the middle of May, just weeks after the earthquake, new building materials were arriving daily by train. Nearly every district had begun rebuilding. The city seemed alive with an air of contagious energy. Hundreds of construction workers arrived from all over the country, knowing that the San Francisco job market was booming.

Many of the tent villages had been dismantled and the displaced families had moved back to their newly repaired homes.

In some cases, as with Gwen and Kingsley Forrester, people lived in rented tents at the sites of their destroyed homes while they cleared the property, prepared new home designs, and searched for loans to rebuild.

For days, Kingsley and Zach had combed through the rubble of their home, salvaging bits and pieces of memories. Finally, the broken boards, sheets of plaster, and roof shingles were carted away, and the land was clear. Only the bricks remained, heaped at the back of the lot, to be used again.

Kingsley had made several trips into the financial district, seeking a loan. Many banks were set up in makeshift offices, sometimes no more than a board stretched across two boxes. Disheartened with each new rejection, he trudged home to tell them the bad news. He wanted the new house built before the end of summer and knew he couldn't wait much longer to begin.

One night, Kingsley came back from the city with the news that he had wired their son, Lawton Forrester, in Sacramento. He had asked Lawton to begin the legal procedures for placing one of the family stores back into Kingsley's name, explaining the need for collateral. The son had readily agreed, but explained that because of the legal entanglements caused by the quake, it would probably take months for the transfer of ownership to be registered, even longer for a loan to be approved.

Lawton had offered to seek the loan in his name, but Kingsley turned him down flat. "As I said before, I don't want to live with the boy," he said to Gwennie, Zach, and Molly. "And I don't want to be beholden to him—or any other part of my family, here or in England." He looked pointedly at Zach, then continued.

"I came to America independent as the day is long. And I'm not ready to roll over and play dead, letting someone else run my affairs. I'm not too old to do this on my own."

Molly's heart went out to Kingsley. She could no longer put off her visit to Winny in San Quentin. They'd exchanged letters, and she knew he had made it through the quake safely. But now it was time to speak to him in person about business matters.

She had been so busy helping with the property cleanup and caring for Gwennie that she had found it difficult to get away for the entire day it would take for the trip, especially because she'd have to travel to the waterfront by bicycle. But now some of the cable cars and trolleys were running, and she needed to go.

On a foggy morning toward the end of May, she rose early to prepare for the trip. After bathing in the small lavatory that Zach had built near their tents, she pulled on a skirt and jacket, twisted her hair into a knot, and put on her straw hat.

As she stuck in the hat pin, Molly thought how the hat, with other clothing items, had been found surprisingly untouched, inside her wardrobe. Gwennie's wardrobe had also survived, leaving her delighted with the unexpected wealth of her own silk undergarments. This was exceeded only by her delight at finding several of her books undamaged—the entire Shakespeare collection, and many of her favorites from the upstairs sitting room bookcases.

Sighing, Molly stepped out of her tent and headed toward the Nob Hill cable car.

"Going my way?" a voice called out.

She turned and smiled. Zach was just steps behind her. "I'm heading to the waterfront, to catch a ferry."

He fell in step with her. "To Sausalito?"

She nodded. "To see Winny."

"I'd wondered when you might be going."

"And you?"

"I've got to see about my purchase."

"Oh, yes, it's about time for your fishing business to begin. The repairs are finished?" She knew that Zach had contacted

159

the seller days after the quake to find that his craft had survived intact. And it had been anchored far enough offshore to escape the waterfront fires. The seller had promised certain other repairs by the first week in June.

Zach nodded slowly. "Any day now. The last time we spoke he was putting on the final touches."

"I'd like to see it." They had walked to the top of the hill, and the cable car tracks were in sight. The creaking of the cable car moving up the hill could be heard in the distance.

"And I'd love nothing more than to show you." He took her elbow as they walked, guiding her around some of the other early-morning travelers heading for the city. "Do you have time today?"

"I'll go with you to the docks first. You can give me a quick tour before I board the ferry."

Molly looked up at Zach, trying to read his expression. Since the day he'd taught her to ride a bicycle, he'd kept at a distance. In fact, this was the first time they'd spoken without Gwennie or Kingsley in their presence. She realized, however, that Zach wasn't entirely at fault. She hadn't encouraged anything that would bring them close, anything that would cause her to lose herself again in his arms.

The cable car drew to a rattling halt, and Zach took Molly's hand, helping her step up and take a seat. With a rattle and jerk, the car started moving back down the steep hill. For a long time, they didn't speak as they rode along. Molly was unsure what to say.

The fog was lifting, and a thin sun tried to break through the mists.

"Molly." Zach finally turned toward her. "I'll be leaving next week."

"I…I thought you planned it for June."

"Yes, originally. But as soon as the boat's ready, I need to take her out, make sure she's seaworthy, before heading down the coast."

"You won't be back?"

"No. If all runs smoothly, I'll just keep sailing south." They passed several tall Victorians in various states of repair. The morning workmen were just arriving. "Before I actually sail, though, I'll be moving on board."

She nodded, unable to speak for a moment. Then drawing in a deep breath, she met his gaze. "When?"

"Probably tomorrow."

"It seems too soon. I'm concerned about Gwennie and Kingsley. How will we—?" Then she stopped, unwilling to admit that he was still needed. Besides, maybe he wasn't. He'd done the work of ten men, clearing the property, seeing to the disposal of the debris. The last loose end was Kingsley's loan so the building could begin. And she planned to see to that herself.

"I…we will miss you, Zach."

"And I you." But instead of elaborating, he turned away from her, and Molly bit her lip to keep the tears from filling her eyes.

By the time they arrived at the terminal, the sun had broken through the morning mist. Zach, ever the gentleman, held Molly's arm, helping her step from the car. They transferred to a trolley, still without speaking, then rode the rest of the way to the waterfront district in silence. The sad quietness between them was so different from the tender and joyous times they'd spent together immediately following the quake.

"Over here." Zach escorted Molly across the bustling wharf

area to the dock where hundreds of small boats bobbed in the choppy waters. Farther out, several schooners lifted their graceful bows to a nearly purple blue sky.

A grizzled old fisherman spotted Zach, waved, then made his way toward them. Zach made the introductions.

"Molly, this is Windjammer."

She looked at the old man in surprise. He gave her a toothless grin. "That's right, Windjammer's what most folks call me. But my friends call me Jam. I'd be obliged to consider anyone who's a friend of my boss," he glanced at Zach, "a friend of mine."

She shook his callused hand. "Then Jam it is."

Zach asked about the vessel. "It's ready?"

"It is, son. Finished up the last bit of painting yesterday." He winked. "If'n you catch my meaning."

Zach patted him on the shoulder. "Then let's have a look, shall we?"

"Sure enough. Sure enough, son. You and the little lady just follow me."

Stepping over coils of ropes and circular crab nets, then wending their way through a maze of drying sails, Zach guided Molly as they followed the man along a newly built dock.

Jam turned and looked at them again with his toothless grin. "Here she is." He stood back to let Molly and Zach step into a tiny, beat-up rowboat.

Molly looked up at Zach in surprise. "This is it?"

For the first time all morning, his expression brightened. He threw back his head and laughed. "No, Molly. This isn't it."

She tilted her head, feeling a bit silly. "This obviously is a tender, to take us to your boat."

He nodded, and beside him the old fisherman chuckled.

"Yours is farther out?"

"Yes."

She looked across the harbor. There were no small fishing boats, only a few graceful schooners anchored solidly a distance from the wharf.

"Sit down, Molly." Zach, still laughing softly, reached for her hand as they settled onto the bench seat, while opposite them the fisherman began to row. "We'll be there in a few minutes."

Soon they neared a three-masted schooner, sails rolled, its white hull gleaming in the sun. It was small, graceful—magnificent. "Oh, Zach," she breathed, "is this it?" She glanced at his face. It was filled with pride.

Zach's smile widened.

"But I thought you'd gotten yourself a fishing boat. This is no boat." She thought about all the times she'd called it that. She turned back to him. "It's beautiful. I had no idea."

"And there's something more." He nodded to the old fisherman who began to turn the tender toward the bow of the vessel. They circled the hull slowly so that Molly could see it from every angle. Finally, they reached the stern and the fisherman stopped rowing.

For a moment, the little rowboat bobbed up and down. Molly's gaze went from the tallest mast to a sweep across the deck. She was about to say something about his needing a crew, when she noticed the vessel's name.

She turned back to Zach. This time, she didn't bite her lip to stop the tears from forming in her eyes.

"Oh, Zach." Her voice was barely a whisper, but it was all she could manage. Then her gaze again took in the name painted in emerald script across the stern. Zach had named his graceful schooner the *Molly Quinn*.

Molly went into his arms, knocking her straw hat askew,

nearly sending it sailing into the water and overturning the little tender. For the longest time, neither of them spoke; Zach just held her tight.

Jam cleared his throat, and with a sheepish laugh, Molly pulled away.

A few minutes later they boarded, and Zach conducted a tour, telling her the schooner's history as they went. The *Molly Quinn,* originally called the *Golden Gate,* had been built for whaling forty years earlier, then taken out of service when the industry came to a close. It had been dry-docked when a San Francisco banker found it and began the refurbishing, only to lose interest in the project. Windjammer had purchased it for a song, finished the repairs himself, then put it on the market—with only one catch to its sale. He wanted to head up the crew that would sail her.

"Jam's sailing with you?"

Zach nodded, looking pleased. Molly couldn't help but feel happy for him. His expression told her that this was exactly where he belonged, on this beautiful vessel, the wind in his hair, the sun on his face, the open seas in his heart.

After a peek into Zach's captain's quarters, Jam helped Molly into the tender and rowed her back to shore to catch the ferry to Sausalito.

Zach didn't accompany her. As she pulled away from the *Molly Quinn,* the old fisherman rowing, she tilted the brim of her hat against the glaring sun. From the deck Zach waved, and she blew him a kiss, waving gaily in return, wanting him to know that she was happy for him.

By the time the tender deposited her on shore, Zach had disappeared from view, and Molly's heart was filled with sadness.

∽∘∾

"Winny!" She reached for her cousin's hands through the wire barrier.

"It's about time you got over. I've been worried about you, Moll. One letter wasn't nearly enough to convince me you're all right." Cousin Winston Carlisle-Jones looked thinner. A shock of red hair fell across his pale forehead, and his freckles stood out almost as if in bas-relief.

"I know, Win. I tried to come sooner. First it was the cable cars, then I couldn't leave Gwennie."

"It wasn't that bad here, but the news from San Francisco was grim. I didn't know if you'd made it."

Molly squeezed his fingers, sorry to have put him through such uncertainty. "I tried to ring you up, but even that was impossible. Most of the lines are still down."

"Tell me everything that happened. Don't leave anything out."

Molly related the details of her ordeal from the first moments of the quake through its fiery aftermath.

"Now," she sighed, after she was through, "I've got something to ask you."

Winny nodded, an expectant look on his face.

"What do you think about going into the banking business?"

"Banking?"

"Savings and loans, only for right now it would be mostly loans."

He looked skeptical. "What do you have in mind? I'm sure it's not an idle question."

Molly explained about the thousands of people who'd lost

everything in the earthquake or fires, only to discover they had no collateral for loans.

"I see it as an opportunity we can't pass up, Winny. What do you think?"

"It's risky." Then he laughed self-consciously. "As if I should worry about that."

"That's why we can charge high interest. The clients would understand that going in. I'm also considering a penalty for early payoff."

"Do you think your clients would agree to that?"

"It's the only way I can get started. If the payoff comes at the wrong time, it may be too late for me to find other clients without collateral. It's the only way I see to avoid having the whole scheme collapse later."

"Some may think it's ruthless, Moll. Are you sure you want to get into this?"

"If they think it's ruthless, they can borrow elsewhere."

"How soon are you planning to get started?"

"Immediately. If you can give me some advice about drawing up legal contracts, I'll see to getting them printed up by the end of the week."

He told her who to contact in the city for advice about interest rates, payment schedules, and payoff penalties. "But before you do anything else," he said, "I want you to contact an old friend of mine in Sacramento. His name is Julian Starr. He's a top-notch lawyer, knows contract law, politics, and the banking business inside out. He'll help you set up the paperwork for your business. Also the legal language for your contracts."

Molly nodded and wrote down Julian's name and address.

Winny grinned. "Besides, I think you'll like him."

She raised an eyebrow. "What do you mean?"

"Let's just say, the ladies find him, well, very attractive. Wealthy. Sophisticated. Erudite. Quite the man about town. He's constantly mentioned in the society sections of the local papers, his name linked with this socialite or that. There are rumors he'll someday be governor."

"Back to business, Winny. I'm not in the least interested."

"Just thought I'd mention it, Moll." Winny shrugged.

"Let's get back to your advice for my business, not my social life."

"Have you wired London for the money?"

"No. I'll do that immediately as well. Though I'm planning on having it sent to a Sacramento bank. Our financial district was completely destroyed. San Jose's also."

"And how about your plans for investments in Monterey?"

She told him what she'd discovered before the quake. "As soon as we've got money ahead, then I'll look into the canning business." She smiled. "I've not forgotten Monterey, believe me."

"Is there some other reason you've got a heightened interest in the Central Coast?"

"There might be," she said simply.

"That must be why you weren't all that keen listening to me tattle on about Julian Starr."

Before Molly could answer, the guard, standing nearby, sidled closer, indicating that the visit was over. Molly squeezed Winny's fingers goodbye.

"Don't stay away so long, Moll." And she promised she wouldn't.

It was dusk when Molly arrived back at the Forresters'. During the afternoon, she'd contacted the legal consultants Winny recommended, ordered the printing of the contracts for her new business, Quinn Investments and Loans, and wired London for the family's funds to be deposited in a Sacramento bank in her name.

After their simple dinner, Zach, Kingsley, Gwen, and Molly sat outside in the balmy spring air sipping their coffee and speaking of Zach's departure the following day.

During a lull in the conversation, Molly cleared her throat nervously. "I have something to tell you," she said to Kingsley. All attention turned to her.

"I'm starting an investment and loan business."

There was a stunned silence.

"You are?" Kingsley's voice held just a hint of a patronizing tone. Molly didn't blame him. After all, as friendly as they were to her, she was still considered a penniless domestic.

"Yes, I am." She went on to explain about the family business she'd been expected to start upon arriving in this country. "It's quite a sum that they've collected. And they're leaving it up to me to decide where, when, and how to invest.

"I've been listening to the difficulties you, and others like you, are having finding loans without collateral."

Kingsley's keen-eyed gaze never left her face. She could feel Zach's appraising stare as well.

"I've decided that's exactly what I'm going to do."

"Make loans without security?" Kingsley's voice was thoughtful. "That's terribly risky, Molly. I'm looking at it from your side of the fence."

She nodded. "I realize that. Which is why I have to charge high interest rates."

"How high?"

"Double the going rate."

Kingsley chuckled. "It sounds like a famous idea to me."

She let out a deep sigh, suddenly realizing she'd been holding her breath. Kingsley's business opinion had been terribly important to her.

"It's so risky that I would also recommend—again, from your side of the fence, not mine—that you charge a good-sized penalty for early payoff."

A slow smile spread across her face. "I was thinking the same thing."

"How much do you have to loan?" There was a look of admiration on the stately older man's face.

She told him.

Kingsley nodded slowly, appreciatively. "That's enough to give you a modest start, with room to expand later, when those payoffs start coming in."

"I'm hoping so."

Finally, Gwennie spoke up. "I'd like for us to be your first customers, Molly."

"I hoped you'd say that."

For the first time in weeks, Kingsley's face lost some of its worry lines. "I think we've got a deal, Miss Molly Quinn, banker extraordinaire! I will be honored to be considered for a loan of, say...." He quoted a figure.

Molly told him that the money would be ready for him within the week. Then she stood and shook his hand. "You can start building that new house, now," she said. "I can't wait to see the plans."

"I can't wait to have breakfast in the rose garden," Gwennie said.

There was an air of celebration among the four. They spoke into the night about their plans: Zach's sailing off to Monterey,

Molly's banking enterprise, and the building of the new house.

The moon was high when Molly finally stood and excused herself to retire to her tent. She kissed Kingsley and Gwen goodnight, then her eyes met Zach's. He rose and walked with her a ways from where they'd been sitting.

"You're leaving tomorrow," she said.

"Actually, I'll be living aboard ship here in the bay for a week or so. Jam's getting the rest of the crew together. We'll sail as soon as he's finished."

"Will you come up to see us before you leave, to say good-bye?"

"Of course." He reached for her hand and lifted it to his lips.

"I'll miss you, Zach. We all will."

"Your investment and loan idea is brilliant, Molly. I have a feeling you're going to find great success." His one-sided smile held a touch of irony. "I'll someday be able to say I knew you when."

She laughed softly. "I hope we're still friends when that day comes."

"Friends?" He raised an eyebrow.

"Can there be anything more? With your dream going one direction, and mine the other?"

The light went out of his eyes. For a moment he didn't speak, then he pressed her fingertips to his lips again. Without another word, he turned abruptly and left her standing in front of the tent.

Moonlight streamed around her, but Molly thought she couldn't bear the shadow that fell over her heart.

14

"TO THE TRAIN STATION IN SACRAMENTO." The sun was just rising as Molly climbed into the hired carriage.

The driver, a muscular young man, nodded as he closed the door after her.

Moments later he flicked reins over the backs of two grays and the carriage pulled away from the Merchant's Trust and Savings Bank in Oak Grove, a small town outside Sacramento. Julian Starr had recommended the bank, owned by a friend of his from Berkeley.

Molly had been in the area since the previous day, consulting with Julian Starr and seeing to the transfer of funds from the London bank to her new account at Merchant's.

She settled into the comfortable leather seat, her valise at her side. Inside, the papers for Quinn Investments and Loans' first transaction were in order, simply awaiting Kingsley's signature. She also carried a bank draft for the loan itself. Kingsley and Gwen would be able to begin work on their new Nob Hill home immediately.

Her thoughts went back to her meeting with Julian Starr. Winny had been right. The man was handsome, almost to a fault. Tall, thin, blond. Eyes the color of bits of sky. Impeccably dressed and a gentleman through and through.

They'd gotten along famously. She was impressed by his brilliant mind, especially his keen interest in her business ideas. Before leaving his office near the Capitol, Molly had put him on retainer, arranging to meet with him to review all new contracts. Instinctively, Molly knew that she could learn a great deal from Julian, and she looked forward to meeting him regularly to work out the details of her transactions.

The carriage rocked, and Molly touched the seat to keep her balance. Outside the windows, the passing landscape was bathed in late spring's pale green grasses and yellow-and-purple wildflowers. Here and there, low hills broke up the lush terrain along the Sacramento River.

As the carriage rolled along, they passed steamers filled with San Franciscans heading inland. She'd heard that many were moving away from the city, deciding to leave the rebuilding to others. Wanting to get away from all reminders of the earthquake, besides moving to cities such as Sacramento, hundreds were heading down the coast to areas such as Carmel and Monterey.

Monterey. She drew in a sharp breath, thinking of Zach. It had been several days since he and Molly had talked outside her tent, and she hadn't seen him since. In fact, Kingsley and Gwennie hadn't heard from him, either. He'd promised to visit before leaving for Monterey, but she knew the time was getting short. He'd said he planned to live on the *Molly Quinn* for a week before sailing.

If his departure calculations were exact, he might be readying to leave immediately. What if today was the day he'd stopped by Kingsley and Gwennie's to say goodbye? And because of her trip to Sacramento, she missed him? Would he leave without seeing her again? It might be months, even years, before they would meet.

Molly swallowed hard, feeling a lump in her throat and a sting behind her eyes. How she would miss him! Even during the bustle of the past week as she visited business contacts in the city, Zach had never been far from her thoughts.

As she rode cable cars and trolleys, or walked to and from her appointments, she would wonder what he was doing. Then she would picture him on the small schooner, the wind ruffling his auburn hair, the sun browning his face. Then as now, she would consider the light in his gray eyes as he gazed at her, and her heart would skip a beat.

The carriage hit a pothole, jolted, and swayed. They were just a few miles away from the landing, when Molly, smiling to herself, picked up her parasol and tapped the carriage ceiling. The driver immediately halted the horses and came around to open the door.

"Can you get me to San Francisco faster than if I take the train?"

The young driver grinned. "Yes, ma'am. It'll only be faster if I get you to the ferry on the east side of the bay, and you take it across. But you'll be in for a wild ride."

"What's the fare?"

He told her, and Molly smiled. "All right, then. Get me to the ferry landing by three o'clock."

"Yes, ma'am," he repeated, giving her a mock salute.

"And hurry."

"That won't be a problem, ma'am."

Minutes later, the carriage was rocking more precariously than ever as they headed west. The driver flicked his reins over the team of grays, and they moved as one across the valley floor, their hooves pounding the dirt road in a powerful cadence.

Several dusty hours later, with only one stop to hitch up fresh horses along the way, the driver drew the team to a halt and opened the door for Molly to exit. She paid him, then, valise in hand, headed toward the east bay ferry. Within another hour, she'd stepped off the vessel in San Francisco's waterfront district and hired a tender to take her to the *Molly Quinn*.

The late afternoon sky was a brilliant cloudless blue. Molly's little skiff glided along as if on glass, the cadence of its captain's oars casting a diamond spray of light across the waters.

As she neared the schooner and its name came into view, Molly thought again of Zach's regard for her. For the thousandth time, she wondered how their emotions could run so deep and their stubbornness so complete that they could say goodbye, perhaps for years, perhaps forever.

Forever? She pushed the thought away. After all, no matter what their lives held in the near future, they had solemnly promised to meet three years from now.

The tender's captain rowed to the ladder at the side of the *Molly Quinn*. He hailed the crew. "Ho, there!" he shouted.

A moment later, Jam's weathered face peered over the side. It broke into its usual toothless grin at the sight of Molly.

"Hold on," the old fisherman called down to her. Then he swung his wiry body down the ladder, took her valise, and helped her onto the deck.

Finally on board, Molly smiled at Jam. "I was worried you'd left. Last I heard, Captain MacAlister said you'd be ready to set sail in a week."

"If you'd waited one more day, you'd've missed us," Jam said, with a nod. "Tomorrow at daybreak's when we're off." His face softened. "Fact is, the cap'n just got back from the city. Been there collectin' the rest of his gear."

"So he's on board?"

"That he is, Miss Quinn. That he is." Then he grinned. "Though last I saw of 'im, he wasn't in too jolly a state. Came back in a stew."

Molly tilted her head, not understanding.

"Seems he didn't get to say all his goodbyes, though I'm surmisin' it now. Didn't know fer sure earlier what the tizzy was all about. Not until I set eyes on your skiff headed this way. Now that I know you weren't there for his farewell..." He gave her a knowing grin, raising his eyebrow.

Molly felt her cheeks redden.

"You want me to fetch him?"

"Yes, Jam. Please."

"Then you just wait here." He nodded to the bow. "And I'll get the cap'n." With another wily smile, Jam sauntered off.

Molly stood at the bow, looking out to the open seas. Tomorrow morning the *Molly Quinn* would unfurl her sails and head out of the bay.

"Molly!"

She turned to see Zach striding across the deck. When he reached her, he grabbed up her hands, his gray eyes filled with delight at the sight of her.

"Zach," she murmured softly.

"I saw Gwennie and Kingsley this morning. When you weren't there..." His voice dropped off for a moment. "I...I worried I wouldn't see you before we sailed."

"Jam tells me you leave tomorrow morning."

He nodded. For a moment he didn't speak. A breeze came up off the bay, mussing his hair. He combed it back absentmindedly with his tanned fingers. Molly noticed his skin had bronzed, and his hair had lightened from the sun. He looked fit and more contented than she'd ever seen him.

"How long until you come back?"

"Not for a while, Molly. This ship is my home. Of course, we'll anchor in Monterey. Though I'll probably be out to sea more than I'll be there."

Molly turned to the railing and held onto it as she looked out at the water. "I'll miss you," she whispered, not knowing whether he heard her or not.

Zach stepped closer, enfolding her in his arms. He placed his cheek against the side of her forehead, and she leaned back against his chest. For a long time, they stood silently. Almost mournfully, Molly thought.

Then Zach turned her gently, so that she faced him. His eyes searched hers. "Molly, you've become a part of my life, my every thought, during the past few months. I can't imagine what it's going to be like not to see you. Not to speak to you."

He sighed, shaking his head slightly. "Being away from you this past week has seemed like forever, even though it's been only seven days. And now the time stretches ahead, weeks, months, perhaps years. I can't help but wonder if it will ever be different, if *we* will ever be different. Will our dreams always keep us apart?"

"Zach, I care deeply for you. You've touched a place in my heart, a place I didn't even know existed. It's almost as if you've awakened me to love, to the possibilities of love. And not in a transient way, but permanent. Everlasting."

He drew her closer, but Molly gently pulled away. "No, let me finish."

He nodded, his expression reflecting her own confusion.

"At the same time, Zach, I'm feeling more vulnerable than I ever have in my life. And scared." She paused, suddenly wanting him to understand. "That day we were in the city—do you remember when you gave me the biking lesson?"

He nodded. "Something changed in you that day."

"Yes. When you were off buying the bikes, I became worried that you wouldn't return. The explosions. The drafting of men off the streets. I became frightened. So, to calm myself, I pictured the same cliff you told me about. Only I was there alone. Something had happened. It was the day we promised to meet, and you weren't there." She bit her lip, feeling the threat of tears just remembering it.

Zach reached for her hand. "Go on, Molly."

"I...I didn't think I could bear it." Her gaze met his, and she drew in a deep breath. "And I didn't like the feeling."

"It goes against your grain."

She nodded. "Yes."

"So you pushed me away, afraid you'd lose yourself, your dreams, because of me."

"Yes," she said again.

"We can't love each other and not be vulnerable," he said. "It goes hand-in-hand with deep caring."

"There's so much I want out of life," she whispered.

"And you're afraid that your love for me will stop you from pursuing those dreams?"

"I think we've talked about this before."

"We have. But I don't think you know how I feel."

"You're right." She laughed softly, a bit embarrassed. "I've been so caught up in my own pursuits that I haven't asked, have I?"

He smiled gently. "I'll wait for you, Molly. I'll never push you to give up your dreams. Ever." He paused, watching her intently.

"But when you come to me, it will be because you've chosen to do so. You'll have 'tasted' the dreams you desire, and you'll come to me in full knowledge of what you're leaving behind. There will be no desperate longing for what might have been. I can't wait forever, but I can wait long enough for you to live your dream and make your choice."

"But we will see each other between now and the day we promised to meet?"

"I hope you'll come to Monterey, soon."

She smiled. "I plan to. But it may not be for quite some time. I won't have any capital to invest until some of my loans are paid off."

"So this will be our goodbye until then."

"I prefer 'farewell.'"

"As do I, Molly." For a moment his gaze carressed her. Then he cupped her face in his hands and tilted it upward, tracing her lips with his thumb. Smiling, he bent down and kissed her, his lips lingering on hers. At first the kiss was tender, then the tenderness deepened into something passionate and wildly alive.

Molly slipped her arms around Zach and returned the kiss. Her heart pounded, and she thought of nothing but the pleasure of being in his arms.

"Oh, Zach," she finally murmured when she could speak. She touched his face, wanting to memorize everything about it. "I don't want to think of life without you."

He kissed her again, then held her fiercely. "Molly," he whispered in a ragged voice. "All my good intentions are melting away." He pulled slightly back so that he could look her in the eyes. "Are you sure of your dream?" Before she could answer, he hurried on. "Marry me. Sail away with me now, my darling.

We'll never be parted again."

Then he seemed to see something in her expression that stopped him from continuing. He laughed softly. "No," he said quickly. "Forget what I just said. Having you in my arms made me forget myself—even my own dream—for a moment."

Molly touched his lips with her fingers to quiet his words. "I'll never forget what you said, Zach. How could I?"

He reached for her, gathering her again into his arms. "Zach, there's something I haven't told you," she said, her cheek resting against his chest.

"What is it?"

"It's something I need to tell you before you sail, before we're parted."

"Go on."

She looked up into his eyes, delighting in the emotion she saw there. She sighed softly. "I love you, Zach," she finally whispered. "I do...oh, so much more than you can know."

"Oh, Molly." He pulled her closer, burying his face in her hair. She could feel his heart pounding and his muscular arms surrounding her as if he would never let go. "Oh, how I love you!" His voice was husky with emotion.

For a long time, they simply held each other, looking out at the bay, speaking of the future, and trying not to dwell on the length of time they would be parted. Nearby, pelicans dipped and soared, competing with the more-graceful sea gulls for space on the fishing boats. Here and there, the bark of a seal or the cry of a swooping gull broke the silence.

When the sun began to slant low across the water, Molly said she needed to get back to the Forresters' before dark. Clouds were forming in the west, promising a vivid orange-and-red sunset.

Finally, they could put if off no longer. Zach walked Molly to the ladder and the tender tied below.

"I'll go with you to shore."

But Molly shook her head. "I want to look back and see you standing on your ship. It will be my last sight of you," she said. "And I want to remember you here on the *Molly Quinn*."

Zach nodded, understanding. "I'll get Jam to take you back." Then he gathered her into his arms one last time. "I'll miss you so much."

She took a deep breath, nibbling her bottom lip to keep from weeping. But when he lifted her face with a gentle touch beneath her chin, her tears were already brimming.

"Oh, Molly," he sighed. "Don't cry. Then I really can't bear it." Holding her face, he wiped away her tears with his thumbs.

"I'm all right," she whispered. "This is just the most difficult thing I've ever done."

"If you change your mind—"

But Molly smiled quickly, and on tiptoe, kissed his lips before he could go on. "I know," she said after a moment. "I know."

A few minutes later, she was seated in the skiff. Zach, who had descended the ladder with her, handed her the valise, gave her another kiss, then climbed back aboard ship, watching as Jam rowed her slowly away.

Zach raised his hand, and Molly waved. Just before the sun slid into the Pacific, the *Molly Quinn* was bathed in the golden light of a glorious sunset. She caught her breath at the sight, knowing it would stay in her memory forever.

She watched Zach until his vessel disappeared behind the other schooners, clippers, and fishing junks. Finally, she turned and faced the shore, speaking lightly to Jam, desperately trying to keep her mind off the man standing on the deck of the *Molly Quinn.*

She forced herself to think about the imminent beginning of her new business, about her new life helping to rebuild the energetic San Francisco, and about a glorious future in which all her dreams would come true.

But without Zach? She tried to shove the thought from her mind. Despite her resolve, however, the sadness of leaving him affected her deeply. And she knew it would be a long time before the ache of missing him lessened.

Zach stood aboard the *Molly Quinn,* watching the tender move toward shore. It slipped in and out of the long shadows cast by the setting sun against the varied fleet of vessels, some readying to leave with sails unfurled.

At first Molly faced him, waving farewell, as Jam's oars skimmed the water, taking her farther away by the moment. He could see her lovely heart-shaped face with its halo of dark curls, strands lifted by the ocean breezes. He could also see her look of determination, as if, even in the sadness of their parting, she would let nothing deter her from the path she'd set for her-self.

He wondered if, when they next met, their feelings for each other would be as tender and loving. Though delicate in stature and gentle of spirit, Molly was strong with a tenacity he had rarely seen in a woman. Or a man, for that matter. Would she change? Would her foray into the hard world of finance harden her, take away those very things he loved in her?

The tender slipped behind a four-masted clipper. Then the tangle of ships and boats and junks became so thick that by the time the sun fell into the sea, Molly's skiff had become lost to him.

The San Francisco shoreline and its twinkling lights became visible. Zach stared across the bay, wondering at the sense of foreboding that overtook him.

THE PLANTING

1907–1908

To give them beauty for ashes,
The oil of joy for mourning,
The garment of praise for the spirit of heaviness;
That they may be called trees of righteousness,
The planting of the LORD, that he may be glorified.

ISAIAH 61:3, NKJV

15

Carmel-by-the-Sea

IT WAS SPRING AGAIN, and a year after he'd begun, Devon O'Rourke had nearly finished the oil painting of Mary Rose and Jesse, now three years old. He'd had to leave the painting for several months while he completed other projects, and now, he was glad to put on the final touches at last during this, their final sitting.

He moved the redwood bench so that Mary Rose was seated in the late-afternoon sunlight. This time of year, her daisies, hollyhocks, and climbing sweet peas added new hues to the background. Cascading wisteria and bougainvillea vines bloomed in vivid light-bathed shades, joining the freshly born roses. At her feet, lacy bleeding heart ferns with their crimson blossoms danced in the ocean breezes, and the wild irises dipped and turned in their delicate purple gowns.

Mary Rose looked up at Devon, smiling tenderly as she settled onto the bench. She wore the same silky, pale blue gown that she'd clothed herself in from the first sitting, and it fell in soft folds around her feet. Her thicket of blond curls shone golden in the sun, and as always happened during the sittings, Devon couldn't keep his gaze from her love-filled eyes.

Jesse climbed onto his mother's lap. Today, Devon planned to touch up the detail on the child's canvas image—his freshly pressed suit with its short pants, small blue tie, and matching leggings. The little boy grinned at the artist; he was still unused to the almost daily regimen of remaining quiet for his portrait.

Light and shadow dappled the garden. Devon, standing at the easel, began to add the final touches to the canvas, working to capture the sunlight touching Mary Rose's and Jesse's faces, the shadows from the leaves of the small olive tree and the Monterey pines that bordered the garden.

He mixed the colors on his palette. "Xavier stopped by this morning," he said, dipping his brush in a dab of yellow ochre. "He got back from Monterey late yesterday."

"Did he have a chance to go by the hotel while he was there?"

"Yes, and I've got news."

"Devon! How can you stand there calmly painting, when our whole future can turn on news from the Del Cortés!" Mary Rose looked prettily exasperated, trying to stay still and talk at the same time. "Tell me!"

He laughed, set down the brush for a moment, and wiped his hands on a cloth. "Actually, dear, if it had been *that* kind of news, I would have told you immediately."

"Then the *Hope* didn't sell...."

He shook his head sadly. "It's actually a step in that direction. But no, it didn't."

"Then what's happened to the painting? Xavier obviously had news from Oliver Duckworth."

Devon grinned. "He spent quite a bit of time with Duckworth. And what he found out is probably the best thing that could happen this side of selling for our asking price." He squeezed some crimson from a bent tube, then picked up the brush and dipped it in. "It seems Duckworth was about to contact me himself. Someone from the governor's office saw the *Hope*, liked it, and asked for it to be delivered to the Capitol. It will be included in a display of up-and-coming California artists."

"That's wonderful, Devon!"

He smiled again, nodding slowly. "It could be the break we're looking for...."

"You're about to add a 'but' to that."

"We didn't sell it, Mary Rose. We needed the *Hope* to bring in some income." His gaze met hers.

"I know, Devon. But this is an opportunity you can't pass up."

"You're right. I've already told Xavier to let Duckworth know I'm agreeing to the painting's transfer to Sacramento. It may lead to something better later. Perhaps it will be seen by someone who *will* buy it for our asking price."

"How about this one, Dev?"

"My painting of you?"

She nodded. "Yes."

"No."

"Why not?"

"You and Jesse are my family. This is for us. It will someday hang in our home."

Mary Rose wasn't to be deterred. "But you have us. You can paint others." She stood to move around to the other side of the easel where she could see the canvas. For a long time, she stood looking at the painting. "You've made us seem alive. I can almost see Jesse breathing." Her voice was soft, awestruck. "And the light, Dev, it's brilliant. The garden seems to shimmer with life and light."

"I don't see how I can let it go."

Mary Rose raised her eyes from the canvas to his face. Her expression was serious. "The great European artists sell their best work. And don't say you're not in the same league. That's why you must sell this. It's not a sentimental decision. It's a practical one. You must have your work seen."

Devon regarded the woman standing in front of him. She never ceased to amaze and delight him. Just when he thought he'd figured her out, she surprised him with her practical wisdom. He thought she would be the sentimental one, holding onto the painting as a symbol of their recent discovery of love. Yet here she was, fighting to let it go, to let it symbolize his talent to the world.

He gave her a lopsided grin, shaking his head. "You're the one who'll have to decide when you're ready to go through this again," he finally said. "If we place this one in the Del Cortés, then I'll insist on doing another. It'll mean another sitting, you know."

Mary Rose made her way back to the bench, scooping up Jesse on her way. "It will be a privilege," she said, as she hugged her son close. "But next time, I want to do the sitting for my husband, not my neighbor." She gave him a pretty smile.

He worked on the painting for a moment as she regarded him. "So that's the real reason you said what you did?" He raised an eyebrow. "It's not so much the talent you want the world to see—"

She laughed, interrupting him. "Dear sir, it's that. Indeed it is. But selling this painting, something that belongs to both of us, is also the only way I can think of to finance our marriage."

He laughed again. "I don't know which I love more about you, Mary Rose. Your artistic sensitivity or your wonderful practicality."

She was trying to hold very still while he worked. But she couldn't help smiling. And when she did, the sunlight touched her face, bringing even greater life to it. She sighed. "Let me tell you what I love most about you, Dev."

"I'm listening," he said, adding a touch of blue to the irises on the canvas.

"Be patient. It'll take me the rest of the afternoon," she teased. "Let me see, I think I'll start with your hair. Have I ever told you I always think of it as the color of wet sand?"

"Ah, spoken like a true artist."

"Or maybe it's your eyes. They remind me of the dawn, filled with light and promise."

"Now I'm getting embarrassed." He grinned, concentrating on adding a dab of yellow to the sunlight in Mary Rose's hair.

"Shall I go on?" Jesse snuggled up against his mother, and Mary Rose rested her cheek on the little boy's golden head, still considering Devon.

"Please do."

"The strength I can see in your neck and shoulders when you're working. That's another of those things I love about you."

"Now there's no doubt, I *am* embarrassed." But he was pleased. He squeezed a ribbon of white onto the palette.

"But do you know what I love most about you?"

He looked up at the change in her voice. The merriment was gone. It was now low and solemn.

"I love the way I feel when I'm with you, Dev."

He set down his brush and met her eyes.

"I'm filled with joy at who we are together, at who we are with Jesse. There's such love and laughter and belonging. It's an emotion so strong, so overwhelming, that I can't find the right words to describe it."

He waited as she searched for the words.

"Sometimes in the mornings, sunlight streams through my kitchen windows, flooding the room with joyous warmth. Fresh flowers are on my little table, the sweet dotted swiss curtains flutter in the ocean breeze, and a loaf of wheat bread bakes in the oven. I step into that place, and my senses are flooded with gladness."

She stood, put Jesse down, and walked toward Devon, reaching for his hand. "I know this may sound silly, Dev, but I have the same overwhelming sense of joy when we're together—gladness, delight, warmth, security. As if you have opened a room inside me, a room silent and dark with mourning and sadness. And your love is flooding it with light."

Devon pulled her closer, holding both her hands. He kissed her knuckles, rough from the hours spent working in her garden. "Every day, Mary Rose, I think it's not possible to love you more. Yet, it happens. I keep discovering new things to love, new things to delight in, new places of depth and caring and understanding." He let out a deep sigh and touched her face. "Right now, if it weren't for these paint-spattered work clothes, I'd like to pull you into my arms to stay forever."

"Me too!" Below them, Jesse tugged at Devon's pant leg.

Smiling broadly, he swept the little boy into his arms. "You too, Jess. You too!"

"And I, for one, don't mind a bit about the paint spatters." She moved into his embrace, then raised her face. He planted a kiss on the tip of Jesse's nose, then another on Mary Rose's lips.

"God's been so good to us, Devon." She smiled.

"Good to us," Jesse murmured, one arm wrapped around Devon's neck, the other around his mother's.

Devon nodded, gathering his little family closer. "And this is just the beginning."

"Let's go to the Del Cortés again as soon as the painting is dry."

"If you're sure, Mary Rose. This was going to be my gift to you."

"I'm sure."

He sighed. "All right. I'll get Xavier to begin constructing a frame. Maybe we can go to Monterey next week or the week after."

As Mary Rose and Jesse again settled onto the redwood bench, Devon concentrated on the painting. "We haven't thought of a name," he murmured absently as he worked. "Any ideas?"

"Mmmm...I've been thinking about it."

"And?"

"It's more a painting of my garden than a portrait. I think *The Garden* has a nice ring to it."

He smiled. "How about *Mary Rose's Garden?*"

"I like that too." She looked pleased.

"Would you mind having your name on the title? If it sells, becomes well known, you'll be giving up something of your privacy."

"I would be anyway. But then, Dev, you are also giving up privacy. It's the nature of what you do as an artist, selling the essence of who you are to the public."

As he worked, he thought about her words.

After a bit of time, she spoke again. "Besides, what difference does it make? Who would ever trek all the way to Carmel on a mission to find the people, or the garden, in your painting? It's the artist who'll get the attention, not the subjects of the art."

He laughed. "Your logic is remarkable, Mary Rose." He looked over the canvas at her, to see the merriment in her eyes. "You've convinced me. *Mary Rose's Garden* it is. I'll get Xavier to make the brass nameplate for mounting."

One week later, with Xavier's help, Devon lifted the newly framed painting into the rear of the padded wagon, then stuffed more padding around its sides for the journey to Monterey.

The day was promising to be hot. Earlier the sun had risen in a brilliant blue sky, and now, as the day progressed, it blazed down on the threesome in the wagon.

Leaving Xavier waving from the boardwalk in front of his shop, Devon flicked the reins over the horse and pulled onto the dirt road. Beside him on the bench, Mary Rose sat holding a wriggling Jesse. She turned and waved to their friend as the old mare plodded up the hill toward Pacific Grove. Devon reached over and lifted Jesse to the seat between them, letting him take a turn holding the reins. The little boy finally sat still.

Mary Rose was lost in thought as they wound into the Monterey pines and cypresses. It had been several months since she and Devon first discussed marriage. And it seemed they were no closer now than they'd been then.

She knew how strongly Devon felt about wanting to support her and Jess. He was too proud a man to marry her and simply move into the house that Carl had built for her and their infant son. Those times she'd tried to convince Devon that it didn't matter to her, that she simply wanted to be his wife—for better, for worse—and that material things didn't matter, he'd told her that he wouldn't even consider such an arrangement. Material or not, he'd said, it had more to do with a man's pride in caring for his family.

She glanced over at his profile as he drove. She never tired of looking at him and marveled that Carl's image had now slipped away so completely.

Sensing her look, Devon turned. "What are you thinking?"

"How much I love you."

He reached for her hand and gave it a squeeze. "Maybe this painting will give us the break we're waiting for, Mary Rose."

"Perhaps a summer wedding is around the corner."

He grinned. "I don't want to get my hopes up, but I'm sure praying for a miracle. We know God's timing is perfect, but I'm sure getting in a hurry."

She nodded, agreeing. "I've been pounding on the doors of heaven myself."

"It's your prayer garden in the painting. Maybe that will help."

"And you've captured it completely. The color, the dappled light. It's perfect. You even captured a bit of me in it—without my likeness, I mean."

"I know. As I've said many times, your garden is an artist's palette. Your composition of color and light is nearly the same that I try to recreate. It's more a part of you than what I do."

"I feel a part of this work. If it sells before the *Hope*, and we can marry because of it, it's almost as if it contains some essence belonging to both of us. It takes on greater meaning somehow."

He looked at her for a long time, and she noticed deep understanding and a sense of wonder in his face. Then the horse shied, and with a wide smile, he looked back to the road.

The sun was already on its downward slant when Devon pulled the wagon up to the front entrance of the elegant Del Cortés Hotel. Within minutes, a gushing Oliver Duckworth had helped them unload the painting. They met with him in his office, agreed on the consignment price, and signed the necessary paperwork.

"The *Hope* is now hanging in the state Capitol," the man said proudly. "I've already heard that it's receiving rave reviews. Everyone wants to know about this 'painter of light' from the Central Coast."

"But no offers?" Devon asked.

"Not yet. But give the *Hope* time. It's only been there a little over a week."

They walked into the large room where workers were deciding on the placement of *Mary Rose's Garden*. Its size required a smaller wall than the *Hope*. Devon pointed to a small alcove just off the front lobby. "There," he said to Oliver Duckworth. "Try it over there."

"Yes, I think you're right," the older man said thoughtfully.

"It's perfect," Mary Rose murmured, holding a sleepy Jesse in her arms. "Perfect light and space."

Devon agreed, and Duckworth ordered his men to move it. Minutes later, the three stood back, admiring the placement.

"This one's an even finer piece than the *Hope*," Duckworth said. "And I never thought I'd see anything I liked better."

Mary Rose looked up at Devon's work. The pale green alcove framed it beautifully, setting off the vivid colors of her garden. As with the *Hope,* Devon had captured a light that seemed to come from within the canvas, rather than from an outside source.

It took her breath away to see it. She glanced at Devon's face, aware that his thoughts were similar to her own. Pride mingled with sadness at leaving it for someone else's purchase.

Were they doing the right thing by letting it go?

"I think we should place a higher price on it," she blurted, without thinking. "Twice what we're asking." She considered it a masterpiece, but she couldn't imagine anyone paying that exorbitant an amount. And barring a miracle, the painting would still belong to them.

Devon and Duckworth turned to her abruptly. Their jaws seemed to drop simultaneously.

"I'm serious." She looked Devon in the eyes. "It's too fine a piece to let go for any less. Please, Dev. Consider it."

He gazed at her for another moment, as if seeing into her soul. Then he smiled slowly and nodded. "I agree," he said. "Let's try it and see what happens."

Duckworth let a low whistle escape his lips. "I hope you know what you're doing," he said. "If it hadn't been for the *Hope* and the acclaim you're now receiving, I wouldn't consider it. But..." He sighed, shaking his head slowly. "For all we know, O'Rourke may be considered the next Renoir. Far be it from me to stand in the way." He drew in a deep breath. "I may be crazy, but all right. I match your consignment price."

Mary Rose met Devon's loving gaze. He gave her a knowing smile as he hoisted Jesse into his arms, then, after their good-byes to Duckworth, they walked slowly to the wagon.

Devon suddenly stopped and reached for her hand. "Why did you do that?"

"Double the price?"

He nodded.

"I suddenly didn't want it to sell. It's too much a part of us. And I couldn't imagine a lifetime of never seeing it again."

He laughed softly. "I thought so."

"Did you feel the same way?"

He nodded. "Yes, but I didn't want to say. We can go back in there and take it home with us, you know."

"I know. But that doesn't seem right, either. I just figured that it's in God's hands. If it's meant to be, the right buyer will come along."

"Though at that price, it's unlikely."

"I know."

"It means we'll have to put off our wedding for a while." He gave her a one-sided smile. "Until I can finish another work."

"I know that, too." She let out a deep sigh. "I hope you'll begin immediately."

He pulled her close and gave her a warm hug. "As soon as we get home, Mary Rose. But keep in mind, the painting may sell for a small fortune. I think the sting of losing it would lessen in light of the joy it would bring us."

"My thoughts exactly." Suddenly the sun seemed brighter, the day even more festive than before. "And what a wedding we'll have to celebrate that joy!"

Devon threw back his head and laughed. Jesse, still in his arms, looked up startled. Then the little boy giggled and nestled his head against Devon's shoulder.

Soon the horse plodded down the road toward Carmel. Mary Rose moved closer to Devon, and he circled his arm around her shoulders. By the time they'd climbed out of Monterey and wound through the coastal pines of Pacific Grove, Jesse slept soundly, his head resting on his mother's lap.

Mary Rose thought she'd never known such contentment.

CHAPTER

16

ZACHARY MACALISTER STRODE through the downtown business section of Monterey. He'd just left the Cabrillo Canning Company. After nearly a year of working with the other canneries, he'd finally signed a contract with Cabrillo. He'd seen them about increasing his supply of salmon, and now he headed toward the bank to deposit the proceeds from his latest catches. The following day, he would need to return to make out the drafts to pay the crew their salaries.

In the months since he'd left San Francisco, his fishing business had steadily improved. New canneries were opening weekly, and the demand for sardines, abalone, clams, and salmon was growing. Most fishermen were cashing in on the sardine and clam trade because harvesting didn't take them far from shore.

But Zach preferred the open seas. Going after salmon fit the *Molly Quinn* and her crew perfectly. In fact, nowadays Zach preferred life as far away from land as possible. He wouldn't enter the city, other than the waterfront, if his business interests didn't require it.

The days were growing longer now, and there was a warm, sunny feel to the air. Zach walked up the hill, a mile or so from the center of town, to the Del Cortés Hotel.

The hotel always offered him a respite from the life of a sea captain. His business required him to stay perhaps once a month, but Zach couldn't deny that he enjoyed the comfort of such an elegant establishment. His attraction to O'Rourke's *Mary Rose's Garden* also kept him returning to the hotel. He'd been drawn to the painting from the first time he saw it. And his delight hadn't lessened with time. It was the one redeeming pleasure he took from being in the city.

He passed the hotel's gardens and crossed the manicured lawns, then took the stairs leading to the entrance two at a time.

"I'd like a room with a bay view," he instructed the woman at the Del Cortés desk a moment later.

"Our only room left is just now being made up," she said pleasantly, recognizing him. "But our maids will be finished in a half hour or so. You may wait in the lobby if you like."

Zach nodded that he would. He walked through the entrance hall, past the salons and shops, toward the heavy, rocky fireplace he could see at one end of the huge room. It was an inviting sight. The fireplace was ablaze with a newly laid fire, and now that the sun was down, the air felt chilly.

But as he was about to stroll into the room, he turned instead to the pale green alcove off to one side. He stopped directly in front of it.

The man he knew to be the hotel manager stepped up behind him. "Beautiful, isn't it?"

Zach turned. "Yes, it's splendid. I'm always glad to see it." He frowned slightly. "Oliver Duckworth, isn't it?"

Duckworth smiled and extended his hand. "Yes, you've got a good memory. I know you're a guest here regularly, but I'm afraid I don't remember your name."

"Zachary MacAlister."

"Nice to have you with us again, Mr. MacAlister." Duckworth turned back to the alcove. "I'm glad you're enjoying the painting. The artist, Devon O'Rourke, has a brilliant way with color, particularly the color of light. You've heard of him?"

"Only since I've been visiting his work here at the Del Cortés."

"He's an up-and-coming young artist out of Carmel-by-the-Sea. Known as the painter of light. One of his works hangs in the Capitol building in Sacramento. Causing quite a stir, from what I hear."

"Have you had any offers for this work?" As usual, Zach couldn't take his eyes from the painting. The artist had indeed captured an ethereal kind of light. It almost shimmered with life.

"As a matter of fact, I've got an art dealer quite interested right now. And he's got no quarrel over the price. He's planning to finalize the deal by week's end."

Zach looked sharply at Duckworth, suddenly wondering if he was being baited. But the hotel manager, a bland expression on his face, regarded Zach calmly. And, after all, the Del Cortés Hotel was considered the finest on the Central Coast, an elegant establishment without blemish. There was no reason to distrust Duckworth.

Zach turned again to the painting, though a sadness now tainted his pleasure. He would miss it when it sold. Duckworth took his leave, saying only that he was available to answer questions about the artist should Zachary need him. The manager then slipped quietly away.

Still waiting for his room to be readied, Zach took a few

more minutes to study the magnificent work. There was something about *Mary Rose's Garden* that reminded him of Molly—it had from the first time he saw it—though the subject of the painting, Mary Rose, looked nothing like her. The artist had painted his subject vitally alive with ruddy-cheeked good health, pretty and blond, eyes shimmering with light as if reflected from the sea. Molly was as delicate as a porcelain doll, with emerald eyes and cascading dark hair.

No, it wasn't a physical likeness. Perhaps it was the young woman's spirit, her bold expression, that reminded him of Molly.

Or perhaps it was the garden.

He remembered her words about creating a work of her own, watching it grow, blossom, bear fruit, like a well-planted garden. Only the garden she wanted to create was a far cry from Mary Rose's, so filled with light and life.

"Sir, your room is ready." The bellman stopped beside him, interrupting his thoughts. "You may pick up your key at the front desk."

He nodded and sadly turned from the alcove, reluctant to leave the painting. By the time he reached his room on the fourth floor, however, Zach had decided. He would buy *Mary Rose's Garden*. For Molly.

The last he'd heard, Molly was building a small house of her own near the Forresters. The property, originally part of the Forrester estate, had been signed over to Molly in lieu of the early-payoff fee from their loan. The O'Rourke would be his housewarming gift. And, he smiled at the thought, he would deliver it himself.

It would probably be another several weeks before Zach's business would allow him to travel to San Francisco. But

Gwennie had told him that their home, and Molly's, would be completed about the same time. Perfect timing, he thought.

Such a purchase would also require dipping into the savings from his family's estate, something he purposely avoided. But the painting had merit far beyond his own sentiments. Zach saw genius in the artistry. He also knew enough about art to realize that works by this young 'painter of light' would be a worthwhile investment, increasing in value with time.

Still, he couldn't help picturing Molly's face when she saw it. And it was sentiment that finally swayed him. He smiled, deciding to find Oliver Duckworth immediately and finalize the sale before the art dealer arrived in the morning. He would bid more than the asking price to ensure ownership, but *Mary Rose's Garden* would be worth every penny.

By nightfall, Zach had completed the transaction with the glittery-eyed Duckworth. As he anticipated, the man had to be convinced not to wait for the art dealer's arrival. When Zach finally wrote out the bank draft, it was for considerably more than the asking price.

He arranged for the O'Rourke's safe transfer to the *Molly Quinn* the following day.

"I…I don't know quite how to tell you this…." A white-faced Oliver Duckworth twisted his hat nervously as he leaned forward to speak to Devon O'Rourke.

The two men sat outside Devon's studio overlooking the bay at Carmel-by-the-Sea. Duckworth had unexpectedly arrived around noon, surprising Devon as he traversed the long, steep pathway, past Mary Rose's cottage and up the stairs leading to the studio.

Devon was getting exasperated. The manager of the Del Cortés was so upset he was inarticulate.

"Go ahead, man. Spit it out. You've obviously got bad news for me."

But Duckworth let out a deep sigh and moved his head slowly side-to-side. "I...I just don't know where to begin," he repeated, haltingly.

"Look. I can probably figure it out. *Mary Rose's Garden* has been at the hotel for six months now. Management has decided that's about six months too long." He shrugged. "You've come to tell me that my work's been kicked out." He sat forward, meeting the man's watery gaze. "Look, Oliver. It's not the end of the world. Artists develop thick skin." Devon wondered why he was trying to make it easier on Duckworth to deliver his bad news.

"No, no. It's not that. It's...worse. Much worse." Duckworth looked down at his hat. Zach noticed his hands were sweating.

"What can be worse than that?"

Again, pale watery eyes met his. "The painting was stolen."

"What?"

"I'm so sorry to have to tell you. I've put it off for days, since the...tragic event."

"How could that happen?" Devon couldn't take it in. "Why would someone do that? It's not as if it were a Cézanne or a Rousseau. Why would anyone bother with an O'Rourke?"

"It's my fault. I should have realized. We marked it with a high price. People may have assumed that it *was* done by one of the great masters. Thought it valuable enough to steal."

"Surely the hotel is liable for my loss."

Duckworth stared at him. "You and I made no such agreement. I'm sorry. I didn't even think of it. Nothing like this has ever happened. I never expected that it would."

"So I'm out a painting. The Del Cortés has lost nothing."

He shrugged. "I'm sorry," he repeated. "The way I see it, we were doing you a favor by letting your work be seen in such an establishment. We have no funds to compensate you. It's not something we've had come up before. You can understand—"

Devon cut him off. "Were Monterey authorities called in to investigate?"

"Of course. But whoever took the painting disappeared without a trace. I have the investigator's report," he reached into his coat pocket, "if you'd care to see it."

Devon took it. Two detectives had signed off on the loss, stating their inability to find any clues to the painting's whereabouts or the perpetrator of the crime. There was also a newspaper clipping stating sketchy details of the heist.

Devon shook his head slowly, still trying to comprehend such a crime.

"There's more to the story than I've told you so far. It will make your loss seem even worse."

"I can't imagine that."

Duckworth leaned back in his chair and crossed his leg, his pallor and his nervousness dissipating. "The evening before the robbery, your painting sold."

Devon sat forward attentively. "What?"

"It's true. A sea captain. We'd planned to complete the transaction the following morning."

"But the painting was stolen during the night?"

"Yes, son. I'm sorry. And he'd agreed to your asking price."

Devon let out a whistling sigh, attempting to understand all he was being told. "Full price?" For a moment he didn't speak. "Did anyone investigate the man himself? I can't be alone in thinking he might have had something to do with the robbery. Was he still at the Del Cortés?"

"Of course. We thought the same thing. But he was there, more upset than the rest of us. It was obvious that he had nothing to do with it. Of course, you're welcome to speak with him if you like."

"No, I don't know what good it would do."

For some reason, Devon noticed a flicker of relief in Oliver Duckworth's eyes. He assumed it was because he'd finished with his delivery of devastating news.

They spoke for a few minutes longer, then Duckworth stood and shook Devon's hand. "For what it's worth," he began, "the Del Cortés is willing to continue with our arrangement. The fact is, your painting very nearly sold for what you wanted. Your next work will command the same price. We will be reviewing our security arrangements so that we can guarantee this will never happen again."

Devon walked with him down the stairs toward the path leading into town. They crossed the bridge near the cottage, and Duckworth stopped.

"I know it's probably too soon for you to think about it, but do let me know if you have any other paintings that you'd like to place with us." He looked at Devon. "And please—accept my most sincere apology for what happened to *Mary Rose's Garden*." He started down the path leading to the road, then suddenly turned back to Devon. "This is the place, isn't it? The garden in the painting."

Devon nodded grimly. "Yes."

"I thought so. Interesting." But he barely gave Mary Rose's garden a glance as he headed back toward the Carmel road.

Suddenly, Devon couldn't wait for Oliver Duckworth to be

out of sight. It was as if his presence cast dark shadows across the garden, across life itself.

Devon agonized over his decision, pacing the small studio, indoors and out. By late evening he finally decided what he must do. In anguish, he walked slowly down the path to the cottage.

Mary Rose met him at the door, her beautiful face brightening.

"Mary Rose," he said without preamble, "something's happened. We must talk."

She nodded and led him to the little table in the corner of the kitchen, seating herself across from him.

"Do you want some tea?" Mary Rose started for the stove, but Devon gently caught her arm and stopped her. She settled back into her chair.

"No. I won't be here that long," he said softly. He felt his heart would break if he didn't get this over quickly.

A look of concern—almost fear—crossed her face, and Devon drew in a deep breath, praying for strength for what he must do. He took her hands in his. "*Mary Rose's Garden* has been stolen from the Del Cortés."

She gasped audibly. "Oh, no!"

"Oliver Duckworth stopped by this afternoon to tell me."

"Oh, Dev." Her voice caught, and tears filled her eyes. "It's gone?"

He nodded. "The worst part is that it almost sold, Mary Rose. The night before the robbery." He laughed bitterly. "For our price."

"Do they have any leads?"

"No. Believe me, I asked all the questions you're about to

ask, and the answer is no on all counts. No trace of the painting. It seems that no one knows anything."

"But maybe we can go to Monterey, investigate ourselves. Maybe there's something that's been overlooked."

"No." He pulled his hands away from hers. It would be easier that way.

Mary Rose looked up at him, puzzled.

"I'm leaving, Mary Rose."

"Oh, Devon. Don't give up. Not now."

"It's not fair to you. Nothing's going to change. And as long as I'm in your life, you're going to remain on the sidelines waiting. Waiting for something that's obviously not going to happen. Waiting for me. Unable to get on with a life of your own."

"Don't say that, Dev. Please!"

For a moment he regarded her, trying not to be moved by the look of disbelief and hurt on her face. But he had to make his words final, for her sake as well as for his. "And truth be told," he continued, "I need some space as well. You've seen how I haven't been able to paint lately. All I could think about was the sale of *Mary Rose's Garden*. The longer we waited to hear from the Del Cortés, the more I dwelt on dollar signs and what it would buy us."

He laughed sarcastically again and shrugged. "And for what? To find out that someone liked my 'masterpiece' well enough to steal it."

She swallowed hard, trying to choke back her tears. But still they traced down her cheeks as she again reached for his hands.

He pulled away from her. "It's better this way, Mary Rose. I need to get away, try to find that place within myself that will allow me to paint."

"Where, Devon? Where will you go?" Her voice was barely a whisper.

"I'm not sure. Find a lighthouse or two that I've not yet attempted to paint. Though, it's ironic. I feel the light's gone out from inside me. Some 'painter of light.'" He laughed again.

She lifted the edge of her apron and wiped at her tears. "All right, then. You've obviously made up your mind."

He nodded. "Yes, I have."

"Without even asking for my thoughts."

"You don't have anything to do with the decision, Mary Rose."

She drew herself up. "I don't have anything to do with this?" This time her laugh was brittle. "I have everything to do with it, Devon. Don't you see how it looks to me? I've forced you into a relationship that killed your artistic spirit." She frowned. "You don't see it, do you? You don't understand me at all. You've not even considered that if I had known, I would have asked you to leave anyway."

She glared at him. He tried to speak, but she held up her hand. "Let me finish." Tears again filled her eyes. "And Devon O'Rourke, don't you dare think I'll forget this day. I ventured out of a dark place in my heart where I'd been since Carl's death. I came out into the light—your light."

He stood and moved toward her, but she pushed him away.

"Now that light is gone," she said, her voice little more than a monotone. "Dead. Extinguished."

"I'm sorry, Mary Rose. I never meant for this to happen. I never meant to hurt you."

"Nor I you." She wouldn't lift her eyes to meet his gaze.

For a moment, a heavy silence filled the room, then Devon started for the door. He reached for the doorknob, then turned once more. But Mary Rose was no longer in the little kitchen.

He stepped out into the dark and made his way up the long path to the studio, planning to be packed and miles away from Carmel by dawn.

17

San Francisco

MOLLY STOOD ABOARD THE SAUSALITO FERRY, heading across the bay to visit Winny in San Quentin. She leaned against the rail at the steamer's bow, breathing in the fresh sea air. The coastal fog hadn't yet crept in, and overhead, sea gulls glided on the wind, white wings gleaming in the sun.

Looking back at San Francisco's skyline, Molly smiled, still amazed at the resilience of the city. Skyscrapers were going up, replacing those demolished in Fearless Freddie's explosions. The burnt-out ruins left by the fires had nearly disappeared, almost as if they never existed. Daily, rebuilt offices opened for business, and still other new buildings were begun.

Quinn Investments and Loans was now doing well enough for Molly to move the business from her makeshift office in her home to a newly rebuilt downtown building. The new location was on the outskirts of the financial district, but close enough to make it convenient for her clients. She had even hired an assistant, a friend of Gwen and Kingsley's, to help with the details of the move, then stay on as a receptionist. Miss Victoria Parrott, hair in a small gray twist at the nape of her neck, was middle-aged, prim, proper, and, Molly could already see, terribly efficient. A no-nonsense kind of woman with a delightful quick and biting humor.

The ferry pulled into the Sausalito terminal. Molly disembarked, then hailed a cabbie to take her to San Quentin. The road to the prison was busier than when Molly had first visited Winny. Since the earthquake, hundreds of families had fled San Francisco for other areas on the bay. New homes dotted the Sausalito hillsides. Even motorcars now putt-putted and back-fired along the narrow, winding roads—Whites, Wintons, and Columbias, with their colorful chassis and leather-rolled upholstery.

Someday, Molly vowed, as soon as her business allowed it, she planned to buy one of the noisy vehicles. Many people discounted them, saying they'd never take the place of a reliable horse-drawn carriage. But Molly could picture herself driving a scarlet roadster, the tulle netting of her hat scarf flowing behind her in the breeze.

The cabbie opened the carriage door at the gates to San Quentin. Molly nodded her thanks, paid him, then hurried to the visitor's section for her visit with Winny.

"Moll, you look wonderful." Her cousin squinted through the iron-mesh barrier, his expression approving. "Better than ever. Business must be booming to give you such a glow."

She smiled at him and nodded. "Indeed it is, dear Winny."

"Tell me the latest. I'm starving for news."

"Any word on when you'll be released?"

"No," he sighed, frowning. "Nothing. Possibility of parole for good behavior was included in my original sentence, but I've not heard anything."

"What about the behavior part?" She raised an eyebrow,

remembering her cousin's temper.

"I've been good, Molly, honest." But his grim expression said otherwise. "Enough of that. I want to hear your news. Tell me everything."

"Quinn Investments is doing well. I've written three new loan contracts just this week."

"That brings you to a total of..." He scratched his head, calculating.

"Twenty-seven since the quake."

"And you're still operating without requiring securities?"

She nodded. "It's the only way I can compete with the bigger banks."

"Has anyone reneged?"

"One smaller loan, just a couple weeks ago. A young family. The husband lost his job."

"You're lucky more haven't fallen through."

"I know," Molly said. "If I had to lose one, at least it didn't set me back much."

"And how about the pay schedules? Still on time?"

She grinned. "You sound like a true financial advisor. Julian would be proud."

"Julian, eh?"

"Back to business, Win. I'll tell you more about your friend Julian Starr a bit later."

Winny gave her a knowing look. "I knew the two of you would hit it off. I just knew it—"

She interrupted with an exasperated sigh. "What else do you want to know about Quinn Investments, Win?"

"You were about to tell me your payment schedule."

"I charge a lavish fee for late payments, just as Julian suggested. That keeps most people on their toes."

"And what about recent payoffs? Any to report?"

"Not since the Hydes and O'Sullivans. They were the last. I think I already told you about the Clarkes last month. Oh, and just recently, the Russells told me that they plan to refinance. Theirs is one of the larger loans, so when they refinance, their payoff of the Quinn loan will add nicely to my capital."

Winston let out a low whistle. "You're a wonder! I can't wait to join you, Moll. We'll be able to double the business."

Molly hesitated. "I don't know, Winny...." Her voice faltered, not knowing what to say.

A look crossed his face that Molly couldn't read. Then he looked away from her. "I'm sure you're thinking that I wouldn't be able to gain the trust of anyone locally after serving time in San Quentin."

She didn't respond.

He turned back to meet her gaze, and she noticed a change in his eyes. Where they'd been friendly and open before, now they seemed shaded, somehow. "But, Moll," he said, keeping his voice even. "I feel that the business is partly mine."

"I'm not going to turn my back on you, Winny. Don't worry. We'll figure out a way to bring you into the business."

"Behind the scenes, I suppose."

"Possibly," she said gently.

Winny leaned forward. "You're getting more investors from England. Maybe when I get out, I could oversee international investments from London."

She nodded, considering his words. "That might be a good solution."

Winny seemed satisfied, and the unsettling flicker in his eyes had gone. He settled back again, lifting an eyebrow. "Now, tell me everything about Julian Starr."

"Actually, there's nothing to tell."

"That's not what I hear from him."

"He's been to see you?"

Winny nodded, grinning like a Cheshire cat. "To ask about you, more than for any other reason. At least, as far as I could tell."

Molly felt her cheeks turn pink. "He did? What did he want to know?"

"The way to your heart, dear cousin. That's all."

"And you said—"

"To support your dream, of course. In any way he can. Am I not right, Molly? Isn't that what you want?"

She nodded slowly. "Of course," she said quietly.

Winny reached for her fingers though the wire barrier that separated them. "I'm sorry, Moll. I spoke in a flippant manner. Suddenly, you look so sad. I didn't mean to dredge up old memories."

Molly squeezed his fingers. The old Winny was back. "It's not your fault. Sometimes I wonder about Zach, that's all. It's been so long since I've heard from him."

"That's why you need to go out with Julian. He's a gentle-man of the highest order. He'll treat you well, Moll. No use moping after a man you may never hear from again."

"Aha, I get it. You told Julian that you'd try to convince me to see him?"

Winston gave her a guilty smile. "I admit that I said I'd try."

She sighed. "If you see him before I do, Win, tell him I'll be happy to see him—for business reasons only."

"Of course." Winny grinned. "I'll tell him."

"I'm serious, Win. I'm not interested in seeing him for any other reason."

The guard moved closer, indicating their time was nearly over. Winny leaned forward, reluctant as always to say goodbye to Molly.

"How about your house, Molly? You said last time that it was almost ready."

She smiled broadly. "I moved in two weeks ago, Win. The house is small, but beautiful. I think I told you that it's a Queen Anne, complete with gables and a small turret. Kingsley's helping me plant an English garden in the front."

"They've become like family, haven't they? Didn't you tell me they gave you the land to build on?"

"It wasn't a gift, Win. Kingsley set it up as part of the penalty payment for early payoff of their loan." She paused. "It was his idea, both to help me out and to keep me close. And I'm glad he thought of it. I don't know what I would do without them being next door."

"I'm sure they feel the same way. I hope I can meet them someday." He paused and gave her a charming grin. "Once my time is served, of course."

Molly didn't answer. She hadn't realized it until now, but thinking about his future somehow unnerved her. She changed the subject. "It's going to be difficult leaving the Forresters once I start working downtown."

"When is Quinn moving?"

"Next week. I think I told you about our new office." She had a hard time keeping the excitement out of her voice. It meant more to her than the little house.

"Yes, you did. I'm proud and envious at the same time, Molly. You've done famously. I just wish I could be there to—"

The guard interrupted. "Time to go, Mister Carlisle-Jones." His tongue rolled over the double name sarcastically. Winny met his mocking stare with a steely look of his own. Molly shivered when she saw it.

"Come again soon, Moll," Winny said as he was led away.

"I will, Winny. I promise."

Molly stepped into the entry hall, kissed Kingsley on the cheek, then bent down to hug Gwennie in her wheelchair. Earlier, the couple had invited her to join them for dinner. She was glad she'd accepted. Her long day in the city, her trip to San Quentin, and the fragrances wafting from Cook Liu's new kitchen made her appetite enormous.

"Come join us. We've been waiting." Kingsley, pushing the wheelchair, led the way into the newly furnished sitting room. Kingsley and Gwennie had combined the best of both their decorating tastes from his old library and from her upstairs sun room in the old Victorian. The result was a smaller room, sunny in the mornings, cozily elegant in the evenings.

After Molly was seated next to Gwennie on a plump settee, the older woman turned to her excitedly, reaching for her hand. "Dear heart," she said, "I didn't think you'd ever get here."

Molly laughed. "That's quite a welcome. I'm glad I came."

"Well, we have a special treat for us all tonight."

"Cook—?"

"Oh, goodness no," she laughed. "He's not made anything special. No, it's something precious and delightful for us all." She looked at Kingsley. "Dearest," she said with a smile, "will you get the letter for me?"

He nodded and rose to fetch it. "It's in the secretary?"

"Top drawer."

As he left the room, Gwennie smiled at Molly. "The letter is from Zachary. Just came this morning."

"And you saved it until I could get here?"

"Oh, yes. It's addressed to all three of us."

But before Kingsley returned, Cook came to the door and announced that the meal was ready to be served. Gwennie patted Molly's hand. "The letter will have to wait till after dinner, dear. Do you mind?"

"No, of course not," though Molly was disappointed. Zach didn't write often. She had heard from him only once since he left, and he'd written the Forresters only three or four times during the year. She pushed Gwennie's wheelchair into the dining room. Within a few minutes, Kingsley joined them, placing the unopened letter beside his plate.

"Now," he said from the head of the table. "Tell us about your day, Molly. You visited your new office this morning?" At his elbow, Cook began carving the roast pork. "Is it ready for the move?"

"And how about your furniture, dear?" Gwennie added, scooping a small helping of potatoes onto her plate. "Have you found a desk for Miss Parrott?"

Molly nodded. "Yes, the details of the move are all in place." She helped herself to a spoonful of applesauce, freshly canned from the previous winter. "As a matter of fact," she began, "I've got some questions for you, Kingsley."

He looked up. "Yes?"

"As you know, people aren't in the hurry they once were to secure a loan."

Nodding, he lifted his fork. "That's true. It's been over a year. I'm sure the initial rush is lessening."

"It also means that my potential clients are getting pickier. I'm no longer the only company offering loans without collateral."

"Ah. Bank of Italy's giving you competition. I figured it was a matter of time." Kingsley didn't appear surprised.

"Yes." Molly nodded thoughtfully, took a few bites, then looked back to Kingsley. "There's another small matter."

"And what is that?" Gwennie asked.

"I'm a woman." Both Gwennie and Kingsley gave her their full attention. "At first, it didn't matter. People were so delighted to find someone who would loan them the money that it wasn't a concern."

"But now?" Kingsley frowned and leaned forward.

"Now it is a concern. Most of my borrowers are men. The investors, too. The truth is, most of them would rather deal with a man than a woman in business matters."

"Have you lost business?" Kingsley asked.

"Not yet. But I can see it coming."

"What can we do to help, dear?" Gwennie touched Molly's arm, and Molly patted the thin hand.

"Actually, Kingsley..." She looked back to the head of the table. "How would you like to come to work for me?"

The white-haired man set down his knife and fork, a slow smile spreading across his face.

"I'm serious," Molly said. "I've given it a lot of thought. The company is growing, and I could use your help, your business expertise. I can offer you a salary, plus a percentage of whatever new business you write."

His smile widened. "It's not the money, Molly, though it would be welcome. What pleases me is that I can be useful again."

Gwennie broke in. "Kingsley, surely you've not thought of yourself in that way—unuseful. The very idea!"

He shook his head as if brushing away his wife's words, his

gaze still on Molly. "Tell me more," he said.

Molly explained the details of what she had in mind. "Then," she concluded, "if you decide it's too much, or that for some other reason you don't want to continue, you could quit at any time."

"I don't know about leaving Gwennie," he said, giving his wife a tender look. "She needs me."

"Dear, dear," Gwennie said, with a bit of a scowl. "I'm not exactly helpless, you know. Though she'll never take our Molly's place, we've got Miss Brown now." She reached for Kingsley's hand. "If you would like to work for Molly's company, I say do it. After all, our new home is finished." She sighed and gave her husband a small smile. "I know how energetic you are, dear. And I think Molly's offer is splendid. You have my blessing, Kingsley, if this is what you want to do."

He turned to Molly without further hesitation. "Then my answer is yes, Molly." He pushed back his chair and reached over to shake her hand.

"Welcome aboard, Kingsley." Molly couldn't stop smiling. Quinn Investments and Loans was now a company of three.

Kingsley leaned back in his chair contentedly. "Now that I'm officially part of the company...," he began.

Molly looked up from the dessert that Cook Liu had just placed in front of her. "Yes?"

"I've been noticing a new area of expansion that we might want to consider."

"What is that?"

"Brick making."

"I've thought of that myself, but right now we don't have the capital to move in that direction."

"What if you bring in another substantial investor?" His gaze was locked on hers. He was now all business.

"You know someone who might be interested?"

He nodded. "You remember, when I paid off my loan to you, that my son had sold my interest in three of the Forrester stores in the Central Valley."

"Yes, I remember."

"I've been waiting to talk with you about investing the proceeds in Quinn. Now, I think, is the perfect time."

Molly caught her breath. "Kingsley..." Then she glanced at a smiling Gwennie, who obviously had known about her husband's intentions, then back to Kingsley. She was astounded by his words. The stores had sold for tens of thousands. She swallowed hard before continuing. "You're sure about this?"

"Never been more sure of anything in my life."

Beside him, Gwennie laughed softly. "You're a gambler, dear. Don't deceive the girl."

Molly laughed with them both. "We're all gamblers at heart, or we wouldn't be doing this. Nothing is sure."

"Now," Kingsley leaned forward and took a bite of berry cobbler, his gaze still on Molly, "let's talk about those bricks people need for rebuilding this beautiful city. There's a nice demand right now, just right for thinking about the supply side of the brick business."

Molly grinned. "Tell me more."

By the time Cook Liu had cleared the dessert dishes and brought the silver coffee server and English china cups and saucers to the table, Kingsley had convinced Molly to buy a brickyard.

"Now," Gwen said, as they lingered over coffee. "Before you leave for home, we've got another item of business." She glanced at the unopened letter beside Kingsley's plate. "I think we've waited long enough. I, for one, cannot bear another moment's delay before hearing Zachary's news. Molly, dear, why don't you read it to us?"

Kingsley handed the envelope to Molly. She lifted the flap and pulled out a single sheet of paper, covered with Zach's bold script. In the right-hand corner he had written the date, April 18, 1907, a year to the day from the great earthquake. She read aloud:

Dear ones,

Since last I wrote to you, the Molly Quinn *has logged hundreds more hours at sea. Business is good. Even the local fishermen say that salmon fishing never has been better than this year. My crew is proving to be solid, and of course, Windjammer—Jam—keeps them, and me, fully in line.*

Monterey Bay continues as our seaport base. We live mostly aboard ship, though I sometimes enjoy lodging at the Del Cortés. The canning industry is still expanding here, so there is a constant demand that will probably not diminish anytime soon. I've been wise, I believe, in limiting the catch of the Molly Quinn *to salmon. Within the past few months, hundreds, perhaps thousands, of new vessels have set sail to fish for sardines. The competition among them is fierce. As you know, the urgencies associated with that kind of 'game' are not for me. That's not why I set off on this venture.*

Which leads me to the reason I did choose this venture. The peace and beauty for which I was searching are here. I have indeed found them. I have only to stand and watch the orange-red sunset as the sun sinks into the ocean...or to look up at the velvet night sky with its spangling of stars to know that this is the life for which I longed. And Molly, I do wish you could stand with me to see the sunrise paint the sky above the Pacific waters. It is truly a splendid sight, one reminiscent of our jeweled dawn, to be sure. Oh, yes. I believe I spotted a sea otter in the distance the other day, though I cannot be certain.

I miss you all. Not a day passes that I do not think of you. I'll be sailing the Molly Quinn *through the Golden Gate for repairs within weeks. I rejoice that I will see you that soon.*

God bless you and keep you.

Until we meet again, I remain yours, very truly,

Zachary MacAlister

Molly folded the letter and placed it back in the envelope. "He's on his way," she said softly. "The letter was posted two weeks ago. He could be here any day."

Gwennie patted Molly's trembling hand. "I know, dear. I know."

18

THE MATRONLY VICTORIA PARROTT tapped on Molly's office door.

Molly, seated at her desk reviewing a contract, looked up. "Yes? Come in."

Victoria opened the door, primly patted her hair, and adjusted her wire-rimmed eyeglasses. "Miss Quinn, you have a visitor."

She pushed back slightly from her desk. "I'm not expecting anyone. Who is it?" Molly had been in her new office less than a week and was still relishing the pleasure of being on the fourth floor of the new Beckworth building above the city.

"He gave his name as Julian Starr from Sacramento."

Molly stood, smiling. "Thank you, Miss Parrott. I'll see him."

A moment later, Julian strode through the door. He rushed over to her, catching her hand in his. "Molly, it's wonderful to see you!" He paused, looking around the room. "And this is marvelous, absolutely marvelous. Better than you described."

She chuckled at his enthusiasm. "It's modest, but it suits QIL's needs quite nicely."

"QIL?"

"It's a mouthful to say Quinn Investments and Loans. I've taken to calling it QIL, as in *quill.*"

"I like it. QIL it is." He walked over to the window. "You overlook the bay. You can watch the ships. Lovely indeed."

Molly moved across the room to stand beside him, gazing out at the marina. "I can see what the rest of the city is doing from up here."

"And anticipate their needs before they do."

She tilted her head, not understanding.

"That's how entrepreneurs make money, Molly. Anticipating supply and demand, then acting before anyone else thinks of it." He laughed lightly. "But I think you're well on your way to discovering that on your own."

Molly didn't answer him, feeling somehow unsettled by his cold assessment.

"Please, sit down, Julian," she said after a moment, nodding to a chair opposite her desk, then settling into her own. "What brings you to San Francisco?"

"Both business and pleasure."

"The business end of it must have something to do with QIL, or you wouldn't be here."

"Actually, you have to do with both reasons, Molly. But let's discuss business before pleasure, shall we?"

She smiled. "Of course. What's on your mind?"

"News of QII's success is spreading."

"I've heard that it is."

"Especially after the profile Hearst did on you in the *Examiner.*"

"It wasn't a profile of me alone. The report was on San Francisco's growth since the earthquake. I was one of many new businesspeople mentioned."

"But the only woman in what's always been a man's domain."

She merely smiled and waited for Julian to continue.

"Nonetheless, the banking community in Sacramento is abuzz with talk of the newest entrepreneur in their midst. You've caught their fancy."

"Whose fancy? Idle speculators or investors?"

"Investors. But they're big fish, Molly. They've asked me to speak with you." He paused. "Though I'm not sure QIL is ready to take them on."

"Why not?" Molly narrowed her eyes.

"Their interest wouldn't be passive."

"What do you mean?"

"They see QIL's potential. They want to be part of its future."

"Go on."

"They want to buy into the company. They see their investments as bringing in a good return and also funding QIL's growth."

"I see nothing wrong with that."

"They want to be at the helm as that happens."

"It's my company. I am at its head. I would never relinquish that position."

"Of course," Julian said. "They respect that. But they've spoken to me about creating a board of directors. You would still head up QIL, but they would be in on the decision making. That kind of active participation would make a difference in the money they invest."

"Wouldn't that require selling shares of QIL?"

He explained that selling shares wouldn't be required, but that it might ensure her ownership as long as she kept the majority. "It's a bit involved and will take some time to set up," he said. "If you're interested in pursuing this, you need to come to Sacramento as soon as possible, meet the gentlemen, make your final decision. At that point, we'll proceed with the legalities of incorporating."

"QIL, a corporation?" She liked the sound of it. "Julian, I would like to meet with them. When do you suggest?"

"By the end of the week if you can get away. Yours isn't the only business in San Francisco they're considering. We'll need to move fast."

She nodded. "Of course. I'll make it a priority."

"I haven't really told you about the men. Shall I?"

"I assume you've already investigated them, or you wouldn't have bothered bringing me their offer."

Julian grinned. "You learn fast, Molly. I've known two of them for years; the other is a newcomer to Sacramento. From the East Coast. New York, I believe, but I've done some background checking. They've all got assets enough to more than back up their offer."

"Which leads me to my next question. Exactly what are they considering investing?"

He told her, and her mouth fell open. Julian nodded slowly, his blue-eyed gaze never leaving her face. "I thought you might be surprised."

Then Molly frowned, stood, and moved to the window overlooking the bay. Below her a mist was rolling in off the Pacific, but it wasn't thick enough to block the view of the clippers and schooners drifting in and out of the harbor. A few gulls made lazy circles, barely visible against the pale gray sky.

After a moment she turned to Julian, who was now standing beside her. "You have really given me your recommendations in this, Julian. I realize that as my legal representative, you were required to present the investors' offer. But, also as my friend and legal advisor, what is your counsel?"

For a moment, Julian didn't speak. "Normally, I would say don't overextend, Molly. Or try to grow too fast. It's a mistake a lot of new businesses make. But usually, that kind of advice has more to do with borrowing against a company's assets than with expanding through new investors." He watched the high-masted ships in the distance for a moment, then turned again to Molly. "In this instance, though you may run into battles for power down the road, I think it's worth moving forward. You've got a keen business mind, and if anyone can handle this kind of growth, it's Molly Quinn."

She smiled. "Thank you, Julian. Your opinion is very important to me."

"I do wonder, though, Molly—and I'm speaking as your friend, now, not your legal advisor—about the toll this may take on your personal life. If you decide to incorporate, the company is going to go through a period of growth that will require all your time and energy. You've told me about the hours you're putting in now." He smiled gently. "How long has it been since you've been asleep before midnight?"

"I couldn't even tell you."

"Are the gains for the company worth the losses you may take personally, Molly?"

She drew in a deep breath. His question reminded her of Zach. It was exactly the sort of thing he would have asked, and she wanted to push it from her mind. Instead of answering, she changed the subject quite suddenly.

"Enough business talk. Now…" She raised a coquettish eyebrow. "What was it you said earlier about being in San Francisco for other reasons?"

Julian laughed. "Forgive me for getting too personal, Molly. It's just that I care. I'm concerned for you. But you're right, it *is* time to turn our conversation to a more lighthearted subject.

"I was wondering if you might attend the opera with me Thursday night. It will be quite a gala affair, a wonderful opportunity to meet people who will help QIL."

He smiled gently, watching her suddenly somber expression. "I am asking you to accompany me as my friend, Molly. And for business reasons. Winston told me about your...ah, hesitancy, and I understand."

She nodded, but didn't give him an answer.

"The proceeds from the tickets will go to rebuilding the opera house," he continued. "Enrico Caruso has returned to show his support—he will even be singing *Carmen* again—though it's a wonder after what happened last time he performed it in San Francisco."

She laughed lightly. "His fear during the earthquake is still being talked about. Did you hear that he thought he'd lost his voice from fright? His conductor told him to stick his head out the window at the Palace and sing anything from *Carmen.*"

Julian chuckled. "Yes. The people who'd run into the streets must have thought the man had lost his mind, not his voice."

Finally, Molly smiled into Julian's eyes. It felt good to laugh again. "Yes, I'll go, Julian. Thank you for asking. But didn't you say we need to be in Sacramento by the end of the week?"

"Yes, I did. If you agree, we can leave early Friday morning, be in Sacramento in time to meet with the investors by mid-afternoon. If you want to proceed, then we'll have all next week to get started on the necessary legal paperwork."

"I'll be ready on both accounts, then, Julian—to accompany you to the opera and to Sacramento."

"You've made me very happy," he said with a warm smile.

She walked with him to the door, and he spoke again of the

coming evening. "Perhaps we can have a late supper at La Scala afterward. The mayor and his wife, Radcliff and Augusta Morgan, will be there. Augusta is in charge of the rebuilding campaign for the opera house."

"It sounds lovely, and for a good cause as well. I'll look forward to it, Julian." She gave him directions to her house.

"Until Thursday, then." He gazed down at her. In spite of his graying temples, he looked boyishly happy. Impulsively, he reached for both her hands and gave them a squeeze.

"Until then," she said, wondering why Zach's image suddenly appeared in her mind.

After he closed the door, Molly sat down at her desk and attempted to concentrate on the contract she'd begun to examine earlier. But her mind kept going back to the commitment she'd just made.

It would be good for her to enjoy a lighter side of life. Many days she worked until midnight or later, reviewing contracts and rates of interest, exploring new ideas for her business.

Besides, she wanted to be part of San Francisco. How better to move up in the social hierarchy than to take in Caruso on the arm of Julian Starr, potential governor of California? And dine at La Scala afterward with the mayor and his wife.

Molly stood and walked over to her window. The fog was heavier now, and she could no longer see the ships entering the Golden Gate. She had taken to watching them carefully, particularly those with three masts.

She would attend the opera with Julian. There was really no harm in it, she decided. Why should she feel uncomfortable, as if she were betraying Zach, when she hadn't heard from him in months? His most recent letter could have been written to his sister, for all the emotion it contained. It hadn't even been addressed to her alone, but to Gwennie and Kingsley as well, as if they were all one big family. As much as she loved the Forresters, she'd been hurt that Zach hadn't posted a more personal letter addressed only to her.

She sighed deeply as the fog completely obscured the bay from her view.

Zachary MacAlister. His name still quickened her heartbeat. What would it be like to see him again? Had their words of love simply been born of their dark circumstances following the earthquake? Or was there still something deeper between them, something lasting?

A tap at the door broke into her thoughts. She turned as it opened. Kingsley poked his head into the office and smiled. "Can you spare a few minutes, Molly?"

"Of course. Always for you."

She pulled her chair around to sit near him without the desk between. "Have you been here all day?"

He nodded and told her about the brickyard deal he was working on. It was an operation that manufactured new bricks and contracted with skilled brick masons and unskilled workers to clean up the mounds of used bricks purchased from burned-out and earthquake-damaged buildings. Molly listened attentively to Kingsley's good news about the company's asking price, glad for his insights and recommendations.

"I agree," she said when he'd finished. "We've got enough capital to cover it. It sounds like a solid investment. And the brickyard is small enough that it won't require much attention. Can the present workers continue?"

He nodded.

"Can you oversee the next steps?" She frowned, scrutinizing the dignified white-haired man in front of her. "And after all is said and done, I'd like to turn over the management of the yard to you as well."

"Thought you'd never ask," Kingsley said with a wide grin.

"There's something else, Kingsley. I need your advice. And I've got an important question for you."

He watched her attentively. "All right."

Molly told him about Julian's visit and about the offer from the Sacramento investors, then listened as Kingsley commented on the pitfalls and the advantages of such a move.

"I would advise you to be cautious, Molly," Kingsley said finally. "You take such joy in running your business, I'd hate to see you lose the ability to do that." He frowned. "If QIL gets too big, that's exactly what could happen."

"That's a concern of mine, too," Molly said.

"At this point, my advice is explore your options. Don't let the big investors influence you just because they've got the assets to do so." He grinned. "But somehow, I don't think they'll sway you easily. You've put more blood, sweat, and tears into this company in one year than most businesspeople put into a calling in a lifetime. I know you'll not give up control of QIL without a good reason."

She smiled and reached for his hand. "I don't know what I'd do without you, Kingsley. Talking with you always helps me see things more clearly." She paused. "Which leads me to my next question."

He raised a white eyebrow. "Sounds serious."

"It is. If I decide to incorporate, will you consider being a member of QII's board of directors? I'll need an ally, a strong ally, if we move forward on this. I want you to be in on every detail."

"I'm honored you asked, Molly. As always, you have my full support."

"Thank you, Kingsley. It means a great deal to me."

They spoke for a few more minutes about personal matters. Molly asked after Gwennie and said to tell her friend that she would stop by to read to her that night.

"By the way," Kingsley said, as he stood to leave. "We're going to the opera Thursday night. Would you care to join us?"

Molly told him about her previous commitment to attend with Julian Starr.

Kingsley nodded as he reached for the door. "Well, another time, dear. But I know that Gwennie will be disappointed." Then he left Molly alone with her thoughts—of QIL, of Julian, and, as always, of Zach.

When Thursday came, business kept Molly in her office until late afternoon, which didn't leave much time to prepare for the opera. On the Nob Hill cable car on her way home, she glanced at her watch, pinned to her lapel. Julian said he'd come for her at 7:00, which allowed her little more than two hours to dress.

She was glad she'd purchased a gown weeks before and hadn't needed to take time away from her obligations at QIL to look for another. She'd found it at the elegantly restored Silvers and Clark for the occasion of a formal dinner which, at the last minute, she was unable to attend. The same garment, with its gossamer folds of silk and lace, would be perfect for tonight's opera, she decided.

After a luxuriant and fragrant bath, Molly slipped into the gown and stood for a moment in front of her wardrobe mirror. The delicate beauty of the dress pleased her enormously, just as it had when she'd first tried it on at Silvers and Clark. The bodice fell in soft pleats from her shoulders to her tiny waist, and long sleeves graced her arms. The neckline—and the swept-up twist of her dark hair—showed off the double strand of pearls she'd fastened around her neck. Her skirt touched the floor prettily, flaring out behind her slightly as she walked.

Molly smiled at her reflection as she added a touch of lip rouge. Her image was a welcome change from the plain long skirts and blazers she wore at QIL.

Molly opened her front door moments after Julian rang the doorbell.

"Come in," she invited and stepped back for him to enter. Dressed in a formal black suit with a high-collared white shirt and gray silk ascot, Julian had never looked more dashing. Even his silver-blond hair added to his look of sophistication. Molly smiled her approval, and he bent to kiss her fingertips.

Molly led him to her sitting room to wait while she went upstairs for her wrap. But before she left him standing before the fireplace, he glanced around the room and complimented her on its decor.

"Thank you," she said. "I had help from Gwennie Forrester. I do so love her taste. She has a knack for recreating the look of fields and gardens indoors, with pastels and florals. I'm not here in the daytime often, but when I am, and the sunlight pours in the windows, I feel as though I'm outdoors in some beautiful, peaceful garden."

"Even now, it's a tranquil place," he said.

"I agree," she said with a smile, then went to gather her short cloak from the wardrobe in her room.

Moments later, they walked to the waiting carriage in front of Molly's house. Julian opened the carriage door, helped her inside, then signaled the driver to start for downtown.

As they pulled away from the curb, she noticed that in

Gwennie and Kingsley's house, every light blazed, as if in some kind of celebration. She knew they were also planning to attend the opera, and she wondered briefly if something had happened to change their minds.

Julian had arranged for box seats toward the front of the auditorium that served as the temporary home of the San Francisco Opera Company. Heads turned and people stared as they exited the carriage at the front portico. Molly quickly dismissed the idea that it might be due to her recent photograph and mention in the *Examiner* and decided instead that her escort's political ambitions were gaining him considerable public notice. He took her arm to guide her to the door, and she couldn't help feeling proud to be with this man.

On their way through the throngs of milling theater patrons, Julian stopped to introduce her to the mayor and his wife, Augusta, a large, feisty woman, and other city officials. She noticed how warmly her escort was welcomed. Someone mentioned the following year's senatorial race, and a knowing look was exchanged between Julian and the mayor. A few others commented favorably, patting Julian on the back.

A smiling and obviously pleased Julian finally took Molly's arm and guided her to their box. Within minutes the heavy velvet curtain lifted, and Enrico Caruso stepped to the center of the stage.

Enthralled, Molly leaned forward slightly in her seat, thrilling to the tenor's resonant voice as he began to sing from *Carmen*.

So mesmerized was she, that it took several minutes for Molly to realize that she was being watched.

She turned, and in the dim light of the theater, she made out the figures of Gwennie and Kingsley in their orchestra seats, just below and slightly to the rear of where she sat with Julian in their box.

Gwennie, as enthralled as Molly had been moments earlier, stared at the stage, never moving her gaze from the great Caruso. Beside her, his arm draped around his wife's shoulders, Kingsley also kept his attention riveted on the performer.

Then Molly noticed a familiar profile on the other side of Gwennie. She leaned forward to get a better look.

The man turned, and Molly's heart nearly stopped. Their eyes met and locked.

It was Zach.

"Molly, is something wrong?" Julian whispered, leaning slightly toward her, at the same time moving to rest his arm on the back of her chair. She looked at him just long enough to say that everything was fine.

He gave her an affectionate hug, then turned his attention back to Caruso. His arm remained circled around Molly's shoulders.

When she turned again to seek Zach's gaze, his seat was empty.

CHAPTER

19

AFTER DINING AT LA SCALA with the mayor, his wife, and a few other friends, Julian hired an open carriage for a romantic ride home. The spring air was balmy, and a full moon cast an ethereal light across the city. Julian rested his arm on the seat behind Molly, gazing at her with open admiration. Throughout the evening, he had been a delightful companion, a lively conversationalist, and a respectful gentleman.

But Molly couldn't keep Zach from intruding into her thoughts. Meeting his gaze so unexpectedly during *Carmen* had unnerved her, and she knew that whatever feelings she'd had for him a year ago were even stronger now. She had to see him, talk with him.

The carriage pulled up in front of her house, and she glanced over at the Forresters', hoping to see a light in the window, indicating they were still up visiting with Zach.

But the house was dark.

Julian helped her step from the carriage, then walked with her to the front door.

"Molly," he said, "this has been a lovely evening. Thank you for accompanying me."

"I've so enjoyed being with you, Julian. Caruso, La Scala, a memorable evening. Thank you—"

Before she could say more, he lowered his face and kissed her gently on the cheek.

She looked into his handsome face in surprise.

"I hope this is the first of many evenings together."

Molly nodded, not knowing how to tell him that it probably wouldn't be—no, couldn't be. She murmured a quick, "Thank you again."

Julian said he would return first thing in the morning to pick her up for their trip to Sacramento. She nodded and, standing on her porch, watched him stride down the walk to the waiting carriage. She waved as he drove away.

That night Molly couldn't sleep. She tossed in her bed, desperately wanting to talk with Zach. Of all the times to have to go to Sacramento! It would have to coincide with Zach's trip home. She sighed deeply, staring at the dark ceiling.

She could cancel the trip, stay in San Francisco to be with him, but it would mean the loss of QII's most important potential investors. And it was impossible to postpone the trip. Julian himself had said that hers was not the only company the investors were looking into.

But Zach! Her heart cried out to him. How could she leave without seeing him?

By dawn, she had finally reached a conclusion. Before leaving with Julian, she would wake the Forrester household, and have them roust Zach so she could speak to him. Then she would explain why she needed to leave, tell him that she would hurry home from Sacramento as quickly as possible, implore him to wait for her.

Finally more at peace with herself, Molly rose to dress for the trip to Sacramento, taking extra pains because she would first see Zach. After a quick breakfast of toast, Gwennie's cherry preserves, and coffee, Molly gave her hair a final touch-up and brushed the folds from her traveling suit.

A thin sun was just rising through the mist when she knocked at the front door of the Forresters'. She drew in a deep breath, feeling that her knees would surely buckle when she was finally face to face with Zach.

She knocked again. The young and pretty Miss Brown answered the door. "Good morning, Miss Quinn," she said, recognizing Molly.

"Is..." Molly hesitated. "Is...Mr. Forrester in?"

Before Miss Brown could answer, Kingsley, still in his bathrobe, came to the door.

"Molly!" he exclaimed happily. "My goodness, you're up and about early this morning. Come in, come in." He stood back to let her enter. "I was just having my usual breakfast alone. Can you join me?"

Molly touched his arm affectionately. "Thank you. But I can only stay a minute. I'm off to Sacramento today."

"Oh, yes, the investors," he said, nodding.

"Yes." She took another shaky breath. "Actually, I've come to see Zach. I saw him with you last night at the opera. I was so sorry he left before we could speak."

Kingsley looked at her kindly. "He's not here, Molly."

"He's not?"

"No, he's staying aboard ship."

"Oh." She felt a sting of tears behind her eyes. "I'm sorry. I thought he would be here."

"How long will you be gone, Molly?"

"Through next week."

Kingsley nodded slowly.

"Has Zach said how long he's going to be in San Francisco?"

"Only a few days, four or five, I think."

Molly didn't know how to respond. Her disappointment threatened to overwhelm her. Finally, she trusted herself to speak again. "Tell him that I'm sorry...so very sorry I missed seeing him," she finally said.

"I'll tell him."

"Oh, Kingsley." She suddenly felt like a little girl again. "What shall I do?" This time, her tears spilled over.

"There, there," he said, gathering her into a bear hug. "There, there, dear," he repeated. He then pulled out a freshly ironed handkerchief and dabbed at her tears. "You'll do what you have to do, Molly. Just as always."

They heard the clopping of horse's hooves from down the street. "I believe Julian is here," Kingsley said, after the vehicle pulled into sight.

Sniffling, Molly dried her tears. "Tell Zach...," she began. Then she sighed. "Never mind, Kingsley. Don't say anything. I don't think he *can* understand why I've got to leave."

Kingsley smiled gently. "I know, Molly. I know."

After giving him a quick kiss on the cheek, she walked next door to gather her satchel and cloak. Minutes later, the carriage pulled away. Kingsley had already returned to his breakfast, and Molly didn't look back.

The week in Sacramento went more smoothly than Molly could have dreamed. She was impressed with the business sense exhibited by all three of the investors. Two of the men, local brothers named Clive and Nevil Richards, had been in banking for two decades. The third, Luke Cornelius from New York, had worked in imports and exports for nearly thirty years.

All three were older, but they didn't attempt to patronize Molly. On two occasions, after their day-long meetings, the gentlemen and their wives joined Molly and Julian for dinner.

By the end of the week, all the legal papers had been signed and filed with the local court, officially declaring Quinn Investments and Loans a corporation. Molly kept her place as president of QIL, with the majority of shares remaining in her name. The others agreed to the addition of Kingsley Forrester as vice president.

The day before Molly was to leave Sacramento, Julian asked her to join him for a tour of the Capitol. She agreed, delighted at the prospect. He stopped by her hotel to pick her up, and as they walked toward the magnificent domed building, he told her about the art exhibit they would see in the rotunda.

"We've got works by some of the state's most talented artists," he explained, as they climbed the stairs to the entrance.

Molly stepped inside the building and looked up into the hollow of the towering dome, feeling dizzy and amazed at the same time. The workmanship, the color, the expanse—every bit of it took her breath away.

Julian, noting her expression, gave her a quick, affectionate hug. "Beautiful, isn't it?"

She nodded and took a deep breath. "It is."

"Would you like to take a look at the artwork before we tour the rest of the building?"

But Molly didn't answer. A large oil painting on the far side of the rotunda had caught her attention. She felt drawn to it and moved across the room to get a closer look.

She had gotten only as far as the center of the rotunda when she stopped. The painting was too powerful to view at close range. It warranted a distance for the emotion it elicited. She couldn't explain, she just knew.

"It's called *Hope*," said Julian, who stood at her side. "It's wonderful, isn't it?"

She nodded. "Who's the artist?"

"His name is O'Rourke. Devon O'Rourke."

"The light," she whispered. "I've never seen anything like it."

"Everyone notices his treatment of light, both artificial and natural. That's part of his genius." Julian also stared at the lighthouse as if unable to move closer. "He's becoming known as 'the painter of light.'"

"I can understand why," she mused. "Are any of his other works here?"

"No. And people can't seem to find out much about him. I do know he's originally from the Central Coast."

"Monterey?"

"Carmel-by-the-Sea."

She nodded. "You said originally?"

"Yes, it's very odd. He's dropped out of sight. At one time, the Del Cortés in Monterey was showing his work. In fact, that's how *Hope* was first discovered, but according to the people he dealt with there, he's turned into a recluse. No one can find him."

"And this is his only known work?"

"Oh, I'm sure there are others. But no one knows where they might be."

Molly shook her head. "O'Rourke's work, his talent, should be celebrated. He needs to be found."

Julian gave her a quick smile. "Spoken like a true patron of the arts."

"That's an idea, Julian. Who knows what the future holds? Perhaps I'll diversify even further. Investments, loans, bricks, canning companies, artists…"

He grinned. "An eclectic mix, to be sure, Molly."

Laughing, they turned from the O'Rourke to stroll past the other oils. But Molly kept looking back at the *Hope*, captivated by the light emanating from the torch in the storm-shrouded lighthouse. She'd never before been touched this way by a work of art. It created simultaneous joy and sadness within her.

An hour later, as they exited the Capitol, the O'Rourke painting pushed everything else she'd just seen from her mind. Perhaps, she thought, as they walked back to the hotel dining room, it was the symbolism of the painting, the torch's soft glow in contrast with the crashing waves.

She imagined a schooner heading toward land in stormy, swollen water. What a welcome sight for the ship's captain—a lighthouse, a signpost warning of danger, a symbol of hope.

"Molly," Julian said, as they entered the restaurant, "I've enjoyed your visit to Sacramento more than I can say."

"It's been a splendid week, Julian. Thank you for all you've done for QIL. We couldn't have put all this together without you."

He pulled out her chair, and Molly seated herself at the linen-covered table. After the server poured water into their goblets and handed them menus, Julian reached for her hand.

"Molly, what I'm trying to say is…" He hesitated, meeting her eyes. His were warm with emotion. "What I'm trying so ineptly to tell you is that I would like our relationship to be more than it is right now."

241

Molly pulled back her hand, gently. "Julian, it's not possible."

He nodded. "This is sudden. I realize that. I also know that it isn't wise to mix our private lives with our business relationship." He sighed. "But when I'm with you—"

Molly interrupted. "Julian, don't do this. You're right. I must insist that we keep our relationship on a professional level."

Julian's gaze met hers, and his eyes were kind. Molly had the feeling that he could see more inside her than she wished him to know.

"I apologize, Molly," he said finally. "I've overstepped the bounds between us. And I understand," he said simply and began to speak of QII's potential for the future.

She hoped that he would never again broach the subject of a relationship between them, unless, of course, she did.

Molly boarded the *Delta Queen,* a paddle wheeler, for the journey back to San Francisco. It would take longer than traveling by carriage or train, but since Zach would already have left the city, there was no hurry. Besides, she needed the added time to sort out her feelings.

She stored her bags, then sat down on a sunny bench outside the cabin, watching the lush delta foliage pass by as the riverboat floated down the Sacramento River.

Her mind was whirling with the proceedings of the week. Now that the Richards brothers and Luke Cornelius were adding capital to QIL, she had much to consider about further investments. They agreed that within a year, a cannery in Monterey would be a serious possibility. If the company continued its rapid expansion, the 'big three,' as they laughingly called themselves, were in favor of purchasing a large operation outright.

As soon as she thought it feasible, Molly would travel to Monterey and look into the options herself, then report back on her findings. Now that QIL had a board of directors, she could no longer make lone decisions. But the men were solid in their perceptions and would bring strengths into the organization that she didn't have.

The first board meeting was already scheduled to be held in San Francisco. At that time, the board members would meet the new vice president, Kingsley Forrester, and each of the five of them were to bring a report on their vision for QII's future. They planned, however, to delay the decision about buying the canning company until after Molly's investigation.

The paddle wheeler glided along, and Molly closed her eyes and leaned her head back against the solid wood of the cabin, seeking solace from her troubling thoughts. She had chosen to pursue QII's business affairs instead of following her heart and staying in San Francisco to be with Zach. It had seemed a sensible choice at the time—in fact, her only choice—but now, in her loneliness for him, she wondered at her wisdom.

What if she had waited to see him? Would there have been other investors if Cornelius and the Richards brothers had decided to go with another company? Probably so, she realized.

Zach. She pictured the strength in his face, the auburn gleam of his wind-swept hair, the light in his eyes. She ached to see him, to hear the husky sound of his voice.

She stood and walked to the railing of the boat, listening to the soothing rhythm of its paddles as it moved through the water. Lifting her face to catch the wind off the river, enjoying its caress on her skin, she wished Zach was beside her and that nothing could intrude on the joy of his presence. Not QIL, nor its board of directors, nor its rapid expansion. Nothing but the two of them, reveling in the beauty of the day and the glory of their feelings for each other.

But would such a day ever come? Molly wondered.

The riverboat headed through a line of dark willows along the riverbanks, and their shadows fell across her. A chill traveled up her spine, and she felt lonelier than ever.

Back in San Francisco, Molly stopped by her office before heading to Nob Hill. As she opened the door, Victoria Parrott looked up from her desk with a quick smile.

"Has Kingsley left?" Molly asked.

"No, he's in. Did things go well in Sacramento?"

"Yes, exceptionally well. In fact, as soon as the legal transactions are completed, we'll need to hire someone to help you. This office will soon be handling ten times the business it does now."

Victoria nodded briskly and adjusted her eyeglasses, looking pleased. Kingsley, hearing their voices, stepped through the open door of his office. "Molly! Welcome home." He paused. "What's this about ten times the business? Things must have gone as well as you expected."

"Better," she said, with a grin, then crossed the room to shake his hand. "Congratulations, Mr. Vice President!"

"They approved of your choice, then?" He looked tremendously pleased.

She went with him into his office, taking a seat near the desk. He pulled up a chair beside her, giving her his full attention as she told him about her week in Sacramento.

"You've done some fine negotiating," he said, when she'd finished. "Good work, Molly. I'm proud of you." A broad smile lit his wrinkled face. "Good work, indeed!" Then he told her about QII's week during her absence.

Molly started to ask him about Zach's stay in San Francisco, when Kingsley leaned forward to speak again, a touch of merriment in his eyes. "You had a visit from the mayor's wife last Monday."

She frowned. "Augusta Morgan?"

"It seems that she and the mayor were quite taken with you the night of the opera."

Molly tilted her head, her instincts telling her there was more to her visit than simply a social call. "And?"

"She's invited you to join her committee for rebuilding the opera house."

"That's delightful news!"

"I'm sure that your participation comes with a price tag."

"After the way things went in Sacramento, I think QIL can afford to contribute," she said. "I'll bring it up at the board meeting."

Kingsley's forehead creased in worry. "Your time is already precious, Molly. I know you're glad to have been asked, but how can you add anything else to your schedule?"

She sighed. "It's too great an honor to turn down, Kingsley. I'll work it in, somehow."

He nodded slowly, and she knew he was right. "I'll be careful, Kingsley. I don't want anything pulling me away from those things, those people, I care for."

"As it did with Zach?"

She nodded slowly. "Yes. My leaving was productive for QIL, but terribly wrong because of Zach."

Kingsley settled back into his chair, his face etched with concern for her. But he said nothing more about Zachary

MacAlister. After a few minutes of discussing the upcoming incorporation, Molly stood to leave.

Kingsley walked her to his door. "Gwennie will be so glad to find you're home. How about joining us for supper tonight?"

"I would love to."

"Wonderful, I'll tell Cook Liu to set an extra place."

"Actually, I can tell him myself. I'm heading home now to unpack and settle in. But I'll stop by first and let Gwennie know I'm home."

"You've got quite a surprise in store when you get there."

"A surprise?" Molly frowned, wondering what it could be. But Kingsley simply gave her a knowing smile and a raised brow as she exited his office.

Molly looked through the mail on her desk, told Victoria she would see her in the morning, and took the elevator to the ground floor.

It was late afternoon by the time she stepped off the Nob Hill cable car and walked the short distance home.

She knocked on the Forresters' front door, planning to see Gwennie before heading across the lawn to her own small house.

Miss Brown opened the door and smiled warmly. "Welcome home, Miss Quinn," she said and escorted Molly into the sitting room.

Gwennie looked up. "Molly! Dear, you're a sight for sore eyes!" She held out her arms for an embrace. "How we've missed you!"

Molly bent to give the older woman a huge hug, then started to settle into a chair near her.

"Now, dear, don't sit down yet. Zach brought you a house-warming gift, and I cannot wait another minute for you to see it."

"He did?" Her voice was an incredulous whisper. "Zach brought me something?"

Gwennie laughed. "Yes, dear heart, he did! Now fetch my wrap." She looked over to the doorway where Miss Brown stood waiting. "Dear," she said to the young woman, "you may have the evening off. Molly will see to my needs."

Miss Brown nodded and exited the room.

"I hope you don't mind," she said, as Molly wheeled her chair through the front entrance and down the ramp. "But there was only one place to leave your gift." She shook her head slowly. "It just wouldn't have been fitting anywhere else."

Molly frowned. "We're heading to my house?"

"Yes, dear. We let Zach place it in your house to await your return."

"I can't imagine what it could be."

"Mmmm. I just wish Zach could have waited to present it himself. It's lovely," Gwennie sighed, as they reached Molly's front door. "You'll soon see. It's so very lovely."

Molly unlocked the door and pushed the wheelchair into the entrance hall.

"Keep going, dear, straight into your sitting room."

She did as Gwennie instructed, but she halted the chair and gasped as they rounded the corner.

Above the fireplace hung the most glorious painting she'd ever seen. She sank into a chair, unable to take her eyes from the light that seemed to shine from someplace within the canvas—through the flowers in a sacred garden—through the faces of the woman and child who stared out at her as if she'd known them forever.

"It's an O'Rourke," she whispered reverently. "O'Rourke, the painter of light!"

"It's called *Mary Rose's Garden*," Gwennie said softly.

But Molly didn't answer. She just sat staring at the painting, feeling the heat of unshed tears behind her eyes. "It's beautiful," she whispered.

20

Carmel-by-the-Sea

JESSE PLAYED QUIETLY IN THE CORNER of the garden, and Mary Rose dug her spade into the rich soil near the lilacs, now again in bloom. Their fragrance filled the air, and the place seemed alive with the music of bees seeking the lavender blossoms' sweet nectar. Several small yellow finches twittered happily from the branches of the olive tree, and a redheaded wood-pecker jabbered from a nearby pine.

Mary Rose had just put in some clumps of tiger lilies near a vine of tiny wild roses, and now she was creating a border of candytufts, newly dug from a shaded place by a streambed in Pacific Grove. Near where she knelt, a box of violets awaited her attention, and they would be next, going in behind the frilly white tufts.

Since Devon's departure, Mary Rose had spent hours in her garden. Especially during the winter, it had brought her solace to work the soil, plant seeds in its dark depths, knowing that, come spring, life would begin afresh.

Many of the winter's bulbs—the tulips she'd ordered from Holland, the daffodils and crocuses—had been watered with her tears as she worked. And now it was spring, and they'd burst into life, an explosion of red and yellow and pink and white, breathtaking in their delicate beauty.

Mary Rose still mourned Devon's absence, but now her thoughts lingered more on the agony he must be feeling rather than of her own anger and loss. She prayed for him constantly, that he would find peace and that he would return to them. But the months had passed without any word.

"Mommy," Jesse said, moving his wooden horse nearer, "I want to go to the beach and look for seashells."

Mary Rose smiled and circled her arm around the tow-headed little boy. "How about after your nap?"

"I don't need one!" he said, with a small frown.

"We'll need lots of energy for our long walk. Then, looking for shells, we'll need even more. How about some lunch, little guy? Then you'll have lots of pep."

Jesse sighed and nodded his head reluctantly.

"Then a rest time so you can run and play and look for lots of seashells at our special beach. How would you like that?"

"Yeah!" he shouted. Mary Rose took his hand and led him back down the path to the cottage. After a lunch of leftover cold fried chicken, canned pears, and a big glass of milk, Jesse's sleepy eyes began to close.

After her son was asleep in his trundle bed, Mary Rose returned to the garden, first to put away her gardening tools, then to have a time of prayer and meditation in her garden's most sacred place.

The sun warmed her shoulders as she climbed the winding path to the prayer garden. She settled onto the redwood bench where Devon had painted *Mary Rose's Garden*. It saddened her to think that the painting had been stolen, and for the thousandth time since it happened, she wondered who might have done such a thing.

During Devon's work on the painting, they had been drawn together, closer than ever before. Yet it was the same painting, with its tragic disappearance, that had created what seemed to be an unbridgeable chasm between them.

"Precious Father in heaven," she breathed, "care for your son Devon. Wherever he may be, let him be aware of your presence. It comforts me to know that he isn't hidden from you.

"You are close to him, perhaps closer now than before because of his pain.

"Restore his joy. May he discover afresh the gifts you've given him and all the gladness that they bring.

"May he rejoice in you and feel your nearness."

She looked around her garden at the blossoming lilacs and roses and newly tamed wildflowers, irises, tiger lilies, the violets. This was her art, her gift. How would she feel if it were destroyed by vandals? She tried to imagine the pain, the hurt, the anger. Gardening—spading the rich soil, discovering new flowers to transplant, watching seedlings become healthy, vigorous plants—brought her gladness. But the garden itself, with the abundance of life it produced—plants, animal, birds, and insects, all of it—was the crowning joy.

Mary Rose opened the small Bible that she always carried with her to the prayer garden. Lately, she had been pondering an obscure passage in the Old Testament, found in the third chapter of Habakkuk. She opened the delicate pages to the place where she'd placed the purple ribbon marker and began to read:

Although the fig tree shall not blossom, neither shall fruit be in the vines; the labour of the olive shall fail, and the fields shall yield no meat; the flock shall be cut off from the fold, and there shall be no herd in the stalls.

Yet I will rejoice in the Lord, I will joy in the God of my salvation.

The Lord God is my strength, and he will make my feet like hinds' feet, and he will make me to walk upon mine high places.

She thought about what the words meant in her own life. Carl, her beloved husband, had died too young, too tragically, leaving Mary Rose with an infant son to raise without a father. Then, miracle of miracles, she had found love again in Devon O'Rourke, only to have him leave her lonely, angry, despairing.

If her life were a garden, she thought, outwardly it would seem that it had indeed been trampled, with fruit destroyed, her labor of love a failure.

"Yet, I will rejoice in my Lord," she murmured, looking heavenward. "I will take joy in you, in you who have saved me. You are my strength. No matter what has happened, you will make me strong enough to walk on the high places. You'll do it even though it seems that everything around me is in ruins."

She drew in a deep breath, feeling a touch of precious understanding flood her soul. Her gaze fell again to the last few words of the passage: *He will make me to walk upon mine high places.*

"My high places...," she mused. "Mine," she whispered again, considering all its implications. *I would want nothing less than to walk in those unique places he has chosen for me.*

Then she thought about her relationship with Devon. What if she hadn't forced the issue of selling *Mary Rose's Garden*? When Devon finished the work, she remembered how he hadn't wanted to sell it. But when the *Hope* was moved to the Capitol, it was she who pushed him to sell *Mary Rose's Garden* so they could marry.

"Oh, Father," she whispered with fresh anguish, "did my headstrong ways cause all this, all the pain and searching that Devon's going through? Did I cause him to leave? Never once did I seek the 'high place' you had for me, for us both. I simply decided that selling the painting was a practical way to solve our financial dilemma. Even my suggestion to double the price may have caused it to be stolen, made it seem even more valuable to the thief."

She buried her face in her hands. "Forgive me, Lord. Oh, how I wish that Devon were here so I could ask his forgiveness, too."

Mary Rose looked heavenward again. "What have I done? How can I undo what I've done to Devon, to us both?"

A sense of quiet settled over the garden. Even the birds hushed their singing. Mary Rose seemed to almost hear the words from somewhere deep in her soul: *Beloved child, you belong to me. Take joy in who I am. Dwell on my compassion, my faithfulness, my power, my truth, my glory, my providence...my grace. Take my hand. I will lead you to those high places. I will strengthen you to walk there. Just trust me to do as I have said, my child. Simply trust me.*

Mary Rose looked up. Sunlight flooded her garden, almost a reflection of the gladness that flooded her heart. "Thank you, precious Father," she whispered. "Thank you for loving me so."

An hour later, Mary Rose, pulling Jesse in his little wooden wagon, headed down the winding path into town. Tucked in behind Jesse were a small bucket and toy shovel for playing in the sand and an old, faded quilt for sunbathing. The wagon rattled along the boardwalk, past the line of small shops.

She had just passed in front of Xavier's picture-framing shop, when the man opened the door and called after her.

"Mary Rose!" he exclaimed, hurrying to catch up, his artist's smock flying out behind him.

She halted Jesse's wagon and turned back, smiling at the

artist. As usual, Xavier sported a neatly trimmed goatee and black beret. He might not be the most successful artist in the colony, but he certainly looked the part.

"Xavier, it's good to see you."

He kissed her on both cheeks, European style. "I assume you're on your way to the beach?"

She nodded.

"Do you mind if I join you for the walk down? I'm on my way to the cove myself."

"We'd love to have you."

"Good," he said, with a quick nod. "I've been meaning to get up to see you at the cottage. I've got news about Devon."

Mary Rose's heart skipped a beat. "You do?" she breathed. "How—?"

"Let me run back and get my things, then we'll talk on the way."

"Of course. We'll wait." But as he sprinted back into his shop, Mary Rose thought she couldn't bear the suspense. *Devon!* She hoped that she would at last find out where he'd gone.

Within minutes, Xavier again flew through the door of his shop, this time carrying his easel, paintbox, and canvas. He fell into step with Mary Rose as she pulled the wagon.

"What a glorious day it is!" Xavier let out a deep, satisfied sigh as they walked along. "I began a seascape weeks ago, just before my trip south for supplies, only to have the mist obscure the very place I'd begun it once I returned." He shook his head and frowned. "The days I could leave the shop, I couldn't paint. What's an artist to do!"

Mary Rose nodded in sympathy, wishing he would get on to his news about Devon.

"But this morning, as soon as I looked out, I knew I would

finally capture the same light I'd found earlier." He adjusted his beret after the breeze nearly caught and lifted it from his head. "And what good fortune to find you outside my door, just as I had decided to head for the cove."

"Xavier, you said you had news?" she asked, as they crossed the street and headed onto a narrower path. Cottages, spaced here and there among a grove of lacy pepper trees, dotted both sides of the winding path.

Xavier suddenly stopped and gasped. "Take a look at that color, Mary Rose. Have you ever seen anything quite so smashing?" He shook his head in awe at a bougainvillea vine sweeping across one of the porch roofs. "I've a mind to stop right here and set up my easel, leave the seascape for another day. This—this is simply too splendid to pass. Don't you agree, dear?" He turned to her, and she could see that Devon was the last thing on his mind.

She let out a deep, impatient breath. "It is beautiful."

"Yes, then it's settled!" he said excitedly, setting up the easel. "My, my, my." Then he frowned, looking befuddled. "Oh, dear. I'll have to return to the shop for another canvas."

"Then maybe you ought to work on the seascape today, save this for another time," she suggested, patiently.

"Yes, of course, you're right, dear. You're so sensible. Not that you don't have an artist's heart. Everyone knows that you do. But, dear, you also have good sense." He picked up the easel and began to walk beside her on the path once more.

"You were going to tell me about Devon? You said you have news."

"Oh, yes. I'd nearly forgotten. Yes, I do."

They arrived at some rocky steps leading downward. The ocean spread before them, sparkling turquoise in the sun, its gentle waves lapping at the smooth, nearly white sand. Above the swells farther out, dozens of gulls cried in mournful voices, gliding in lazy circles.

Again, Xavier stopped. "I never get weary of this. I can gaze at it dozens—no, hundreds of times in a year, and then I come across it on a day like today, and it seems I've never seen such glory before."

Mary Rose nodded and helped Jesse climb out of the wagon. Then letting the wagon bounce down the steps behind them, she led her son to the beach. Xavier followed.

She spread the quilt and removed Jesse's shoes. Even at four years of age, the little boy still giggled as he felt the warm sand on his toes. After a few minutes, he sat beside Mary Rose, digging tunnels and building castles in the sand.

Xavier settled down beside them. "I came across Devon last week," he finally said. "He's painting again. From what he said, he hadn't even lifted a paintbrush for months."

Mary Rose turned to him. "Where is he?"

"I saw him in Santa Barbara, though he was just in town for supplies. He's been painting north of there, around Point Conception. A lighthouse, I believe he said."

"Did he..." Her voice faltered. "Did he say anything about coming back?"

Xavier's expression was sympathetic. He shook his head slowly. "I'm sorry, Mary Rose. He didn't really say."

She didn't respond, but looked out toward the breaking surf.

"But, dear, he looked fit. Though I might add, he didn't look any too happy." He smiled gently. "And he did ask after you."

"He did?"

"Yes. He asked if you and your son were well."

"That's all? Just if we were well?"

"This is hard on you, isn't it, dear?" Xavier's expression was thoughtful.

Mary Rose nodded, not trusting her voice.

"Everyone here in town knew that you were thinking of marriage. And for what it's worth now, we were cheering you on. We care for you both. Still do. After what you went through with Carl and a new baby…" His voice dropped. "I'm sorry, dear, I'm getting much too personal. Carmel is such a small town that we all tend to mind each other's business."

Mary Rose touched his arm. "It's all right, Xavier. Really, it is. I've come to terms with Devon's leaving, and so, apparently, has he."

The artist stood, adjusted his beret, then picked up his easel and paintbox. "If you ever need anything, Mary Rose, I'm here," he said kindly.

"Thank you, Xavier. I'll remember." Shading her eyes with her hand, she looked up at him from where she sat on the quilt.

"Well, until later, dear. You take care now."

"Goodbye, Xavier."

The sprightly artist had walked a short distance from her, when he turned around with a frown. "I forgot to ask. Have you seen Sterling lately?"

"No, I haven't."

"I thought he might have stopped by your cottage on the way to his place behind Devon's…ah, the studio."

"I haven't seen him recently."

"He's been in Monterey during the past week. Just got back yesterday. Stopped by my shop this morning."

Mary Rose waited for him to continue.

"Seems he stayed at the Del Cortés, just as he usually does. And while he was there, he heard a strange rumor."

She tilted her head, still shading her eyes from the sun.
"What was it?"

"You remember Duckworth? Oliver Duckworth?"

"Of course. He's handled Devon's work. He even came here
to tell us about the theft."

"Sterling heard that Duckworth's being investigated. The
hotel's called in a detective—incognito, of course."

Mary Rose stood and walked toward Xavier, while keeping
an eye on Jesse, who had followed her the short distance and
was now looking for seashells. "Investigated?" Mary Rose asked.

Xavier nodded. "Unrelated to what happened to you, but
the Del Cortés is looking at some discrepancies in his book-
keeping."

"How did Sterling find out?"

Xavier grinned, rubbing his goatee. "Seems he and the lovely
daughter of the Del Cortés owner are, shall we say, friends." He
raised an eyebrow. "She told Sterling, though right now it's still
very hush-hush. No one at the Del Cortés, not even
Duckworth, knows he's in hot water."

"Could it be that *Mary Rose's Garden* wasn't stolen after all?
Maybe he took it himself, or it sold and he kept the money."

"Well, dear. That's a pretty big leap. But it might be worth
checking. One never knows."

But Mary Rose's mind was racing ahead. If Duckworth was an
embezzler, perhaps he was guilty of other crimes as well. "Please,
Xavier, let me know the minute you hear anything more."

He nodded. "I will, dear. You can be assured of that."

"There's more involved with this than just the painting."

"I had a feeling there might be. Now you get back to your
sunbathing, and I'd better get to my seascape before the light
changes."

Mary Rose gave him a quick peck on the cheek. He smiled, his pale cheeks turning pink. "My goodness, dear, you've just made my day," he murmured as he trudged off in the sand.

"And you've just made mine a lot sunnier," she called after him, before turning back to Jesse.

Devon carried his recently finished painting of the Point Conception lighthouse into the Santa Barbara gallery.

"This is the work I was telling you about," he said to the proprietor. He leaned the painting against the counter.

The man walked over to Devon, shook his hand, then stood beside him, staring at the painting. "Mmmm," he said, frowning as he studied it. For several moments, he didn't speak.

Devon waited patiently. A clock somewhere in the back of the shop chimed five o'clock, and he sighed, worried that he wouldn't be able to take a look at the studio he was considering before dusk.

"You've done an interesting study of light," the proprietor finally said. "I don't think I've seen anything like it. But your darkness is greater than the glow of the lantern. Interesting."

"Are you interested in carrying my work?"

"Oh, yes. Very much. You've got a unique style. Do you have any other work?"

Devon nodded. "I've recently begun painting again after a bit of a hiatus. But I can have more for you within months."

"I'll take as many as you can produce."

"Thank you. It will be a pleasure to have my work shown here. Your gallery is the finest in town."

"Thank you, Devon. And are you planning on making Santa Barbara your home permanently?"

"Yes."

"Judging from just this one painting, I think I can safely say that we're fortunate you've picked us. And I hope this is the beginning of a very long business partnership."

"Thank you, sir."

Devon signed the necessary papers and headed up the street to the real estate office. There would be just enough daylight left to see the studio he'd inquired about earlier.

It was nearly sundown, though, when Devon climbed the stairs to the studio. Much like the studio he'd rented in Carmel, the place offered him an ocean view, without the forest of Monterey pines and cypress trees—without Mary Rose's garden below him, or her little cottage, as it had been before.

The sun began to slide into the mist-covered ocean, casting a lavender-gray glow across the water. It was a lonely color, and he turned away quickly, unable to bear the sadness.

Mary Rose. Would he ever be able to banish his thoughts of her, his memories of their times together, from his heart? He had tried to forget her, but the image of her face with its splash of freckles, the gold of her hair, the sea green of her eyes, simply would not leave him.

She occupied his first thoughts in the morning, his last at night.

Oh, Mary Rose, what have we done? he cried out in silent anguish as the last of the sunlight faded into darkness.

21

Monterey

MOLLY STEPPED FROM THE TRAIN at the Monterey station, dodging the other travelers. In the distance, the clatter and blast of an incoming train rattled the station. Then it neared the platform, its rods and cylinders clacking, its metal wheels screeching as it ground to a stop, disappearing into a cloud of steam. All around Molly, people were hurrying, laughing, and talking—new arrivals, their friends and relatives, porters and conductors.

It had been nearly a year since Zach had left his housewarming gift, *Mary Rose's Garden,* in her parlor. She had wanted to come to Monterey sooner but had been consumed by QII's rapid growth—and more than a little afraid of Zach's rebuff. She had written to him once thanking him for the oil, but Zach hadn't answered. His silence spoke volumes, and Molly decided it was best to keep her distance.

But now, at last, she had come to Monterey, Zach's beautiful little village by the bay. A breeze off the ocean ruffled her hair. Holding her straw hat in place with one hand, she tucked away a stray curl as she surveyed the platform. Wagons and carts clattered along, moving in and out of the small mountains of trunks, satchels, and luggage. Along with her fellow travelers,

Molly had just gotten off the Del Cortés Special out of Salinas. Now they all stood about, waiting for the vehicles that would take them to the hotel.

Molly had left San Francisco that morning, stopped briefly in Salinas to change trains, then boarded the Del Cortés Special to Monterey. The latter part of the line, its cars sporting the most luxurious furnishings she'd ever seen on a train, had been built expressly to transport guests to the resort hotel.

There was a spirit about Monterey that intrigued Molly from the moment she stepped off the train. The town was built on a gently sloping hillside, lush with foliage and stands of pine. From the station, she could see some of its shops and homes. They were fashioned of adobe, their thick whitewashed walls gleaming in the late afternoon sun.

Molly walked to the edge of the platform, looking toward the waterfront. In the distance, Monterey Bay stretched before her in the shape of a crescent moon. Glistening like a blue-green mirror, the bay was dotted with vessels of every style, color, and size. From clippers to Chinese junks, from schooners to paddle wheelers, they bobbed in the water's gentle swells. Farther out, a few moved gracefully under sail; closer to shore, they shifted lazily against their anchors. Others darted along, leaving frothing white trails behind them.

Dozens of schooners, sails furled, were anchored beyond the wharf in the bay; others, their white sails filled with wind, sailed toward shore. She wondered if the *Molly Quinn* was among them. Perhaps Zach and his crew were unloading their catch as she watched. She only hoped he hadn't taken the vessel out on an extended voyage....

"All guests awaiting transport to the Del Cortés, your carriages have arrived." The driver's call broke into Molly's thoughts. Picking up her satchel, she signaled for help with her luggage, then boarded the Del Cortés carriage.

As the vehicle clattered along the waterfront, Molly's thoughts were only of Zach, the joyful expectancy of soon being reunited with him, the fear that somehow it wouldn't happen.

The next morning, Molly rose at dawn. She pulled on a long flared skirt and dark blazer, with a lace-trimmed, pleated blouse, and fastened her hair into a high twist. She'd bought a new hat just for the trip, and now she pinned it in place, smiling at the result in the mirror. The hat's wide brim framed her face, its soft pink roses providing a feminine contrast to the businesslike suit.

Stepping out of the hotel into a sunny and cloudless day, she decided to walk the short distance to the landing where she hoped to find word of the *Molly Quinn*. The sun had risen high by the time she reached Alvarado Street to the wharf.

An old fisherman sat on one side of the wharf, fishing rod in hand, wicker creel beside him.

Molly approached him, nodding her greeting. "Do you know of the *Molly Quinn?*" she asked when he looked up.

"Sure, I know her. Most folks do…nice rig."

"Do you know anything about her schedule? When she'll be in port?"

"Last I heard, Missy, she headed out yesterday morning. I don't know when she'll be back," the old fisherman told her. Then he chuckled. "Her cap'n don't check in with me."

Molly turned away, overcome by disappointment. Now that she was here, so close to Zach, she thought she couldn't bear being away from him another moment.

Drawing a deep breath, she concentrated on the morning sun that warmed her shoulders as she headed back into town, the ocean breeze that caressed her skin. She savored the clear, sweet air with its scent of sand and sea as she walked.

Her disappointment lessened. Here she was in Monterey, near the place Zach loved. She couldn't leave without seeing him! Surely he would return soon.

With thoughts of Zach spurring her on, Molly headed toward Ocean View Avenue and its row of canneries to look into the businesses that Julian Starr had suggested. Just before leaving San Francisco, Julian had stopped by Molly's office. He'd offered to meet her in Monterey to prepare the necessary paperwork for the board if she decided to make an offer on one of the canneries.

Molly had agreed. She wanted to spend as much time as possible with Zach, and Julian's help with the transaction would hurry along the purchase, allowing her even more time.

The first factory Molly visited was the Portola Canning Company, a long low building made of corrugated tin and weathered wood. She was introduced to the general manager, a portly older man. She didn't tell him of her intent to buy a cannery but spoke in vague terms about getting into the fishing end of the business. He raised a condescending brow, and Molly wondered if he might pat her on the head, but he told all about the growth of the canning business in Monterey, especially about Portola's part of the operation.

She learned the steps from catch to canning. First the deep-laden fishing boats pulled in against the docks adjoining the cannery and unloaded their catch into chutes that poured the silver rivers of fish directly into the building. At the same time, the cannery whistles called workers from all over town to clean the fish.

She next visited the Monterey Canning Company. Its building was even more dilapidated than the first. She asked many of the same questions, particularly about the details of factories competing with the company. One of the worst-run companies, she was told, was the cannery at the far end of Ocean View Avenue, the Cabrillo Canning Company. Many other canneries were converting to sardine canning, but Cabrillo was the only factory still dealing exclusively with salmon. It was owned, she was told, by Mr. John Cabrillo, who insisted to everyone he met that he was a descendent of the sixteenth century Spanish explorer, Juan Rodríguez Cabrillo.

Without even raising an eyebrow at that improbable news, Molly nodded her thanks, then walked immediately to the building at the end of the street. Even from a distance, it was a dismal sight, a sagging structure made of tin and rusted iron and splintered wood.

A stooped man with a pinched face met her at the door. Molly explained why she was there, and he graciously showed her around. He was the only manager to take her through the entire operation. She followed him from room to room, through the fish-cleaning areas with their long tables and bins, to the packing rooms where rows of workers placed silver and pink chunks of salmon in cans, to still another room where more workers fastened lids and affixed labels.

Molly was struck by the dreary lot of the workers. Their demeanor was that of the downhearted with no goals or ambitions. It made her wonder if new ownership could better their lot, give them reason to improve their outlook and their productivity. She knew from her own experience that if a person was contented, even challenged on the job, the work would improve.

As she shook the manager's hand, she wondered at the man's own outlook. What if he were given positive incentives to improve the operation? She wondered about giving the workers part ownership of the Cabrillo. How would that change their productivity? It couldn't help but improve it. But she also would need to weigh the profit and loss on QII's part, if they undertook such a radical move.

She decided, if QIL and Cabrillo Canning Company did agree to a selling price, she would take her management ideas to QII's board members at their next meeting and ask their opinions as experienced businessmen. It was an intriguing idea, one she would work with and consider until then.

Before sunup the next day, Molly had dressed and hired a carriage to take her to Carmel-by-the-Sea. The driver took her on a road that wound along the rocky shoreline with crashing waves on one side and thick and verdant forests on the other. Zach had told her about the Central Coast, but she hadn't been prepared for such beauty. Finally, the road curved upward, climbing to the top of the sea cliff, then across the hillside leading into town.

They passed the Carmel mission church, wound around another hillside, then suddenly, the tiny village appeared before them.

The driver explained as they went along that though the colony was founded as Carmel-by-the-Sea, nowadays, most folks called it simply Carmel.

The carriage rattled onto Main Street, and Molly called to the driver. "You can pull over here."

He did as she asked, then came around to open her door.

She stepped onto a boardwalk in front of an artist's framing shop. If anyone could tell her the whereabouts of Devon O'Rourke, it would be someone such as this. She paid the driver and he pulled away, leaving her standing at the front of the small business.

The bell atop the door jingled as she entered the shop. A wiry man with a goatee and beret looked up.

Molly smiled. "Hello, I'm looking for an artist. His name is Devon O'Rourke."

"You won't find him around these parts any more. He used to live here, in fact, was here for a number of years. But he moved away months ago."

"I'm sorry to hear that. I've come quite a distance to find him."

"Did you see his work in the Capitol? That's where most folks hear of him." The man came around the counter to stand near Molly.

"Yes, I've seen his work there and—"

"That's what I thought. That where most people hear of him, our famous 'painter of light.'" He smiled. "I'm sorry. I'm being rude." He stuck out his hand. "My name is Xavier."

Molly shook his hand. "I'm Molly Quinn, Mr. Xavier. From San Francisco."

He laughed lightly. "No. Just Xavier. No Mr. in front of it. I go by only one name."

She nodded amiably. "Do you know where Devon O'Rourke has gone?"

"As a matter of fact, I was just telling Mary Rose yesterday that I'd run into him. None of us in the colony knew until I found him, just where he'd run off to—"

She interrupted as soon as he paused to take a breath. "Mary Rose?"

"Yes, do you know her?"

"It's the name of my painting."

"Your painting?" Xavier watched her intently.

"I mean my O'Rourke. It's called *Mary Rose's Garden.*"

Xavier gasped, dramatically bringing his hand to his mouth. *"Mary Rose's Garden?* Are you sure it's an O'Rourke?"

Molly frowned. "Of course I'm sure. I've seen the *Hope.* His style is unmistakable."

Xavier removed the beret and scratched his head. "Tell me how you came by the painting."

"A friend purchased it for me. Why? Can you tell me why the concern, the doubt? The questions?"

Suddenly, a slow, knowing smile covered Xavier's face. "I think you've just solved a mystery that's had the whole colony stumped, young lady." His voice held awe. "And I've got someone you need to meet." He quickly stepped to the door and turned over the welcome sign, then escorted Molly from the shop.

"Please, tell me why you're concerned," Molly said, as they hurried up the boardwalk, past the few shops that made up the small town. "Where are we going?"

"You're about to meet Mary Rose," Xavier said. "And I have a feeling the two of you are going to have a lot to talk about." His eyes were merry.

He led Molly along a winding path toward a small cottage among the pines. Moments later, he held open a wooden gate, then followed her up the stepping stones to the door.

He rapped softly. Molly could hear the sound of footsteps inside. Then the door opened, and a young woman smiled, first at Xavier, then quizzically at Molly. She was even lovelier in person than in the oil painting.

"Mary Rose," Molly whispered, feeling almost as if she already knew her.

Xavier stepped up quickly to introduce them. "Mary Rose, this is Molly Quinn from San Francisco. Molly, Mary Rose Sheffield." He drew in a deep breath. "Molly's come here looking for Devon."

A barely perceptible shadow crossed the young woman's face. "Devon?" she said softly. "Didn't you tell her that he's left?"

"Yes, I did, dear. But she's got some news that I think you need to hear right away. That's why I brought her."

Mary Rose nodded, her gaze meeting Molly's. "I was just about to go up to my garden. It's such a beautiful day, would you like to join me?"

"That would be lovely," Molly said to her.

Xavier cleared his throat. "I think I'll leave you ladies to your discussion. If you'll excuse me?"

Mary Rose walked with him to the gate, then turned back to Molly. "Please, come with me," she said and led the way around the house and into her garden. They climbed the small path, past rows of tender green, newly planted vegetables, through beds of flowers and shrubs. Molly had never seen such color and variety; she couldn't even have guessed the names of most. Throughout the garden, the music of birds and insects rose into the fragrant air. Molly didn't think she'd ever been in a more pleasant spot.

Finally, arriving at a level terrace at the top of the garden, Mary Rose nodded toward a redwood bench under an olive tree. "Please, sit down," she smiled.

Mary Rose settled onto the seat beside Molly, then turned toward her. Behind them, a rushing creek added to the music of the afternoon.

"You've come looking for Devon?" Mary Rose asked.

Molly nodded. "I was disappointed when Xavier told me that he'd gone. I have one of his paintings, and I looked forward to meeting him, perhaps purchasing another." She smiled gently at Mary Rose, understanding intuitively that Devon O'Rourke's leaving was somehow painful for her.

But Mary Rose looked pleased, her face lighting at the mention of O'Rourke. "You must have the *Hope*. I hadn't heard that it sold. That will be such good news for Devon."

"No. It's *Mary Rose's Garden* that I have."

"That's not—" Mary Rose began, then stopped midsentence, frowning. "How did you get it?"

"It was a gift. But Xavier indicated that there was some mystery involved. Can you tell me why? He seemed adamant that we talk."

"It was stolen from the Del Cortés. At least, that's what we were told."

"Stolen?"

Mary Rose nodded. "It was heartbreaking to hear of it. Nearly a year ago, Oliver Duckworth, the hotel manager, drove down here from Monterey to tell Devon. He said he had an interested buyer. Then that night the painting disappeared. The buyer had nothing to do with it. According to Oliver, it was simply coincidental." A sad expression crossed the young woman's face. She paused before going on. "Devon was devastated, as was I. He...*we* had put a very high price on the painting, in more than one regard. Our future was dependent on it."

"That's why he left?" Molly asked gently.

Mary Rose nodded, looking out at her garden. "Duckworth is at fault. Xavier heard that he's being investigated on other charges. Now I think we can add one more charge to the list."

She turned back to Molly. "You said the painting was a gift?"

Molly nodded.

"The person who gave it to you?"

"His name is Zachary MacAlister."

Mary Rose went on excitedly. "Do you think he will testify to the facts regarding his purchase?"

"He's a sea captain out of Monterey. I'm not sure when he'll be back, but as soon as he is, I'll tell him what has happened. I'm sure he'll want to help you."

Mary Rose leaned toward Molly. "You have no idea what this means to me, what it will mean to Devon." Then she smiled. "I haven't even asked how you like the painting."

"When you opened the door of your cottage a few minutes ago, I felt as though I'd already met you." She shook her head slightly. "The painting hangs above my fireplace, and it fills me with peace each time I look at it. I'm involved in a world that can sometimes be overwhelming. But I look at it, at the garden, and I feel much the way I do sitting here today with you. It's as if the light in the painting really exists, a place really exists, where there is peace and joy and comfort and love." She smiled, laughing softly. "I think that's why Zach gave it to me. He knows that the world I've stepped into can cheat me of those things. And he suspects that deep down I miss them."

"He—your Zach, must know you quite well."

Molly nodded slowly. "Yes, he does. One time I told him that creating a successful business of my own would be like planting a garden and watching it grow." She paused, thinking about the night she'd said the words, how much had changed since that long-ago evening in another garden, Kingsley's, before it was destroyed in the earthquake. "And your garden, in the painting, with all its light and shadow and color and glory, made him remember my words. This," she looked out at the lush and glorious surroundings, "connected us to each other, just when I thought he'd forgotten."

Mary Rose nodded, a look of understanding on her face. "And the same painting was created to bring Devon and me together in marriage. Yet a deception, a crime committed with the same work tore us apart." She sighed. "You have no idea how terrible it was for Devon. This was such a work of love, a work that brought together so many elements of his artistry, color, composition, his study of light. He really didn't want to sell it."

Molly was surprised, though she didn't say so.

"Since he left I've been struggling with my own guilt at pushing its sale." She smiled sheepishly. "Devon is a very proud man. You see, I'm widowed. I have a small child."

"The baby in the painting..."

"Yes, Jesse. He's napping right now, but as soon as he wakes, I'll introduce you."

"I'd like that."

"Anyway, as I was saying, Devon's a very proud man. But like most artists, he lives on the income from his paintings. And he hasn't sold more than just enough to buy supplies. We spoke of marriage, but he wouldn't consider it, unless, of course, the *Hope* or *Mary Rose's Garden* sold."

"Then the *Hope* went to the Capitol for display, and *Mary Rose's Garden* was stolen."

"Yes, but how did you know about the display in the Capitol?"

Molly shook her head. "Let me tell you about a remarkable coincidence. I was in Sacramento on business, and a friend took me by the Capitol. I saw the exhibit and was immediately drawn to the O'Rourke lighthouse. I'd never seen such power and depth in a painting. And of course, the light. Everyone at the exhibit was talking about it. I could have spent the entire day just absorbing that one oil."

Mary Rose watched her attentively with a knowing look.

"Then something extraordinary happened. The day I returned to San Francisco, I walked into my home and found an O'Rourke hanging in my sitting room, a housewarming gift from Zach." She let out a small sigh. "The coincidence of it all. I'm still in awe."

Mary Rose nodded. "It wasn't a coincidence, Molly."

Molly gave her a quick look.

"It was meant to be. God is using this painting." Then, noticing Molly's puzzled expression, she laughed lightly. "And from all appearances, he's not through with it yet."

"I hadn't thought about it in quite that way. Perhaps you're right." She frowned. "You know, Mary Rose, the first time I looked at your garden in the painting, it seemed to be an almost sacred place. And now, sitting here with you, I get the same feeling. You're a very religious person, aren't you?"

"Religious?" Mary Rose laughed. "I hope not!"

Molly raised an eyebrow at the unexpected response.

"People who call themselves religious may as well wear a sign around their necks, proclaiming a self-righteousness that makes everyone they meet uncomfortable."

Molly laughed, liking Mary Rose more than ever. "Now that you mention it, I've known people like that. They seem to glory in their own 'goodness.'"

"And it has nothing to do with God or who they are in him."

"Well, that's a bit beyond my experience. I believe in God

the Creator and that we're all part of his creation. But that's about where he ends and I begin."

"God helps the one who helps herself?"

Molly laughed again. "That could very well be my credo." Then she became serious. "You said something about people who are 'in God.' I don't think I've ever heard anyone mention a relationship with him as personal as that."

"There's a verse in the Bible that speaks about God as being a vine, with us as branches." Mary Rose smiled, looking around at her garden. "I can understand what that means. He wants us to abide in him just as a branch is connected to a vine. I've always thought of abiding as a life-blood connection that flows from him to me, a continual conversation in which he hears the thoughts of my heart, and I listen to his."

Molly opened her eyes wide. "You listen to God?"

Mary Rose laughed quietly. "I didn't mean for it to sound quite so extreme. It's not like I hear voices or anything." Her expression softened. "I just find that when I take the time to sit down and be quiet...such as here in the garden, I read his Word—"

"You mean the Bible?"

She nodded. "Then I open my heart to his thoughts. I can't explain it. It's just a time of visiting with my friend and listening to him speak to me through what I've just read, or through verses or phrases I've read at other times." She smiled at Molly. "But I'm going on and on about this. Are you sure you want to hear it?"

"*Mary Rose's Garden* is a part of my home. Just now, listening to you speak, it's occurred to me that every time I look at my painting, I'll remember you, Mary Rose, and your garden...especially why it's such a sacred place." She paused.

"What are some of those heart-thoughts you've heard when listening to God? I want to remember those, too."

"Some things that come to mind are from the Book of Isaiah: 'You are precious and honored in my sight and I love you.... I have called you by name; you are mine.' He tells us in the Psalms, 'I will watch over you.' And in Jeremiah, he says, 'I have loved you with an everlasting love.... I have brought you to me with loving-kindness.'"

"Those words are beautiful. You really believe that God said, or is saying them about you?"

Mary Rose nodded slowly. "Yes."

"It must give you great comfort to know you are loved, watched over, and cared for."

"Yes, it does," she said.

Molly looked around the garden. "I know now why, even in the painting, this appears to be such a place." She turned back to Mary Rose. "I'll remember those words, those thoughts, every time I look at *Mary Rose's Garden*. Thank you for telling me."

"Devon will be so glad to know how his work has affected you, Molly, especially after thinking it was forever lost. I can't wait to tell him."

"Tell me about Devon. You said that you had planned to be married. I could tell he loved the subject of the painting. And he painted such love in your eyes."

Mary Rose sighed deeply. "Devon told me goodbye right after Duckworth's visit. Then he cleaned out his studio and left, not telling me where he was going." Her eyes teared as she spoke, and she swallowed hard. "At first I was angry with him for not staying and fighting to get his work known. I felt betrayed and abandoned." She shrugged.

"You don't sound angry now."

"I'm not. I've come to terms with what happened, especially my part in it."

"Do you know where he is now? Has anyone a clue?"

Mary Rose smiled. "Yes, I may be able to find him. Xavier saw him in Santa Barbara not too long ago. We think that's where he's made his home, though he leaves on extended trips to paint lighthouses."

A small voice called from the cottage.

"Jesse?" Molly asked.

"Yes, but please wait here. I'll get him and be right back." Mary Rose started down the path. Then she stopped suddenly and turned to look back. "Molly, I haven't talked to anyone about Devon since he left, I mean about what happened between us. It's felt good, actually, it's felt right to tell you. Thank you for listening. It's as if..." She frowned, searching for the right words.

"As if we're going to become good friends?" Molly smiled. "I've been thinking that myself."

"From the painting?"

"Yes, from the painting."

Jesse called out again, and Mary Rose hurried to retrieve him. Moments later, she held his hand as they walked up the path to meet Molly. The little boy's cheeks were rosy from sleep. He rubbed his eyes, giving Molly a shy smile.

"He's even more beautiful in person. May I hold him?" Molly held out her arms, and the towheaded Jesse climbed onto her lap. "I've been thinking about a plan," she said. "It's something I'd considered even before I met you. In fact, it's what prompted my visit in the first place. But after talking with you, I'm more certain than ever it's what I want to do."

Mary Rose, now seated again beside Molly, looked up attentively.

"Devon's talent is too important to remain hidden. He must have the support to continue on without interruption. I want to have a part in helping him do that."

A tremulous smile spread across Mary Rose's face. "Molly, I...I don't know what to say." Her voice was barely more than a whisper.

"You told me that Devon's a very proud man. Do you think he'll accept my help as a patron?"

"I can't speak for him, but I'll do my best to find him and ask." A shadow crossed her face. "Though, at this point, I'm not even sure of the reception I'll get when I find him, *if* I can find him."

Molly smiled gently. "I understand, but my offer will remain open until you do have a chance to ask him."

Mary Rose nodded.

"Do you think you'll go to Santa Barbara?" Molly asked.

"That will be my starting place."

"Why don't you come into Monterey first, before I leave? I'll introduce you to Zach. Then you'll have evidence to take to the authorities and to Devon. I'm here on other business, but I'll help you as much as I can."

The two young women sat and talked well into the afternoon, Jesse playing happily nearby, the brook bubbling and singing behind them. Mary Rose served them tea and sandwiches under the pepper tree, and when Molly stood finally to say goodbye, the late afternoon sunlight was flooding the garden.

Molly felt that she'd never been in a more peaceful place.

22

MOLLY WAITED THREE DAYS for the *Molly Quinn* to return, but still there was no sign of the schooner. On the morning of the fourth day, as usual, she checked at the wharf before going about her business in town. When Zach wasn't there, she began to face returning home without seeing him. Julian was due on the afternoon train to finalize the Cabrillo Canning Company offer, and Mary Rose planned to join her the following day to look into the Duckworth affair. By the end of the week, Molly would have no reason to further delay her journey back to San Francisco.

The old fisherman at the wharf recognized Molly on sight now, and gave her a toothless grin as she walked toward him. "Nah, no word of the *Molly Quinn*," he said, as she drew nearer. "She usually doesn't stay out this long. Sorry, Missy."

Molly nodded.

"You must have some important business with her." He stuck a piece of smelly fish bait on his line.

"I need to speak with her captain."

"Well, Missy, there's a storm brewing. It'll be drivin' in the best of 'em. If I see your cap'n, who shall I say's lookin' for him?"

"Tell him Molly Quinn has been here asking about him."

"Molly Quinn?" He looked up at her incredulously.

"Yes, Molly Quinn." She smiled.

The old man guffawed. "Well, if that ain't somethin'. Molly Quinn, the real Molly Quinn, comin' to see the cap'n of the *Molly Quinn,* eh?" He slapped his knee. "Well, now, if that just ain't somethin'."

She chuckled with him. "Just tell him I was here, if you see him, please?"

"That I will, Missy. You can just bet I will."

Molly walked back into town, heading straight to a livery stable where she rented a small one-horse surrey. If she couldn't see Zach, she would do the next best thing, drive to the place he had told her about, the place of the jeweled dawn. She might not be able to find the exact location, but on her trip into Carmel, she had noticed the beautiful beaches near Pacific Grove. They had reminded her of Zach's descriptions, and she planned to head there now, before Julian or Mary Rose arrived and she got too busy to break away. She wanted some time alone with her thoughts of Zach, with her memories.

The stable hand hitched a bay mare to the surrey. Molly took the reins, flicked them lightly above the horse's back, and headed the animal onto a main road leading south.

The carriage rattled along, and soon they were out of Monterey on a narrow, winding road at the ocean's edge. She passed other travelers, some on horseback, others in carriages or motorcars. At first, she held the reins tightly, worried the horse would spook at the sound of backfiring cars. But the mare clopped along calmly.

A short distance past Lovers Point, she headed onto Lighthouse Road toward Point Piños. Soon the lighthouse shone in the sunlight, the waves behind it spraying onto a rock-strewn beach. Molly recognized it as the same that Devon O'Rourke had painted in the *Hope*. The people in Monterey were proud of the landmark, one of eight lighthouses that had been built on the Pacific Coast in 1855. Its charm delighted her as the carriage rattled past, and she understood why O'Rourke had chosen it as his subject.

From time to time, as the vehicle rattled and swayed along, she stopped to gaze at the ocean, thrilling to the sheer power in its crashing waves. Toward the west, she could see that the old fisherman had been right. A bank of clouds heralded a coming storm, causing the surf to pound wildly, its mist carrying on the wind.

Soon the road wound away from the beach and up into the woodland cliffs above the water. Molly was glad that the traffic was lighter here, with fewer travelers and no loud automobiles. The sounds of the forest were peaceful, and the music of the breaking waves faded into the distance. The trees grew thicker as the mare pulled the surrey up the hillside, the pines now so dense that they obscured her view of the ocean.

Finally, she rounded a curve and spotted a clearing. There before her spread the ocean, its color ever changing in the coming storm. She could see every shade of green and blue and turquoise, even a lavender gray where the horizon met the dark bank of storm clouds. This might not be the place that Zach had told her about, but she had never seen anything quite like it.

Pulling the surrey to the side of the road near a stand of trees, she looked out at the expanse of ocean. The storm was closer now, and its brisk wind whipped at her face and clothes, loosening her hair. But the sun still warmed her shoulders, and she decided to stay awhile.

After fastening the mare's reins to a small shrub, she walked out to a granite point and stood, drinking in the beauty and watching the storm as it moved toward shore. It had taken her only a half-hour to drive out. She felt sure there was plenty of time to head the surrey back down the cliffs and into town before the storm hit.

Sighing, Molly settled against a rocky cairn. Some distance out, she could see clippers and schooners heading back to Monterey Bay. She wondered if Zach's might be one of them. Perhaps, as the fisherman had said, the storm would bring the *Molly Quinn* into port by the end of the day.

Lost in thought, she didn't hear the lone horseback rider approaching, until her mare whinnied nervously from where she was tied. Molly turned to look back to the road, but the clearing was obscured by the cypress trees.

She moved toward the road, still unable to see the rider. The wind whipped her hair across her face, and Molly reached up to brush it back with her fingers.

At the same time, the rider dismounted and turned to her.

She caught her breath, afraid to hope.

"Molly," the rider finally said.

It was Zach!

Molly remained motionless—afraid to run to him, afraid to speak his name—afraid he might have changed toward her.

Zach strode closer, and Molly bit her lip, watching his every step. His gaze never left hers. At last she could see into the depths of his eyes, the light they held. The love!

Then Zach stopped a few feet in front of her, searching her face. "Molly?" he repeated hoarsely.

She caught her hand to her mouth and felt unbidden tears fill her eyes.

Then Zach held open his arms. With a small cry, she ran to him.

Zach grabbed her with fierce abandon and pressed her close. "Oh, Molly," he murmured into her hair, not letting her go.

Molly clung to him, still unable to believe he was really here and that she was in his arms.

Finally, she leaned back to look into his eyes. She touched his face with her fingertips. His skin had turned a golden brown from the sun, and he seemed leaner and more muscular than she remembered. "How did you find me?" she finally managed.

He grinned. "You made quite an impression on the old fisherman at the wharf. We'd barely unloaded the morning's catch when he was at my heels telling me all about your visits."

"But here? How did you know?"

He hugged her close again, and she could feel the steady rhythm of his heart. "I just guessed, Molly," he said. "The old man told me that he saw you pull out of the livery and head south. I hoped I'd find you somewhere along this stretch of the beach."

She looked up at him. "Is this it, Zach? The place you told me about?"

"No. But it's not far. Would you like me to take you?"

"Very much."

He squinted, looking out at the storm. "I think we've got time before it hits. Why don't you follow me?"

She nodded.

Within minutes, Zach had mounted his Appaloosa and rode beside her as she drove the surrey. They headed through a grove of Monterey pines and across a gently sloping hillside near the water. A towering cliff met them on the other side.

Zach halted the Appaloosa and signaled Molly to stop.

"Here's where the road ends. The surrey and mare will never make it to the top." He looked up the hillside. "We'll need to leave them down here. You can ride with me."

Molly nodded, laughing slightly. "I'll have to ride in front, though, sidesaddle. My long skirt will hardly double as riding attire."

"That will just give me another excuse to hold you in my arms, Molly." He gave her a smile that caused her cheeks to flame. Then he helped her tie the mare securely to a cypress tree in a clearing off the main road. With one swift, strong movement, he lifted her onto the saddle. He mounted behind her and, true to his word, held Molly securely in place. She settled against him, feeling the strength of his arms around her holding the reins on either side.

He nudged the Appaloosa's flanks, and the big horse climbed the steep hillside. The higher they went, the more spectacular the view as Molly turned to look back.

It took only a few minutes to arrive at the top. Rather than the rocky ocean cliff Molly had pictured, a beautiful meadow lay in front of her, surrounded on three sides by a forest of Monterey pines. Wildflowers of every description covered the bright spring grasses, and off to one side, near a small brook, three deer—a doe and her two yearlings—grazed, their ears flicking as they watched Zach and Molly.

Zach helped Molly from the saddle. He let the Appaloosa graze in the meadow and walked with Molly to the edge of the hillside.

She caught her breath in wonder. Below them stretched the Pacific, dark, powerful, and mysterious—but no less beautiful— as the sun slipped behind the layer of building clouds.

"Oh, Zach," Molly whispered. "It's splendid." She turned back to him. "I can only imagine what it looks like at dawn."

But Zach was looking at her, not the ocean. "Molly, how I've missed you," he murmured, as he gently gathered her into his arms again.

She slid her arms around him. He bent his head, touching her lips with his. His mouth met hers with such tenderness, that Molly felt tears sting her eyes. She returned the kiss.

After a moment, Zach looked into her eyes and Molly felt her knees grow weak. She swallowed hard as he touched her face, tracing his fingers along her cheek, around her chin, then with the backs of his fingers, gently touched her temple. He brushed back a few errant curls, tucking one behind her ear, then bent to kiss her again.

Molly was almost afraid to breathe, afraid she would somehow break the precious and fragile moment. Never in her life had she felt so cherished, so loved.

She slipped her arms around his neck, and on tiptoe, softly touched his lips with hers. Then she pulled back slightly and looked up at him. "It feels so right to be in your arms, so very right."

"Molly," he breathed. "I wonder if you have any idea how I feel about you."

She gave him a small smile. "Tell me."

"Since that night in San Francisco, I've dreamed about holding you in my arms again—kissing you, feeling your lips on mine, your arms around my neck."

His fingers under her chin, he gently tilted her face toward his. For a moment he didn't speak, just looked deep into her eyes. His voice was husky when he finally continued. "You've captured my heart, Molly. I don't know for sure when it happened. It might have been when I saw you fixing your flower-covered hat at the Forresters' front door the day you first arrived. Or it might have been when I danced with you in the rain. Or maybe when I held you in my arms the first time."

He frowned in his earnestness. "It seems that you've always been part of my life, my thoughts." He paused, his voice dropping. "And now, Molly, I can't imagine my life without you. I don't want to imagine my life without you."

Zach drew her closer and pressed his lips more passionately against hers. After a moment, Molly looked up at him, breathless, her heart pounding so loudly against her ribs she thought he surely could hear it.

"Zach," she whispered, her voice tremulous, "at night, I dream of you. And in the daytime, I think of you." She tilted her head, her eyes still meeting his. "Constantly." Her smile widened.

He frowned slightly. "I saw you in San Francisco with another man."

"Julian? He's—" she began, but Zach touched her lips to quiet her.

"There's no need to explain, Molly." A shadow crossed his face. "We have no formal commitment. And it had been so long..." His voice broke off. "I had no reason to believe—"

This time, she interrupted him. "You don't understand. I had so hoped to see you, to speak with you. Then that night at the opera, I looked down and there you were. My heart nearly stood still." She sighed. "Then just as suddenly, you were gone."

She touched his face again, caressing his cheek. "Zach, I decided to leave San Francisco before we could speak. The trip to Sacramento was for my business, an opportunity I thought wouldn't come round again. I thought I needed to act quickly. I made a choice, and it was the wrong one." She looked out at the darkening sea, unable to meet his gaze. "I need time, Zach," she finally said.

Zach turned her gently, lifting her face toward his. "Will one more year allow you enough time to follow your dreams, Molly?"

"One year." she repeated softly. "The day of our promise."

"You didn't answer my question. Is it enough time?"

"I'll be here, Zach. At dawn. It's a promise that's dearer than life to me." She still hadn't answered his question

He seemed to understand and didn't repeat it. Instead, he asked, "Can I talk you into making it sooner?"

She swallowed hard, shaking her head. "I'm sorry."

"Sometimes, Molly," he said after a moment, "I feel I can wait forever. Other times..." His voice broke off, and he didn't go on.

She reached her hands around his neck and gently pulled his face toward hers. Her lips again met his. The kiss made her want to weep, to stop the world from spinning so fast, and to cry out from the fear of losing him.

As they walked back to the Appaloosa, Zach heard the latest news from San Francisco, especially about Gwennie and Kingsley, and about Molly's company, QIL, as she now called it. As Molly spoke about QIL and her move to incorporate, he noticed he'd never seen her look so devastatingly radiant. He wondered if it was because they were together or if it was because of her delight in telling him about her business. With a stab of sadness, he suspected it was the latter.

Then the conversation turned to his fishing business, and Zach found that Molly was keenly interested in every detail. He couldn't help thinking about the women he knew whose faces went blank after the first word uttered about salmon runs in the Pacific. Yes, Molly was unique in every way.

"Do you ever think of expanding?" she asked, after hearing of his progress. "Buy another ship, hire on another crew?"

Zach laughed. "I seem to remember having this conversation before. You're the one who said you'd never be content with a single fishing boat. You said something to the effect that you'd not be happy until you owned the whole fleet."

But Molly frowned. "I'm serious, Zach. You've created a successful enterprise. There's a demand for salmon, especially now that most fishermen have switched to sardines. The time to expand is now. There's no reason you can't. I'll speak to QII's board. Perhaps we can provide the capital you need."

"No," Zach interrupted. "I don't want help. I don't want to expand. My small fishing business is perfect just the way it is. I want nothing more." He gave her a wry grin. "Besides, it would be difficult to think that I was working for you."

She didn't smile. "But you wouldn't be, Zach. QIL would simply be investing in your business."

"As in a loan without collateral?"

For a moment she didn't speak. "The *Molly Quinn* would provide your collateral," she finally said.

"That's what I thought." He searched her eyes for understanding of his point of view. "My independence is very important to me, Molly. I thought you knew that."

"I do," she said. But Zach judged from her expression that she didn't.

"Do you know what it would do to us for you to own my ship, my business, in any way?"

She didn't answer.

"That would be the one thing that would drive us apart, Molly."

Molly reached up and touched his face. "Nothing can drive us apart, Zach. We're too entwined in each other's lives." He caught her hand and kissed her palm, hoping that she truly understood the gravity of what he'd told her.

They had walked halfway into the meadow when Molly suddenly stopped and looked up at him. "The painting," she said softly.

"*Mary Rose's Garden?*"

She nodded. "I got so carried away just seeing you again, I nearly forgot to mention it." She let out a small sigh. "Zach, words can't describe how I felt when I saw it."

"The day I first saw it at the Del Cortés, I felt the same way. I knew you had to have it."

"It's perfect." Then she frowned. "But why didn't you answer my letter? I wrote you right after you left the painting."

"I'm sorry, Molly. Your letter just seemed so...stilted, businesslike. After your leaving so abruptly, I just assumed that you wanted to keep it that way."

"Nothing could be further from the truth."

"I know that now." His eyes smiled into hers. "But I didn't then."

Molly went on to describe her trip to Carmel-by-the-Sea. Zach watched the animation in her expression as she related the story of Devon O'Rourke and Mary Rose, their love, and how their upcoming wedding was canceled due to the theft of the painting.

"Theft?" Zach repeated incredulously. He couldn't believe what he'd just heard. "Do you mean, the proceeds of the sale never got to Devon O'Rourke?"

"Apparently, Duckworth pocketed the money and led everyone, including Devon and Mary Rose, to believe the painting had been stolen right from under your nose."

Zach let out a long sigh. "I had no idea. We must go after him immediately, tell the authorities. This wrong must be made right as soon as possible." He paused. "I can only imagine what this has done to Devon O'Rourke."

"That's why he left."

"Does Mary Rose know where he is?"

Molly shook her head slowly. "There's a chance he's now living near Santa Barbara, but no one is certain."

"My next trip out, I'll be heading south. I wonder if there's anything I can do." Zach wondered if he would be able to take the time to search for the missing artist. Where would he even begin to look?

Molly suddenly brightened. "Maybe you could take a passenger with you?"

"You?" He smiled at the delightful thought.

"No. Mary Rose. She said something about going to look for Devon. I don't think she has much money, and the trip would be a hardship."

"If that would help. The *Molly Quinn* isn't luxurious by any stretch, but we have the room to accommodate a passenger." He paused, thoughtfully considering Molly's suggestion. "Yes," he finally said. "I'd be happy to take her to Santa Barbara."

Molly nodded. "She's coming to Monterey tomorrow. How about meeting us for late afternoon tea at the Del Cortés?"

"I'll look forward to it."

The Appaloosa stood in the center of the meadow. The storm was nearly ashore now, and the strong wind whipped unobstructed from the sea. Zach started to lift Molly into the saddle. But as he reached his hands around her waist, she gazed up at him.

"Zach," she murmured, "thank you for coming out here today."

He gave her a half-grin. "I wouldn't have missed seeing you for the world, Molly."

She touched his cheek. "When do you sail?"

"Day after tomorrow. And when are you going back to San Francisco?"

"The same day."

He sighed and lifted her into the saddle. Seconds later, he swung a leg over the Appaloosa behind her and nudged the big horse forward. They rode into the wind, and after a few minutes, clambered down the cliff to the road below.

"Molly," he said, as she stepped into the little surrey, "there's something else I wanted to tell you."

She looked up at him, the wind whipping her hair, her cheeks pink from the damp cold.

"The meadow where we just stood?"

She nodded.

"I bought it three weeks ago."

"Zach, you did? That's wonderful!" A smile of wonder lit her lovely face.

"It's for us someday, Molly."

"Oh, Zach," she whispered. She regarded him a moment without speaking. "But too often I wonder," she said finally, "if that someday will ever come."

"I know," he said quietly. "I know."

CHAPTER

23

As Molly and Zach pulled into the stables, a light rain had started to fall, and they hurried for the shelter of the nearly deserted livery. Zach said he had business to attend to in town, and Molly planned to return to the hotel.

"Until tomorrow, then?" Zach brushed her lips with his in a goodbye kiss. "I want to be with you every moment of the day." He smiled. "I don't think I'll let you out of my sight."

Molly sighed. "I've some business I need to handle in the morning. Shall we meet for tea with Mary Rose, then spend the rest of the evening together?"

"And for the evening, I have something special in mind."

"Can you give me a hint?"

He smiled. "Picture the moonlit surf and a candlelight supper."

"It sounds beautiful."

Zach searched her face and frowned. "Molly, is something wrong?"

"It's just that it will be our last day together. And it's just now striking me that I don't know when we'll be together again."

He pulled her closer. "I know, my darling, I know. I don't want to think of it either."

She settled into his arms, feeling strangely uneasy. The rain continued to fall, hitting the puddles in a sad and mournful rhythm. Molly shivered and tried to shut out the sound.

After hailing a horse-drawn cab, Molly arrived at the Del Cortés and found that Julian Starr had registered during the afternoon. She sent a message to the lawyer's room, and moments later he strode in to meet her in the ornately furnished lobby.

They settled into two plush chairs near the fireplace.

"The climate must be invigorating, Molly. You look wonderful," he said, with an appraising gaze.

Molly patted her still-damp hair. "I can only imagine. I've just returned from a buggy ride out in the elements. But yes, the climate—though not that different from San Francisco's—does agree with me." She laughed lightly, thinking about the meadow on the hill.

Then they settled down to business. "Tell me what you've found."

"Cabrillo Canning Company is perfect," Molly began and told him why she thought it would be a good place for QIL to invest. Julian nodded attentively, taking notes and asking questions from time to time. "I'd like to make an offer tomorrow morning," she concluded. "That is, if you agree."

He told her that the other board members were awaiting his wire and would respond with their recommendations. "By tomorrow night," Julian said finally, "Cabrillo Canning Company will probably belong to you, Molly." He smiled and shook her hand in congratulations as they stood to part. "Good work, and I like your management ideas," he said, as they moved from the room. "I would suggest that we wait until after the next board meeting to implement them, however."

She nodded in agreement. "I'll wait, but I feel very strongly about this."

"I know you do, Molly. And it's a sound idea. But you don't want to alienate the 'big three.'" He took a deep breath. "For all the reasons we've talked about."

"I know, Julian. And thank you for meeting me here to pull this together." They had reached the elevator, and as the doors opened, Molly stepped in.

Julian held up his hand, and the elevator operator kept the door open. "Do you have dinner plans?" Julian asked Molly.

She hesitated.

"I have some other QIL business I'd like to discuss before our meeting with Cabrillo tomorrow."

The last thing Molly wanted to do was spend the evening with Julian, but he was probably right. They needed to talk over the details of tomorrow's offer. Besides, the more business they could handle tonight, the more time she would have for Zach tomorrow. "All right, Julian," she finally said. "I'll meet you in the hotel dining room." The delight on his face was transparent as the elevator doors closed, but Molly felt uncomfortable about their meeting as she rode to her floor.

At seven o'clock, Julian rose to meet her, pulling out the chair beside him for her. During dinner and their conversation afterward, Julian was the erudite gentleman, charming, witty, and attentive. He followed her lead and kept the conversation light, primarily speaking about business matters. He spoke of Sacramento politics, the increasing rumors of his running for political office, and his inclination to do so.

The evening raced by, and Molly enjoyed his conversation and company. Still, she was grateful when business had been concluded and the evening drew to a close. They spoke of meeting the following morning and riding together to the cannery. Julian said he would order a carriage to be ready for them at eight o'clock

It was late when Julian stood to escort Molly to the elevator. As they passed the saloon next to the dining room, raucous late-evening revelers were standing about. Julian took her arm, walking beside Molly protectively.

They passed through the nearly empty lobby, and Julian stopped near the flickering fireplace. He turned to Molly, taking her hand in his.

"Molly," he began. "This evening—"

"Julian, please," she said, pulling her hand away. "Our relationship can only continue on a professional level." Though a capable lawyer and up-and-coming tough politician, he remained a gentle soul. She didn't want to make an issue of something that could be handled in a straightforward manner. If he weren't such a loyal and excellent attorney, she would send him packing.

But instead, she smiled up at him. "Julian," she sighed, "I told you before, nothing can come of this. The fact is..." Though she didn't like to talk about her personal life, perhaps it was the very thing that would deter him. "The fact is, there is someone else in my life."

He raised an eyebrow. "There is?" He hesitated. "Oh, Molly, I feel like such a fool. I should never have pursued this." For all his sophisticated ways, he suddenly reminded her of an awkward schoolboy. "I'm sorry I put you in this awkward position...having to tell me..."

She placed her hand on his arm, tilting her head to meet his gaze. "Please, Julian. Don't be embarrassed. I treasure your friendship. You've been wonderful for QIL, for me as well. You've brought us through the rockiest of times, introduced me to the 'big three.' You've been wonderful. I consider you among my dearest friends."

A look of consternation crossed his handsome face. "Friends?" he croaked. "I still feel foolish."

She smiled, shaking her head slightly. "Julian, I could never think of you as foolish. And there might have been more to our...ah, friendship...except that..." She faltered, searching for the right words. "There's someone so important to me, someone I will love until the day I die. I'm simply not interested in anyone else, and I don't think I ever could be."

He looked so dejected that she touched his cheek. "I'm sorry," she added.

Suddenly, Julian grinned at her and chucked her under the chin. "You've just broken my heart, Molly Quinn," he said. "I wanted to take you with me all the way to Washington, D.C."

"Well, when you get there, dear," she said, smiling up at him, happy the awkwardness had passed, "at least invite me to a state dinner. And I can say, I knew you when."

He gave her a quick hug, laughing with her. "It's a promise. It is indeed." He turned to look affectionately down at her again. "Your intended, whoever he is, is a lucky man. I hope he knows that, Molly. And if anything should ever happen and you find yourself, your heart, free..." He let his words hang.

"Thank you, Julian," she said. "I'll remember that." But she couldn't imagine anything that could sever her bond with Zach.

They were so caught up in conversation that neither Molly nor Julian saw another guest enter the lobby and stand by the registration desk. Zach had been there several minutes, silently watching them as they looked into each other's eyes by the fireplace, then as they talked so intimately together while strolling to the elevator. He recognized the man immediately. He was the same person who had accompanied Molly to the opera in San Francisco.

Heartsick, Zach turned to leave as the elevator doors closed and Molly rode to her floor somewhere above him. He'd planned to stay the night in the Del Cortés, but now he didn't want to be anywhere near her, not even in the same building. He needed time to think about the scene he'd just witnessed.

Zach hailed a cab and stepped inside for the ride to another hotel downtown. He hadn't doubted a word that Molly had said to him that afternoon. How could he? The truth of her affection was in her eyes. At least he'd thought so. But what kind of game was she playing? And why?

It didn't surprise him that she had suitors. A woman of such beauty and spirit would be sought after by every eligible bachelor she came across, of that he had no doubt.

Perhaps the man was somehow involved in QIL. She had said she was in Monterey on business, though she hadn't said why. Would Molly go to such lengths to cultivate a business deal?

The whole idea angered him, disappointed him, sickened him. By the time he reached his hotel, he seriously wondered if the chasm between them was too deep to overcome.

As the carriage bumped along the road, Zach closed his

eyes, trying to shut out the image of Molly touching the face of another man. But the image wouldn't flee. He felt betrayed. Angry for falling in love with such a woman.

Minutes later, Zach stepped from the cab into the night drizzle. Looking out at the mist-shrouded bay, he thought of the schooner and decided he would set sail by sundown the following day. If it were not for business at his cannery in the morning and for the promised meeting with Mary Rose, he would sail at dawn. Though it wasn't his legal responsibility, he wanted to help Devon O'Rourke recover his stolen funds. The meeting was necessary, even though it would be difficult to see Molly again.

All along, Molly had asked for more time before making a commitment. Now, even if she changed her mind, Zach knew that he was the one who needed the time—and distance—from her. But he wondered, as he stepped through the hotel entrance, if either could heal his pain.

Molly and Julian headed by carriage to the Cabrillo Canning Company shortly after eight o'clock. Their meeting with the owner was set for eight-thirty, and she hoped that by noon the sale would be final.

The drizzle from the previous day's storm had stopped, but a heavy fog had settled like a damp, cold blanket onto the small town. Molly shivered and pulled her cloak closer. Seated across from her, Julian noticed and smiled.

"Was that from the cold or from a case of pre-sale jitters?"

She laughed lightly. "Probably both. Though I was just thinking about how inclement weather affects the fishing industry."

He laughed with her. "Always the businesswoman." He looked out the window of the slow-moving carriage. "But you're right, I doubt that fishing boats leave port on a day like this. I doubt that, overall, the weather makes much difference. The fish in the bay are so abundant that a few days of bad weather probably don't matter."

Molly's gaze took in the dark gray outside the window. "I should think that even the lighthouse couldn't lead a ship through this."

"There've been some tragic shipwrecks because of it."

She thought of Zach and the *Molly Quinn* and was glad the schooner lay at anchor in the bay. She hated to think of him navigating through this dangerous, heavy shroud. Quickly, she tried to think of something more pleasant than shipwrecks.

The carriage picked up speed as it turned down Ocean View Avenue. Molly thought of her meeting with Zach and Mary Rose at four o'clock. Just the thought of seeing him again lightened her heart. Then she sighed happily, her mind on the romantic dinner he planned overlooking the bay.

She'd been awake most of the night, reliving their tender moments in the meadow. All night long, her heart had nearly burst with joy at the memory of being in Zach's arms.

Tonight, she'd decided toward dawn, she would tell him that she didn't want to wait another year until their promised tryst. She wasn't sure she wanted to wait at all.

Smiling to herself, Molly snuggled back into the carriage seat, thinking of the surprise on Zach's face when she told him. Suddenly, nothing mattered—not even QIL or her expanding holdings—more than Zach and her love for him.

Zach, she thought, still looking out at the dark, gray mist, *how I love you! My heart...my all...belongs to you.*

The meeting with John Cabrillo, the portly owner of the canning company, went more smoothly than Molly had imagined. After enduring the tale of Cabrillo's heritage, complete with details for his believing that he was directly descended from Juan Rodríguez Cabrillo, Molly let Julian begin negotiations on QII's behalf.

It turned out that John Cabrillo was more than ready to sell, though before negotiations were completed, he quoted an asking price that was slightly more than Molly had been told originally. However, during a brief caucus outside the office, Julian assured her that Cabrillo's price was still within the limits agreed to by Clive and Nevil Richards, Luke Cornelius, and Kingsley Forrester. He also advised that it was fair, considering the company's potential.

By noon, the papers had been drawn up and signed, with approval from QII's board members, who had been notified by wire and had responded favorably, in the same manner. QII's funds were wired from the Sacramento bank, and a cashier's draft was soon passed into the hands of John Cabrillo.

Cabrillo smiled broadly and nodded as he looked at the draft. "It's all yours, Miss Quinn," he said finally and stood to shake her hand.

Julian stood and took her hand as well. "Congratulations," he said. She could see from his pleased expression that he knew how much this transaction meant to her.

Just then there was a knock at the office door.

"Yes?" Cabrillo called out.

The pinch-faced manager who'd originally shown Molly the premises stuck in his head. "One of the fishermen wants a word with you, Mr. Cabrillo," he said gruffly.

"Send him in," Cabrillo replied with a grin. "We'll introduce him to Cabrillo's new owner."

The manager disappeared, then after a moment, the door opened again, wider. When he stepped back into the room, the fisherman followed behind him.

At the same time, Molly stood and turned to face the two men as she was introduced. Julian stood by her side.

The fisherman moved out from behind the manager, and Molly gasped. It was Zach. His eyes met hers without expression.

A beaming John Cabrillo cleared his throat, his smile stretching across his face. "I'd like to be the first to introduce you to your new boss," he said with a chuckle. "Miss Molly Quinn, President of QIL Enterprises, is Cabrillo Canning Company's new owner."

For a moment, the room was filled with a heavy silence. Then John Cabrillo cleared his throat again, his gaze still on the surprised faces of the men standing before him. "Any questions either of you have," he continued, "can be directed to Miss Quinn." Then, with a flourish, he picked up his hat from a corner chair, tipped it jauntily on his head, grabbed his brass-tipped walking stick, and without another word, exited the room.

Molly extended her hand to the still-stunned manager. He smiled and congratulated her, pumping her arm up and down. Julian stepped forward to speak to him about the future plans for Cabrillo Canning Company, and Molly, disengaging herself from the man at last, turned to speak to Zach.

But the doorway where he'd been standing moments earlier was empty. She ran to the door and glanced about, but Zach had left the premises without a word.

Molly's heart sank. Zach had asked her just yesterday if she knew what it would do to their love for her to be in control of his business in any way. He'd said it was the one thing that could divide them.

Standing in the doorway of her newest business enterprise, Molly looked out at the fog-shrouded ocean. Another chill traveled down her spine. But this time she knew it wasn't the inclement weather that had caused it.

CHAPTER

24

MOLLY TOOK EXTRA PAINS with her appearance as she prepared for tea with Zach and Mary Rose. She changed from the business suit she'd worn to Cabrillo Canning Company and pulled on a pale pink dress of gauze and lace, its pleated sleeves reaching to her wrists with lacy points. The collar rose high on her delicate throat, and she fastened a pearl-framed cameo in its center.

Checking her reflection in the mirror, she arranged her dark curls into a loose twist atop her head, with tendrilled wisps at her temples. She added just a touch of lip rouge and pinched her cheeks for a bit more color.

Finally, she stood and made her way to the door, trying to ignore her thudding heart. She hoped she could speak with Zach before Mary Rose's arrival. She had to convince him that she knew nothing about his contract with Cabrillo. Then she let out a deep sigh. What if he wouldn't listen? The knowledge that her actions might have driven him away filled her with sadness.

By the time she reached the elevator, Molly had lifted her chin high, determined to speak with Zach privately. It was the only way. She would sell the company tomorrow, if it would make a difference, and she intended to tell him so.

Feeling immensely better, Molly stepped from the elevator and crossed the lobby to the Del Cortés tea room, just off the main dining area.

The earlier fog had lifted, and the tearoom, facing the hotel's extensive gardens, was filled with sunlight. She described whom she was meeting to the maître d', and he beckoned for her to follow. She moved across the room to a more private alcove behind some small palms and pots of fresh flowers.

Rounding the corner, she stopped abruptly when she spotted their table. Mary Rose and Zach obviously had introduced themselves and were already deep in conversation.

Facing her, Zach was the first to look up, but he avoided her gaze as he stood. Mary Rose let out a joyful exclamation and also stood, giving Molly a quick hug.

Molly smiled at them both, then settled into the seat that the maître d' pulled out for her, just between Zach and Mary Rose at the round, linen-covered table.

"I see you've already made introductions," Molly said pleasantly. She dared not look at Zach, afraid his cool expression would so break her heart that she wouldn't be able to make it through tea. So she directed her words to Mary Rose. She needn't have worried, because Mary Rose, so delighted to be with them, kept the conversation moving, telling Zach the details of Devon's transactions with Oliver Duckworth.

"Have you seen him here since you arrived?" Molly asked Mary Rose. She knew that Mary Rose had registered at the Del Cortés earlier that morning.

"No. I asked for him at the front desk, only to be told that he is no longer employed here."

Zach spoke up. "I think it's important for us to go to the

police, Mary Rose. You were a witness to the original transaction, and I have the papers to prove that I bought the painting. We can get the investigation of Oliver Duckworth started, though I think they'll also need Devon's testimony of his conversation with Duckworth about the theft."

Mary Rose nodded. "When will you be leaving Monterey?"

"Very soon, but we can go to the police after we're through here, if you like."

Nothing had been said about Molly accompanying them, and she knew that Zach was purposely excluding her. She cleared her throat softly. "Perhaps I should go too. After all, the painting is now in my possession."

For the first time, Zach's gaze met hers. It was as cold as ice. "That's true," he said without emotion. "You now own the painting, though I don't believe the police will care about present ownership. All they need is my receipt from the purchase."

"But come with us anyway, Molly," Mary Rose said quickly, reaching for her hand. A frown crossed her face, and Molly could see that she was trying to understand the coolness between Zach and her. She knew it would only prolong the agonizing tension between them if she went along, so she graciously declined.

The server brought a pot of steaming tea and set out their ornate bone china teacups and saucers. He poured the fragrant liquid into their cups, then left only to return moments later with a silver platter filled with pastries, fruits, and cheeses.

Molly took a bite of an almond-covered Neapolitan creme puff, but it could as well have been made of paper. The sadness of her loss had spoiled any appetite she might have had.

She ventured another glance at Zach over the rim of her teacup. Staring into a piece of chocolate cake, he looked as miserable as she felt. Finally, he seemed to give up on eating and placed his fork at an angle on his plate, indicating to the waiter that he was finished.

Then he smiled at Mary Rose, who was still looking a bit confused. "You know, Molly had a wonderful idea that we spoke about earlier."

Mary Rose had lifted her teacup for a sip. "Yes?" she said, when she'd set it down again.

"I know you're very anxious to get in touch with Devon. Molly said that you'd heard he's in Santa Barbara."

She nodded. "That was some time ago. I don't know if he's still there."

"But that's where you'll start your search?"

"Yes," she said with a smile. "It is. As soon as I can make arrangements."

"Is Jesse with you?" Molly asked.

"I thought the trip might be too much for him. He'll be staying with some friends in Carmel." She looked sad. "I can't tell you how much I miss him."

Zach broke in, his expression kind. "I'll be sailing south when I leave. Would you like to accompany me on the *Molly Quinn?* You can be in Santa Barbara within a few days, though perhaps no faster than if you go by train."

Mary Rose's eyes opened wide, and a smile lit her face. "When are you leaving?"

"Before dusk tonight."

Molly swallowed hard. She had hoped beyond all hope that he would at least keep their plans for dinner that night.

They spoke of other details of the trip—getting Mary Rose's trunk from the hotel to the ship and hurrying to the police station before it closed to begin the proceedings against

Duckworth. Molly only half listened, biding her time to make a graceful exit.

The waiter filled their teacups another time, then brought the check. Molly hesitated, then reached for it at the same time that Zach did. His hand touched hers, and a jolt like electricity went through her. She pulled her hand away. Zach gave her a cold smile. "I'll take care of it," he said. "You may be my boss, but I think I can still be the gentleman among us."

Wordlessly, Molly nodded.

After the server had brought him change, the three stood and moved toward the exit.

At the elevator, Mary Rose gave Molly a quick hug. "Thank you for everything," she whispered. "Your visit brought all this about. It will make all the difference in the world."

Molly nodded. "Remember what I said..."

Not understanding, Mary Rose lifted a brow and tilted her head slightly.

"About becoming Devon's patron. When you see him, tell him I've invited both of you to San Francisco. If he agrees, we'll work out the details there."

Mary Rose hugged her again. "Molly, if you only knew the hope you've given me." Her eyes misted. "I'll be praying for you."

And Molly knew she meant it. She nodded. "Thank you, Mary Rose. Now you two had better be on your way." Her eyes met Zach's as she spoke. "You've got a lot to do and a long way to go before dusk."

Zach gave her a curt nod and took Mary Rose's arm to escort her to the registration desk to take care of transferring her luggage to the *Molly Quinn*.

They had walked a few feet when Molly called after them. "Zach?"

He turned.

"May I speak with you just a moment?"

Mary Rose went on to the desk, and he stood in the same place, not moving any closer to Molly. "Is this an order from my boss?"

She shook her head slowly. "Zach, please. Is there someplace we can talk privately before you go?"

He gave a short and brittle laugh. "I think it's too late for that, Molly."

She walked closer to him, since he seemed unwilling to move. "Please, Zach. I want to explain. I had no idea—"

He interrupted with another laugh. "You want to explain? Explain what?" He practically spat the words. "That's the least of your problems, Molly. I honestly think you don't know what you want."

"Zach," she implored, her voice a hoarse whisper. "Don't do this. You're throwing away something so precious. You're throwing away our—"

He cut in again. "I am, Molly? You're the one who's destroyed our love. Not me."

Molly felt as though he had slapped her. For a moment they stared at each other in silence.

Then she looked up to see Mary Rose walking toward them from across the room.

"Goodbye, Zach," Molly whispered. But he didn't hear her. He'd already turned to meet Mary Rose, and they left the hotel, her arm tucked in his. He didn't glance back even once.

Molly took the elevator to her room, opened the door, and collapsed on her bed. It was then that she looked up to see an envelope on her dresser, obviously left there by the concierge. Her name was scrawled across the front in Zach's strong script. She quickly opened it and began to read.

> *Molly,*
>
> *I cannot meet you for supper tonight as we had earlier planned. I believe you understand the circumstances preventing it.*
>
> *Life has a strange way of sorting itself out, and I believe that is what has happened to us. From the first day I became enchanted by you, my own stubbornness blinded me to the obvious: your drive and ambition are far more precious to you than love. It is what defines you. It makes you who you are today and who you will be tomorrow. I should have realized that immutable fact before now.*
>
> *It is time to take off my blinders. In fact, one could say they have been ripped from my eyes even against my will. I see you, Molly, and understand you better now than I have since the day we met. Though I would not be telling you the truth if I did not also say that this new understanding has left me aggrieved. It has, for I thought you to be very different than who I have discovered you to be.*
>
> *It is better that we part now. I will make no further attempt to see you. And I ask that you afford me the same courtesy.*
>
> *Regards,*
> *Zachary MacAlister*

Molly bowed her head as the tears began. She covered her eyes with her hands, and a desperate sadness washed over her. Later, she couldn't remember how long she cried.

But when she rose and washed her face and hands, a new resolve had hardened somewhere inside her. No one, least of all Zach, would ever know the depth of her mourning.

She had been tempted to let go of QIL because of her love for him. She remembered bitterly that she had even planned to tell him this night.

But now?

It was time to build her life around other things, her business, her new friends in San Francisco, the energy she drew from helping the city rebuild itself.

Drying her eyes and blowing her nose, she squared her shoulders. Yes, life would go on very nicely without Zachary MacAlister.

And it was time to get back to San Francisco without further delay. She quickly packed her bags, straightened her rumpled dress, and fussed a bit with her hair. Then she headed for the elevator and the front desk to ask for a carriage to transport her to the train station. Hoping to be back in San Francisco by morning, she planned to catch the next train to Salinas.

Within the hour, the Del Cortés Special pulled out of the station. Molly settled back into her seat, not knowing when she'd be back, if ever. And, she told herself, she didn't care. Behind her, Monterey Bay, its clippers and schooners and fishing boats, disappeared into the growing dusk.

Aboard the *Molly Quinn,* Zach introduced Mary Rose to the crew. Windjammer quickly said to call him Jam, and to plain ol' call him, he added with a wink, if she needed anything on their short voyage. Then Jam took the baggage below to her quarters, and Mary Rose followed.

Zach was relieved to finally be alone. Both hands firmly on the helm, he steered the *Molly Quinn* out into the open seas. Sails unfurled, she caught the wind and moved swiftly away from land.

By sundown, the bay shores lay far behind. A few clouds were on the horizon, and they turned every shade of purple and crimson as the sun sank into the water.

With a pang, Zach thought of Molly. Her presence at tea had nearly undone him. She'd walked in, and he'd been overwhelmed by her delicate beauty. When she looked up at him, her liquid emerald eyes had filled with hurt and confusion. Briefly, he'd even wondered if he'd been mistaken.

How could he have been so wrong about her? Even now, no matter what she'd done, she filled his every thought.

"Zach?" Mary Rose's voice was soft as she approached him.

He nodded a greeting. "Are you getting your sea legs yet?" He grinned at her.

"Actually, the water is so calm, I've not had any trouble." She raised an eyebrow. "So far," she added with a laugh. "My father was a sea captain, and I've been on plenty of seagoing vessels. You might say this is much like coming home."

He chuckled. "There are many who would disagree about the sea ever becoming home."

"Molly?"

He looked at her sharply. "No, I don't really think Molly's ever given it that much thought."

"I...I could tell things were pretty dismal between you today." Mary Rose seemed shy about bringing it up.

"To say the least." He stared out at the horizon, almost invisible in the pale gray twilight.

"I'm sorry. It's just that I can see how much she cares for you. It's in her face."

He gave her a short and bitter laugh. "There was a time I might have believed you."

"That day she came to see me, we talked of many things. Especially about *Mary Rose's Garden*. She told me how affected she'd been by the gift you'd given her." She smiled. "And it wasn't just the painting she was referring to."

310

He looked at her quizzically.

"She said that you know her better than anyone else, her hopes and dreams and failings, that you understood her need for remembering a real garden, that the painting had connected the two of you, just when she thought you'd forgotten her." She paused. "It was the gift of your remembrance that touched her more, I think, than the painting itself."

Zach let silence fall between them. "Molly is a determined young woman," he said after a moment. "And talented. But she is letting that business head determine her life's direction. There's room for nothing—make that, no one else."

"And you think she has no heart?"

He drew in a deep breath. "Let's just say she's lost sight of it."

"I think you're wrong, Zach." Her voice was thoughtful. "Molly and I spent just one afternoon together, but she impressed me with the depth of her emotions. Not once did we speak of her business. Instead, she asked me all about my garden."

"Your garden?"

She nodded. "Yes, she said that it seemed sacred. She'd noticed it in Devon's oil, and she felt it again as she sat in the garden with me. I remember her saying that even in the painting she recognized it as a place where peace and joy and love really exist. She wanted to know why the garden affected her so, and if I felt it too."

"And you told her?"

"We talked for hours about it."

"And?" Zach's eyes searched the darkening water as the *Molly Quinn* sailed southward. Above, dim pinpoints of starlight came into view across the sky.

Mary Rose smiled softly, then let out a small sigh. "Now

we're getting into a subject that is among my favorites."

"Gardening?" He glanced over at the pretty blond woman beside him. Even before he asked, he knew the answer wouldn't be that simple.

She grinned. "I suppose in a way. We spoke of vines and branches and what they have to do with us, and with God. I told Molly that my prayer garden is a sacred place. I've created it to be a small sanctuary, and I go there for times of quiet prayer and song."

"Ah…," he said with a slow nod, wondering where this conversation might lead, and also trying to imagine Molly speaking to Mary Rose about such things. This was a side of Molly he didn't know. "Vines and branches," he mused. "I seem to remember my grandmother reading something to me from the Bible about that."

Mary Rose smiled. "Molly wanted to know what it means to be 'in him.' I explained that, to me, it means that he wants us to abide in him just as a branch is connected to a vine, a lifeblood connection that flows from him to us." Her expression softened. "I told her that being in him is almost as if you're having an unending conversation with a friend who knows you so well that he understands the thoughts of your heart without words. He listens to your deepest yearnings and cares, and you open your heart to listen to him."

"My grandmother said that God was her dearest friend," Zach said. "I think she understood the kind of relationship you're describing."

"There's nothing quite so comforting and joyous as knowing God and being known, completely, by him."

"That's what comes through in the painting. I saw it too. Not only is the garden a place of love and light, a sacred place, it's a place where you, the subject, are known and loved by the artist."

"It strikes me," Mary Rose said thoughtfully, "that we are the subjects of our Creator's artistry. We are known and loved. And when we are 'in him,' he creates a sacred place of light and love within us. His dwelling place." She sighed deeply, reverently. "Talk about a sacred garden."

Below them the waves lapped gently against the ship and above, the navy sky provided a backdrop for millions of stars that seemed to have been strewn across the heavens.

"What about the shadows?" Zach asked suddenly, a brittle edge creeping back into his voice. "Life isn't made up of just love and light. Anyone who thinks it is, is deluding himself."

"Of course it isn't," Mary Rose said. Zach couldn't see her face in the darkness, but she sounded sad. "Life is made up of pain, disappointment, deep discouragement. People we love die tragically, or sometimes they simply go away. Life doesn't always turn out the way we'd like, or the way we planned."

"How do you deal with it? You seem so content." He turned to her. "Molly told me that you lost your husband and were left to raise your baby alone. I would think you'd be bitter. Weren't you tempted to shake your fist at God in anger?"

For several minutes, Mary Rose didn't speak. She was looking away from him, turned toward the bow of the ship. The wind lifted her blond curls from her face. "I did," she finally said, softly. "For months I cried out in rage against God. Carl's death was unfair. Why should I have had to suffer? And what about my innocent child who would go through life without a daddy? Of course I was angry." Zach could hear the sorrow in her voice.

He reached out and touched her shoulder. "I'm sorry. I

shouldn't have asked you about this."

She had turned again to face him. "No, Zach. Don't apologize. You see, I learned some very important lessons during that dark time. First of all, God's love is so complete—for you see, he created me—that he already knows the worst about me, yet loves me anyway." She tilted her head in wonder, regarding him. "In my pit of despair, he cared for me, even as I shook my fist at him. Can you imagine such love?"

Zach didn't answer, trying to take in all she was telling him.

"Now, when I look back on that time, I see myself as if I were a small child, crying out in anger and frustration at a parent. God lifted me into his arms, the same way I do my son, and held me close to his heart even as I cried. At the time, I was too distraught to know where I was. But now I look back, and I can see that he was there, holding me, the whole time."

"You said there were other lessons."

Mary Rose nodded. "About the shadows that you mentioned earlier. When I've watched Devon paint light, I've noticed that its glow is brightest when it's outlined by shadows, or darkness. The lighthouse in the *Hope* would not be so exquisitely brilliant if it had not been for the storm."

"So you think that our lives need times of darkness for the brightness of the light to be meaningful?"

"Something like that." Then she shrugged and laughed lightly. "I hope I haven't bored you with my philosophical rantings."

"You're a deep thinker, Mary Rose. And I've not been a bit bored."

"My hours in the garden allow me a lot of time to ponder life's mysteries." She smiled up at him.

"Mmmm...we return again to the garden," he mused. *"Mary*

Rose's Garden. Somehow I feel the painting, the way it's brought us all together, was no accident."

She laughed again. "That's exactly what I told Molly," she said.

They talked for a few more minutes about the voyage to Santa Barbara, then Mary Rose excused herself to go below and freshen up for dinner.

Jam took over the helm, and Zach strode to the ship's bow to stand alone and consider all that Mary Rose had told him.

His thoughts again turned to Molly, his hurt at seeing her with another man, his anger that she'd purchased the company he worked for. He knew the darkness of anger and lost love. He knew the desperate emptiness that losing Molly had caused.

He raised his eyes to the velvet-black heaven and its canopy of silver starlight. He didn't doubt the existence of a Creator. Life on earth, in the universe, contained too much order to have come from chaos. But a God such as Mary Rose described, someone who cared intimately about every detail of his life?

In the dark days following the earthquake, Zach had pondered some of the same questions. At the time, he'd wondered if this same God could have brought Molly and him through the cataclysm, to bring them light and love and deep joy later.

He considered the contrast of shadows and light Mary Rose had just talked about, remembering the words his grandmother read to him from her well-worn Bible. In his present darkness, he could almost feel God's arms around him, saying, *I have loved you with an everlasting love. Fear not...I am with you.* And suddenly the darkness seemed less dense, less impenetrable.

Again, Zach's thoughts turned to Molly. He considered his loneliness. Was it Molly alone who could fill it? Or was there something far deeper inside his soul that was missing? Mary

Rose had just described a God of unchanging, everlasting compassion, a God who loved him without condition.

What was it she'd said? His love is so complete that he already knows the worst about us, yet loves us anyway.

Zach looked up at the skies, somehow knowing that his emptiness could only be filled by his Creator. But how could he move into such a relationship with God? The chasm seemed too great between man and God, no matter how loving he was. He wondered if it would always seem so.

CHAPTER

25

MARY ROSE MOVED FROM THE TENDER onto the Santa Barbara wharf. Zach stepped out just behind her, carrying her carpetbag. She smiled up at him, touched by his protective expression. "Zach, you've been so kind. Thank you."

He swung her bag into the carriage, and she climbed in, but held the door open for a moment as they said goodbye.

Zach gave her a warm grin and a nod. "God speed, Mary Rose. I hope you find Devon. I wish I could do more to help."

"So do I, Zach," she whispered, almost as if to herself. "So do I."

Leaning forward, she laid her hand lightly on his arm. "You've done so much already, Zach. You and Molly," he winced as she spoke Molly's name, "are about to turn Devon's career around."

"All the same, it doesn't seem right just leaving you here alone."

She smiled softly. "I'm not alone, Zach."

He nodded, and she could see that he understood her meaning. After they said goodbye, he closed the carriage door firmly and she settled back into her seat.

The driver flicked the reins, and the carriage rumbled away

from the wharf. Mary Rose drew in a deep breath and considered her surroundings.

Santa Barbara lay sparkling and beautiful in the midmorning light. Much like Monterey, its architecture was mostly Spanish, and its California-style adobes gleamed in the sun, red-clay roofs providing a texture and color unlike the villages on the Central Coast. The town lay on a slope of land rising above a sapphire ocean.

She headed to a small Victorian hotel she had spotted not far from the beach. It looked clean, though modest. Green wooden boxes filled with red geraniums graced each window, and a pebble-covered path led to the entrance. Its look was so inviting that Mary Rose figured it must once have been someone's home. She dismissed the cabbie as soon as she found there was a room available, and moments later she unlocked her door and placed her bags on the single small bed.

When she opened the window, she could hear the pounding surf just yards away. Overhead, pelicans dipped and circled among the sea gulls, calling out in their eerily pleasant voices. She drew in a deep breath, relishing the smell of the surf and sand and sea creatures.

Knowing that her search for Devon would probably take her out of town, Mary Rose changed into clothes more suitable for horseback riding—a long, full split skirt with a matching jacket blouse. She tied a ribbon around her thicket of blond curls at the nape of her neck.

Moments later, she was headed up the main boulevard into town. She'd already decided on a course of action. She would visit all artist's supply stores and art galleries, asking about Devon. She had no doubt he'd already become known in the area. Of course, it would be another challenge entirely to discover his present whereabouts.

About halfway up the street, she turned into a corner art supply store.

The proprietor, a middle-aged woman, looked up as the door opened and Mary Rose let herself in.

"I'm looking for an artist named O'Rourke. Devon O'Rourke."

The woman removed her wire-rimmed eyeglasses and squinted in thought. "O'Rourke? Mmmm...no, I'm afraid not. What does he look like? Maybe I just don't know him by name."

Mary Rose described Devon.

But the woman simply shook her head again and replaced her eye glasses. "No, I'm sorry. I don't know him."

Mary Rose thanked her and headed to the next shop. Still there was no recognition of name or physical description. So she moved along the boulevard to another. This time, a young man looked up as she entered, seeming to brighten as she described Devon.

"Yes," he said. "I've heard of him. He's a painter of light."

"Yes," Mary Rose whispered, almost afraid to hope. "That's him."

Then he shook his head slowly. "But I'm sorry. I have no idea where he might be. For a while, I heard that he'd planned to paint all eight of the lighthouses on the West Coast. If that's true, no telling which direction he went to begin." Then he shrugged, and a frown furrowed his brow. "Though, now that I think about it, I also heard he'd grown interested in the California missions. Most of them are in ruins, so maybe that information was inaccurate." He shrugged again. "I'm sorry. I'm not being much help."

Mary Rose assured him that he had helped. She started to

leave, then turned back. "Do you know if a local gallery might be carrying his work?"

The man smiled broadly. "Ah...now why didn't I think of that? Yes, I do know. The gallery just up the street—left side about three shops up—has an O'Rourke. Perhaps more than one. I don't know, but it's worth going by to ask."

Mary Rose thanked him again and headed out the door. The sun beat down on her shoulders as she strode up the tree-lined street. It was now nearing noontime, and the sidewalk was filled with bustling people of all ages. Motorcars putted and backfired along the street, and horse-drawn carriages clattered by.

She pushed open the door of the elegant gallery. Before she even met the proprietor's gaze, her eyes focused on three paintings at the end of the long room.

"You've got O'Rourkes," she managed to whisper.

The proprietor moved from behind his desk to stand beside her as she gazed at them.

"He's an extraordinary talent."

"I know," she said simply, taking them in one by one. Devon had done another lighthouse. As usual, the glow from the mirrored kerosene lantern dominated the gloom of raging surf and storm. One of the others was a simple, rough-hewn wooden shack at the ocean's edge. It was dusk, and a mist laced in among some dark and mysterious pines. But through the shack's window, a single lamp's glow transformed the dreariness of the small house and its surroundings. The third painting was of a California mission. Its crumbling adobe walls were in ruins, but a light came from behind the still-intact chapel and fell in the shape of a cross upon a garden.

The garden was hers, painted from Devon's memory. There was the olive tree, the redwood bench he'd made for her, the irises, the lilacs, the roses—all of her prayer garden was there. She drew in a deep, shaky breath.

"It's indeed beautiful, isn't it?" the proprietor asked.

Unable to speak for a moment, she simply nodded, swallowing hard. "Yes, it is," she finally managed.

Then she turned to him. "I'm looking for Devon O'Rourke. Do you have any idea where I can find him?"

The proprietor's eyes flickered uncertainly for a moment. "Why is it you ask?"

"I'm a friend of his. I have important news about the sale of one of his paintings."

"I thought I was handling his work exclusively."

"Devon thought this particular painting had been stolen, when in fact, it had been sold. It happened long before he came to Santa Barbara." She narrowed her eyes slightly in a no-nonsense look. "It's important that I find him right away."

The man flushed noticeably, and his expression softened. "Yes, yes. I'm sorry I questioned you. It's just that O'Rourke seems to be a very private man. I didn't want him disturbed, if this was not..." His voice faltered.

"Important," she finished for him. "He is a private man, but he will be pleased with this news. Believe me."

"Yes, yes. I understand." He sighed. "All right, then. I'll tell you where he's painting. He's been working out at the Santa Ynez Mission ruins." He went to his desk and pulled out a sheet of paper. "I'll draw you a map. By horseback or carriage it shouldn't take you too long to get there."

Mary Rose nodded and watched him as he worked. Moments later, he folded the paper and handed it to her. "Good luck," he said, as she turned to leave. "But I hope this doesn't mean he'll be going back where he came from. He's never said where that was, but I figured something tragic had driven him away."

Mary Rose merely smiled and thanked him again before moving through the door to the street.

Devon stood in the once-verdant vineyard of the crumbling mission. Around him, hundred-year-old vines still struggled to survive in the dry earth, covering a decaying arbor with leaves that wouldn't die. Beyond him was the padre's cemetery, headstones and grave markers scattered in disarray.

An empty fountain stood to one side, cracked and chipped. Around it, also refusing to die, wild roses had wound their vines into a delightful tangle of colorful life.

It was midafternoon, and ordinarily Devon would be putting away his easel and paints. But today the air was clear and the long late-afternoon shadows would hold purples and blues that ordinarily couldn't be seen. He waited also for a certain slant of light from the setting sun.

He'd chosen the spot because of the contrast between death and life. He wanted to step beyond the light he usually painted in his work and show its connection with life. He'd attempted it in *Mary Rose's Garden*, concentrating on Mary Rose's face more than he did the light in her garden. Now, he wanted to attempt it with the ruined mission.

He gazed at the old arbor, the crumbling chapel, the broken water fountain, and thought about what they symbolized. Death.

And life? There was a rough-hewn cross at the top of the chapel, and when the slant of the sun was just right, its prominence overpowered the rest of the scene. Its profound simplicity didn't change. But it was as if the cross, and the life it represented, overcame the symbols of death surrounding it.

Since it would be a few hours until the sun slanted toward the mission, Devon left his paints and walked to the top of a nearby incline. This time of year, the gentle, rolling hills were covered with pale green grasses and wildflowers. Even a few poppies had started to show their golden heads. Earlier, an ocean breeze had kicked up, cooling the air and turning the flowers in a gentle dance.

The road leading to the mission wound lazily along the hillside, weaving through an unkempt apple orchard from the mission's latter years. Devon had ridden up during the predawn hours, and now his horse, a sorrel, grazed a short distance away.

Devon heard the rider approaching before he actually saw the horse. Seconds later, the horse and its rider emerged from behind a stand of trees. But they were still too far away to identify.

He walked back down the hill toward the mission, figuring the rider was heading there. Not many visitors came to the ruins, and he was surprised anyone would bother this time of day.

The rider drew nearer. He saw her hair, its color of liquid sunshine, and he knew it was Mary Rose. His heart quickened, and he began to race down the hill to greet her.

At the same time, she looked up to see him running toward her. She slowed the horse and dismounted, waiting for Devon to reach her. He could see by her expression that she was feeling shy about their meeting. She brushed a few wisps of hair from her forehead.

But by the time he reached her and drew her into his arms, she gave a little cry of joy and reached around his neck.

"Oh, Dev," she murmured with a half-sob, burying her face against his chest.

Devon didn't trust his voice to speak. Mutely, he held her,

breathing in her special fragrance of violets and soap and ocean breezes.

Finally, he stepped back to gaze into her eyes. "Oh, my darling," he breathed. "How I've missed you."

She touched his face. "I didn't know how you'd feel about seeing me again. The way you left, it seemed so final."

"It was a terrible and dark time, Mary Rose. I can only ask your forgiveness. I thought I was giving you the chance to go on with your life. After I realized my mistake, I thought it was too late to return." He swallowed hard. "I didn't know if you'd have me back."

She smiled up at him, her eyes bright with compassion. "Dev, there's not a day that's passed that I haven't thought of you, prayed for you. You should know by now that my heart is so filled with love there could never be anyone else."

He caught her palm in his hand and kissed it tenderly. "I love you," he said, his voice hoarse. He gently lifted her face upward with both hands, then he bent over her, touching his lips to hers. The kiss was gentle, then he looked into her eyes, saw her answering love, and he covered her mouth with his again.

This time the kiss was passionate, and Devon thought he might drown in the whirl of emotion that filled him.

Finally, Mary Rose pulled back a bit, gazing up into his eyes once more. "I need to ask your forgiveness, Dev," she said quietly. "Since you left, I've thought about how I wronged you."

"You wronged me? Oh, Mary Rose," he sighed. "It wasn't you."

She touched his lips. "No. Let me finish. I practically forced you to sell *Mary Rose's Garden*. My timing got in the way of God's. I should have been more trusting. It was my idea to place that enormous price tag on it. Inadvertently, that alone may have resulted in the deception that followed."

"Dearest," he said, his voice husky, "there's nothing to forgive. We both made the decision to sell the painting." Then he frowned. "You said 'deception.' You mean the theft?"

Mary Rose took in a deep breath. "I've got something to tell you," she said, finally. She moved away from him, looking down the small grassy hill toward the mission.

Devon stepped up beside her. "*Mary Rose's Garden* has been found?"

She turned to look up at him. "In a manner of speaking."

"Tell me."

"Oliver Duckworth sold the painting, pocketed the money, then rode to Carmel to tell you it had been stolen."

Devon didn't know whether to laugh or cry. "It sold?"

She nodded slowly. "Yes."

"How did you find out? Did he confess?"

Mary Rose went on to tell him about Zach MacAlister and Molly Quinn and the strange turn of events that had connected them all.

"So Molly Quinn now owns the painting?"

"Yes, it hangs in her new home in San Francisco." She smiled. "She treasures it."

"And it was purchased by Zach MacAlister as a gift for her."

She nodded again. "Yes, and he has already gone with me to the authorities in Monterey to testify that he indeed purchased the painting. In fact, Dev, he paid more than the asking price, and he's got the receipt to prove it."

"Has an arrest been made?"

"No, it seems that before our discovery, the hotel began investigating Duckworth on other matters. He got wind of it and disappeared."

Devon thought about what she'd told him, trying to take it all in. "Even if he's found," he said after a moment, "there's no guarantee that we'll recover the money from the sale."

Mary Rose let out a deep breath. "That's right, Dev. I'm sorry."

"So, we're no closer to solving our financial dilemma." Her face fell, and he touched her shoulder. "I'm sorry, Mary Rose. I didn't mean to bring it up again." He wondered whether he should tell her there had been no sales in Santa Barbara either.

They'd started walking toward the mission when Mary Rose spoke again. "There's something else, Dev." He could see from her expression that it was important. But there was another emotion in her eyes. Reluctance perhaps?

"What I have to tell you is about Molly Quinn, the woman who owns *Mary Rose's Garden*. She is a woman who has attained some means during the past year or two. She's head of QIL, dealing primarily in investments and loans."

"What does that have to do with us?"

Mary Rose stopped and her eyes narrowed. "It has everything to do with us, Dev."

He waited for her to go on, somehow afraid of what she was going to say next.

"Even before Zach gave her *Mary Rose's Garden*, she'd seen the *Hope* in Sacramento. She was profoundly affected by it. She understands your work. Then, after receiving Zach's gift, she was all the more determined to find you, to discover more of your work. That's why she initially came to Carmel—to find you."

"She wants to purchase another?"

Mary Rose shook her head. "No. She wants to become your patron."

Devon knew that Mary Rose was waiting for him to react in

some ecstatic manner—throw his arms around her and twirl her in the air—exclaim that all their money woes were behind them—anything but what he was doing, which was standing as if rooted to the spot, unable to do what she wanted.

"Oh, Mary Rose," he finally breathed, watching understanding and disappointment seep into her eyes. He shook his head sadly. "A patron can dictate style, numbers of paintings to be produced, where they are displayed or purchased. I don't know if I'm willing to give up what I'm doing right now."

"Does it have to be that way? I mean, aren't there contracts in which the artist dictates his own terms?"

He nodded slowly. "The reality is, they're rarely written to benefit the artist. The patron wants return on his or her money. Especially a patron who is not involved in the arts. And from what you've told me, this young woman—Molly Quinn—is more interested in investments and loans than in art."

"But you haven't met Molly. I think if you did, you'd see that she understands your work. I don't believe she would presume to tamper with what you do." Mary Rose's voice dropped in sadness, and Devon sensed her deep hurt.

He gathered her into his arms. "Dearest," he whispered, "forgive me for disappointing you. But I can't see giving up who I am as an artist to please a patron who might have other motives for helping me. It would be like selling my soul."

But Mary Rose stepped back. "Won't you just talk with her, Dev? Come with me to San Francisco and meet her before you make a final decision."

He regarded her for a moment. The sun had cast a palette of vivid color across the sky. And Mary Rose's face was caught in its reflection. She'd never looked more beautiful as her eyes implored him to agree.

Molly Quinn's offer meant everything to Mary Rose. It meant that they could at last be married.

"I don't know," he finally breathed, shaking his head slowly. "I'm sorry, I know how much this means to you. But my work is here now. I can't just drop everything and run to San Francisco."

"Then nothing has changed, has it, Dev?"

Without another word, Mary Rose turned from him and walked back toward her horse.

"Mary Rose!"

She turned toward him, her face a portrait of sadness. "It's not the financial independence you want and need, Dev," she said softly, tears brimming, as he walked closer. "I think it's independence. Period. I should have realized it from the beginning."

Then she mounted, still looking down at him.

"Mary Rose, don't go. Not like this."

She nudged the mare's flanks. The horse started forward, but Devon reached for the reins. "I can't let you leave like this," he whispered raggedly, his gaze still on Mary Rose's face. He let go of the reins and gently took hold of her hand. "Please, don't go."

Her eyes met his, and he caught his breath. The horse danced sideways.

"Please," he finally said, still holding her fingers in his. "I can't promise anything, but please tell me more about this Molly Quinn."

With a smile, Mary Rose slid from the saddle.

CHAPTER

26

San Francisco

MOLLY RETURNED TO SAN FRANCISCO with a renewed determination to set her mind only on QIL. She pushed Zachary MacAlister from her thoughts, attempting to forget him by diving into the business at hand.

Before leaving Monterey—to stay as far away from the area as possible—she had placed Julian in charge of handling Cabrillo Canning Company. He, in turn, had left it in the capable hands of the current manager, though in the ensuing weeks Julian had found it necessary to travel from Sacramento to Monterey to oversee the operation. When he reported on his trips, she purposely didn't ask if he'd run into Zach.

The next board meeting was coming soon and took most of her attention. Molly wanted to present a radical new management plan to the board members. She stayed up nights reading about others who had experimented with employee ownership and how it translated into productivity. The more she read about the experiments, the more she was determined to try it with Cabrillo.

As the weeks and months passed, her days settled into a comfortable pattern. She spent her mornings at the QIL office, often riding in on the cable car with Kingsley. After reviewing loan applications and investment inquiries, she turned to discussions, again with Kingsley, of future opportunities. It was becoming apparent that the two of them could no longer handle the volume of work now being generated. Victoria Parrott was a big help, but she handled only the general office work.

"It's time to hire another investment counselor, Kingsley," Molly announced one morning over coffee. She had just settled into her office chair, and Kingsley sat down opposite her.

"I don't think one will do it," he chuckled. "QIL's growing at such a rapid rate, we might as well take on two or three."

"I wish Julian Starr could join us full time," Molly said. "But now that he's running for U.S. senator, he has less time than ever for QIL."

Kingsley nodded. "Perhaps it's also time to think about adding a full-time lawyer. Julian has done a good job on retainer, but I feel we need someone in the office to handle all our legal documents."

"I agree, Kingsley. Perhaps Clive or Nevil, since they know both Sacramento and San Francisco, can suggest someone." She sighed. "We've got quite an agenda for this board meeting."

"And it's still a week away." He laughed and took a sip of coffee. "No telling what else we'll come up with between now and then. By the way, how's your proposal for Cabrillo coming along?"

"Nicely. Though I'm not sure I can convince everyone else to try such a radical plan." She described what she wanted to do, and Kingsley listened thoughtfully, nodding his distinguished silver-haired head. "Julian has spent the last week there, gathering the comments of the manager and the employees. He'll be reporting in this afternoon."

"It sounds good, Molly," Kingsley said, then gave her a

searching look. "Do any of your plans include Zach?"

She shook her head. "No. He is to be treated as any other employee or contract fisherman." She'd told Gwennie and Kingsley about Zach's reaction when he found out that she'd purchased Cabrillo Canning Company. "No better, no worse," she added.

Kingsley nodded. "But he'll have the same opportunity to buy into Cabrillo, if he would want to."

She gave him a wry smile. "I can almost guarantee that he will not even consider such an offer."

"You may not know him as well as you think, Molly," Kingsley said quietly. But he didn't elaborate, and they went on to discuss other matters about Cabrillo.

After a few minutes, Kingsley stood to return to his office.

"I saw Winny the other day," Molly said, as she walked him to the door.

"And how is your cousin?"

"About to be released. He's certain he'll be out within six months."

Kingsley stopped at the door and turned toward Molly, peering at her intently. "You knew it would happen eventually."

"Yes, though I thought it would be sooner." She let out a troubled sigh. "I find myself in something of a dilemma."

"Having to do with offering him a job?"

"Yes. He's my cousin. We've always been close."

"But Molly," Kingsley touched her arm affectionately, "any connection with QIL could bring down all you've worked so hard to build. Your cousin is a convicted felon. Even his relationship to you could cause irreparable damage to the company."

"I don't know that we would be judged so harshly, Kingsley. Every family has a black sheep."

"I disagree. You may not think you've got enemies, but envy can cause even people you thought were your friends to turn against you. If someone got hold of Winny's embezzlement story, his prison record, his association with you..." Kingsley didn't finish, just shook his head slowly.

"But he's family. I don't know how I can possibly turn my back on him."

"I don't want to sound coldhearted, Molly. But don't have anything to do with him. Especially, don't invite him to stay with you while he gets back on his feet."

"I've spoken with him about heading up our international investments division. He could be based in London."

Kingsley considered her words a moment, then frowned. "Even that would be a mistake. And I would strongly advise against it. So would Clive and Nevil Richards and Luke Cornelius, if they knew." Then he paused, looking at her more sharply. "Do they know anything about your cousin Winston?"

"No. It never came up. I guess I assumed Julian would mention it if he thought it was necessary. After all, he's Winny's friend, too."

"Perhaps it should be mentioned at the board meeting. As investment partners in QIL, I believe they have a right to know."

Molly nodded. "I'll think about it."

"You need to do more than just think about it, Molly," he said, with a fatherly tone in his voice. "I know this is difficult, and I suppose I should have given it more thought myself before now. But I believe you're obligated to be completely candid with the board about Winston and his crime."

"What if Clive, Nevil, and Luke decide to pull out? QIL would collapse without their money. All our recent purchases—

Cabrillo, the brickyards," her voice faltered.

"I know. But it must be done. I don't see that you have a choice."

She swallowed hard. "Of course, you're right. And I'll handle the situation with Winny."

Kingsley reached for the door, then stopped again, frowning. "Molly, I don't mean to imply anything by this, but..." He shook his head slightly, as if unsure of how to continue. "How well do you know Winston? I mean, especially since he's been in prison?"

"What are you getting at, Kingsley?"

"You do realize, don't you, that he must be aware of the potential damage his relationship with you can cause?"

"I'm sure he's aware of that." She paused. "In fact, he's brought it up himself."

"What I mean to say, Molly," he went on gently, "is that in prison, people change. Even if they went in for a minor crime, something they didn't intend to do..." He paused, drawing in a deep breath. "They come out hardened somehow, part of life's seamier side. And in some instances, that life is an easier fit than any other."

"You're saying that Winny may leave San Quentin changed—a true criminal?"

Kingsley nodded. "It's a possibility."

"You're also warning me about what he might do to me, to QIL?"

"It's occurred to me that he could use your family relationship against you."

Molly drew in a deep breath. "Blackmail?"

Kingsley nodded slowly, sadly. "Yes, dear. That's what has me worried."

Long after Kingsley had left her office, Molly considered his words. She thought about Winny, her sweet and favorite cousin. Could Kingsley possibly be right? She'd seen Winny only once or twice since her trip to Monterey, and she'd noticed a change in him. But it was so subtle, she hadn't given it much thought.

Now that she looked back on his attitude and actions, he did seem to have hardened somehow. She'd attributed it to his bleak existence over the past few years, but perhaps it was more than that. Perhaps Kingsley was right.

Molly's appointments filled the rest of the day, but she decided that as soon as she could, she would pay another visit to Winston. Besides examining his emotional state, she needed to speak with him about his plans following his release. She would offer to pay his passage back to England, perhaps set him up in business there, a business unrelated to QIL. If she could get Winny to agree, then when she divulged the information to the board members, perhaps their concerns wouldn't be as great.

She checked with Miss Parrott about her appointments for the following day. Tomorrow morning was free, and she decided she would visit Winny without further delay.

Then, she turned back to her calendar for the day. Her next meeting was with the mayor's wife, Augusta Morgan, regarding the campaign to rebuild the opera house.

Minutes later, the big woman bustled through the door.

"Molly!" Augusta exclaimed, reaching for her hands in greeting.

Molly shook Augusta's hand, then walked with her to the sitting area. "It's good to see you again," she said, as Augusta settled heavily onto a floral-print settee that was flanked by two

Queen Anne silk-brocade chairs. A fresh bouquet of flowers arranged in a Chinese vase rested atop a cherrywood table at the sitting area's center.

Victoria Parrott entered the room a moment later with the silver tea service and a plate of sweets. She left, closing the door behind her.

Augusta draped her fox boa across the back of the settee. "Dear, I have something important to ask you."

"Something to do with the opera house committee, I'm sure, Augusta," Molly said, as she sat in the high-backed chair next to her. "But first, may I offer you some tea?" She poured a cup for each of them.

Molly stirred a lump of sugar into her cup, and settled back to hear what the mayor's wife had come to discuss.

"Dear, I'm here on behalf of the entire committee." She leaned forward in her earnestness. "We'd like to ask you to take on a special responsibility." Augusta smiled prettily, set down her cup and saucer, then folded her hands.

For nearly a year, Molly had been working with the committee—mostly on the sidelines—to raise funds for the opera house. She had also contributed thousands of dollars of her own money. She smiled at Augusta. "What can I do to help?"

"We'd like to ask you to take charge of the effort."

"Take charge?" Molly asked, unable to believe so much confidence was being placed in her, a relative newcomer to San Francisco society.

"Chairwoman." Augusta's round face broke into a smile. "With your growing reputation, dear, you're perfect. All of San Francisco has noticed that everything you touch turns to gold."

"I...I don't know what to say." Molly was terribly flattered, but she also knew the hard work that would be involved. "I'm honored to be asked, but…" Her voice dropped as she shook her head slowly.

Augusta was now sitting on the edge of her chair. "Just say you'll do it, Molly. For us. For the city."

Molly took a deep breath. "Tell me what all will be involved."

"We need someone strong at the helm. Someone who knows how to convince donors that they're needed." She gave Molly a wry look. "And most important, someone who knows how to get them to part with their money." She chuckled.

Molly nodded. "Fund-raising events?"

"Banquets, soirees, balls—yes. You, or your designated representative, will meet with potential donors. Tell them what they will get in return for investing in the opera house—in San Francisco."

"Such as contributing to the culture of the city," Molly said.

"Or their names on a brass plaque in the foyer." She chuckled. "The size of the name depending on the amount they contribute, of course."

Molly laughed with her. "For the right money, I suppose they could have a statue in their image erected at the entrance."

"That's the spirit!" Augusta was laughing harder. "Or the stage named after them."

"Why not the entire opera house?"

"Dear, you're perfect for the post. When can you start?"

Molly agreed to take on the job, wondering, even as she said the words, how she could possibly fit anything more into her busy days. But she liked Augusta and would enjoy working even more closely on the committee with her.

After reminding Molly of the date of the next meeting, Augusta stood to take her leave. "By the way, dear," she said, as she gathered her fox boa, "I hear our mutual friend, Julian Starr, is going to win the election hands down next November." She winked at Molly. "But don't you dare tell anyone, least of all Julian, that I told you."

"I'll not say a word."

"It's my thinking, dear, that it would be quite appropriate to hold a—shall we say, soiree—immediately following the election."

"To celebrate Julian's victory?"

"Not exactly, though his presence as our newest U.S. senator would be a coup, now, wouldn't it? No, I was thinking that the timing of his victory will come just in time for a Christmas gala." Her face dimpled. "You do see where I'm going with this, don't you, dear?"

"I think you've lost me," Molly chuckled. "Are you talking about a gala to raise funds for the opera house?"

Augusta nodded vigorously. "With Julian in attendance, his connections in both Sacramento and Washington—don't you see, dear, how the publicity would benefit our little project?" She raised an eyebrow, awaiting Molly's agreement.

"And the other potential donors that publicity might bring?" Molly ventured.

"Exactly, dear." Augusta sighed. "Julian will be at your side, of course, and seated at the head table. Mmmm...I can see it now." She laughed. "Can't you, dear? All those who want to meet our rising star, so to speak, before he leaves for Washington will attend. It will be open to the city...to the entire state, for that matter."

"At an exorbitant price per plate," Molly interjected, wondering what she'd just gotten herself into.

"I like that, dear. Quite a lot actually," she said, with another chuckle. "It will be the event of the season. Perhaps of the century." With that, she dramatically swept the boa around her shoulders and moved toward the door.

After the big woman left, it seemed to Molly that her office had been hit by a tornado literally bursting with energy. She sighed and walked to her desk to check the next appointment of the day.

Then she smiled, surprised she'd forgotten, as she read the name: Julian. And he was probably on his way up the elevator right now. At least his presence would be calming after the whirlwind named Augusta Morgan.

Moments later, Julian poked his head in the doorway and smiled.

Molly rose from her desk. "Julian, come in. When did you get back?"

He strode across the room and took her hands. "Molly, you look more glorious than ever. And to answer your question, I only just arrived. Took the train in from Salinas this morning."

She nodded to the sitting area. "Please, come sit down. Tell me everything you've found out.

"First of all," she said, after they were seated, "the name—what have they come up with?"

Julian chuckled. "It was a grand idea to ask them to rename their company, Molly. The workers were delighted that you'd given them the opportunity."

"If we turn over the ownership, the name will be even more important. What did they come up with?"

"They chose two, then couldn't decide between them. They want you, and QIL, to make the final decision. They said they'd be happy with either."

"And they are?"

He gave her an affectionate smile. "Molly's Canning Company and People's Choice."

"Molly's Canning Company?" She chuckled, but shook her head. "It was nice of them to suggest it, but no, I don't think so."

"They're quite taken with you, Molly. It's a sign of their regard."

"And it's also a token of my respect for them to go with their second selection. It's perfect. Not only is it the workers' choice, we hope the product's sales will match its name. It's brilliant. I think the board will agree."

Victoria came in with a fresh pot of hot tea and set it on the tray. Molly poured for Julian and refilled her own cup. "Now, how are the operations running? Is production still on schedule for this time of year?"

He nodded. "Couldn't be running better. News has gotten out about your ideas for employee ownership. It's boosted morale a great deal already. I hope the board will go for it though, Molly, or we'll have some tremendously disappointed people."

"I know, Julian. But I've been working on my board proposal. I've done research on other companies that've tried it. The results are encouraging. I have a feeling they'll let us give it a go." She took a sip of tea. "With the board's approval, I would also like to improve the plant itself...update the equipment, increase the drying area, give the place a fresh coat of paint, and, of course, put up the new sign: People's Choice."

He grinned. "A nice touch, and one that will make the employees very proud." He looked thoughtful. "There's something else I need to talk with you about, Molly."

She raised an eyebrow. "Sounds serious. I'm listening."

"One of the fishermen came in to see me while I was there. Wants out of his contract."

Molly drew in a deep breath. "Zachary MacAlister."

Julian didn't look surprised that she knew. "I told him that from a legal standpoint, his term isn't up. The contract is binding until then."

"Did he tell you why he wanted out?"

Julian shook his head. "No, he didn't. "

"I want you to draw up the necessary legal papers to let him out of his contract."

"That might be a mistake. If other outfits attempt to get out of their contracts, the company could run into trouble. As you know, many of the canneries operate without binding contracts with the fishermen. John Cabrillo thought this might stabilize his operation. He wanted fishermen to work exclusively for him at a fair price. That way no other cannery could offer a fleet a better price for their catch, buying his product right out from under his nose.

"If we lose our contracted salmon fleet, we'd have to buy the fish at a daily market price at the wharf. It's not as risky if you're dealing with salmon *and* sardines, perhaps abalone as well, but we're the only cannery dealing exclusively with salmon."

"I understand the risks," Molly said finally, after considering his words. "But I still want you to draw up the necessary papers and let Zachary MacAlister out of his contract."

For a moment, Julian didn't speak, then his eyes met Molly's. "He's the one, isn't he?"

She tilted her head.

"The man you told me about that night in Monterey. The man you said you'd love until the day you die."

Molly took a sip of tea, looking at Julian over the rim of her teacup, considering how much she should say. He'd already guessed that Zach was the man she'd been referring to that night. There was no reason not to confirm it. Setting down her cup, she let out a sigh. "I once had deep feelings for Zachary MacAlister." She paused. "And, yes, he's the man I told you about. But all that is in the past. Our relationship is over."

"It was the canning company—his working for you—that did it, wasn't it?" He regarded her, his expression unreadable. "I could see it in his face when he asked about you."

Suddenly, Molly felt hot tears threaten to well in her eyes. She'd kept her thoughts of Zach at a distance for so long, the still-raw feelings took her by surprise. She drew in a shaky breath.

"Oh, Molly. I'm sorry. I didn't mean to open old wounds." He moved to the settee to sit beside her, handing her a mono-grammed handkerchief. "I am so sorry."

"I'm surprised at myself, Julian." She attempted to compose herself, but still the tears flowed.

Julian moved closer, laid one arm on the small sofa behind her, and gathered her into his arms. "Go ahead and cry," he murmured. "I'm here…I'm here."

Shutting all thoughts of Zach from her mind, she relaxed in the warmth of Julian's embrace. Her world of despair and dis-appointment seemed to fade as she remained there, consciously shutting out everything except the soothing comfort of his voice.

"I'll always be here for you, Molly," he breathed again, stroking her hair and resting his cheek against her head.

27

THE WEEK-LONG BOARD MEETINGS were held in the new wing of QIL. Molly had sought for and received approval to expand their office space, including a board room just down the hall from her office. The board room was a rich meld of wood and leather with a highly polished oak table ringed by six high-backed leather chairs. Windows, with draperies tied back, lined the length of the wall, affording a view of the bay.

Clive and Nevil Richards sat on one side of the long table, Luke Cornelius across from them. Julian Starr sat to the right of Molly's place at the head, and Kingsley Forrester faced her at the far end.

The early sessions were amiable. Julian opened by presenting reports on the financial status of the newly incorporated company, now officially called QIL Enterprises. With the news of their growing assets and increased return, Clive and Nevil Richards and Luke Cornelius were pleasantly open to Molly's proposals of central office and personnel expansion.

Surprisingly, they also agreed to her plans for Cabrillo Canning Company and approved the new name, People's Choice. When she explained her plan for employee ownership of People's Choice shares, with QIL Enterprises contributing matching funds, the men discussed the possible outcome at great length. There were a few raised eyebrows when she added that quarterly the workers would receive a portion of the company's profits—translating into a gradual vesting that would eventually mean full shares—thus giving them greater incentive to work harder and faster. But in the end, she convinced them that it was worth a short-term try.

Finally, during the last session of the board meeting when all other business had been voted on, Molly stood, telling the board members that she had another issue to discuss. She exchanged a quick glance with Julian who was seated at her right. He gave her a nearly imperceptible nod, and she was glad for his support.

"Gentlemen," she said, "as you know, I arrived in San Francisco just a few years ago. What you don't know is that I came here to join my cousin in an investment business that he had put together. The young man was a rising star in a growing investment firm here in the city. And it seemed that nothing would stop him. He wrote of his success, and my extended family contributed funds to send me to join him. They also gathered funds for my cousin to invest—money from inheritances, small investments, savings accounts—everything they could get their hands on, sometimes at great sacrifice.

"This was deposited in a London bank awaiting word from me to transfer by wire and invest in my cousin's enterprises."

Molly leaned forward intently. "But gentlemen, when I arrived here, I found my cousin had taken up a new residence."

They looked up at her, quizzically, expectantly.

"My cousin, Winston Carlisle-Jones, had been incarcerated at San Quentin. His crime—other than greed, of course? Winny had been caught and convicted of embezzling from the investment firm."

There was murmuring among the men at the table. The Richards brothers exchanged grim looks.

"Why did you keep this from us?" Luke Cornelius asked.

Molly took a deep breath. "I didn't think it was anything more than a family matter. Winston had turned out to be the black sheep. My loyalties were with the rest of my family and our friends in England. I set out to do what I could on my own, to give them some return on their investments and to start fresh on my own. Other than visiting Winston a few times, I really didn't give him, or his relationship to me, much thought."

There were a few nods, then Cornelius cleared his throat. "Why now? I sense from your reluctance to tell us about your cousin, that there's more to your narrative."

Molly looked at him squarely in the face, then met each of their gazes in turn without flinching. "First of all," she said calmly, "I want to tell you that I did not mean to keep this from you. Kingsley Forrester brought it to my attention a week ago, right after I told him that my cousin will be released within the next six months."

This time there was obvious displeasure at the news. "Please, gentlemen, let me finish," she said loudly. But they kept speaking among themselves. "Please," she said again.

Kingsley tried to gain their attention, but they ignored him as soundly as they had Molly.

Finally, Julian stood. "Gentlemen," he said, his voice booming through the board room. "Gentlemen, Miss Quinn, if I may speak?" He looked to Molly for her nod. She gave it, then sat down. Julian went on, the room now uncomfortably quiet.

"Miss Quinn and I have been considering the, ah, problem

that Winston Carlisle-Jones presents to QIL Enterprises. I would like to add my comments to hers, also the solution that both of us would like to present to you."

There were nods of approval urging him to continue.

"Winston would not pose such a threat to QIL Enterprises if his crime were not related to the investment business. But because he embezzled investors' funds from another firm similar to ours, any association with Miss Quinn or our company could have grave results. Miss Quinn is quite aware of this." He glanced down at Molly and she nodded.

"After discussing the situation at great length, I believe we can make an offer to Winston that will eliminate any threat to us."

An indignant Nevil Richards interrupted Julian. "An offer! You surely didn't take it upon yourselves to bring him into the company." His words were laced with anger. Molly fought her dismay at the turn of events and kept her chin high.

Julian's voice was strong, even soothing, as he continued. "I think you'll find this is a reasonable solution to the dilemma we face."

"Go on. We're listening," Luke Cornelius muttered, shaking his head slowly as he spoke. He began stacking his papers as if readying to leave.

"We will propose to Winston that he open a small branch office in Canberra."

"Canberra, Australia?" Clive Richards said appreciatively. There was chuckling around the long table.

"Brilliant show, Julian," Cornelius added. "No wonder you're on your way to becoming our next senator." With that statement, Molly knew that the mood had switched. She also knew that she had lost leadership ground, and at the same time, Julian's stature had risen.

The men watched Julian attentively, respectfully. He went on to tell them about the contract he'd written in which Winston Carlisle-Jones would agree to leaving the country immediately upon release from prison. A sizable remuneration (from Molly Quinn's private funds) would be awaiting him in Australia, to be used only for starting an investment and loan business. Winston would be periodically audited by QIL Enterprises, but he would not be considered part of the organization. If any discrepancies were seen in his records, he would be reported to Australian authorities immediately.

Molly stood again. "Gentlemen, as you can see, we've done our best to find a solution to the concerns about my cousin. But I want to add a personal word to what Julian has told you."

They watched her quietly.

"I give you my word that if Winston Carlisle-Jones breathes even a hint of threat toward QIL Enterprises, I will resign my position immediately and walk away from the company. I will distance myself from you to control whatever damage my association with him might bring."

There were some raised eyebrows and murmuring among the board members.

Finally, Luke Cornelius spoke. "We appreciate your candor, Miss Quinn. But I think all of us agree that if your cousin hasn't signed the contract by the time he's released, we may have to consider your resignation, with or without your willingness to offer it."

There were nods of approval from the Richards brothers. Julian and Kingsley vehemently defended Molly, and a heated discussion followed.

Finally, Molly stood and cleared her throat. "Gentlemen,

nothing can be solved here today. For all we know, Winston may sign this contract the instant it's presented to him. Until he does or doesn't leave the country, until we do have to make a leadership decision, I remain fully in control of QIL Enterprises.

"I suggest that we leave the Winston Carlisle-Jones question open until we've explored all avenues. Let's get back to the business at hand—how to best increase our holdings and get the most out of those we have."

By the time the meeting was adjourned the issue had been dropped, but the mood remained somber. Molly thanked the men for their attendance and exited the board room to return to her office.

She'd just settled onto the settee with a cup of tea when Julian tapped lightly and came into her office.

"An excellent job, Molly, even though the Winny question was extremely difficult to present," he said, as he sank into a chair beside her.

"I thought we'd lost them," she said, feeling her exhaustion.

He reached for her hand. "Board meetings are notorious for their abrupt changes of direction. I actually thought this went more smoothly than most."

"Thank you, Julian. But you're the one they eventually listened to. It doesn't matter that I began QIL Enterprises and have led it from its beginning. In the long run—I'm a woman. Young enough to be their daughter. They see me as some sort of pleasant aberration as long as everything is going along nicely." She shook her head slowly, sighing. "But when something threatens their equilibrium, they instinctively turn to a man for leadership."

Julian was silent for a moment. She knew from his expression that he agreed. Finally he spoke again. "There is something else, Molly. After you left, Cornelius brought up the point we'd feared."

"Blackmail?"

He nodded. "Yes. I think they're all aware of the potential. Winny has the capability to hurt us, whether he leaves the country or not."

"I know, Julian."

"I think it's time to present the contract to Winny. See if we can at least get that question solved. Shall we go see him tomorrow?"

Winny had become increasingly difficult, even nasty, to deal with. Molly let out a sigh. "All right."

"Now, with our board meeting and Winny's dilemma out of the way..." Julian poured himself a cup of tea and rested his head against the back of his chair, briefly closing his eyes. Then he opened them, looking straight into Molly's. "Let's go to dinner and celebrate tonight. How about it?"

"I don't know, Julian...." Since the day that she had cried in his arms, Molly had purposely kept her distance. No matter what had happened with Zach, she couldn't bring herself to care for anyone else. She felt comfortable with Julian, but she didn't want him to think there could be anything more between them.

He reached for her hand again. "No strings attached, Molly," he said softly. "Just two friends enjoying an evening together." He smiled. "Besides, I want to tell you the latest about my campaign. I've got some speeches to make in the next few weeks. Different organizations around the area. I'd like you to accompany me."

His words reminded Molly that she did need to talk with him about the upcoming Christmas gala and his role, if he would agree. "All right," she finally said. "Dinner does sound lovely. I'd be delighted to come."

He stood. "I'll pick you up at your house, eight o'clock?"

"Perfect. I'll be ready."

"Oh, and Molly," he turned after he reached the door. "I've got a bit of a surprise. Something to show you."

Still seated, she raised an eyebrow. "Give me a hint."

He laughed. "You'll guess it if I do. Just be ready. And wear a hat."

"A hat?" She tilted her head in wonder. "A hat?"

But he didn't answer. Molly could hear him chuckling to himself as he strode through the outer office toward the elevators.

Molly put her head back on the settee and closed her eyes. She felt completely consumed by her emotional battle with the board members. She wondered if it would ever get easier.

She found some solace in the time she spent with the Forresters. Each night she read to Gwennie from a new leather-bound volume of Jane Austen's works, her recent gift to the older woman. She brushed her long gray hair one hundred strokes, then tucked her into bed. Gwen made no bones about preferring Molly's voice and touch to Miss Brown's.

After her special time with the Forresters, Molly would make her way home through the hedge and flower bed that Kingsley had planted for her.

But her favorite time of day was after she'd bathed and prepared for bed. In her dressing gown, Molly would curl up in the sofa that faced *Mary Rose's Garden* and soak in its beauty by candlelight.

It was only then that she allowed herself to feel both the pain of missing Zach and the joy of the painting. And she would remember the words that Mary Rose had told her, words from the Bible about God's love and intimate care.

As she considered the painting's garden, its shading and light, she thought about her life. About the business she'd once told Zach would be like such a place.

Drawing in a deep sigh, she wondered how long she would need to keep the frantic pace of recent months. She planned her schedule meticulously so that she wouldn't have time to dwell on Zach or the deep, aching emptiness that had settled into her soul.

She had supposed that with every triumph, every personal success, the emptiness would lessen. But so far, it hadn't changed.

Without love, she concluded nearly every evening, her garden was made up more of shadows than light.

Victoria Parrott knocked at the office door, interrupting Molly's reverie. "Yes?" she called out. She had nearly fallen asleep after Julian's departure minutes earlier.

"You have visitors in the waiting room," Victoria said, as she entered.

Molly stood and walked to her desk to consult her calendar. "I don't have any appointments, do I Victoria?"

"No, you don't. But the couple seem sure that you'll see them."

"Did they give their names...or their business?" She figured they must be connected with the opera house.

"A Mr. Devon O'Rourke and a Mary Rose Sheffield," Victoria

Parrott announced, with a prim pat to her tight twist of graying hair. "And strange as it may seem, they want to speak to you about Mr. O'Rourke's artwork. I started to shoo them off, but they're insisting." She gave an impatient sigh.

Molly smiled broadly, suddenly feeling better than she had in days. "That's quite all right, Victoria. Please show them in."

A moment later, Victoria opened the door, then stepped back as Mary Rose entered, followed by a sandy haired, rather ordinary-looking man with extraordinary eyes. They were deep pools of curiosity and life, taking in everything around him.

Molly gave Mary Rose an affectionate hug.

The blond woman beamed. "Molly, it's so good to see you." Then she looked up into the face of the young man beside her. "I'd like to introduce Devon O'Rourke."

Molly took his solid and callused hand. "I'm honored, Devon. I've heard so much about you from Mary Rose."

He laughed a little self-consciously. "We'll have to compare notes. Mary Rose has spoken so often, and in such glowing terms, of you and your visit that I decided I had to meet you for myself."

"Please, come in and sit down. We have much to talk about." Molly gestured to the sitting area, and the two joined her around the cherrywood table.

"Now," Molly said, after they'd settled into their seats, "what has happened since I saw you?"

Devon and Mary Rose looked at each other lovingly. First Mary Rose told of her trip on the *Molly Quinn* to Santa Barbara, then related her trip by horseback to the San Ynez Mission.

"We almost parted again right then and there," Devon added sheepishly. "My stubbornness took over, and I almost let her go. After she'd come all that way to see me."

351

"Then we talked over our, shall I say, differences of opinion." She grinned up at him. "And reached a compromise."

Molly chuckled. "Maybe I shouldn't ask about those differences. You can skip over that part, if you like."

Devon frowned. "Actually, our differences had to do with your offer."

"That's coming right to the point," Molly said, though not unkindly.

The young man went on. "Mary Rose told me about your offer to sponsor my art, to become my patron."

"And you didn't like the idea." It wasn't a question. She could see his independence in his eyes. "You said you reached a compromise. Is that why you've come now?"

Devon smiled. "I wanted, first, to finish my work in Santa Barbara, and second, to see if any of those paintings might sell."

"And?" Molly raised an eyebrow.

"I finished, and yes, two paintings did sell."

"If your paintings are selling, then...?" She left the question hanging.

Devon gave her a half-grin. "Then why did I come here?"

"Yes."

"Mary Rose has told me about your interest in my work."

"I have *Mary Rose's Garden* hanging in my sitting room. And I've seen the *Hope*. They have both touched me, each in a different way."

"I would like to see my work get some exposure here in San Francisco. I thought you might know of art dealers, or galleries or museums that might be interested."

Molly sat back, thoughtfully considering his words. "Of course, my answer is yes, I will do what I can. But as you probably know, most of our galleries and museums were destroyed in the quake. They're in the process of being rebuilt, but certainly aren't ready to handle works of art." She frowned. "I do have an idea that might help, though."

"In what way?" Mary Rose asked.

"A means of getting your name known by the right people. People, I mean, who can afford your work."

Mary Rose and Devon exchanged glances. "How do you propose to do that?"

"The event of the year is coming up just before Christmas. A banquet followed by a formal ball. It will be attended by all the dignitaries of the city, and many from Sacramento, as well. The entire affair is being put on specifically to raise money for rebuilding the opera house." She paused. "What would you think about auctioning the *Hope?* We would start the auction at whatever price you would want to put on it. When it sells, that amount would be yours to keep. Whatever is raised above that would go to the rebuilding campaign."

Devon let out a low whistle.

"If you'd like," Molly continued, "think it over. You can let me know."

Devon interrupted, a look of wonder on his face. "I can't speak for you, Mary Rose." He glanced at her wide smile, then back to Molly. "But I think this idea is nothing short of miraculous. And the answer is yes!"

Molly smiled at the two. "I'll also speak to people I know at the *Examiner* to see if they'll run an article on you before the event, who you are, a bit about your style, and of course your generous donation to the opera house fund. It will be great publicity for your work."

They spoke excitedly for several minutes about the event, the time they would need to spend in San Francisco preceding it. "And," Molly said finally, "I would like the two of you to be my guests at the event."

They readily agreed.

"We have another request," Mary Rose said, after a bit. "Actually, two."

"As if what you've done isn't enough," Devon said with a chuckle.

"And those requests would be?" Molly asked.

"We'd like to invite you to our wedding." Mary Rose looked lovingly into Devon's eyes.

Molly laughed softly. "I would be honored. When is it?"

"In the early spring, in Carmel."

"I'll be there," Molly said. "And the other request?"

"We'd like to see *Mary Rose's Garden.*"

"And I can think of nothing I would rather do than show it to you. Will you still be here tomorrow?"

They nodded.

"Wonderful. How about joining me for dinner? Tomorrow night about seven o'clock?"

Mary Rose glanced happily at Devon. "We'd love to," she said.

They spoke for a few minutes about Carmel and Monterey. "Tell me," Molly said, after a few minutes, "what has happened with the charges against Oliver Duckworth? Was he ever found? Your money recovered?"

Devon shook his head. "No, though he was spotted south of here."

Mary Rose spoke up. "It was Zach who saw him, Molly."

"Zach?"

"Yes, he'd anchored off Morro Bay and had taken the tender into town. He spotted Duckworth coming out of a saloon up the street. By the time he reached the place, though, Duckworth had disappeared. Zach spent two days trying to trace him, but the man had apparently seen Zach. He's vanished again without a trace."

"I'm sorry," Molly said, then added softly, "and Zach? How is he?"

Mary Rose met Molly's gaze, her look understanding. "He misses you, Molly."

"Did he tell you that?"

"No. I can see it in his eyes when your name is mentioned."

Molly looked away. Any thought of Zach only gouged another wound into her heart. "He knew you were coming to see me?"

"Yes," Mary Rose said.

"But he sent no word, no message?"

Mary Rose's voice dropped. "No. I'm sorry, Molly."

The conversation turned again to Oliver Duckworth and his whereabouts. A short time later, Mary Rose and Devon stood to leave.

After walking them to the door, Molly moved to the window overlooking the bay. The clippers and schooners glided by, wind filling their billowing sails.

She thought about the *Molly Quinn* and wondered if Zach still thought of her. Did he remember the joy they'd felt in each other's arms? Did he look forward to the day that they'd promised to meet? It was months away, but she wondered if he would be there.

The way things stood, he probably would not bother. She sighed, turning away from the window. Not that it mattered. She probably wouldn't go, either.

28

LATER THAT EVENING, Molly was dressed and ready when Julian arrived at her door. She invited him in.

"I see you've worn your hat," he said, with a wink and a smile of approval.

"I can't imagine why you'd insist on it," Molly said with a laugh, touching the mound of silk flowers on the brim. "I've been trying to solve the riddle all afternoon."

"You'll soon see." He helped her into her wrap, and moments later they headed down the walkway to the street.

"How did you get here?" There was no waiting carriage, and she looked up at him, puzzled.

"You'll see," he said again, mysteriously, and held open the front gate.

Streetlights cast a soft glow as they strolled up the street, and carriages passed by them, horse's hooves clip-clopping along. Julian gently took her arm, leading her around a corner.

Molly halted and put her fingers over her mouth in wonder. They stood before a sleek automobile parked directly beneath a streetlight.

"Julian!" she exclaimed. "Is it yours?"

He nodded, unable to stop smiling. "Do you like it?" he asked needlessly.

"Oh, Julian. It's beautiful," Molly breathed. She didn't know the make, but it was shiny and sturdy-looking with an open top and elegant leather seats. It was obviously pricey, and it struck her fancy right off.

"Madam, are you ready?" He bowed formally and opened the door on the passenger's side.

Molly slipped onto the seat, and Julian handed her a pair of goggles. Delighted, she tied them on. Then, with a flourish, he presented her with a length of net tulle. Molly straightened her hat, making sure it was well anchored, and Julian bent over her, looped the netting over her face, and knotted it behind, its tails free to dance in the breeze once they started.

He touched her veiled face and smiled approvingly. "Perfect," he said, raising an eyebrow. "Now the difficult part." And he went around to the front of the motorcar.

Molly waited expectantly while he gave the crankshaft a turn. After a few tries, it putt-putted to life, the whole roadster shuddering and coughing.

Quickly, Julian tied on his own goggles, then slid in behind the steering wheel. After a barely visible wink in her direction, he began to operate the clutch, then the accelerator. Then he flicked on the lights, and with another shake, the auto ground into gear and shimmied forward.

They swerved onto the road, picking up speed as they headed down Nob Hill. They quickly overtook horse-drawn carriages and other autos. Julian, with a boyish chuckle, squeezed the bulb of the horn, and horses shied and bucked. His exhilaration was contagious. Molly felt the wind in her face, whipping the tulle netting. She threw back her head, laughing up at the stars, feeling like a girl again, responsibilities, heartaches, and worries pushed from her mind.

Julian drove to a quiet restaurant overlooking the bay a few miles from the city. It was small, but elegant. The maître d' obviously knew Julian and led them to a private window table covered with a linen cloth and set with crystal and silver. A candle flickered at the table's center, surrounded by an arrangement of golden-hued autumn flowers.

Julian allowed the maître d' to seat Molly, then sat beside her rather than across the table. They both faced the view of the bay. A moon was out, just bright enough to illumine the rippling water.

Molly turned to Julian, who was regarding her with an affectionate expression in the candlelight. She was struck by his almost lighthearted behavior tonight. It was a delightful contrast to his normal sophisticated reserve. His hair was mussed from the breeze in the automobile, and her gaze settled on the perfect contours of his face, the attentive way he considered her.

After they'd ordered their meal, Julian entertained Molly with the latest news from Sacramento, especially about his bid for the U.S. Senate. As he spoke, he became more serious, particularly as he related details of the upcoming election by the state legislature.

"We'll know the outcome by the end of November," he said. "But that leaves only a few weeks for campaigning. As I mentioned this afternoon, Molly, it would be delightful if you could accompany me to some of my appearances."

She frowned slightly. "It depends on when and where, Julian. You know how difficult it is for me to get away from QIL Enterprises."

He took a sip of wine from a crystal goblet. "There will be two or three upcoming in San Francisco. Perhaps those?" He lifted an eyebrow.

358

She nodded, looking at him from above the rim of her own goblet. "I'd love to." She smiled.

"And," he began, watching her expectantly, "the coup de grâce." He gave her a big smile. "The governor's hosting a dinner for me in two weeks. That's probably the most important of all. Is there any chance—?"

She grinned, lifting her glass, and leaning toward him. "For that, Mr. Senator, there's every chance." He clinked his goblet against hers and smiled into her eyes.

They went on to discuss the dates and times of his appearances. By the time their plates of roasted mountain quail in rosemary-basil sauce and wild rice had been set before them, the conversation had turned to the Christmas gala. Molly related the details of Augusta Morgan's visit and her agreement to chair the drive to raise funds for the opera house.

Julian lifted his glass again. "You'll soon be the toast of San Francisco, Molly. Congratulations."

She nodded her thanks. "All I see now, though, Julian, is the hard work ahead. It's going to be difficult to fit it all in."

"I'll help out. Just let me know what I can do, especially with the gala."

"Actually, Julian, I would love for you to attend, as my escort, of course." She laughed lightly. "Augusta has it in mind that your attendance as our next senator will draw other dignitaries to lend their presence."

"Whether I win the election or not, I'll verbally add my endorsement to your efforts in Sacramento," he said solemnly. "And I'll be honored to be at your side."

"Speaking of Sacramento…" Molly told Julian about Mary Rose and Devon's meeting with her that afternoon. "I mentioned holding an auction at the gala," she concluded, "both to raise funds for the opera house and to get the O'Rourke name in the news." She took another bite of the delicious quail.

"It's a wonderful idea. But since you mentioned Sacramento, you must be thinking of the *Hope*."

She nodded slowly, sensing he had news of the painting.

He smiled. "You can be the first to break the news to Devon O'Rourke. He'll need to paint another for the gala, because the *Hope*—"

"It sold?" she breathed, delighted.

"Yes, I just heard myself. And for quite a nice sum, I might add."

"Do you know who bought it?"

"No. It seems the buyer wanted to be anonymous."

Molly put a hand on Julian's arm. "You must be there when I tell Devon and Mary Rose. Can you come to dinner tomorrow night?"

He smiled into her eyes. "Again, I'd be honored."

"You keep saying that," she said, with a light laugh.

He set down his fork and looked at her adoringly. "Because I do feel honored when I'm with you, Molly. Honored and delighted. Always."

She quickly changed the subject, and by the time their flaming brandied peaches arrived, they were laughing amiably about Julian's new auto and the raised eyebrows it would cause among the stuffier, old-guard politicians.

The waiter cleared their plates and served coffee. Molly looked out at the navy blue water of the bay, its gentle ripples sparkling in the moonlight.

"Molly?" Julian said thoughtfully, and she turned toward him. "I hope this doesn't come as too much of a shock to you." He combed his fingers nervously through the shock of blond hair at his forehead, taking a deep breath at the same time. "But I have something terribly important to ask you."

She waited for him to continue, but he seemed to be struggling with his thoughts. "What do you mean?" she finally prompted, though something told her that perhaps she shouldn't have asked.

He reached for her hand. "I know when we talked in Monterey several months ago, you tried to discourage my attentions. You told me that you were in love with another man, with Zachary MacAlister."

With the mention of his name, Molly tried to push Zach's image from her mind, her heart. She caught her breath and listened.

His tone was low, impassioned. "I know things have changed between you and Zachary. I've watched your pain, Molly. So many times I've wanted to step in and ease it somehow.

"I had planned to wait to ask you...." His voice faltered. "But tonight—just hearing you laugh again, watching you enjoy yourself—has prompted me to speak. I want to bring happiness back into your life. More than anything, I want you to smile again. Always." He paused. "I care deeply for you, Molly."

Their server suddenly hovered near the table, filling their coffee cups and water glasses. Molly took a sip of coffee and met Julian's eyes over the rim of her cup. He looked as shy and uncertain as a schoolboy. She was touched to see this side of the tough and erudite attorney.

"You don't need to give an answer tonight. All I ask is that you consider it." He squeezed her hand. "I want to ask you to marry me, Molly."

The waiter chose the moment to return with the bill.

"Marry you?" she finally breathed, when the man had gone.

"Maybe it's too soon for you to love someone else." Julian frowned. "Or perhaps, Molly, you'll find that love is different than you thought."

He lifted her hand and pressed it to his lips. "Maybe love is meant to be comfortable, a calm harbor in life's storms. Respect and high regard and well-matched interests also speak of love, Molly."

She thought of Zach and the bitter sadness she too often felt at the mere mention of his name. Perhaps a calm harbor, a comfortable affection, was what she needed. A safe place where she could finally push him from her heart. "I agree," she finally said. "There are different kinds of love, Julian. And maybe now's the time to consider them."

He kissed her fingertips again. "Molly, I'm almost afraid to ask, but does this mean you will consider my proposal?"

"I can't give you an answer yet, Julian." She smiled gently. "Will you give me some time, time to get used to the idea?"

"I'll wait, Molly," he said, his eyes warm. "Believe me, I'll wait."

The next morning, a cold blanket of gray fog drifted far inland. Molly left her house, shivering as she headed for the Nob Hill cable car, barely visible through the mist.

A half-hour later, she'd made the connection to the trolley in town and headed toward the waterfront Ferry Building where she planned to meet Julian.

As she walked toward the ferry at the waterfront, she thought about the old grizzled fisherman, Jam, and the magnificent three-masted *Molly Quinn*. And, of course, Zach. How delightful that day had been when she discovered that he'd named his ship after her! She wondered if he had kept the name, and if he had, why. Perhaps it was simply too complicated to change.

She strolled into the Ferry Building and smiled when she saw Julian. He waved and strode toward her. He carried a leather valise, which Molly knew contained the contract they were going to discuss with Winny. As usual, Julian was dressed impeccably, in an expensively cut suit and Italian shoes. When he reached her, he took her arm protectively and led her through the milling crowd to the waiting Sausalito ferry.

As they boarded, Molly could see that the fog had lifted somewhat, though the day remained dank and clammy.

"Are you ready to face him?" Julian asked as they took their seats near the bow.

"This is going to be difficult for me, Julian. Winny has always been my favorite cousin. We played together as children, dreamed dreams." She shook her head sadly. "It hurts me to have to send him away. When it comes right down to it, I'm not sure I can force the issue."

"Family loyalty versus losing your company?"

She gave him a half-smile. "You'd think it would be a simple choice, wouldn't you?"

Julian took her hand. "Your loyalties run deep, Molly. And friendships are extremely important to you. I can see how this may hurt you."

"And family," she murmured, considering her mother and father and aunts and uncles back home in England. Would they ever understand why she had to send Winny away?

"But how about you, Julian? You befriended Winny when he first arrived. You stuck with him through his trial and sentencing. This can't be easy on you, either."

Julian nodded slowly. He didn't answer but looked out over the gray, choppy Pacific.

By the time they disembarked in Sausalito, the fog had lifted into a white overcast. When they stepped into the hired carriage, blue sky was at last showing through, and Molly settled back into the cracked leather seat.

The carriage rumbled and jerked along the dirt road leading to San Quentin, as they planned various approaches to their presentation of the contract.

Finally they arrived, and Molly, stepping down from the carriage, smoothed her skirt and straightened her hat. Julian took her elbow and escorted her into the prison.

"Both of you visiting at the same time," Winny said as he seated himself on the other side of the iron mesh. A guard stood near him. "To what do I owe this great honor?" There was an edge to his voice.

Molly touched his fingers through the barrier. "Winny, it's good to see you."

"Is it?" Winny's gaze met hers, and Molly was sad to see the light gone from his eyes. How different he was than when she had first visited him in San Quentin.

"It is," she said softly. "Is there any more word on your release?"

"Six months, like I told you." He shrugged.

Julian pulled his chair closer. "Winny, we've got some business to discuss with you today."

"Does it have to do with my job at QIL Enterprises?" Winny laughed. "If it doesn't, I don't want to hear it."

"In a manner of speaking, yes, it does," Julian said.

Winny shrugged again. "Then go ahead."

Molly spoke, keeping her voice low and earnest. "Winny, I've got a proposition. I would like to start you in the investment business again."

Winny threw back his head and guffawed. Then he looked up with a half-grin, running his fingers through his rust-colored hair. "That's a good one, Molly. As if anyone would come to me for investment advice."

"Not here, Winny. Outside the country." Molly looked at him evenly.

He raised an eyebrow. "England? We talked about that once."

Molly shook her head. "No, Winny. How would you like to go to Australia?"

"Australia?" He laughed. "Why would I want to go there?"

"Because we're paying you to go there," Julian broke in, his voice laced with exasperation.

Winny stared at him. "Sounds like something you're trying to force on me. I go, I get paid. I don't go, I don't get paid. Right, old friend?"

"Maybe," Julian said quietly. "But if you care at all for your cousin, you'll think about it."

Winston looked back to Molly. "Tell me more," he said.

Molly outlined the plan, trying to present the best possible scenario. "We've chosen Canberra," she said. "Since Australia's nationhood, the place has been chosen as the capital. It's already becoming as cosmopolitan as San Francisco. Great plans have been laid. Your business can grow with the country, Winny. It's your chance to start over. No one there will know about what happened here."

He seemed receptive. Molly went on with the details.

"Just like that, you're sending me away, Molly?" he asked, when she'd finished. "After all I've done to get QIL Enterprises started? How can you think of doing this to me?" He narrowed his eyes. "In my way of thinking, QIL Enterprises is half mine. I gave you the leads for investments. The money that was sent from England was half mine. Ask anyone there, and they'll tell you. They didn't send you to America to take a chance with their nest egg. It was both of us."

"Winny, please—"

"I'm not going away. Not for any amount of money."

Julian broke in. "Perhaps when you find out the amount Molly plans to invest in your business…"

Winny cocked an eyebrow and listened as Molly told him the sum. Then he took a deep breath. "If you're willing to hand me that much money if I agree to go to Australia," he said, with an innocent smile, "I can only imagine what you'll be willing to give me if I stay."

"What are you talking about?" Julian growled, leaning forward.

Winny smiled again. "Just think about it, old friend." Then he stood, signaling to the guard that he was ready to go. "Just think about it."

As Julian and Molly ferried back to the city, they discussed Winny and the contract. He obviously wasn't going to cooperate, but Molly was just as determined not to give up on him. "I refuse to think that he won't listen to us—to me—in the end," she told Julian.

But Julian looked worried. "We need to be ready for the worst," he mused. "There's no need to alert the board, yet.

We've got six months to work on Winny. We'll hope for the best, but diligently prepare for the worst."

She looked at him sharply. "You mean my stepping down?"

He nodded slowly and took her hand. "There are several contingencies to consider...," he began, then let his voice drop.

Molly pulled her hand away and looked out at the bay's choppy gray water, lost in thought.

Molly tried to keep her mind off her visit with Winny as she prepared for the evening's dinner. She'd borrowed Cook Liu for the day, also inviting Kingsley and Gwennie to attend the dinner party for Devon and Mary Rose.

Even before the guests arrived, the little Queen Anne cottage was filled with the fragrance of Cook Liu's ministrations in the kitchen. Molly had let him plan the menu. For the main course, he'd marinated a tender cut of venison in wine sauce, then roasted it with golden acorn squash and baby parsnips. For an accompaniment, he'd made, on Molly's request, his specialty—a succulent minced lamb and rosemary pie in a flaky pastry.

Molly had set the table in her dining room with dishes from England and sterling cutlery given to her by Gwennie and Kingsley. Tapered candles in silver holders graced the center of the table, and she'd cut fresh flowers from her garden and placed them in low arrangements on either end. Gleaming crystal goblets, ordered from Ireland, reflected the candlelight.

Just off the dining area was the sitting room, its fireplace and *Mary Rose's Garden* on the wall above it dominating the entire room. A fire had been carefully laid behind the grate and now crackled cheerfully, its warmth reaching into the dining room.

Devon and Mary Rose arrived in their hired carriage just as Julian drove up, the gleaming roadster putt-putting, backfiring, and shimmying as he parked in front of Molly's house.

It was an immediate sensation. Within minutes, Gwennie and Kingsley had joined the others around the automobile, discussing its six cylinders and highly polished chassis and leather seats, even the delightfully silly horn.

Even Gwennie tried the horn, her wrinkled face breaking into a smile as she squeezed the bulb.

"What a splendid and wonderful machine!" Gwennie exclaimed, just as Molly stepped through the gate to join them. "How I would love to drive it!"

"Then how about taking a spin with me later? I'll teach you the rudiments," Julian said, jovially.

"I see you've already made introductions," Molly said, after giving Mary Rose a quick hug and shaking Devon's hand. Julian kissed her cheek and took her arm as they walked back up the stone walk, through the small garden, and into Molly's house.

Molly led the way to the sitting room, turned up the lamp, then stood back so that Mary Rose and Devon could see the painting.

As the group moved toward the fireplace, there was a moment of awed silence. Devon put his arm around Mary Rose, and they stood looking up at the oil as if no one else was in the room.

"Oh, Devon," she whispered. "It's more beautiful than I remembered."

"It's because of you," he murmured. "This painting shows the light within you." He paused. "And just look at Jesse. How much he's grown since then!"

Mary Rose nodded, her eyes still on the oil. Standing silently to one side, Molly could see the range of emotions—joy, sadness, regret—in her face. She knew how difficult it must be for them to see it again, knowing how its disposition had driven them apart.

Mary Rose turned to Molly. "When we were told of its theft, I never thought we'd see it again. I think that's what makes it all the more precious to us."

Molly nodded, understanding.

"Thank you, Molly," Devon said. "It's perfect here. I feel that God has given us a special gift in allowing us to see where it hangs and to see how much it is appreciated."

"It's also brought us together in a unique way," Molly added. "And for that, I thank you. I treasure not only your art, but both of you and our growing friendship." She tried not to think about Zach and his part in all this. She missed him more than ever, standing here with Mary Rose and Devon, before the oil with its garden filled with light. How she wished, suddenly and achingly, that Zach were standing beside them. Beside her.

Julian moved toward her and took her arm. "Dear, I believe Cook is trying to tell us something."

Molly looked toward the dining room where Cook Liu was trying to get her attention. Smiling, she turned again toward her guests. "Dinner is served," she said.

As soon as everyone was seated, Molly nodded to Cook Liu to begin serving. She was seated at the head of the table, Julian opposite her at the far end, Devon and Mary Rose facing the sitting room so they could see the painting, and Kingsley and Gwennie across from them. The lights from the candles cast a pleasant glow across the group.

"I have some good news," Molly said, smiling at Devon and Mary Rose. "Just before Julian left for Monterey, he heard something that I believe will interest you, Devon."

Everyone turned toward her, setting down knives and forks or glasses. "The *Hope* has sold!" she said, still watching Mary Rose and Devon.

There was an audible gasp from Mary Rose.

"It has?" Devon asked quietly, shaking his head in disbelief.

Molly nodded. Julian took up the conversation, relating the details of the sale to an anonymous art collector.

After several minutes of animated conversation, with Gwennie murmuring, "Dear, dear," from time to time, and Kingsley trying to guess who the buyer could be, Molly again broke in. "That does leave us in a dilemma, albeit the best kind of dilemma I can imagine."

"The *Hope* can't be auctioned," Devon said. "It's wonderful that it's sold, but I was looking forward to the gala."

"Do you have any others ready? I would still like to auction one of your works," Molly said, lifting her fork.

Devon and Mary Rose exchanged a glance, and Molly noticed a slight frown cross Mary Rose's brow.

It was Mary Rose who answered Molly. "There is one," she said. "It's a magnificent piece. It was partially commissioned, then the buyer's circumstances changed. It's available again, and I think it would be perfect." She smiled a bit sheepishly. "With each new piece Devon produces, I'm convinced it's his finest effort. But there is something about this oil that is very special." Her gaze traveled to the next room where she could see *Mary Rose's Garden*. "Even though this will always be my favorite," she nodded toward the oil. "The painting we're speaking of is truly remarkable."

Devon seemed to watch Molly curiously, then he added, "If you'd like, we can have it transported to San Francisco in time for the event."

"I would. Thank you," she said. "And I'll begin making the

arrangements for its unveiling." She lifted her wine goblet toward Mary Rose and Devon.

Around the table, the others followed suit.

"To love and happiness," she said solemnly, as they clinked the glasses together, then sipped the deep red liquid.

"And to marriage," Julian added, lifting his glass, but smiling at Molly instead of the betrothed couple.

The others turned toward Molly with puzzled expressions, but she merely smiled. "I think a toast 'to love' is enough for tonight," she said with a smile.

"To love!" she repeated. And they all clinked their glasses again.

The next morning, Mary Rose stopped by Molly's office before the couple left to return to Carmel-by-the-Sea.

"Devon's at the *Examiner*," she explained, as the two women walked to the sitting area. "And I wanted to stop by and thank you again for the lovely dinner."

Molly, smiling, nodded to the settee. "Please sit down. I'm glad Devon was able to make time for his interview, and it gives us time for a nice visit." She settled into a chair across from Mary Rose. "I wanted to let you know how happy I am that things have worked out for you and Devon."

"They almost didn't," Mary Rose said. "If it hadn't been for you and Zach—" She stopped abruptly, as if knowing Molly's pain. "I'm sorry. I probably shouldn't have mentioned him."

"No," Molly said quietly, "don't apologize. I know that you and Devon have become friends with Zach. I also consider you my friends." She laughed softly. "You can't avoid mentioning our names to each other."

Mary Rose looked serious. "Devon and I pray for you, that God will work in both your lives."

"Thank you." Molly noticed the caring in her friend's eyes. "I've never forgotten those things you told me about his love. Sometimes when I'm especially lonely or troubled, I sit in front of the painting and remember your garden. I think about how you meet God there and talk with him. Just thinking about it brings me peace. I can't explain it; it's just there."

Mary Rose nodded. "You know, Molly, you're welcome to come visit anytime you need to get away from all this. My home, my garden, is yours for as long as you want to stay."

Molly smiled. "I just may take you up on that, sooner than you think. I've got some weighty decisions to make, in my business and in my personal life."

"Do either have to do with Julian?" Mary Rose met Molly's gaze evenly.

"Yes," Molly sighed. "He's asked me to marry him."

"Do you love him?"

For a moment Molly didn't answer. She turned to the window, as always, focusing on the three-masted schooners gliding across the bay. "I thought I knew what love is," she said finally. "With Zach, I was so sure." She turned back to Mary Rose. "But I didn't think love could hurt so much."

"It happened fast, didn't it? I remember hearing how much you cared for each other one day, and you were barely speaking the next."

"Zach turned from me after I bought the canning company."

"Cabrillo?"

"Yes, though we're calling it People's Choice now." She shook her head slowly. "I had no idea he worked for Cabrillo. I can understand why he was angry, initially." She shook her head. "But when he refused to speak with me about it, I was disappointed in him, in his lack of respect for me. I felt he at least owed me that."

Mary Rose nibbled at her bottom lip as if deciding whether to say more. "There is something else, Molly," she said, finally. "When I was on the *Molly Quinn* with Zach, we had a chance to speak quite openly. He was mourning for you during that voyage."

"Mourning?"

"Yes," she said quietly, drawing a deep breath. "He told me how you'd met at the sea cliffs, then parted. You returned to the hotel, and he had business in town."

Molly nodded, remembering.

"He told me that he decided to register at the same hotel so you could have time together in the morning. It was late by the time he got there, but while he was standing at the registrar's desk he saw you with Julian. He said that you were strolling from the dining room arm-in-arm, engaged in intimate conversation." She looked sad. "That's why Zach turned away. The other—the canning company purchase—was meaningless in comparison."

Molly fell back in her chair, stunned. "I met Julian that night to discuss the offer for Cabrillo. He'd come from Sacramento specifically to handle the legal part of the transaction. Whatever Zach saw had nothing to do with any romantic feelings between Julian and me."

"Yet you're considering marrying Julian?"

"I wouldn't have given it a second thought at the time Zach saw us. But now?" She shrugged. "I will never feel about anyone the way I felt for Zach. I wouldn't want to. It's too painful. But Julian is offering me a comfortable and stable life." She paused, letting out a small sigh. "So, the answer is, yes, I am considering it. Maybe Zach was right after all. He did see something between us that night, something even I didn't know was there."

"Or something that wasn't there at all, Molly," Mary Rose said gently. "And never can be."

Molly didn't respond.

"Molly," Mary Rose said, leaning forward and touching her hand. "Don't close the door on possibilities. If you have any love left in your heart for Zach, don't close that door."

"If I thought there was any hope at all...," she began, then stopped. She shook her head sadly, then stood and walked to the window overlooking the bay. A moment later, Mary Rose joined her.

"Where there's love, there's hope, Molly," she said softly. "Always."

"I once thought so, too, Mary Rose. But not now."

A few minutes later they said goodbye, and Mary Rose left to join Devon at the train station.

But for a long time, Molly stood at her window, thinking of Zach. Always Zach.

29

THE WEEKS PRECEDING THE ELECTION passed swiftly. Molly's social activities were reported in the *Examiner* almost daily, mentioned as being on the arm of the candidate as they attended political functions, or with Augusta Morgan and the other committee members as they prepared for the Opera House Gala, as it was now being called.

More often now, she and Julian were seen as a couple, and their relationship had become the object of gossip throughout Central California. The rumor was that they would be married before the year's end. A feature article, written after the governor's endorsement dinner in Sacramento, referred to Julian and Molly as the "Golden Couple of the Golden State" and speculated that the coveted guest list for their wedding would include Teddy Roosevelt.

When the day finally arrived and it was announced that Julian Starr had won the election, Molly and Julian were dining with the mayor and his wife in the city. A young reporter burst into the elegant restaurant with the news, shouting it to the entire roomful of Julian's supporters.

Hats soared into the air, and shouts of victory resounded.

Before the hubbub had died down, Julian had taken Molly

into his arms and planted a jubilant kiss on her lips. There was cheering all around, and people called for a speech.

Toasts were made, and Julian moved to the dais at one end of the room to more cheers. Molly stood beside him as he gave his victory speech. When he was finished, another reporter called out: "Kiss your soon-to-be Missus again, Senator, and tell us when the big day is going to be!"

Molly felt her cheeks redden, and Julian looked down at her expectantly.

The room was suddenly silent.

Then, playing to the crowd, Julian bent down and kissed her cheek again. As the cheers went up, reporters scribbled notes in their notebooks.

The headline on the next morning's *Examiner* read, SENA-TOR-ELECT JULIAN STARR CELEBRATES WITH BRIDE-TO-BE. And the article beneath the headline, after laying out the details of the election and its meaning for the state, described in perfect detail the new senator's exuberant embrace with the beautiful Miss Molly Quinn.

Molly was appalled when Victoria Parrott brought her the morning *Examiner.* She'd been caught up in the celebration the night before, and though comments had been made about her relationship with Julian, she'd dismissed them as mere speculation.

Julian had already left for Sacramento on the morning train, so he couldn't help get the newspaper to correct the error. After a few minutes of fuming, she had just about decided to march over to the *Examiner* office herself, when Victoria announced a visitor, Augusta Morgan.

"Darling," Augusta said, breezing in with the tails of her boa flying behind her, "everyone's talking about the news."

"Julian's election?" Molly knew that wasn't the news she meant.

Augusta helped herself to a chair, settling heavily into it. "You know that, of course, I mean the news of your betrothal."

"I haven't said that I'll marry Julian, Augusta. We've made no plans."

Augusta chuckled. "But you haven't said you *won't* marry him, have you?"

Molly shook her head. "No."

"Well, then, dear. Let the public have their heyday. There's no harm in it, is there?"

"I don't appreciate being talked about. The speculation..." She frowned. "It seems that my life is not my own anymore. I've had too many dinners to attend with Julian, too many meetings for the opera house campaign, then with my work here at QIL Enterprises..." She sighed. "I don't remember when I've had an evening to myself, to visit with friends or to sit in front of my fire."

Augusta didn't seem to have heard her. "You'll be having to make a choice soon, won't you, dear?"

"What's that?"

"If you go to Washington in January as Julian's wife, you'll have to give up QIL Enterprises."

As Augusta droned on about Washington, Molly thought about the ongoing difficulties with Winny. Washington, D.C., *would* be a solution to that problem. But she barely considered it. Of course she wouldn't give up QIL Enterprises. In fact, the more she thought about it, the more determined she was to finally settle the speculation about Julian once and for all. It seemed Augusta's busybody questions had made her suddenly aware that she was not going to marry Julian. She hadn't given him an answer to his proposal, but now, with acute clarity, she realized how wrong she'd been to consider marrying him.

And, of course, her indecision had caused great commotion in the Hearst papers and others as well. She needed to be honest with Julian. He deserved that from her. He needed to understand there could never be anything romantic between them. But she said nothing of all that to Augusta.

"As I've told you, Augusta," she said pleasantly, when Augusta paused to take a breath, "we have no plans for the future."

Augusta gave her a knowing smile, and Molly changed the subject to the art auction. The big woman beamed at the mention of the other well-known artists that Molly had lined up to participate. Besides Devon O'Rourke, six others were donating the proceeds from the auction of their works.

"A clever idea, Molly, the unveiling of the newest works by each. The fanfare. I predict the auction will be hugely successful!"

"Thank you," Molly said, as the older woman at last stood to leave. "But if it hadn't been for Devon O'Rourke, I would never have thought of it."

Augusta raised an eyebrow as she wound the ever-present fur boa around her shoulders.

Molly chuckled as she escorted Augusta to the door. "It's a long story." But she didn't go on.

"I have a feeling there's more involved than what you'd care to tell," Augusta said, with a wink. "Or maybe it's more a question of who's involved that you don't care to talk about."

Molly didn't answer.

"Just don't let anything or anyone interfere with your upcoming engagement, dear."

Molly narrowed her eyes. "As I said before, Augusta—"

"I know, I know," the mayor's wife interrupted with a jolly laugh. She lifted a brow again. "It's just that I know a good catch when I see one."

Molly opened the door for the woman to exit. Augusta bussed her cheek with a quick kiss, then sailed from QIL Enterprises' suite of offices.

It was midafternoon when Zach strode from the office of People's Choice cannery. Around him, workers were busily pounding nails into the new headers and removing rust from the old corrugated building. Already the painting had begun at one end. When completed, the building would be a pale gray trimmed in navy blue with a bright red door. He assumed the workers had made the decision, and as he had since the day he first found out Molly's employee-ownership plans, he applauded their initiative.

The inside of the plant was improving as well. New equipment had been installed, even new chutes that reached the fishing boats and ships to make unloading their catches easier.

But it was the spirit of the place that had changed the most. There was a new camaraderie, and workers took pride in their jobs. The transformation was obvious to anyone visiting the cannery.

He looked up at the new sign, with its bright red, white, and blue lettering. PEOPLE'S CHOICE, it read. Zach had heard about the workers' first pick. They'd wanted to name their company after Molly, their new champion. To her credit, he thought, she'd turned it down.

Zach had been offered a cancellation of his contract with the cannery. He knew that it was Molly's doing. For months he'd been planning to walk away from People's Choice if given the opportunity. But when the chance came, he'd decided to stay on to watch the results of her experiment. More often than not nowadays, he approved her every innovation, her every effort on behalf of People's Choice workers.

As he walked along the waterfront, he breathed in the sea air. People passed him, nodding greetings. A horse-drawn buggy rattled along the street, and one of the town's few automobiles putt-putted by, causing the horse to snort and dance sideways.

Then he turned up Alvarado, past the shops and businesses, toward the center of town. He planned to buy a copy of the *Examiner* on his way to the Del Cortés, where he'd be spending the night before sailing north the next day with Devon and Mary Rose.

He had agreed to accompany them to San Francisco to attend the Opera House Gala and auction. And he was planning to see Molly. After talking to Mary Rose about her visit with Molly and searching his soul about his deep feelings for her, he'd finally written.

Zach strode up Alvarado Street, stopping briefly to buy a newspaper from a paperboy on the corner. He tucked it under his arm and headed up the hill toward the Del Cortés.

In his room, he pulled off his shoes and, sighing heavily, settled into a chair near the window. As usual, he'd requested a room with a bay view, and he looked out, trying to spot the *Molly Quinn*. She was anchored a ways out, and he'd rowed in on the tender with Jam. Now he squinted into the hazy sunset, trying to distinguish her from the other schooners.

The earlier mist was moving back onshore, obscuring his view. Even the sun was merely a small orange ball sinking into a pale gray sea.

Zach had been up since before daybreak. He closed his eyes, planning to rest before meeting Mary Rose and Devon in the hotel dining room. But as usual, his thoughts turned to Molly. Within days he would see her. He wondered at her reaction to his letter. He'd heard nothing in response, though that wasn't unexpected. He'd told her he would contact her once he was in San Francisco.

His only nagging thought had to do with Julian Starr. Mary Rose had said that, though the man was trying to court Molly, she'd seen no love between them. And Zach had at last set aside his assumptions about what he'd seen at the Del Cortés that night long ago. But Molly and Julian were together socially and in business. If Julian were elected senator, Molly would make a fine politician's wife, as he was surely aware.

Thinking of the election, Zach remembered the newspaper. Yesterday, the Judiciary Committee had voted on California's next U.S. senator, and he wondered briefly if in fact Julian had won, as most pundits predicted. The paper would tell him.

He stood and walked over to the bed where he'd tossed the *Examiner*, then crossed the room and turned on the light. Settling into the chair again, he flipped the newspaper open to the front page.

The headline stunned him: SENATOR-ELECT JULIAN STARR CELEBRATES WITH BRIDE-TO-BE. His heart seemed to stop beating as he quickly scanned the article. For a long time afterward he sat stunned, unable to move or even to think.

Then, slowly, he crumpled the paper into a ball and threw it into the trash.

How could he have been so foolish? Why hadn't he followed logic instead of his heart?

Grimly, he dressed for his dinner with Mary Rose and Devon, wishing he could back out of the voyage. If it hadn't been too late for them to plan other transportation to San Francisco, there would be no question. But Devon's painting for the auction was already carefully packed aboard the schooner and they were set to sail at sunrise.

He might not be able to get out of the voyage. But attending the Opera House Gala? That was another matter.

One thing was for certain, he would not be meeting with Molly Quinn. He only wished he hadn't posted the letter.

For the first time in weeks, Molly made time to be with Kingsley and Gwennie. Miss Brown had the night off, and Molly looked forward to an intimate evening alone with her dear friends. In honor of the occasion, Cook Liu fixed his minced lamb and rosemary pie.

"We've missed you so," said Gwennie, as they settled into the sitting room after an early dinner.

"And I've missed you both more than you can imagine," Molly said, getting up to kiss Gwen's cheek and give her another hug. "I see Kingsley nearly every day in the office, but it's just not the same."

Kingsley cleared his throat. "Now that we're here together, just family," he said, picking up a copy of the *Examiner* from a nearby table, "Molly, what is this all about? Is there any truth to it?"

She drew in a deep breath. "Julian *has* asked me to marry him."

"Are you considering it?"

Molly shook her head. "He's a good friend, but no, I can't marry him. I've only just realized all the reasons I can't."

"Is one of the reasons Zach, dear?" Gwennie's pale blue eyes seemed to pierce her soul.

Molly might lie to herself, but she couldn't lie to Gwennie. "It has everything to do with him," she finally whispered. "But knowing it doesn't matter as far as Zach is concerned. Whatever was between us is over. That's probably the only reason I considered marrying Julian."

"Maybe it's time for you to see this then, dear," Gwennie said softly. She pulled an envelope from her pocket. "I've had it here for a few weeks now, waiting for the right time to present it. Zach sent it along with a little package of things he'd gathered for Kingsley and me in his travels. He asked me to choose the right time to give it to you." She smiled gently and reached over to pat Molly's hand. "Don't read it here. I want you to go home and curl up in front of the painting you love so much. Then open this letter, Molly, and read it with your heart."

Molly looked at the letter after Gwennie handed it to her. Her name was written in Zach's distinctive scrawl across the front of the envelope. She hesitated, and Gwennie, as if reading her mind, chuckled. "I know you came over intending to read Jane Austen and curl my hair, but dear, tonight I want you to go home. Tomorrow, we can get back to our reading. In fact, I've been meaning to tell you, I've been in the mood for Cervantes lately."

Molly smiled. *Don Quixote?* Gwennie's eclectic reading choices never failed to surprise and delight her.

"Yes, you go now, dear. Tonight I'll dream of tilting at windmills."

As Molly walked along the little path between her house and the Forresters', she wondered if the letter and its symbol of hope and love was just as much a fantasy.

At home, she turned up a table light in the sitting room, placed Zach's letter next to the lamp, then laid a few pieces of wood in the fireplace. As always, when she entered the room, her vision was drawn to *Mary Rose's Garden*. After she lit the fire she looked up at it and felt a sense of peace. What was it that Mary Rose had said? Where there's love, there's hope. She glanced back at the letter and sighed. Just touching the paper on which Zach had written gladdened her heart.

Finally, she settled into a chair and picked up the envelope. Her fingers trembled slightly as she pulled out the two pages, unfolded them, and began to read.

My dearest Molly,

My heart is full as I pen this letter to you. But there is so much I need to say, and I'm not sure these pages will give me adequate space.

First, my dearest, I must ask your forgiveness. I cut myself off from you without giving you a chance to speak from your heart. When last we saw each other in Monterey, I took on the role of judge and jury, sentencing both of us without regard for the witness of your feelings or interpretation of your actions. Please forgive me, Molly, for my blind and arrogant behavior.

Next, I need to tell you that there has not been a moment since Monterey that I have not thought of you, holding you precious and dear in my heart. No matter what transpired between us—or what I thought had transpired—I could not get you out of my mind, Molly. I thought about our time together at the place of the jeweled dawn, and I could not believe you did not mean your words of love to me.

Then, I remembered those things that occurred afterward, and I thought I was holding claim to false hope and counterfeit love. I did my best to stop loving you, but Molly, I've found it quite impossible.

I am writing because I cannot let go of that love until I hear from your lips that my hopes and prayers are impossible. This leads me to my question and primary reason for this missive. Molly, will you see me?

Devon and Mary Rose have asked me to accompany them to the Opera House Gala in December. (They will be sailing with me to San Francisco for the event.) If you agree to see me, perhaps we can meet during this time. The three of us will be staying aboard ship during our visit, but I will be coming into the city to see Gwennie and Kingsley.

I may be at sea when you receive this, so you will not be able to get word of your answer to me. I will contact you when I arrive in San Francisco.

Until then, I will pen the words that have been on my heart so long that they seem to have been etched there—I love you, Molly Quinn, and I believe I always shall.

I remain forever yours,
Zachary MacAlister

Molly didn't realize she was weeping until her tears caused splotches of ink to run. *Oh, my darling,* she breathed clutching the pages close, *I've never stopped loving you. I love you, Zach...I love you.*

The same night, Zach strode into the dining room at the Del Cortés. At the elegantly laid table, Mary Rose and Devon sat waiting.

Mary Rose looked up with a smile as he approached, then frowned when she saw his expression. "Is something wrong?" Devon matched her look of concern.

Zach thrust the wrinkled newspaper toward them. He'd retrieved it from the trash, smoothing it out so they could see the news firsthand. Besides, he'd thought he might choke on the words if he tried to utter them. After all, how could he nonchalantly announce, "Molly's marrying Julian Starr"?

When they'd finished reading the article, Mary Rose spoke first. "I had no idea she would actually marry him."

Devon shook his head slowly. "The night we had dinner with Molly, Julian seemed overly eager to establish some sort of proprietary claim. But I saw no response from Molly. She accepted him as a friend and business partner, but that was the extent of it. Did you think so, Mary Rose?"

She nodded in agreement. "And when I asked her about it the following day, she shrugged it off, as if his attentions— though she clearly understood them—didn't matter. There's got to be some mistake."

"There's been some mistake, all right," Zach muttered. "And I've made the biggest of all."

"The painting for the auction?" Devon frowned. "Do you still want to go through with it?"

"Ahh, yes. The painting." Zach laughed bitterly, shaking his head. "Do we have a choice?"

Mary Rose touched his hand. "No," she said softly. "We really don't."

Devon looked from one to the other. "I disagree. Zach, if you want to pull it out, we will."

Zach shook his head. "I'm sorry I'm sounding so bitter about it all. It's just that the news has knocked me off kilter." He took a deep breath. "In reality, I wouldn't pull it out of the auction now, Dev, for your sake, if for no other reason. The painting's one of your finest works. No matter how I feel, it deserves to be seen."

Devon nodded. "Thank you, friend." But he and Mary Rose exchanged worried glances.

CHAPTER

30

AFTER A WEEK OF HEAVY STORMS, December in San Francisco
began with crystal-clear days, purple skies, and sparkling bay
waters. It had now been nearly three years since the great earthquake of 1906, and San Francisco still held an air of excitement
as carpenters, brick masons, architects, and engineers worked
to rebuild the beautiful city.

The skyline was changing almost daily, with the skeleton
frames of new skyscrapers rising to soaring heights. Some of
the city's favorite landmarks were in various stages of repair or
rebuilding. The new Palace Hotel was still in the planning
stages, designed to be bigger and grander than before.

A new hotel, the Queen Victoria, had been completed in the
fall, and San Franciscans were proud of its courtly design and
how it symbolized the city's return to its former look of afflu-
ence and economic well-being. The towering structure was
built on a hill overlooking the bay, with terraces surrounding its
downstairs ballrooms and banquet halls. Every detail, from the
crystal chandeliers to the ornate gold-leaf fixtures, from the
Persian carpets to the seven-foot Chinese vases of fresh-cut sea-
sonal flowers, spoke of tasteful elegance. The rectangular structure was built around a cobbled courtyard with bubbling

brooks, water fountains, and sculptured gardens.

Molly and the planning committee chose the grand banquet room and adjoining ballroom of the Queen Victoria for the Opera House Gala. San Franciscans, proud of their world-famous opera company, had responded in overwhelming numbers when they received their invitations. Though the cost per ticket was in the hundreds of dollars, more than a thousand people were expected to attend.

As the time grew near, even though Molly was wrapped up in the final details of the affair, she waited with growing anticipation to hear from Zach. But the days before the Christmas gala quickly passed, and there was no word from Mary Rose, Devon, or Zach.

Augusta approached her the day before the gala. "Have all the artists arrived with their paintings?" she asked.

"All but one," Molly replied absently, as she directed workers to move a large curtained easel onto the dais. "Strangely, it's Devon O'Rourke."

Augusta didn't look concerned. "As long as he gets here before tomorrow night. Have you seen the other works?"

"No. They're being stored in the hotel's vault. They'll not be revealed until the auction."

"The curtain's a nice touch." She nodded to the easel on the platform.

Molly smiled. "I just hope the bids are high enough to give the artists satisfaction and bring in funds for our cause."

She looked up in surprise to see Julian walking across the large ballroom to where she stood talking with Augusta. She'd given him her answer about marriage days earlier, and he'd taken it in stride, asking only that they keep the news to themselves until he left for Washington. Knowing that it was important for him politically to save face, she'd agreed, hugely relieved that he'd accepted her decision with such grace.

"I'm at your beck and call," he announced grandly as Augusta, after winking at Molly, busied herself with a flower arrangement. "How can I help?"

Molly smiled. He'd been a great support already, agreeing to split the duties of hosting the event with the mayor, Augusta's husband, Radcliff Morgan. He'd also offered advice on the hire of a professional auctioneer from Sacramento to handle the artwork and put the committee in touch with a small ensemble from the San Francisco Symphony Orchestra to play during dinner and later to provide music for dancing.

"I don't know what I'd do without you," she said.

He gave her a wry look, and Molly took his arm as they walked across the ballroom floor toward the vault, asking him to see about the paintings in the vault. Some artists had brought more than one work, and she needed to know the exact number. They had just about reached the doorway dividing the ballroom from the banquet area, when Julian stopped.

"There's Devon O'Rourke now," he said. "And Mary Rose."

Molly looked through the open hallway toward the elaborate, chandeliered entrance to the Queen Victoria. Julian was right. The young couple, after asking directions from a uniformed concierge, turned and spotted Molly and Julian. Mary Rose waved and, Devon beside her, hurried toward them.

The two women hugged. "It's so good to see you again, Molly!" Mary Rose exclaimed, as Julian and Devon shook hands. "It seemed to take forever to get here. We were delayed off the coast by last week's storms."

"You came on the *Molly Quinn?*" Julian asked.

Molly noticed that something flickered in Mary Rose's eyes, then quickly disappeared. "Yes," she said. "Zach brought us."

"Where...where is he now?" Molly asked, feeling breathless in her desire to see him. Again, she noticed an unreadable expression crossing Mary Rose's face.

"He's still aboard the schooner," Devon said. Molly wondered if she imagined a coolness in him.

For an awkward moment no one spoke. "Well," Molly said, finally. "We'd better see to the painting. Is it with you?"

"We've made arrangements for its delivery tomorrow," said Mary Rose. "It's scheduled to be brought here by noon, if that's all right."

Julian joined them to explain the procedure for the following day, pointing out where they would be seated with the artists and dignitaries during the banquet and auction.

After a few minutes, Mary Rose and Devon told Molly goodbye and exited the room, walking with Julian toward the front office so that he could show them the location of the vault.

Molly watched them leave, wondering about the disquiet that had so suddenly swept over her. She tried to push it aside, remembering the words Zach had penned in his letter, words she'd practically memorized, especially his words of love.

She sighed, dismissing her fears. Instead, she concentrated on being in his arms again. And smiling to herself, she went back to work.

When Molly still hadn't heard from Zach the following afternoon, she knew something was terribly amiss. Even Gwennie and Kingsley hadn't seen him or heard anything from him.

As she began preparing for the evening, Molly consoled

herself, thinking that Zach probably planned to see her at the gala.

She laid her gown across her bed. It was white, fashioned of organza and Swiss lace. Its high collar was lace trimmed, and its sleeves circled her slim arms, with luscious fullness at her shoulders and lace at her wrists, matching that of the collar. Tiny pleats fell from the gown's neckline to her ankles, interrupted only by a wide embroidered lace trim at the hem. A matching cape, sleeveless to show off the full sleeves, would add a look of royalty.

Molly swept her hair upward, fastened it high, then wove a delicate crown of pearls among the loose plaits. When she finished, she pulled on the gown and satin shoes, then looked in the mirror as she added a touch of lip rouge. The white gown was a perfect contrast to her dark hair. There was soft color in her porcelain skin, due, she thought, to the prospect of seeing Zach.

Julian called for her at six o'clock, and though the gala wouldn't begin until seven o'clock, they both needed to arrive early to oversee the last-minute details.

"Has the O'Rourke painting been delivered?" she asked, as he helped her into her cape.

"Yes, around eleven this morning. It's in the vault, safe and sound." He opened the door for her, and they walked down the little path, through her garden, toward his automobile. Molly was glad to see he'd lifted the top so they wouldn't get blown to pieces by the wind.

It was already dark, and soon Julian turned the vehicle up the drive to the stately hotel. Victorian streetlights flanked the avenue leading to the immense portico entrance. Already a queue of horse-drawn carriages and motorcars had formed along the street, awaiting the hotel's formally dressed valets.

The auto idled in line for several minutes, then Julian at last pulled up to the portico. He had just escorted Molly into the lobby with its gold-leaf and crystal chandeliers, gleaming marble floors, and Persian rugs when she looked up, sensing she was being watched.

She glanced about, scanning the groups of chatting women in their floating gossamer gowns, their escorts in top hats and formal suits.

Then, her gaze halted on a man who stood watching her from across the room, leaning against a pillar, legs casually crossed at the ankles, arms crossed at his chest.

Her heart skipped a beat, and heat flooded her face.

His eyes met hers.

She'd never seen Zach dressed in such elegant attire. He was wearing a high-collared shirt, gray silk ascot, top hat, and an exquisitely cut jacket. Molly swallowed hard. Zachary Mac-Alister, captain of the *Molly Quinn*, had disappeared. Tonight, he was truly the son of an English duke.

Zach made no move to approach her. And Molly stood rooted to the spot just beneath the huge crystal chandelier. She wanted to run to him, feel his arms around her, hear his husky voice whisper in her ear. But something stopped her from moving at all, from smiling or acknowledging that she'd seen him. It was the expression in his eyes, even from the distance that separated them, that chilled her.

In that moment of silent communication between them, she knew that she'd lost him. Whatever he'd written in her letter no longer mattered, because something within him had changed toward her.

Beside Molly, Julian had stopped to speak to a group of

friends from Sacramento. She heard the sound of his laughter in response to an aside someone uttered.

Julian.

A sinking realization sickened her. *Julian.* Of course. That was it. Zach had somehow heard the mistaken news of their engagement. That's why she hadn't heard from him. That's why he'd given her the cold look from across the room.

Without a word of explanation, she left the group of people who'd gathered to speak to Julian. She hurried to the place where she'd seen Zach moments earlier, but he was gone.

She had to find him. She had to explain what had happened. She remembered the night at the opera when he'd left before its conclusion after seeing her with Julian. She couldn't let that happen again.

She wound her way among the gathering guests, smiling and chatting, but always looking for Zach. Dozens of people stood talking in small groups. Cheerful laughter carried across the lobby and down the wide hall.

Then her attention was temporarily diverted by Mayor Radcliff Morgan, graying and dignified, and Augusta, in a bright, lusciously plumed hat, strolling toward her with Julian. The four stood together commenting on the numbers of gathering guests, then Radcliff and Julian spoke of the evening ahead, comparing notes for their shared master-of-ceremony roles.

After a few minutes, Julian took Molly's arm again as the two couples walked toward the banquet hall. Molly searched the faces in the growing crowd, but still, she couldn't see Zach anywhere.

The banquet hall was breathtakingly beautiful. Six chandeliers hung from recessed alcoves in the elegant mirrored ceiling. A long row of tables had been set near the dais, for the masters of ceremonies, artists, and dignitaries. Besides Mayor Radcliff Morgan, the governor would be in attendance, as well as state senators and members of the Assembly, Julian as one of the two U.S. senators, city government officials, and the opera house rebuilding committee members.

In the main hall, round tables had been set with linen cloths. At the center of each was a candle surrounded by pine boughs, cones, and white-and-gold ribbons. Each table was laid for ten, and seating for hundreds spread across the huge room in a sea of candlelight, sparkling china, crystal, and silver.

Molly, Julian, the mayor, and Augusta entered the banquet hall. After finding their seats at the head table, Radcliff and Augusta moved away to welcome city officials they had spotted hesitating near the entrance. Molly and Julian circulated, welcoming the artists and showing them to their places.

At last, Mary Rose and Devon entered the room, and Molly hurried over to greet them. Mary Rose looked beautiful in a simple pale green gown, setting off her blond curls and gray-green eyes. She smiled at Molly, and on Devon's arm, followed Molly to the head table.

After they'd reached their places, Mary Rose touched Molly's arm. "Molly," she said, her voice low. "There are three of us. Is there room?"

"Zach's with you?"

Mary Rose nodded, her expression giving nothing away.

"I saw him in the lobby." She swallowed hard. "Of course he can join you." Molly didn't add that she and Julian would be seated across from them.

One of the other artists, a friend of Devon's, joined them, discussing the festivities excitedly. He was especially complimentary of Molly's idea for the auction and the opportunity to participate. Gradually, other artists and their families joined the circle, and Molly excused herself, moving on to another group. As ever, she watched for Zach.

By seven o'clock the elegant banquet hall was filled. The mayor, Julian, and the opera house rebuilding committee members stepped onto the dais.

The mayor introduced Julian Starr as the state's newest U.S. senator, friend of San Francisco and the rebuilding efforts throughout the city. When he mentioned that Julian was a special friend to the opera house rebuilding committee, someone at one of the front tables quipped, "especially to one particular committee member." Molly felt her cheeks redden. There was laughter from those who'd heard the man's words. Julian grinned, acknowledging the man's comments, as he took his place behind the lectern and made the rest of the introductions. Then he greeted the crowd on behalf of the entire opera house committee and called for Father Timothy Ryan, an Episcopal priest, to come forward to give the invocation.

At the prayer's conclusion, Julian took Molly's arm as they stepped from the platform. As they moved to their places at the head table, people called out their congratulations to the new senator and there was a smattering of applause.

"Good show! We knew you were the best man for the job," an older man said as they moved by, and Julian nodded graciously. "Good luck in Washington," a younger woman called out, and Julian smiled as they finally reached their seats.

Julian pulled out Molly's chair, waited for her to settle into it, then sat down next to her. Molly, almost afraid to look, finally gazed around at the other nearby guests, recognizing most of them. She surveyed the seats to her left, nodding and smiling at two rather Bohemian-looking artists who were seated directly across from Julian and herself. Two others, more conservative in their dress, were seated adjacent to them. As she expected, Radcliff and Augusta were seated on Julian's left.

Mary Rose and Devon smiled at her from across the table. But her vision moved no further than the guest seated next to them.

Zach's cool, assessing gaze met hers. She wondered how she could possibly break through the emotional barrier he'd raised, long enough to explain her relationship with Julian. For a moment that seemed to last through eternity, they stared at each other, until at last, Mary Rose spoke.

"Molly," she said. "I didn't have a chance to tell you earlier, but you look absolutely radiant tonight."

Molly gave her a small grateful smile. "Thank you, Mary Rose. I was about to tell you the same thing."

Then conversation across the large hall quieted as the small ensemble of violins, violas, a cello, and flutes seated near the dais began playing a Mozart aria. A small army of servers entered the room, silver trays in hand, and moved to the various tables.

Several waiters assigned to the head table set their covered trays on nearby stands and began to serve the first course. As the supper progressed, all around Molly, the guests praised the chefs' creations, the French wines, and exquisite breads and pastries. But to her it was all a blur. The death of hope made every bite taste like ashes in her mouth. Unable to bear looking at Zach, she kept her attention to the left side of the table, speaking mostly to Julian and the Morgans.

At last dinner was over, and as people lingered over their coffees, teas, or port wines, Julian and Radcliff again took their places on the platform. One by one, the artists were introduced and asked to join the others on the dais.

Devon was last and rose to stride to the podium as he was being introduced.

Julian told the audience of Devon O'Rourke's work painting light, achieving what few others had been able to do with oils. He mentioned the *Hope,* that many of the guests had seen at the Capitol, and Molly could hear words of excitement and awe from some of the guests seated nearby.

Molly glanced at Mary Rose, whose love and pride shone as brightly as lamplight on her face. She smiled at her friend's expression, so wondrously glad she was for the young couple. They'd discovered, and were holding onto, something very precious. She sensed Zach watching her, and for a heartbeat, she caught his eye before turning her attention back to the podium.

Julian introduced the auctioneer, who detailed the rules of the auction. Then he nodded to a couple of uniformed security officers at the room's wide doorway. The men disappeared for a short time, then reentered carrying the first painting.

It was set on the large easel on the dais, still draped, and the crowd hushed in anticipation. The auctioneer told about the artist and his other works, mentioning the prices for which they'd sold. He gave the painting's title and the starting bid amount, briefly mentioned the rules again, then with a grand flourish, lifted the drape from the painting, a bright rendition of San Francisco waterfront before the earthquake, done in the style of Gauguin.

Sounds of awe carried through the room, and the bidding began. Molly was surprised that the bidding so rapidly increased. It was beyond all her expectations. Augusta Morgan leaned forward and caught her attention, lifting a pleased brow when the painting finally sold for more than twice the expected bid.

Molly settled back to watch the activities proceed with the second painting, a still life. The auctioneer spoke of the texture, lines, shapes, and color values. It was a magnificent piece, and the bidding increased as rapidly as it had with the first painting.

As each painting was brought out, the excitement seemed to grow in the room. Again and again, Augusta looked over at Molly, her face a wreath of gladness and awe. By the time the draped O'Rourke was carried to the easel, Molly had lost count of the money already raised for the opera house.

"This next painting," the auctioneer began, "is a Devon O'Rourke. As you heard when he was introduced, O'Rourke is becoming known throughout the state as a painter of light. His works are already being compared to some of the great masters. We are privileged to have even one of his works with us tonight." He cleared his throat and checked his notes before continuing. "He has titled this work *The Jeweled Dawn.*"

He went on to give the opening bid, but Molly wasn't listening. She shot a glance at Zach to see if he was as surprised as she by the painting's title. But his expressionless gaze was locked on the auctioneer. Then Molly looked to Mary Rose, but in her excitement, she had eyes only for Devon, still seated on the dais.

"And now for the unveiling," the auctioneer said, with a flourish. The drape was lifted, and there were sounds of approval and awe from throughout the room. The bidding began.

But Molly sat, stunned. The painting was of a dark haired young woman dressed in white, standing on the rocky cliffs overlooking the sea. Behind her was a meadow filled with wildflowers, rimmed by the dark and mysterious Monterey pines. A doe and two fawns grazed there, barely visible among the pale green grasses. A blue-green mirror reflecting prisms of light resembling jewels. Though the woman's face wasn't clearly visible, Molly knew without a doubt who it was.

She turned to Zach with questioning eyes, but still he refused to meet her gaze. Around her, the hubbub of frenzied bidding continued.

Suddenly, Molly understood. Zach had commissioned the painting. She remembered now that Devon and Mary Rose had mentioned it the night they found out about the sale of the *Hope*. They'd also said that the person who'd commissioned the work had changed his mind, which left the painting available for the auction.

That Zach would allow it to be sold before her eyes spoke greater volumes than any words of contempt he could utter.

The place of the jeweled dawn was precious and known only to them. She had thought until now that it was as sacred to Zach as it was to her.

She couldn't sit in his presence a moment longer. The bidding was still in progress, but Molly didn't care. Blinded by tears, she stood, not caring what anyone in the room might think, even if they did notice her departure, and swiftly made her way to the exit.

Fighting to keep her composure, she swept through the wide doorway and into the hall. Wanting simply to be alone in her grief, she walked hurriedly to the grand ballroom, thinking it would be empty. But the ensemble was setting up to play for the ball that would immediately follow the auction.

Seeing that the large stone terrace just outside the ballroom was dark. Molly hurried through the glass doors, struggling to catch a breath, trying to stop the threatening flood of tears, when she heard footsteps behind her. She didn't turn, hoping that the intruder would move on, leaving her alone.

Blinking back her tears, she looked out at the gardens beyond the terrace, her back still turned.

"Molly…"

It was Zach. Her back stiffened, and she continued to gaze into the dark gardens, unwilling to face him.

"Molly," he said again, and she could hear him moving closer.

At last she turned.

31

"MOLLY," ZACH SAID AGAIN, MOVING CLOSER.

Molly drew in a deep, shaky breath and raised her eyes to his. "What has happened to us?" Her voice was little more than a ragged whisper.

For a moment, he didn't speak. "Will you walk with me?" he finally asked. "In a few minutes we won't have much privacy."

She nodded, and placing his arm around her shoulders, he gently turned her toward the terrace stairs leading into the dark garden. They walked in silence along the stone path until they reached a clearing. A three-tiered marble fountain, a sculpted cherub gracing its crown, was at the center of the clearing, circled by clay pots filled with winter flowers.

Zach stopped near the fountain, and Molly turned toward him. "Your letter...," she began. Then her voice faltered. She didn't know how to go on.

"I meant everything I said in it, Molly. Every word."

"I thought you wanted to talk with me, that you were going to contact me. Then tonight I saw the look in your eyes, and I knew I'd been mistaken."

"After the news of your engagement to Julian, I thought there wouldn't be any point to it."

"So it *was* Julian," she mused, half to herself. For a moment only the sounds of the fountain's cascading waters could be heard in the garden. "There was—no, there *is* no betrothal between Julian and me," she said. "And there never has been. He is my business colleague and friend. Nothing more."

"The *Examiner* was wrong, then..."

"Oh, yes. Terribly wrong. The whole thing has been a source of embarrassment to Julian and me. If we'd made them print a retraction, we felt it would cause even greater attention, so we just let it go."

"I should have come to you." Zach's face, even in the dim light of the garden, reflected his deep anguish. "But I reacted with my heart, not my mind. I'd poured out my soul in my letter to you. When I read the news of your coming marriage to Julian, all I could think of was how foolish I'd been, how foolish you must think me."

Molly concentrated on the fountain, turning away from Zach and trying to make sense of her own thoughts. The night air was cool and crisp. A mist off the ocean had begun lacing itself through the garden's shrubs and trees, and in the distance, an owl hooted.

"What about the painting, Zach?" she asked, turning back to him. "*The Jeweled Dawn?* You commissioned it?"

"Yes." But he didn't elaborate.

"Then why did you allow it to be auctioned here?" She didn't think anything he could say would help her understand.

He looked at her from across the clearing, making no move to draw closer. His expression was sad. "I had asked Devon to paint it a long time ago, Molly. Then things changed between us, and I didn't think I could bear looking at it. When the opportunity came for a presentation here, I gave him my blessing."

"But it's of our sacred place…" Her voice faltered, and she swallowed hard before going on. "When I saw the painting tonight, dreams and memories and love all seemed to turn into ashes." She searched his face for understanding.

Now Zach moved nearer, so near that she could almost reach out and touch him. Then he stopped, his gaze never leaving hers. "Our sacred place." He repeated her words softly. "After all that's happened between us—my foolishness, the silence?" He paused. "You still think of it that way?"

She gave him a small smile. "Yes," she whispered.

He moved closer still and touched her cheek with his fingertips. Molly caught her breath, feeling her heart thudding beneath her ribs. His touch was gentle, and the expression on his face spoke of wonder. She remained motionless, and his touch moved to her temple where he brushed back a dark tendril. Then he traced the backs of his fingers along her jaw, and she reached up to take his hand.

She opened it and gently rubbed his calluses with her thumb. Then lifting his hand to her lips, she kissed his palm, her eyes never leaving his.

In the distance, the music of the ballroom ensemble drifted toward them, blending with the bubbling water of the fountain.

Zach drew Molly closer, and her arms slid around him. His voice was husky when he breathed her name. "Molly," he said, "I don't ever want to be without you again."

Then he lowered his head and kissed her. Molly melted into his embrace, feeling her heart pound wildly.

After a moment she pulled back and, smiling into his eyes, reached up to touch his face, marveling at the strength she saw in it. "I'm the one who's been foolish," she whispered. "I should have realized—"

But Zach touched her lips, not letting her continue. "No, Molly. You're not at fault. The distance between us, the time that passes so quickly, not seeing each other to communicate, to reach out to each other—those things are equally at fault." He frowned. "I don't know how we can go on like this."

Molly let out a small sigh. "I don't either, Zach." She considered him a moment. "You once said you'd give me time to dream my dreams." She laughed lightly, thinking of how she'd often thought she wouldn't give up QIL Enterprises for Julian, for anyone. "I think, dearest, that it's time to make some changes in my life."

Surprise registered on Zach's face. "I think you need to explain, Molly, before I jump to some very serious conclusions."

"Give me some time to 'get my house in order' at QIL Enterprises."

He frowned. "I don't want you to give up your life's dream for me. You've been hugely successful, and from what I hear, QIL Enterprises is growing by leaps and bounds. Are you sure you want to walk away from the company you built?"

She laughed lightly. "Actually, I wasn't considering walking away entirely. I just need to think about a compromise, something that will allow me to do it all." Feeling better than she had in weeks, she flashed him a smile. "Can you give me a few months to figure it out?"

"If anyone can figure it out, it's you, Molly Quinn." And he pulled her into his arms again. "It's you," he murmured into her hair.

Standing on tiptoe, Molly reached up to cup his face with her hands. She traced his lips lightly with her fingers, then kissed the corner of his mouth. She could feel his heart pounding beneath his ribs. For an endless moment, neither of them moved. Then their lips met again.

"I love you," Molly said finally, looking into his eyes and feeling herself sink into their depths.

His arms again curled her into an embrace. "I need to ask you something." His expression was serious.

She nodded.

He drew in a deep breath. "I can't imagine a lifetime without you. Even after I thought you were going to marry Julian, I entertained the idea of sailing up here and stealing you away."

Molly laughed softly. "My knight in shining armor. I would love to have seen it." She touched his cheek. "And your question?" she asked, though she thought she knew.

"Will you be my wife, Molly?"

Molly regarded him silently, almost afraid to breathe because the moment was so precious.

"No, wait," Zach said. "Don't answer yet." He brushed a thick strand of hair back from his forehead, grinning. Then capturing her hand, he led her to a stone bench near the water fountain. He laid his coat carefully across it, and as he gave her a small bow, she settled onto the bench.

His expression serious, he dropped to one knee before Molly, her hand still resting gently in his. He kissed her fingertips, then looked into her eyes. "Molly Quinn," he said, his voice hoarse, "will you marry me?"

Molly regarded Zach. Emotions deeper than she'd ever known welled from someplace inside. She considered how, just a short time ago, she'd thought she'd lost him. That knowledge made this moment even more precious. She lifted his hand to her lips. "My beloved...," she breathed. "Yes...Oh, yes!"

A wide smile spread across Zach's face, then he stood and,

his arm cradling her, gently drew her to her feet. "I love you, Molly," he whispered and kissed her again. "How I love you!"

The guests had now filed into the ballroom behind them, and the ensemble began their music for dancing. The strains of it spilled into the garden, mixed with the sounds of laughter and festive voices. Nearby, the water rivulets splashed in the fountain and an owl called from the top of a pine.

Zach gathered her into his arms and they began to dance, Molly's cheek against his shoulder. As they waltzed, and later as they sat in the garden, they spoke of their future: Zach's return to Monterey and Molly's disposition of QIL Enterprises.

She told Zach about Winny and the board of directors, and the problems that she needed to resolve before changing her position in the company. "I've already told the board that I'll step down if Winny doesn't agree to leaving the country," she said.

"Wouldn't it be a logical step?"

Molly shook her head uncertainly. "Perhaps, but I've got to see it through to the end. I don't want to leave defeated. I want QIL Enterprises to be in its healthiest position ever."

"Do you want to continue as part of the company?"

She nodded. "Besides staying on the board, I'd like to run People's Choice." Then she looked up at him, smiling a bit coquettishly. "That is, Zach, if you don't mind tearing up your contract. I'm told you haven't done it yet."

He looked at her affectionately. "I'm so proud of your ideas, your way of running things, that I've moved past any concerns I might have mentioned before."

"Concerns? If I may quote you, dear sir, you said that any involvement I might have in your company would destroy our relationship."

He looked sheepish. "As I said, that was before I'd seen Molly Quinn in action."

Molly's tone was serious when she spoke again. "Zach, I never had a chance to tell you, but I didn't know when I bought Cabrillo that it was your cannery. I wouldn't have done it, otherwise."

"I know that now, Molly. But that wasn't what distressed me most."

She drew in a troubled breath. "Mary Rose told me what you saw that night between Julian and me." He raised a hand to stop her from going on, but she shook her head. "No, my relationship with him has caused too many difficulties between us. You need to hear this."

"All right."

"Julian has been a steady influence on QIL Enterprises from the very beginning. I began this company as a novice." She shook her head. "I was so naive. I dreamed of investing in a small company that would eventually expand. I thought I would have plenty of time to experiment, study the markets, learn what I was doing. But along came the earthquake, and with it, opportunities for people like me, with a dream and a bit of cash to dream with to start a successful business. That same opportunity also created rapid growth, so rapid that I didn't have time for the studying and experimenting I needed to do.

"Then along came Julian, with people to join me as investment partners, with advice, with legal expertise. I counted on him, and he's been a solid and faithful friend and advisor." She sighed, watching Zach's expression as she spoke. "But he wanted more from the relationship than that."

Zach remained silent, and Molly continued. "That night you

saw us at the Del Cortés, he'd just told me of his growing affection." She lifted her eyes to meet Zach's. "I told him that there
was someone else, someone I would love until the day I died."

"I'm sorry, Molly. I didn't know."

"After you turned away from me, Julian and I did begin seeing each other socially. He even asked me to marry him."

"Did you consider it?"

She smiled. "I never said yes, though, as you know, we were
linked together romantically in the papers." She touched his
hand. "That's all, Zach. There was nothing more."

Taking her hand, Zach drew her again into his embrace.
"I'm glad you told me, Molly," he murmured.

"I don't ever want anything like this to come between us
again, Zach. The hurt is too great when love is so deep."

"How well I know," he breathed. For a long time, they stood
holding each other, listening to the distant music and laughter.
Then he turned Molly gently, and with his arm still circling her,
they walked back up the path, across the stone terrace, and into
the ballroom. The chandeliers had been turned low. Millions of
tiny reflected lights danced across the ceiling's recessed mirrors.

Zach pulled Molly into his arms once more, and they began
to dance among the other couples. Within minutes, however, it
was evident that they were causing quite a stir. But Molly didn't
care what anyone thought about the woman they assumed was
their new senator's bride-to-be. All she cared about was the
man who held her in his arms.

Suddenly, Augusta Morgan appeared at Molly's elbow, halt-
ing their dance. After Molly introduced her to Zach, she
exclaimed, "Dear! Wherever have you been hiding? I've scoured
the premises looking for you."

Molly glanced at Zach, who stifled a grin.

But Augusta didn't give Molly a chance to answer. "I saw you leave before *The Jeweled Dawn* was auctioned off. Have you heard about its selling price?" Her voice was filled with awe.

Molly shook her head, and Augusta proceeded to tell them both. Molly's mouth fell open. Augusta beamed, pleased to be first with the astounding news.

When the woman moved on, Molly turned to Zach. "I didn't wish it because of Devon and Mary Rose, but I had hoped it wouldn't sell."

Zach drew her again into his arms, and they began to dance to a Strauss waltz. The music swelled around them. "I know, dearest," he murmured. "Though I'm not surprised it sold for such an enormous sum. I think it's Devon's finest work."

A short distance from Zach and Molly, another couple whirled around the dance floor.

Devon looked down at Mary Rose as they moved to the waltz. Her gaze met his, and he smiled into her sea-green eyes, nearly feeling lost in their depths.

"I am the most blessed of men," he said.

"Because of *The Jeweled Dawn's* sale?" she asked.

"No," he said, "because you're here with me, in my arms. God has been good to us, Mary Rose. A year ago I would never have thought tonight would be possible, as an artist, as your future husband."

"I never gave up hoping things would work out, Dev, for your art, for us to be together. But this is beyond anything I could have dreamed." She looked around at the ballroom. "Though I wonder about it all. The gala is for a good cause. I have no doubt about that." She frowned. "But the grandeur seems somehow false. When I think of real beauty, I don't picture chandeliers or ornate gold sculptures of cherubs and angels and scrollwork."

Devon watched her expression. He loved listening to her thoughts. More often than not, her ideas echoed feelings he'd never put into words. Soul mates. That's how he'd grown to think of this woman God had chosen for him. Mary Rose was his soul mate.

They moved to the music, whirling and stepping with the other couples. The Strauss waltz rose to a crescendo, and Devon pulled Mary Rose closer, marveling at her light-footed grace.

She continued. "There's no greater beauty than what God has created," she said, looking up at him. "Or what is reflected in art like yours."

He chuckled softly, knowing where she was headed. "What I think you're trying to tell me, Mary Rose, is that you'd rather be in your garden than whirling among celebrities and dignitaries in California's most elegant ballroom."

She laughed. "You're right. I'd rather be working in my garden, or standing in your studio as you create another masterpiece. Or watching Jesse's face as he turns over a seashell. The simplest things are the most beautiful."

"How do you know my own heart so well?" he mused. He pulled her closer as the waltz came to an end and rested his cheek against her head.

"Have you noticed Molly and Zach?" Mary Rose asked as the music stopped.

Devon looked over at the couple who, as if they were the only two people in the room, gazed adoringly into each other's faces.

He smiled. "It seems they've discovered the love they thought they'd lost."

"Just as we almost did."

Devon nodded slowly, drawing Mary Rose into his arms as the music began again.

"Do you think he'll tell her?" Mary Rose asked.

"About *The Jeweled Dawn?*" He raised an eyebrow. "I'm sure when the time is right, he'll tell her what happened."

Mary Rose let out a small sigh. "I'm still in awe about how God has used your work to bring us all together, Dev." She watched Molly and Zach moving to the music, Molly now leaning her head against Zach's shoulder. "I consider them both so dear."

"I don't think God's finished with us yet, Mary Rose. With my art, its influence on us all." He frowned. "Or with his influence in our lives, with the intertwining of our friendships and loves."

She laughed softly. "I don't think he ever will be."

Devon's gaze moved from Molly and Zach dancing under the glitter of lights to where Senator-elect Julian Starr stood watching the couple, legs and arms crossed, a dark look on his handsome face.

The intertwining of their lives also had brought a tangle of separate stories, unsolved problems, uncertain futures. Oh, yes. There was more ahead for them all. Devon wondered why a chill suddenly traveled up his spine.

He cradled Mary Rose in his arms, and again they began to dance. As the music from the violins and flutes and cellos drifted toward them, Devon prayed silently for them all, especially for Molly and Zach.

THE DAWN

1909

I will build you with stones of turquoise,
your foundations with sapphires.
I will make your battlements of rubies,
your gates of sparkling jewels,
and all your walls of precious stones.

ISAIAH 54:11,12, NIV

CHAPTER

32

MOLLY LOOKED FROM HER OFFICE WINDOW toward the waterfront and the bay beyond. It had rained steadily for days following Zach's departure for Monterey, and her heart felt as dark as the gray skies, she missed him so.

During the past few weeks, she'd thrown herself into the work at QIL with renewed zeal, preparing for the spring board meeting, especially for the presentation of her ideas concerning the company's future.

Her goal now was to free herself of running QIL in San Francisco. She had devised a plan for the board in which she would be involved from a distance, perhaps journeying from Monterey to San Francisco four times a year for board meetings. She planned to recommend that Kingsley take her place as president of QIL. She still owned the majority of shares, giving her leverage. Of course, Winny still posed a problem that could change the balance of power.

Julian was due to meet her at any moment. He had kept a distance since the gala, and she knew he had been distressed by the sudden turn of events with Zach. But she hoped their easy friendship would be reestablished as they worked together. It would be difficult to break the news of her upcoming marriage, but nonetheless, it had to be done. And though he was no longer formally on retainer, she needed his help to implement her plan.

A light knock sounded at the door.

"Come in." She turned as Victoria Parrott opened the door a few inches.

"Senator Starr to see you, Molly."

"Thank you, Victoria. Send him in, please." It would be the first time she had seen him since he was sworn in. She stood to greet him.

A moment later, Julian strode through the door. "Molly," he said formally, with a nod.

"Julian," she said, noticing his cool, assessing look. "Please, come in and sit down." She walked with him to the sitting area. "How have you been, Julian? It's been weeks since I've seen you."

"Busy," he said. "I'm leaving for Washington within days."

She smiled, trying to break the ice. "That's right, Senator," she said. "A new life is about to begin."

But he didn't smile in return. "Molly, you've asked me here for a purpose. Let's get on with it, shall we? I'm sorry, but I really don't have much time."

Molly nodded, attempting to overlook the rebuff. "I need your advice, Julian. I'm planning to step down as head of QIL Enterprises, and I've come up with a plan to present to the board."

"Step down?" He raised an eyebrow, and his words were heavy with sarcasm when he continued. "I didn't think I'd ever see that happen. May I ask, to what do we owe this turn of events?"

Molly stood, not knowing whether to dismiss him curtly, without his advice, or to attempt to smooth his obviously ruffled feathers. She walked to the window by her desk and looked out.

"I'm sorry, Molly," he said finally. He stood and moved

toward her. She turned and saw an unreadable expression in his face. "This hasn't been an easy time for me. I won't go into all the reasons, but I've come here to help you. Please let me know how I can do that."

She nodded. "All right. I'll get right to it, Julian. I'm getting married in the spring." Something dark flickered behind his eyes, but she hurried on. "I'll be living in Monterey. I've come up with a plan for QIL in which I can still be actively involved from a distance, travel here a few times during the year, run part of the company from there. I'd like you to take a look at it, let me know the feasibility, the legalities...." She smiled.

"Do you have it written out?"

She nodded and handed him the draft plan. He took it, already beginning to read, and walked back to the settee. She followed and sat across from him.

After several minutes, he looked up with a slow nod. "It looks good, Molly. As usual."

"Thank you. But what's your guess about the board's reaction?"

"I think that this," he thumped the papers, still in his hand, "is the least of your worries right now with QIL."

"You're referring to Winny?"

He nodded. "We both know his capabilities."

"Have you seen him recently?" Molly asked.

"I can't afford to be seen visiting a felon. I haven't seen him since the election."

"I've seen him once," Molly said. "He still refuses to accept going to Australia. In fact, his threats are even more blatant. He's saying that he may not wait for his release to come after his part of QIL Enterprises." She drew in a deep breath. "He's changed. He's a bitter, angry man. I never thought he'd turn against me. We were once so close."

"Anger can spark strange emotions in people," Julian said. Something in his expression made her think he spoke of himself, not Winny.

"I don't know what else to offer him. If he carries out his threats, all of QII's investors would suffer, not just me."

"Then it seems obvious, Molly, that you should step down." Julian's voice was cold. "You want a lesser role anyway. Why not walk away from QIL altogether?"

She leaned forward earnestly, trying to break through his bitterness. "Julian, you of all people know what this company means to me. I refuse to be blackmailed into leaving. I don't want to hurt our investors, but I can't walk away from QIL that way."

He nodded slowly. "You may not have a choice, Molly." He narrowed his eyes. Then, taking a deep breath, he settled back and crossed his legs. "What then?" he asked, lifting a brow.

"I only hope I don't have to make that decision," she said evenly. After a moment of uncomfortable silence, she spoke again. "What is your advice about my proposal, Julian, if any?"

He shrugged. "I suppose I have none. Everything is in order. I can't see any reason for the board to object."

"And about Winny?"

"That's a more difficult issue. I would advise you not to see him again in person. Write him, if you like, with threats of your own, perhaps."

"Threats?"

"It could be that's the only language he understands."

"What kinds of threats are you talking about?"

But Julian merely smiled. "Use your imagination, Molly. Imagine yourself in his place and find his weaknesses. Dwell on those awhile, then use them against him."

"I couldn't do that, Julian."

Julian laughed, his tone lightening. "No, I don't suppose you could. But that's exactly what he's doing to you." He leaned forward again, setting the document on the low table between them. "I suppose when it comes right down to it, Molly, it depends on how badly you want to walk away from this company with your head up. Something tells me that QIL means more to you than you are willing to admit. Quinn Investments and Loans is your life. You draw the very air you breathe from running it—right here at the top."

"What are you talking about, Julian?"

"I don't think you can give it up as easily as you presume. I don't think you'll give it up for Winny, for the board, or even for your Zachary MacAlister."

Molly felt heat rise in her cheeks. "I think that's quite enough, Julian. You're going far beyond—"

He interrupted with a quick laugh. "I struck a nerve, didn't I?" He sat back still chuckling.

"Please leave now, Julian. I don't think I or QIL will be requiring your services any longer."

"As you wish," he said, standing.

She escorted him to the door. "I'm sorry it had to end this way, Julian," she said.

But Senator Starr gave her one more inscrutable look, then turned to stride through the door without another word.

That night after dinner, Molly told Kingsley and Gwennie about Julian's visit. The three of them had just settled into the sitting room, Kingsley leaning back in his overstuffed chair, and Gwennie in her wheelchair next to Molly, who sat on the small sofa. Miss

Brown, after joining them for the meal, had left to help Cook Liu prepare a special blackberry tart.

"Men whose amorous attentions have been rejected can turn bitter, Molly," Kingsley said. "No matter what he said at the time, Julian had hoped to marry you."

Gwennie, who was leafing through Molly's latest catalogue of wedding fashions from Paris, *La Mode Illustrée*, looked up. "I saw how he wanted us to think you belonged to him the night you had us all for dinner. You remember—that night with Mary Rose and Devon?"

Molly nodded. It seemed like such a long time ago.

Gwennie held her new wire-rimmed eyeglasses to the light from a nearby lamp, wiped them, then placed them back on her nose. "I worry about Julian, now that you and Zach have announced your plans to marry. A man that possessive might have a mean streak in him."

"I don't worry about him that way, Gwennie," Molly said, though not knowing why she bothered to defend Julian.

"I don't like what he said about threatening Winny, Molly," said Kingsley. "That he could think you're capable of such an act..." His voice dropped, and he shook his head slowly. "I can't exactly put my finger on why it bothers me so. It just does."

"I felt the same sense of foreboding, Kingsley." She thought over Julian's words. "I've decided, though, that the one thing he told me not to do—visit Winny—is exactly what I plan to do. I think I'll visit him again soon."

"Just be careful, Molly. There's something about all this that we don't understand."

She agreed, then turned the conversation to the upcoming wedding.

"Ohhh. I like this one," Gwennie said, pointing to an illus-tration of a wedding gown.

Molly recognized it and smiled. "It's my favorite too."

"Listen to this, Kingsley," Gwennie said with a sigh, and she began to read: "'A bridal gown of ivory *mousseline de soie* trimmed with garlands of roses and green leaves. The draped bodice, framing a tucked yoke with a high collar, crosses in front and is held by a spray of orange blossoms. A tulle veil attached under a wreath of roses completes the ensemble.'

"It is splendid, Molly," Gwennie sighed when she'd finished. "I can just see you floating down the aisle in a cloud of white tulle and rose garlands."

"Then I think I'll have it begun immediately."

Gwennie clapped her hands in delight. "Molly, don't tell me you've finally made your decision after all these weeks." She snapped her fingers. "You made it just like that."

"But we have one more to pick out," Molly said, smiling into Gwennie's face.

Gwennie looked up at Molly, her blue eyes questioning.

Molly smiled, and reached over to turn a few pages. "How do you like this one?"

Gwennie adjusted her eyeglasses and squinted carefully at the page. After a moment of studying the illustration, she said, "Why, child, it says that it's a gown for the mother of the bride. It's made of silver-gray taffeta."

Molly reached for the older woman's hand. "Gwennie, would you do me the honor of attending me in my mother's place on my wedding day?" Then she stood and kissed Gwennie's cheek.

The older woman's eyes filled with tears. "You've made me so happy, child." She reached up and patted Molly's cheek. "I'm the one who's honored. And of course, my answer's yes. I would be delighted."

"Then we'll go to the seamstress tomorrow and start our fittings."

Gwennie's smile spread across her wrinkled face. "You and Zach, married at last!" A dreamy look shone in her eyes.

Molly turned to Kingsley. "I have a question for you as well," she said. He nodded and smiled as if he knew what she was about to ask. "Since my father can't be here, will you stand in for him? Escort me down the aisle?"

He grinned. "I'd be delighted, dear." And he rose to kiss her cheek. "And as Gwennie already said, I'm honored, truly honored." He cleared his throat. "You know, Molly, dear, when you came into our house three years ago, our lives became richer. You've been a breath of fresh air to Gwennie. And to me? Well," he sighed, "you've made an old man feel young and vigorous."

He smiled in his dignified way, raising a silver brow. "And useful, Molly. That's probably the most important. You gave me reason to feel useful again."

Miss Brown proudly carried in the tarts on a silver tray and served dessert and coffee before withdrawing for the evening.

Molly, Kingsley, and Gwennie talked into the night about Zach and his fishing business, QIL Enterprises—and most of all, about the wedding.

Molly stepped onto the cable car atop Nob Hill. A heavy fog had moved inland during the night, and as she moved to her seat, she looked out, hoping it would lift before she reached the waterfront. The damp cold seemed to chill her to the bone. Shivering, Molly pulled her cape closer.

As the cable car rattled along, she thought about what she would say to Winny when she reached San Quentin. It would be a difficult visit, but then, it seemed all of them were.

It had been two weeks since her conversation with Julian, and she had finally reached a conclusion. She couldn't let Winny dictate the conditions any longer. It was time to stand up to him, let him know what he stood to lose if he didn't go along with the Australia plan. In her mind, she enumerated the points she was going to make: Winny would lose her friendship, a friendship that had lasted since childhood; he would lose the good graces of their family in England—so far they hadn't been told of his whereabouts; and he would lose out on any monetary reward. She would set him up in business, but only if he left the country. Half the funds would be wired to Sydney, awaiting his arrival. The second half would arrive at some future date, when he'd established himself and shown good progress with his company.

Molly wondered why Winny was being so obstinate about the plan. She was setting him up with a great deal more than he'd had when he first arrived in America. Why, she wondered, had he such an aversion to doing as she asked?

The old Winny would have snapped it up without a contrary thought. But now? She mused on it, wondering who it was that might be influencing him, if anyone.

A short time later, she strode along the waterfront to the Ferry Building, checked the schedule, then settled onto a bench to await the Sausalito ferry. The fog had lifted, just as she had hoped, and the ferries were running on time.

When at last she boarded, she noticed there weren't as many passengers as usual, probably because of the early hour. Nervous about her meeting with Winny, she strolled about the deck, looking out at the choppy gray water.

The sun was about to slide from behind the thin winter clouds, creating a glare of gray and white. Gulls called as they circled, and their voices seemed more melancholy than usual. Sighing, Molly turned away from the deck railing and concentrated on the other passengers. Mostly they were workmen on their way to jobs in Sausalito. A few families, perhaps of San Quentin inmates, strolled about the deck.

The ferry pulled up to the Sausalito dock, and Molly took her place in line, awaiting her turn to step off the ferry.

She was absently scanning the crowd on shore, when a tall, blond man caught her attention. He had just stepped from a carriage, similar to those that Molly took when visiting Winny, and was turned away from her. She frowned, trying to get a better look. A passenger stepped in front of her, and she moved to one side.

The man had moved, and now only his back was visible. Exasperated, Molly walked closer to the railing and peered into the crowd. She spotted him again.

This time there was no doubt. It was Julian. At first, she was delighted. He'd changed his mind and decided to see Winny on her behalf after all. Then she remembered, he'd told her that as U.S. senator, he couldn't afford to be connected with a felon. He'd also said that he was leaving for Washington long before now.

She tried to understand why Julian would be here if he hadn't come to visit Winny. There was no reason.

When it was her turn to disembark, Molly tried to slip in among the other passengers. She wasn't sure why, but she didn't want Julian to see her. She waited until he'd boarded before she hired the carriage to take her to San Quentin.

424

As the carriage rumbled swiftly along the road, Molly tried to collect her thoughts. She wondered if she should press Winny to tell her about his visitor, or if she should even let on she'd seen him.

She puzzled over it during the short journey to the prison, but still hadn't reached a decision when the vehicle pulled up in front of the gates.

It really didn't matter, because when she asked to see Winston Carlisle-Jones, she was told that he could see no visitors. No reason was given, and no one seemed to know when the order would be rescinded.

As Molly stepped onto the ferry to return to San Francisco, she was more puzzled and troubled than ever.

33

ON THE MORNING OF MOLLY'S last wedding gown fitting, the seamstress attached the long veil to a crown of pale pink silk roses and placed it on her head. Molly found herself unable to speak as she gazed in the mirror. Her breath caught as she thought of Zach and the deep joy she would feel as she walked down the aisle to become his bride, his wife.

Her love for him had continued to grow even stronger since they'd been parted. In a short time, she would leave for Monterey and Carmel for Mary Rose and Devon's wedding. And she would be with Zach, who planned to meet her in Monterey, making the final plans for their wedding the following month. In April, she would become Mrs. Zachary MacAlister, the name she would cherish for the rest of her life.

She smiled at herself in the mirror, turning sideways to catch a glimpse of the veil, floating cloud-like in gentle folds of tulle to the floor.

Behind her, in the wheelchair, Gwennie sighed, a dreamy expression on her wrinkled face. "I've never seen you look more beautiful, Molly," she said with pride.

As the seamstress stepped nearer to help her out of the gown and veil, Molly held up her hand. "Give me just a few more minutes," she said softly. "This is the last time I'll wear it until my wedding day."

She turned again in front of the mirror, watching her image. The gown was more exquisitely beautiful than all her expectations. It symbolized her love and commitment to the man she would marry. They would come together as one and remain as one until death parted them. She sighed deeply, her love for Zach bubbling up like a fountain inside her heart.

"All right," she finally whispered, though reluctantly. "I'm ready." The seamstress came forward to unfasten the tiny satin-covered buttons at the gown's back. Moments later, Molly again wore her long gored skirt and matching jacket. She attached the wide-brimmed straw hat with a long pearl-tipped hat pin, fussed a moment with her hair, then stepped from the shop, pushing Gwennie's wheelchair.

The motorcar and uniformed driver Molly had hired for the morning waited at the curb. With a nod, the chauffeur helped the women into the vehicle, then hoisted Gwennie's chair into the rear. Then he gave the crankshaft a spin, waited, then gave it another. The auto shook and sputtered and vibrated to a start.

"Dear, dear, I like these things," Gwennie said with a wide smile as they turned up Market Street. "I'd learn to drive one myself, if I could." The car rumbled along.

Molly remembered the night Julian had promised Gwennie a ride in his roadster. A shadow crossed the otherwise happy morning. She still hadn't found out why she'd seen him in Sausalito, presumably after visiting Winny. The board would meet next week, and she was no closer to solving the problem with her cousin than she had been at the last meeting. And now she no longer had her ally and friend, Julian, by her side.

She drew in a deep breath, trying to shake the web of foreboding thoughts threatening to strangle her joy.

"Mine is the next office on the right," she called to the

chauffeur a few minutes later. He swung the motorcar to the side of the road and came around to open Molly's door. After giving Gwennie a quick kiss, Molly stepped onto the sidewalk in front of her building.

Molly watched until the vehicle had rounded the corner on its way back to Gwennie's house atop Nob Hill.

As Molly left the elevator and walked down the hall, she looked about, satisfied at the bustling activity that now comprised QII's working hours. In recent weeks, seven new associates had been brought into the company. Victoria Parrott, who oversaw the office operations, also had hired an assistant, a red-haired young man named Jimmy Green, who reminded Molly of Winny when he was younger. He had a contagious grin, and they'd hit it off from the first time he brought coffee to her office.

She turned into her suite, said good morning to Victoria and Jimmy in the front reception area, then entered her office. As was his morning custom, Jimmy brought her a pot of fresh coffee, setting it on the table near her settee. Beside it, he placed the morning's *Examiner.*

Just after he exited the room, Kingsley knocked lightly, then stepped through the doorway. He looked worried.

"Kingsley, good morning," Molly stood to greet him. "I've just now arrived. Gwennie and I had a delightful time. Your idea for hiring a car was a stroke of genius! For Gwennie's sake, I wish I'd thought of it earlier."

Kingsley said good morning and gave her a half-smile. They walked over to the sitting area, and Molly nodded toward the settee. "Will you join me for coffee? I was just about to pour some for myself."

Kingsley nodded and reached for the cup and saucer after she had filled it with the hot, steaming liquid.

Molly poured herself a cup, then settled into the high-backed chair across from him, still noting his worried expression.

"Kingsley, what is it?"

He looked down at the still-folded newspaper lying on the table. "You haven't heard this morning's news, have you, Molly?" She shook her head and reached for the paper, but before she could open it, Kingsley went on. "There was a breakout at San Quentin last night, Molly." She knew what he was going to say before he uttered the words.

"Winny...," she breathed.

He nodded. "He's escaped, Molly. There were three who attempted it, two were caught, but Winny got away. They don't have any idea where he might be."

"Was anyone hurt?"

"A guard was stabbed but is still hanging onto life. He's unconscious."

"Who stabbed him?"

Kingsley's forehead furrowed in thought. "It's not surprising that both of the inmates who were caught say it was Winny's doing—his plan, his leadership that got them into the mess. They're also saying he wielded the knife that almost killed the guard."

Molly nodded, feeling physically sick. "Tell me everything you've heard, Kingsley. Don't leave anything out."

"They said the guard had been harassing him from the beginning of his incarceration," Kingsley said. Molly remembered the guard who, in front of her, had ribbed Winny with a tone of mocking British royalty. "Apparently," Kingsley continued, "the encounters had escalated, become quite physical during recent months."

"No wonder he was so angry and bitter," Molly mused frowning. "He was due to be released sometime this spring."

"This is the strange part," Kingsley said. "According to the newspaper, his hearing for early release was rescinded quite suddenly."

"For misbehavior?"

"No one knows. But the two prisoners who were caught said quite the opposite. Until the escape, Winny was the model prisoner. They had nothing to gain for saying it."

"Which gives their words more credibility." Molly sighed, trying to take it all in.

Kingsley nodded, his face a portrait of sadness and concern for her.

"I don't understand, Kingsley." Molly stood and moved over to the window, looking out at the bay. Everything was as it should be, bright skies above the blue-mirrored water, workers bustling along the waterfront, ships and boats gliding in and out of the harbor, gulls wheeling and calling, wings gleaming silver-white in the sun. Even around her, in the offices beyond her suite, QIL employees went about their business, increasing the holdings of the company, writing contracts for even more loans, researching investment opportunities.

Yet Molly couldn't shake the feeling that her world was about to fall apart. The board would meet next week, and she would have to tell them about Winny. How could she now present her proposal for QII's restructure? She knew the answer even before she'd considered it: She couldn't. Not until the problem with Winny was resolved.

"Is there anything I can do?" Concern etched Kinglsey's face.

"This changes everything," she whispered, not looking up. "Everything."

430

"I know, dear."

"I can't step down from QIL until this is resolved. I just can't...." Her voice broke off. She swallowed hard, shaking her head. "I can't leave now, Kingsley. I can't just walk away."

"You're saying you can't marry Zach?"

"Not until all this has been taken care of, Kingsley."

For a moment he regarded her, not speaking. "Then you must go to him and tell him in person. News such as this can't be conveyed in a letter. Even if you think you can't get away from QIL right now, you must do this, for Zach, for yourself."

"I can't tell him when I'll be free to leave QIL...to marry him." She pressed her lips together and drew in a shaky breath. "I don't know if he'll wait this time."

"If you leave tomorrow, you can return for the board meeting next week. Until then, I'll handle things here, divert attention from the Winny problem, if need be."

"Actually," she whispered, as Kingsley gave her shoulders a fatherly squeeze, "I'll leave on tonight's train for Salinas. That way I can be in Monterey first thing in the morning."

After giving a few instructions to Victoria Parrott, Molly left QIL Enterprises for her little Queen Anne cottage. She packed the few clothes she thought she'd need, and while she awaited her transportation to the train station, she stopped by to let Gwennie know what had happened.

Gwennie's eyes were bright with tears when Molly hugged her goodbye. "Follow your heart, dearest child," she said, just before Molly left the house. "Follow your heart."

Spotting Gwennie peering through the lace curtains of the sitting room, Molly blew her a kiss as she stepped into the waiting motorcar. The chauffeur wound the crankshaft and slid into the driver's seat, and the car jerked and putt-putted forward.

The train ride to Salinas was longer than Molly had remembered. She gazed out the window at the flat, green valley, and the miles passed with an almost intolerable monotony. Normally, she would enjoy the landscape, much of it covered with tender young plants, freshly sprouted from the spring plantings. But as the late afternoon sun sank low to the west, all she felt was growing impatience.

She leaned her head back against the seat, shutting out the voices of other passengers. Never had her emotions been in such turmoil. Her heart skipped at the thought of seeing Zach again after their long weeks of separation. But she also dreaded the words she had to tell him. More than anything, she couldn't bear to picture his face.

She thought of Mary Rose and Devon, realizing that probably she would have to miss their wedding. She and Zach had agreed on their gift for the young couple, and she smiled at the thought of the joy it would bring them. Because she was unsure when she could return to Monterey, she'd packed the gift, *Mary Rose's Garden,* and brought it with her on the train, planning for Zach to deliver it on the couple's wedding day.

Even the thought of Zach's going alone caused her anguish. But she had to remain strong for what was ahead. She lifted her chin with new resolve and tried to put aside her sadness, concentrating instead on solutions to her dilemma at QIL.

But no matter her resolve, her thoughts kept returning to her uncertain future.

Suddenly, her focus settled on the heavy package that she'd had the porter place on the seat beside her. Though it was wrapped, she considered its contents, the painting, *Mary Rose's Garden.*

What had Mary Rose told her about God's care…about his

intimate concern with the details of her life? She had spoken about a Bible verse, and Molly couldn't remember the exact words, but it had something to do with being precious in God's sight...*I love you. I have called you by name; you are mine.* There were others, from the Psalms, Molly thought, or perhaps Jeremiah. She couldn't remember which, only that the thoughts had remained as if printed indelibly in her mind: *I have loved you with an everlasting love.... I have brought you to me with loving-kindness.*

She remembered Mary Rose's confidence about the future when they'd spoken in the garden. She seemed to have an inner joy and peace, looking forward to a future that she'd left in her Lord's hands. Molly had known at the time that Mary Rose experienced deep sadness and heartache from the loss of her husband, then from Devon's leaving her.

Molly looked out again at the darkening fields. Did God know her troubled thoughts—about Winny—about Zach— even about running QIL? And did he care? she wondered.

A vineyard covered the slopes of some nearby hills, but the branches were barren of fruit and leaves. She remembered Mary Rose's words about how God wants his people to abide in him just as a branch is connected to a vine. She'd said abiding was a lifeblood connection that flowed into her heart, a continual conversation in which he heard the thoughts of her heart.

What would it be like to be loved, watched over, and cared for in such a way? Molly mused. "Heavenly Father," she breathed, still gazing out at the vineyard, "I want to know you. I need you, but I don't know how to find you."

She sighed and looked out at the twilight skies, a whisper of gray-pink to the west, fading to magenta, then a deep navy velvet overhead. On the hillside, silhouettes of the vines stood out against the western skies. By summer, they would be filled with new growth, and by autumn, they would be heavy with grape clusters.

Molly considered them, noting that a peace had settled into her soul. But at the same time, there was a longing in her heart, as if a place was being readied for Someone to come in. The shape of it—if it could be called a shape—Molly knew, was such that only God himself could fill.

The train pulled into the Salinas station. Molly spent the night at a nearby inn, then caught the first Del Cortés Special leaving for Monterey the following morning.

As soon as she moved from the train onto the noisy platform in Monterey, a breeze off the bay chilled her to the bone. She held her hat, as the wind gusted wildly around her.

Shivering, Molly gathered her things and took the new Del Cortés motorbus to the hotel. By midmorning, she'd registered for a room, had her luggage delivered, and arranged for the still-wrapped painting to be placed in the hotel's vault. As she did so, she wondered if Oliver Duckworth's whereabouts had ever been discovered and made a mental note to check when things settled down.

She changed into a dark skirt and fitted jacket, and grabbed her hat before strolling to the waterfront. She'd just arrived at the wharf when she spotted Jam rowing to shore.

Tilting the wide brim of her hat to shield her eyes against the sun, she looked farther out. The *Molly Quinn* was anchored about a mile from shore, and she let out a sigh of relief.

Jam's weathered face broke into a smile as he rowed closer. He lifted his hand in a friendly wave. "Ho, there!" he shouted across the water. "Well, I'll be. It's Molly Quinn!"

Molly returned his wave, and he pulled up beside the wharf. "Or maybe I should practice sayin', it's Molly MacAlister!" he exclaimed happily. After he tied the small boat to a piling and extricated himself, he joined Molly on the wharf.

"My goodness!" he said with a grin. "You're a sight for sore eyes, Molly. Does the cap'n know you're due?"

She shook her head. "No." She laughed lightly. "I thought I'd surprise him."

"Well, that'll surely be the case when he sees you, Missy."

"Where is he Jam? Aboard ship?"

"No, he's out at the property," Jam said, and Molly knew he meant the seacliff meadow. "Been out there since daybreak workin' on—" He stopped abruptly, giving her a sly grin. "Probably'll be there till dusk. You've got a good chance of catchin' him, I'd say, if you go right now."

"I'll do just that, Jam. Thank you."

"But mind you, be careful. I believe there's a storm a-brewin'." He squinted to the northwest. "Most've these spring storms are worse'n the ones in winter." Then he turned again and looked at her, frowning in worry. "You hang onto your flowery hat, Missy. This storm's gonna be worse than most we've seen lately around these parts."

"I'll be careful," she said. "I promise. And thank you, Jam."

She headed to the small livery just up the street. While the stable owner hitched a small roan to a covered buggy, Molly swept a length of tulle around her hat so it wouldn't fly off in the wind. Soon she'd climbed into the driver's seat, reins in hand, and was on her way through Pacific Grove and onto Lighthouse Road.

She flicked the reins over the horse's back, and it trotted along, seeming unconcerned with the still-gusting winds. Molly wondered at the coming storm. The last time she'd ridden to the seacliff meadow, a storm had also been churning the waters and turning the skies a threatening gray. She pushed the sense of gloom from her mind and concentrated instead on keeping the buggy on the road.

When Molly reached the turnoff to the meadow cliffs, she was surprised to see that Zach had graded a small, steep dirt road up to his property. Within minutes they reached the top, and she halted the roan at the edge of the meadow, then looked across the stretch of pale green grasses.

There, tucked into the pines, was a house, so well blended with the terrain that it almost seemed one with it. Its sides were made of stained wood, smooth river stones, and glass. From the distance, it seemed to be two-story, circled entirely by wide porches with views of the Pacific and its crashing surf.

Molly caught her breath. It was their house. He'd built it himself. Quick tears sprang to her eyes, and she bit her lip, feeling an intense bittersweet awareness wash over her.

At the same moment, Zach, who'd just come around the house with a ladder, looked up and spotted her across the meadow. A wide grin covered his face. He dropped the ladder and ran toward her.

Molly jumped from the buggy. She yanked off her hat and tossed it aside, letting her dark hair tumble down her back. Her heart pounding, she made her way toward him through the tall meadow grasses.

In a heartbeat, Zach reached her. He swept her into his arms, holding her as if he would never let go.

"Oh, Molly," he breathed. "Molly, you're here at last!"

Clinging to him, Molly buried her head in his embrace, wondering how she could utter the words she needed to say.

CHAPTER

34

"OH, MY DARLING," ZACH MURMURED, still holding Molly close. "How I've longed to see you!" Then he pulled back and looked into her face. "I didn't think you were coming until Devon and Mary Rose's wedding. That's still two weeks away." He frowned. "There's something wrong, isn't there?"

Molly swallowed hard and nodded.

Zach cupped her face with his hands. "Molly? What is it, darling?"

"Oh, Zach," she finally breathed, "Winny's escaped from prison."

For a moment, Zach seemed uncomprehending. Then a slow realization showed in his eyes.

"I don't know what he might do, Zach," she said. "To me. To QIL."

He nodded slowly but didn't speak.

She swallowed again. "There's more."

"The wedding," he said, at last, his voice hoarse. "You want to call it off."

"Oh, no." She touched his jaw, her fingers lingering on its rough texture. "Not that. I would never do that. I just need more time. I've got to see this through."

"I see."

"Please understand, Zach. Please tell me that you do."

"Molly," he began, watching her intently, his eyes filled with sudden sadness. "I know what QIL means to you. I've known from the beginning. But I'm realizing that perhaps you can't give it up."

Molly remembered Julian's prediction, so similar to Zach's, and was momentarily stunned. "Are you asking me to make a choice right now, Zach?" She frowned. "Surely you wouldn't do that. Not now, with so much at stake."

"At stake for QIL, Molly? Or at stake for us? Which is more important to you?"

"You...us, of course." But suddenly, she was unsure.

"You've always wanted it all. You've told me you thought you could have it." He shook his head slowly. "Maybe it's just not possible."

"But this is only for a little while, Zach. I'm just asking you for more time, that's all."

"What then, Molly? What if there's another crisis that you must see through for your investors? What then?"

Molly felt her heart breaking. She couldn't answer him. "Can't you see, Zach? With Winny's escape, it changed everything. I'd already drawn up a proposal to present to the board next week. I'm planning on stepping down."

"You're still planning to present it?"

"No." Her voice was small. "I can't until the situation with Winny is resolved."

For a moment neither spoke. Then Zach said quietly. "What if he's not found, Molly? What will you do then?"

She couldn't answer, because she didn't know. Mutely, she shook her head.

Zach turned her gently, and with his arm encircling her,

they began to walk to the meadow's edge. After a few minutes, they stood in the sea grasses and wildflowers atop the rocky cliffs overlooking the ocean.

"*The Jeweled Dawn*," Molly murmured. "This is where Devon painted it, isn't it?"

Zach smiled softly, as if holding onto a secret memory. "Yes."

For a long time, they stood looking out at the sea. The surf was wild, pounding the sand below with a sound that carried upward on the wind.

Molly looked up into his clear gray eyes. She remembered how, when she first met him, their color had reminded her of the sky before dawn. "Where do we go from here?" she whispered, feeling somehow lost. "Will you wait, Zach?"

He turned to look out to sea again. Only the sounds of the crashing waves and the cries of gulls could be heard. Molly pressed her lips together to keep her chin from trembling. She didn't want to cry. Not now. But she thought she wouldn't last through the eternal moment it took for him to answer.

At last, he let out a ragged sigh. "Oh, Molly," he said, "I can't imagine life without you." Placing his hands on either side of her face, he lifted her chin upward, caressing her face with his gaze. He frowned, gently touching her cheeks with his thumbs. Then he kissed her on the lips, tenderly, as if she were fragile. "I love you, Molly Quinn," he said. "I don't know how long I can wait, but I'll love you forever."

With a small cry, Molly slid her arms around his neck, holding him tightly. "Oh, Zach! I love you," she cried.

After a moment, he pulled back and looked at her lovingly. Then he turned her toward the house, now illumined by a pool of sunlight. "This was to be your wedding present, Molly. It's nearly finished."

For several minutes, she couldn't speak. The house spoke of love and family and laughter and joy. She looked up at him. "Can't we say, it is my wedding present?"

He laughed softly. "I think you've got greater hope than I do in that regard, Molly. But no matter what happens, it will never belong to anyone else." He gave her a tender smile. "It's for you, Molly."

"It's beautiful, Zach," she breathed in awe, again taking in its elegant design. She glanced up at him. "Can we go in? I want to see inside every nook and cranny."

"That, I *will* keep as a surprise for our wedding day."

They walked through the meadow toward Molly's buggy. "I brought *Mary Rose's Garden* with me, Zach. I doubt that I can get away for Mary Rose and Devon's wedding." She gave him a sad look. "I thought you could take it on behalf of us both."

"I've got a better idea." He reached for her hand and squeezed it as they walked. "You're at the Del Cortés?"

She nodded.

"How long can you stay?"

"Only a few days. I've got to get back for next week's board meeting."

He stopped and turned toward her. "Let's spend as much time as we can together."

"I was hoping you'd say that."

"Starting with dinner tomorrow night?"

She nodded, happily. "And your better idea?"

"Let's drive to Carmel the day after and deliver the painting together."

Molly smiled. "I'd love to, Zach. It sounds perfect."

He frowned, glancing briefly at the northwestern sky. "I can't be with you tomorrow. I promised I'd take Devon out to the ruins of an old lighthouse near Point Sur. He wants to paint it from a different perspective."

Molly was alarmed. "But what about the storm? Jam said it'll be blowing in tomorrow."

Zach laughed, shaking his head slightly. "That's part of what Devon wants to experience. He's painted lighthouses in the swelling surf and crashing waves from shore, but never from the other side."

"You're taking the *Molly Quinn?*"

"No, I don't want to bother the crew with this. I'm borrowing a fishing boat from a friend." He looked into her eyes, noticing their troubled look. "Molly, it'll be all right. We're only going down the coast as far as Point Sur." He smiled, trying to lift her spirits. "We're leaving at sunup and should be back in time for supper."

They continued walking through the grass toward the buggy. Zach grabbed her hat from where she'd earlier tossed it. When they reached the rig, Zach patted the horse on the neck.

Molly noticed the gentle touch of his callused hand as he stroked the roan. "This is the last I'll see you then, until you get back?" The wind lifted strands of her hair, whipping and turning them across her face. She reached up and tucked the errant wisps behind her ears.

He pulled her close, resting his cheek on her hair. "I'm sorry, but I've got some business to take care of with the crew tonight. I would've made other arrangements, if I'd known you were going to be here."

"Don't apologize," she said, then on tiptoes reached up to give him a kiss.

Taking her hand, he helped her into the driver's seat. He stepped back, and she lifted the reins, then hesitated for a moment before dropping her hands to her lap.

She turned to Zach who stood watching her in the sunlight. Suddenly, she was so overwhelmed by her love for him that she couldn't move. With a small cry, she nearly flew from the carriage into his arms, pressing him close. She didn't want to let go. She couldn't let go.

Surprised, he drew her nearer. "What is it, Molly?" he asked. "Is there something else, something you haven't told me?"

"I love you, Zach," she whispered, her voice husky with the depths of her emotion. "I just needed to tell you once more." Clinging tightly to him, she whispered the words again. "I love you!"

Zach tightened his hold, and murmured his answering words of love into the thicket of her hair. "Molly Quinn," he said, "you are my life. I will love you until the day I die."

The following morning dawned bright and sunny. Molly looked out her hotel room window, thinking that Jam had been mistaken. She smiled, thinking about how she would tease him about his powers of storm prediction the next time they met.

Taking her time, she had a leisurely and fragrant bath and laid out her gown for the evening's dinner with Zach. She'd slept well. Her last thoughts before drifting off and those when she awoke were of Zach and the life they would someday have together. Since seeing him the day before, she had new resolve to return to San Francisco, face the board with the news of Winny's escape, and take swift action to circumvent any problems. For the first time since hearing the dismaying news from Kingsley, she felt strong enough to face whatever was ahead.

Since Molly had the whole day to herself, she decided to

spend it in town. After lingering over a sumptuous breakfast in the Del Cortés dining room, she walked briskly down Alvarado to the waterfront where she looked for Jam. He wasn't anywhere to be seen, so she strolled on toward cannery row and People's Choice.

She was delighted with the changes in the factory. It was now bright and clean, with evidence of new paint and equipment and attitude. Many of the workers recognized her and called out greetings as she toured the plant with the manager.

"Has the salmon catch come in today?" she asked the manager just before leaving.

He smiled amiably. "No. The weather's too uncertain. Seems there's hurricane winds making landfall north of here."

Molly tilted her head. "But it's sunny and clear out. Yesterday it looked like something might be headed this way. But not now."

He laughed. "That's the trouble with these Pacific storms. They're deceptive. Sometimes they linger offshore while they pick up speed and power. That's why most experienced fishermen keep their feet on dry land when they hear something like this is brewing."

Molly felt herself go pale. She reached for a nearby steel rail for support. After she had asked a few more questions about the company, she hurried outside.

Zach probably figured he'd be back in the bay by the time the storm hit. And, she chided herself, there was no point in worrying. She drew in a deep breath, feeling better, and began the long walk back to the Del Cortés.

As she passed the Monterey Police Department, she decided to check on the Oliver Duckworth case. A sergeant looked up from his desk as she approached. "Good morning," he said amiably.

Molly gave him a smile and quick nod. "I'm wondering if you can tell me what happened with the Oliver Duckworth case." She filled in the details about the theft connected to *Mary Rose's Garden,* explaining her interest because she owned the painting.

"Ahh, yes," he said, when she'd finished. "An interesting case. We had investigators following Duckworth all over the state. He eluded us every time we got close." He shook his head slowly. "Then Duckworth got careless. Seems he just couldn't resist getting back into the hotel business. Not just any hotel, mind you. He tried to get on with the new Queen Victoria Hotel in San Francisco. Do you know it?"

She said yes, she did, and the police sergeant went on. "Well, he applied for a job there under a fictitious name, just a few weeks ago. Someone who'd seen him at the Del Cortés recognized him and got suspicious. The hotel contacted the owner of the Del Cortés. Of course, he let us know immediately. Duckworth was arrested days after." He grinned, obviously pleased.

"Has he gone to trial yet?"

"No, there won't be any trial. He confessed to everything."

"How about the recovery of the funds he stole?"

The sergeant shook his head, frowning. "We're still working on that. At first, he said nothing was left. He'd spent it all. But when we started bargaining with him for a reduced sentence, he came up with a different story."

Molly sighed. "Then there's a chance the money owed Devon O'Rourke will be recovered?"

"A good chance, I suppose, for at least part of it. Though I'm really not at liberty to divulge the details of the agreement. That'll have to wait until the negotiations between Duckworth and the State of California are finalized."

"I understand," Molly said, feeling happy for Devon and Mary Rose. What a nest egg that would be for their coming marriage!

She thanked the sergeant for the information, then stepped out into the thin afternoon sun. Moving her gaze across the bay to the horizon, she searched for signs of the coming storm. In the north, thin streaks of clouds were spreading across the sky, though they certainly didn't appear ominous.

By the time she reached her room, however, and looked out the window toward the bay, whitecaps were whipping up in the normally placid waters. Clouds now darkened the sun, and the skies faded to gray as she watched.

By nightfall, the storm had hit. Howling winds bent the trees and heavy rain slashed against the windows.

Zach still hadn't arrived by suppertime, and Molly fought to keep her fear under control. Finally, she went to the dining room alone, more for the company of others than because she was hungry. But the normally bustling room was eerily empty.

She ordered a bowl of hot soup and some fresh-baked bread, staring dejectedly out at the rain while she attempted to eat. But the food was tasteless, and she finally pushed the bowl to the center of the table.

"Quite a storm," her waiter said, as he brought the bill.

She nodded.

"I hear there's sandbagging at the waterfront tonight."

"Sandbagging?" She hadn't heard of it.

"They're stacking them like bricks—making a wall to keep the high tide from flooding the town. The mayor, businessfolk, fishermen, factory workers—they're all down there working side by side."

Fishermen. Molly thought of Jam and the crew. Maybe they would be there. They might have information about Zach and Devon. She paid the waiter and hurried to her room for her overshoes and a cape.

She asked at the front desk for transportation to the waterfront. The clerk arched his brow in surprise, then quickly informed her that none was available on such an inclement night.

Molly thanked him and headed for the door. Stepping into the rain, she caught her breath. It was coming down in sheets. She pulled the hood of her cape over her head, but before she'd turned onto Alvarado, the wool cloth was soaked through.

Gingerly, she picked her way across the small rivers that had formed at the sides of the street. She strode along in the dark, alone and miserable. But her thoughts were with Zach and Devon. What if they were still out at sea? She pushed the thought from her mind.

The wind gusted and howled, and the slicing rain stung her skin. Molly held onto her hood, trying to protect her face. By the time she reached the waterfront, now lit by lanterns, she could see the workers frantically stacking burlap bags of sand.

More than a hundred people were there. Molly could see that it would be impossible to find Jam. Dejectedly, she walked toward the wharf and stood looking out into the raging surf.

The rain poured down, splashing against her face. It was going on ten o'clock, and Zach would have been home long ago, had he been able to. She could no longer doubt that he must have run into serious trouble.

"Missy," a gruff voice said behind her. "What're you doin' out on a night like this?"

She turned to see Jam, his face wrinkled with concern in the dim lantern light. "It's Zach," she said. "He's not back, is he?"

Jam shook his head. "No, Missy. He didn't get here when he said he would."

She swayed, feeling faint, and Jam put an awkward arm around her. "Now, don't you fret. Oftentimes, we put up in a safe harbor to wait out storms. Not unheard of at all. No, ma'am."

Molly nodded, drawing in a shaky breath. Maybe he was right.

"Now, you remember this, Missy. You'll have to wait until the storm's over and the ocean quiets down a bit to know for sure. But the cap'n knows this coastline like the back of his hand. You hang onto that hope till you hear otherwise. You hear?"

She pressed her lips together and nodded her head again. "All right, Jam. But will you let me know if you find out anything? I'm staying at the Del Cortés."

He patted her arm. "You can count on it, Missy." But a trace of something in his tone canceled the comfort his words were meant to bring.

She managed a small, shaky smile. After giving her another gruff hug, Jam turned to the sandbags, and Molly trudged through the rain back up the hill to the Del Cortés.

CHAPTER

35

THE RAIN CONTINUED FOR THREE DAYS. The morning of the fourth day finally dawned bright and clear, and Molly again walked to the docks, just as she had every day of the storm.

She waved to Jam, who was just leaving in the tender to check on the *Molly Quinn*. Each time they met, the old fisherman had looked grimmer, and today, his weathered face drooped with concern.

"There's still no word, Missy," he said, when he looked up. "But I'm going out with the crew later, sail down to Point Sur and have a look-see."

"I'll be in Carmel, visiting Mary Rose Sheffield," Molly said. "But I'll be back later today. Probably by the time you are." She hated to leave for even that long, but she needed to tell Mary Rose what had happened.

Soon Molly was on her way in the same rig she'd rented just days before. The road to Carmel was treacherous. Where it wound along the seaside, it had washed out in places and required time-consuming detours. Several times she had to halt the horse and lead it by the reins across the muddy ruts and shallow gullies. As she passed the turnoff, Molly didn't stop at Zach's property. She kept her eyes on the road ahead, trying not to think about the last time she'd been there.

It was well past noon when she pulled up in front of Mary Rose's cottage. She tethered the roan to a post out front, then let herself through the gate.

After knocking lightly, she heard the sounds of scurrying feet racing toward the entrance. Seconds later, Jesse threw open the door.

Molly hadn't seen him for over a year, and she was surprised at how tall he'd grown. He still had Mary Rose's fair, freckled skin and blond hair. Even his eyes matched the sea-green shade of hers. But he'd lost his babyish look and now had the expression and build of a rough-and-tumble boy of five years.

"Hi, Jesse," Molly said with a smile. He scrunched his nose and frowned, not recognizing her. "My name is Molly Quinn, and I haven't seen you since you were about this big." She held her hand out a little ways from the ground.

He grinned just as Mary Rose stepped to the doorway behind him. She wiped her hands on her long apron. Molly could see that her eyes were red-rimmed and swollen.

"Molly!" she exclaimed, hurrying across the threshold to hug her friend. She pulled back. "What are you doing here? I thought you were still in San Francisco." Behind her, Jesse scampered back into the house.

"I came a few days ago, just before Zach and Devon left."

"You know they're missing then? I was going to wire you today."

"Have you heard anything?"

Mary Rose shook her head slowly. "No, I haven't." Then she gave Molly a small smile. "Look at me! I'm not much of a hostess, am I? Please, come in, or would you rather sit out in the garden? I'll put on some tea."

"The garden sounds lovely, Mary Rose. So does the tea."

"I'll get the things for tea. Why don't you go on up? I'll meet you there." Then she touched Molly's arm. "You don't know how glad I am to see you, Molly."

"And I you," Molly said with a soft smile.

She made her way along the path to the upper part of the garden. As she passed by the abundance of spring growth—the kitchen garden, the blossoming shrubs and trees and flowers—she felt her soul fill with unexpected peace.

She spotted the clearing under the olive tree and settled onto the carved redwood bench. Nearby, lilacs bloomed, filling the air with their sweet scent. Tiny gray birds with jaunty top-knots sang as they hopped from bush to bush, and behind her, the brook she remembered from her earlier visit murmured as it bubbled along its banks.

After a few minutes, Mary Rose opened the back door and, tea tray in her hands, walked up the steep pathway to join Molly.

She set the tray on a redwood table, settled onto the bench beside Molly, and poured tea from a delicate china teapot.

"I've just put Jesse down for a rest," Mary Rose said, as she stirred in a spoonful of sugar. "He doesn't need long naps any-more, but he's such a little bundle of energy he wears himself out before the day's half done."

"He's a beautiful child, Mary Rose."

"He's a blessing, especially right now."

Molly nodded slowly. "It's been four days. Jam said that they may have taken safe harbor someplace to wait out the storm. It could be that they're trying to get back to us right now. He was going to take the *Molly Quinn* out today to look for them."

"I'm glad to hear it. Maybe we'll have some good news soon." She sighed deeply. "I've been praying for them constantly."

She shook her head as if to keep her thoughts from slipping into further sadness. "Tell me what brought you to Monterey this early. Zach told us you weren't going to be here until right before the wedding."

"I came early to see Zach." She described the events that led to her arrival, sparing no detail, including her guilt for sending Zach away in such anguish. "Because of his love, he agreed to postpone the wedding. But I could see his sadness. And I'd caused it. If only I could roll back time and take away his pain."

Mary Rose gave her hand a squeeze. "God is in control of all this. It doesn't change our sadness, but it helps to know that none of this is taking him by surprise. He knows where Zach and Devon are right now. Even now they may be on their way home to us...."

But her voice broke off, betraying her anguish. "Maybe I'm being unrealistic, but I just can't accept that they're..." Molly hesitated, "not coming home."

"I know, Molly."

"God wouldn't allow it, would he? Allow them to die?"

"They're with him. No matter what's happened, they can't be separated from his love." She hesitated, as if wondering if she should say more, then she continued. "When we belong to God, he holds us in the palm of his hand, in life and in death. He overcame death's hold on us when he died on the cross, then rose from the grave."

Molly nodded slowly, trying to understand.

"There's something else, Molly," Mary Rose finally said softly. "Zach's been on a journey to find meaning in his life, to find God. One night, a few weeks ago, he and Dev sat here in the garden until well after midnight, talking about it."

Molly considered her own recent musings about God. "I

know about those thoughts," she said, almost as if to herself.

"Zach told you?"

"No, the same thoughts and questions have been mine."

"About God?"

She nodded. "On the way to Monterey, out in the Salinas Valley, I spotted some grapevines and remembered what you said about abiding in him and he in you...letting his lifeblood flow into you as if you were the branch attached to his vine."

Mary Rose nodded in understanding, and Molly went on. "My life has been filled with good things, things that bring me great joy. But still there's something missing. An emptiness that goes unsatisfied no matter what I do. I looked at those grapevines and considered how any one of the branches would die if it were cut off from the vine." She looked into Mary Rose's eyes. "I thought I was looking at myself."

Mary Rose remained silent, letting Molly speak from her heart.

"I love Zach with every part of my being. But this barren place inside has nothing to do with human love." She turned toward Mary Rose. "I can't really explain it, but it's just different."

"I understand," Mary Rose finally said.

"I asked God to show me the way, and I feel drawn to him. But there's still something I'm missing. A bridge I need to cross." Molly had never before opened her heart's innermost thoughts to anyone else's scrutiny. But as she considered Mary Rose's loving expression, she knew that nothing she said would be misconstrued or made light of. She let out a sigh.

"You're talking about the most important relationship in your life." Mary Rose was quiet for a moment, and only the sounds of the birds and murmuring stream could be heard. "The bridge you mentioned..."

Molly nodded.

"That bridge is Jesus Christ, Molly. He is the way to the Father...the only way. The Bible tells us that the only way to the Father is through accepting Jesus, his Son, into our lives."

"There's that word *in* again, as in abiding *in* him. It seems that nothing about all this is external."

"It isn't, Molly. It's one thing to believe that God is who he says he is, such as believing that he's the creator of the earth and all that's in it. Or believing that a man—even God's Son Jesus, the Savior—was born of a young virgin and died on a cross for the sins of humanity. Even believing all this isn't enough to cross that bridge you're talking about."

"Belief isn't enough?"

"I think our journey starts with belief." Mary Rose frowned in thought. "When I was a child, I remember touching a rose petal and wondering about the God who'd created it. One day outside my bedroom window, in a nest in an apple tree, I saw a baby robin peck through its shell. It was through nature," she gestured around the garden, "that I first began to understand there is a God. A Creator. And that he is both powerful and tenderhearted." She paused. "There's a Bible verse that says 'for the invisible things of him from the creation of the world are clearly seen, being understood by the things that are made....'"

Molly nodded uncertainly. "You're saying that creation is evidence of his existence?"

"Yes, but acknowledging that isn't the same as knowing him. He's still at a distance."

"On the other side of the bridge." It was something Molly wanted to consider someday, but not right now. Zach's life, and Devon's, might depend on her action. There would always be time to think about God, but suddenly she could wait no longer to do what she could for them. "Someday I'm going to think about all this," she said finally. "When Zach and Devon are found and all the problems with QIL are solved, I'm going to think about what all this could mean in my life."

"Don't wait too long," Mary Rose said simply. But she said nothing more about it.

They talked awhile longer, mostly about Zach and Devon, then Molly said she needed to get back.

"What are you going to do now, Molly?" Mary Rose asked. "Do you need to return to San Francisco right away?"

"No, I'm going to have Kingsley handle things for me. Postpone the board meeting." She sighed. "Right now QIL—or anything connected to it—doesn't seem very important."

"You're welcome to stay here if you like."

Molly bit her lip, looking into the sun-dappled garden. "I must get back to Monterey," she said, her voice suddenly stronger. "If the *Molly Quinn* comes back without Zach and Devon, I plan to launch the largest rescue effort the Central Coast has ever seen."

Mary Rose's smile widened. "Molly! That's wonderful. I can't tell you what hope that gives me."

"I don't care how long we need to search, or how much money it costs, we'll go over every inch of this coast until they're found." She took a deep breath. "As soon as Jam returns, I plan to hire every ship, every fishing boat, every Chinese junk in Monterey. I'll pay them double what they would get for each day's catch." She lifted her chin. "And I'll offer a reward for everyone aboard the first vessel that finds them." Then her voice quieted. "But all this planning may be for naught. Our men may be waiting on the dock for us in Monterey."

Mary Rose squeezed her hand, and Molly could see tears fill her eyes.

They talked for another few minutes, and Molly said she would be in touch as soon as there was any news of Zach and Devon. As they walked through the garden to the front gate of the little cottage, Mary Rose suddenly turned to Molly. "I have something for you," she said. "Wait here." And she headed back into the house.

After she returned, she handed Molly a key. "It's the spare to Zach's house in the meadow," she explained. "If anything..." She hesitated. "If anything happens and you need to go there, I thought you might like it."

Molly clutched the key in her hand. "Thank you," she whispered, not wanting to think about the circumstances that might warrant it.

Then Mary Rose pulled a small leatherbound book from her pocket. "And something else..."

Molly nodded.

"We ordered this for Zach, but we hadn't had a chance to present it to him." She opened the front cover. "Dev and I had both signed it with our love, and just now, I added your name by Zach's."

Mary Rose placed it in Molly's hands. It was a Bible, the first she'd ever owned. She clutched it to her heart. "Thank you," she whispered again as they embraced. "Thank you for everything."

Then Molly unfastened the roan's tether and climbed into the buggy. Mary Rose stood by the gate watching as Molly drove away.

Four days later, the *Molly Quinn* hadn't returned. On the fifth day, Molly saw the three-master enter the bay and hurried to the dock. But she knew by the look on Jam's face as he rowed the tender toward her that the news wasn't good.

"I'm sorry, Missy," the old fisherman said, as he stepped from the small boat onto the dock. "They've disappeared. Not a trace." He shook his head sadly. "But we didn't find a ship-wreck." His shoulders were slumped in discouragement. "So maybe they're still out there, somewhere." But his tone said he didn't believe they were.

Molly listened only long enough to hear where they'd searched, then she told him her plan. He smiled sadly. "All we can do is try, just try, Miss Molly. But I don't know how much good it will do."

Molly lifted her chin. "We're going to search till we find them, Jam. You spread the word. Tell everyone my offer. I hope every ship and boat in this bay is heading out by tomorrow's dawn."

Jam nodded. "Yes, ma'am." But he didn't look convinced.

The next morning, however, there was a hubbub of activity at the dock. Molly was there before sunup, orchestrating the rescue. She spoke with many of the fishermen and sea captains herself, asking them to pass on the information about the catch compensation and reward to others. A short time later dozens of vessels set sail.

All day Molly awaited word. By nightfall, a few ships had returned with no news. Those that stayed out all night returned in the morning, also with nothing to report. But Molly refused to be discouraged.

The search continued throughout that first week. Each day, Molly set out with new determination, ignoring the pitying looks from the men who daily reported their progress.

At the end of the second week, Mary Rose joined her at the

Del Cortés, walking with Molly to the wharf when the search vessels returned. But still, there was no good news. After a few days, a downhearted Mary Rose returned to her little Jesse in Carmel.

Finally, three weeks after Zach and Devon disappeared, a shout went up from a small fishing boat at it neared shore. Molly had just arrived from town and watched tearfully as waterlogged pieces of wood were dropped noisily on the dock. "Are you sure that's from Zach's?" she asked.

Jam walked up beside her. "Can't be for certain-sure, Missy," he said quietly. "But it looks it to me. Same color. Been in the water 'bout long enough."

"If you're not sure," Molly said decisively, "the search will go on." She ignored the exchanged glances among the fishermen and workers on the dock. "Anyone who wants to continue will receive the same pay as before, and I'm doubling the reward."

Jam moved closer. "Missy," he said, his voice raspy. "None of us wants to admit that the cap'n ain't comin' back. But we don't like takin' your money like this either."

Molly remained silent, knowing what he was going to say next, but not wanting to hear it.

"He's not comin' back, Miss Molly. I know it breaks your heart to hear it. And I wish I didn't have to say it. But it's been nearly a month now." He patted her arm. "Zach took a boat out in one of the worst storms in recent memory. There's no sign of him anywhere. Only these few pieces of waterlogged wood."

"But he could still be out there," Molly said, her gaze taking in the expanse of gray-green ocean. "What if..." She felt the sting of tears behind her eyes. "What if Zach...and Devon...are out there? Somewhere. And we stop looking? And they can't get back without us?" She couldn't let the searchers stop. She just couldn't. To do so would be admitting that Zach was dead.

"If'n there was a chance, I'd be the first to tell you. But honey, they're not comin' back. Everybody knows it but you."

"Keep searching," Molly said, refusing to listen. "Tell them I'll pay double."

Jam looked troubled. "They're sayin' they won't do it, Missy. They're sayin' it's like robbin' you. They won't do it for any amount of money."

She nodded. "I see."

He looked stricken. "But I'll keep lookin' if'n you want me to."

Molly kept her eyes on the horizon, just as she had every day of the search. Jam was right. She turned back to the old fisherman. "You tell the men," she finally said, "that the search is over."

"I'll tell 'em."

Molly turned away.

"But Missy," Jam called after her, "they all said to tell you while we're out there fishin' none of us are gonna give up. Every day we'll still be lookin' for the cap'n and his friend."

She nodded, but couldn't answer. The pain of her loss suddenly swept over her in waves. She didn't allow herself to think about the search that was ending. Because if she did, the tears would begin. And when they did, she knew they wouldn't stop.

It was over. Zach wasn't coming home.

The next morning, Molly flicked the reins above the horse, urging her up the steep hill. Within minutes, they reached the top, and across the meadow stood the beautiful house. It hurt too much to consider the place where she'd last been in Zach's arms, so she kept the horse trotting along the road that wound to the house.

She unhitched the mare and turned her out to pasture, then pulled the house key from her pocket as she walked up the rock-lined path to the front door. Moments later, she pushed open the heavy door.

At first, the entry was too dim to see much, and she let her eyes adjust before looking for a lamp to light. She headed for the room that she thought might be the kitchen, found a lamp on the table, with kerosene and matches nearby.

Carrying the lamp, she began a tour of the house. As she stepped from room to room, her wonder grew. The inside design was as much a part of the landscape as the exterior. Everything was natural, from the stained wood to the river-rock fireplace. Across the front of the house, which faced the ocean, windows rose from floor to ceiling.

Molly wandered throughout the house, feeling Zach's presence everywhere she looked. He had built it for her, but the house exuded his personality. It spoke of his strength, his attention to detail, his appreciation of natural beauty.

At last, she came to a large room upstairs off the main hallway. Holding the lamp in one hand, she turned the brass handle and pushed open the double door.

Stepping in, she paused in awe. The L-shaped room had floors of polished wood, graced by rich-colored Persian carpets. A stately ebony grand piano stood at one end, a towering stone fireplace at the corner where the room turned into a smaller wing.

As she moved into the room, her attention was caught by a painting over the fireplace. She walked closer, lifting the lamp. By the time she stopped in front of it, her heart was aching with love and sorrow. It was *The Jeweled Dawn.*

It had been Zach who bought it after all. She didn't know how he'd arranged it. A bid by proxy, perhaps? She smiled—it really didn't matter. For a long time, she gazed at the oil, unable to move.

At last, she stepped over to the window and gazed out. It was dark now, but she knew that the view of the ocean from this room would be more spectacular than from anywhere else in the house. *The Jeweled Dawn* faced the window. If she looked out at a certain time of morning, when the sun was just right— just as Zach had told her on that long-ago, terrifying night after the earthquake—she knew she would see the jewels in the sea.

But she also knew that she wouldn't look out. Not alone. Not ever, unless Zach was here with her.

She moved away from the window and rounded the corner to the room's smaller wing. It served as a library, and was filled floor to ceiling with books. Zach had placed a desk across from this side of the fireplace, and Molly moved over to it, setting the lamp to one side, and settling into Zach's luxurious leather chair.

Then she looked up at the painting opposite her, a smile of recognition dawning on her face.

She leaned back in the chair, feeling a gentle peace ebb into her soul. It was as if Zach had left her a message of hope.

There on the wall was the O'Rourke that had first captured her attention at the Capitol.

It was the *Hope.*

Molly looked at the swirling seas in the painting, then she moved her gaze to the lighthouse and its warm glow.

Suddenly, she knew why Devon painted light. His light wasn't an inanimate illumination. No, he painted living light, a symbol of the One who was the light of the world.

In the middle of life's uncertainty, tragedy, or confusion, darkness prevailed. It caused pain and sorrow and bitterness and desperation...much like the dark waves that crashed near the lighthouse in his painting.

Yet the light shone brightly, penetrating the darkness, bringing safe passage to those lost at sea.

Molly looked up at the lighthouse. She didn't want to perish in her darkness. She wanted to know, to be filled with light, *the* Light.

She bowed her head. "Jesus, my Lord," she breathed, "I'm new at this. I don't know that I've ever talked with you before...I mean as if you were a real person, actually listening to me, caring about what I might say to you. So forgive me, if I stumble with my words."

She swallowed, aware of a sweet and powerful presence with her in the room. "I believe in who you are, that you came to earth to die in my place, to die for the sins of all of us. I can't imagine the love that would cause you to do that for me."

She paused again, considering the agony Jesus endured on the cross, the humiliation that God's Son endured at the hands of his creation. "What love," she whispered. "Would you have done it just for me?" She felt certain of it and began to weep. "How can it be that you could love someone who has never acknowledged your presence?"

For a long time, Molly considered the love of her Father. She didn't speak, but just let the sweet knowledge of it enfold her, flow over her, fill her. Then, taking a deep breath, she murmured, "Will you come into that place that you created in my heart to fill with yourself?"

Again, she kept her head bowed in silence, letting her

thoughts dwell only on God's power to change lives. It struck her suddenly that if he'd created such a place inside, he'd known her intimately from the moment she was conceived. He *knew* her better than she knew herself. He knew everything about her, the good and the bad. Yet he loved her anyway!

She looked up, startled by the joy of the thought. She was loved and accepted by the God of the universe! He'd created her—along with the stars and the moon and the sun—yet he also knew every intimate thing about her.

Molly thought she couldn't contain her joy. She looked up at the *Hope* with new eyes, and her thoughts again turned to Zach. Had he discovered the same joy? Was that why he'd placed the painting in front of his desk?

She reached into her pocket and pulled out the Bible that Mary Rose had given to her weeks earlier. Opening the cover, she touched her fingers to the inscription:

> *To Zachary...and to Molly,*
> *With love and friendship,*
> *Devon and Mary Rose*

She could see that her name had been added later, and Mary Rose had written next to it, *Isaiah 54:11*. She thumbed through the thin pages to the place and began to read:

> *Behold, I will lay thy stones with fair colours. And lay thy foundations with sapphires. I will make your windows of agates...and all your borders of precious stones.*

At first, she took the words literally, and wondered why Mary Rose had chosen that particular passage. Her next thought was that perhaps it was a message about heaven. Then, with a small frown, she read it again. She took in a sharp breath, almost as if the words were audibly spoken by God to her.

Could it be that real jewels were not those she'd been trying to gather for herself through QIL? She'd come to America seeking riches and wealth, even power. Perhaps the jewels in the verse symbolized those things God was giving to her of himself—forgiveness, grace, joy, peace, faithfulness, and love. Perhaps those precious "jewels" were the foundation stones of her new life in him.

They were of eternal value. And she considered QIL Enterprises, the wealth she'd acquired through her efforts. Those riches paled in comparison.

"I surrender everything," she whispered, her eyes focusing on the lighthouse and its glow. "I give you all I am...all I can ever be. It belongs to you, Lord. I belong to you, completely."

CHAPTER

MOLLY STAYED AT THE HOUSE on the sea cliffs for more than a week, going into Carmel only once for provisions. She spent every day in prayer, often sitting alone on an outcropping of stones, overlooking the ocean. She lost herself in the books of Psalms, Isaiah, and John. Other times she talked with God, speaking to him as to a precious friend, and her time with him brought a sweet balm to her anxious soul.

Each day she prayed for Zach's and Devon's safety, clinging to the hope that they might somehow still be alive. Mary Rose and Jesse visited, and the three of them walked down to the beach to picnic, and Jesse played in the sand. Mary Rose and Molly developed an even deeper bond of friendship as they cried together, laughed together, and prayed together.

Molly opened her heart to her friend. "I'm struggling with a decision," she said one morning as they walked to the beach. "I need some time away from QIL. If Zach doesn't come back…" Her voice faltered.

Mary Rose gave her an understanding look.

Molly took a deep breath. "I could stay at QIL, continue running it just as I am now. But something keeps me from committing my heart and soul to it again." She stepped from the rocky path onto the sand. Mary Rose followed, holding Jesse's hand.

"Something...or Someone?" Mary Rose said, as Jesse ran out to splash in a small wave.

Molly knew she meant God. "That's why I may go away for a while, perhaps to England. Or the Continent. The *Prince Edward* will be docked in San Francisco soon." She sighed, then shook her head sadly. "Yet when I consider booking passage, something stops me. I picture Zach alive and well and on his way home."

They each took hold of the corners of a small chenille bedspread, laid it on the sand, then settled onto it.

Molly squinted out at the calm sea. "But I can't stay here forever." Then she sighed. "I just wish I knew what to do."

"You'll know the right thing to do when the time comes, Molly," Mary Rose said. "You've prayed for guidance, and God is with you. You'll know."

"How about you, Mary Rose? What will you do?"

Mary Rose turned her gaze from the open sea to look at Molly. "I haven't given up hope. Even after the weeks of search, I just can't give up hope."

The following day, Molly hitched up the buggy, drove into Monterey, and wired Kingsley, asking him to let the board members know that she was at last ready to meet with them— and for the last time. She also asked him to book passage on the *Prince Edward* for her.

That evening, on her ride back to the sea cliffs, her heart was troubled. Deciding to leave made Zach's disappearance seem final. She fought back tears and prayed for him, desperately holding onto the hope that he might still be alive.

The sun had risen high the next morning when a knock sounded at the door. She opened it slowly, surprised when she saw Mary Rose's ashen face.

Then she gasped.

It was Devon! Haggard and thin, he stood with an arm around Mary Rose.

"Devon?" she whispered, not believing her eyes. How could it be? And where was Zach?

The young man stepped forward and pulled her into his arms. "I'm sorry, Molly," he said hoarsely.

Then she knew.

"It's Zach, isn't it?" she cried softly, looking up at him. "It's Zach."

Devon and Mary Rose cradled her in their arms. "I'm so sorry," Mary Rose murmured.

Molly thought her knees would fold beneath her, and she held onto them both for support. "Please," Molly finally said, "let's go inside. You need to tell me what happened."

Mary Rose and Devon entered the house, and Molly led them into the small downstairs sitting room. She stood by the front window, looking out at the sea. Devon and Mary Rose moved to stand beside her.

"Tell me…," Molly said at last, not looking at either of them.

"The storm took us by surprise, Molly," Devon said. "We thought we'd have plenty of time to make it back to Monterey before it hit."

She nodded, biting her lip.

"The current slammed the boat against the Point Sur cliffs," he went on softly. "After the boat broke apart, Zach and I held onto separate pieces of the wreckage. Miraculously though, we were able to swim away from the cliffs.

"We managed to stay near each other…until we became too weak to keep up the effort. Then, just a few hours after the accident, we were hit by driving rain and waves that swept over us. A wave—larger than any I'd ever seen in the Pacific—towered up above us, then crashed down, pushing us under." He paused. "Right before it hit, Molly, that's the last time I saw him.

"I paddled toward the place, yelling for him. Waiting for him to reappear. Hours passed. Then a day. Maybe more. I don't remember. I gave in to the current. The rain continued, and I couldn't see land. I didn't know whether it was because of the fog or if I had been carried too far out to sea. Then the scrap of hull I'd been hanging onto began falling apart, and I gave up hope."

Devon's voice was low. "The water was so cold, so very cold. I remember just letting go." He sighed. "I woke up days later in a hospital, battered and unable to breathe. Pneumonia, they said. Someone had found me, near death. On a beach not far from where we foundered." He swallowed hard. "But they didn't find Zach, Molly. I'm sorry."

"But you made it," Molly said turning to him. "That's got to mean that Zach could have made it too!" She wanted to believe it.

Devon shook his head. "I saw the wave pull him under, Molly. It was thunderous. He never came back to the surface." He paused, then added sadly, "It would have taken a miracle to survive something like that."

"No!" she cried, refusing to accept that Zach could be dead. "No!" Mary Rose gathered her into her arms, and Devon held them both. "No, it can't be!" she wept, overcome by pain and sorrow.

᷑ᴏ᷒

Mary Rose and Devon stayed with Molly that night, their presence a welcome comfort. Molly went to bed before sundown. Until tonight, she'd held onto the hope that Zach would return. But Devon had seen him die.

Zach was gone.

Her dreams were ashes. She thought about her new faith, but somehow, she couldn't see beyond her sorrow to find God.

Mary Rose tapped on her door a few hours later, bringing her tea and some soup. Molly couldn't eat, so Mary Rose just sat beside her bed, holding her hand.

"I miss him so much," Molly said. "I didn't realize how much I was hanging onto the hope that Zach was alive. But now, it's so final. My hope is gone. And I feel so empty. Where is the solace I felt earlier? Where is God?"

Molly squeezed her hand. "He's holding you, Molly. When we can't walk, or talk, or even see him in times like these, he carries us close to his heart. He's there, Molly. Remember— nothing can separate you from his love, not even death. God's with you this very minute, with you in your heartache. Cling to that knowledge, Molly."

Mary Rose sat with Molly through the night. When the sun finally rose, Molly slept at last. And still Mary Rose and Devon stayed in the house watching over her.

In the afternoon, Molly sat with them in the room under *The Jeweled Dawn,* speaking of her plans for the future. "I've decided to return to England for a while," she said, taking a deep breath. "But before I go, I'll meet with the board and arrange to take a leave. I want to find out what God has ahead for me." She gave them a small smile. "So far in my life, I've determined my own future—or thought I did. This time, I'm going to let my Lord take the helm."

"Just listen to his voice, Molly," said Mary Rose. "I know he'll lead you."

Molly smiled sadly. "It's strange, but even in the darkest hour of my sorrow, there is a light that I'm drawn to, knowing somehow that as I approach it, joy will be restored. Perhaps not soon. But someday."

"He heals our heartaches," Devon said. "He is the light you're drawn to, and it's healing from our sorrows, Molly, that he offers."

She swallowed hard. "I've got a lot to learn." She stood and looked out over the meadow to the sea beyond. "But I suppose I've got nothing but time in which to learn it. His time."

By late afternoon, Devon and Mary Rose had left, and Molly prepared to do the same the following morning. She packed her things, leaving only *Mary Rose's Garden,* the wedding gift she and Zach had planned to give the couple, in the great room. The gift would have to wait. Devon and Mary Rose hadn't said when they now planned to marry.

Molly arrived at the train station in Monterey in time to catch the noon Del Cortés Special to Salinas. She watched blindly as the countryside passed outside the train window. In Salinas, she changed trains, taking the midafternoon flier into San Francisco. By dusk she was on a cable car, heading up Nob Hill.

She stopped at the entrance to her cottage and unlocked the front door. Then, frowning, she paused in the foyer. Instead of the musty smell of a closed-up house, the distinct fragrance of cooking food wafted from the kitchen.

Feeling her way along in the darkness, she moved down the long hallway to the sitting room. As soon as she turned the corner, she saw a dim light beneath the kitchen door.

Who would be here without her?

She tried to dismiss her worry, thinking it was probably Cook Liu. Maybe he'd slipped out of the Forresters' house when he'd heard she was home, and now he was preparing a special dish in welcome.

Briskly, she walked toward the door and swung it open.

A tall red-haired man, stirring a pot in front of the stove, turned in surprise.

"Winny!" she exclaimed. "What are you doing here?"

"Well, if it isn't the famous Molly Quinn!" he said with a grin. "Cousin of the infamous Winston Carlisle-Jones." He gave her a mock bow with an elegant flourish of the wooden spoon he held in his hand.

"Winny," Molly whispered and sank into a chair at the small table at the room's center. "How long have you been here?"

He raised a light red eyebrow. "Since the day you left, Molly." The grin was gone from his face. "I watched from the back of the house until you'd put your bags and things in the hired motorcar. Then I just let myself in. I hope you don't mind."

"Mind?" She let out a long sigh, shaking her head slowly. "You're an escaped convict, accused of stabbing a guard."

"He didn't die, Molly. And it was in self-defense. He'd been after me for months. When I tried to escape, he came after me with the knife. We fought, and I ended up hurting him. It was him or me." He shrugged, his expression sad. "I chose to live." Gone was the careless demeanor she'd first seen when she entered the room.

"Were there witnesses?"

"None I could rely on." He sat down at the table, across from her. "I'm sorry, Molly. I've muddled things, haven't I?"

She nodded. "Why did you escape, Winny? You had only a few weeks to go."

He let out a short, brittle laugh. "Oh, you didn't hear about that, did you? I'm sure our dear friend, Senator Starr, hasn't told you about his part in all this."

Molly caught her breath, remembering Julian's visit to San Quentin. She had hoped he wasn't involved. "No," she said sadly. "I haven't seen him. Did he put you up to this, Winny?"

He laughed again. "Put me up to it? You could say he shoved me into it."

"I'm sorry, Win. He was trying to get back at me—"

Winny interrupted, squinting at her. "Get back at you? What he pulled was hardly the way to do it. Unless keeping me behind bars would've saddened you, somehow. And after the trouble I've caused, I should think it would have had quite the opposite effect, Molly."

"What do you mean?" She frowned, trying to comprehend.

"He pulled some political strings and had my parole revoked. I was due to get out in weeks, Molly. Think of it." He shook his head. "Weeks! Then our dear friend appeared and spoke to the board before I came up for final review."

Molly was stunned. Julian had tried to help her, after all.

"Not only that, he had me placed in solitary confinement. He wanted me completely out of touch with the world. For your sake, I dare say, dear Molly." He hurried on. "You know me. That is the worst thing anyone could do. I had to get out. I thought I'd die if I didn't."

"Oh, Winny..." Molly reached across the table and took his

hand. He didn't pull away. "What are you going to do now?"

"Will you still help me, Moll? You said you'd set me up in business in Australia. I've got connections. I can get out of the country. The authorities will never expect to look for me in— where was it to be?"

"Canberra."

"In Canberra. No one will think to look for me there. I can start all over again, Moll." His face brightened with new excitement. "Begin a new life. Stay out of trouble. I've been thinking about it the whole time you were gone. If you'll back me—and I promise I'll not make any trouble by making myself known— maybe I can make a fortune for us both. Will you help me?"

Molly looked into his face. She could see a glimpse of the old Winny in his expression—scheming for the future, dreaming of riches. There was no malice or bitterness toward her now. Though perhaps it was simply because he needed her help.

"I can't, Winny. I'm sorry."

"We're family, Moll. You can't turn your back on me."

"I'll stand by you if you turn yourself in. But I won't help you escape."

"Turn myself in? Do you know what they'll do to me, Molly? I'll be in prison for years. I'd rather die than go back."

"I know."

There was anguish in his eyes.

"I'll pay for your defense. We'll get you the best lawyer money can buy, find witnesses to back up your claim of self-defense. That's the only way I can help, Win. Nothing else."

He stood and walked to the stove, gave the pot of beans a stir, then turned back to face her. "You haven't said you'd turn me in. Would you do that to me?"

"No," she whispered. "You've got to make your own decision. All I can tell you is that I'll go with you, arrange for your legal help, and stand by you through your trial. I'll do whatever it takes to help you...*if* you do the right thing." She looked at her favorite cousin, caring deeply for him. A feeling of sadness for him swept over her. "But if you decide against my help," she went on, "I want you out of my house by morning, Winny."

"Molly," he said as she stood to leave the room.

She'd nearly reached the door when she remembered the small book in her pocket. She turned back to Winny.

"If you go, I've got something I want you to take with you."

He looked at her, surprised.

She walked over to him and placed in his hands the small Bible that Mary Rose had given her. Then on tiptoe, she kissed him on the cheek, and left the room.

The next morning Winny and the Bible were gone.

One week later, Molly sat behind her office desk at QIL. She'd been making notes for the board meeting, but as too often happened now, she found it difficult to keep her mind on business. Perhaps, she thought, because QIL no longer mattered. Since Zach had left her, everything had changed. She wondered how long she would feel the desperate sadness and loss.

She turned her chair toward the window to gaze out. The *Prince Edward,* one of the prestigious Cunard vessels, was anchored in the bay. Molly's trunks had already been delivered, and she would embark this afternoon, immediately after addressing the members of QIL's board of directors at their opening meeting.

A knock interrupted her thoughts, and she turned to the door. "Come in."

Kingsley entered and strode across the room toward her. "Are you ready?"

She nodded, standing to greet him. "Yes."

"You're sure you want to do this, Molly? It's not too late to change your mind."

"I'm sure. Shall we go?"

They walked into the board room where the others had already gathered. Molly took her place at the head of the long table. On one side sat Clive and Nevil Richards, and across from them, Luke Cornelius. Kingsley sat opposite Molly. He gave her a smile of encouragement as he settled into his chair.

"Gentlemen," Molly began without preamble, "this is the last time I will address you as president of QIL Enterprises. After a time of deep searching, I have decided to step down.

"You received a proposal from me by courier a few days ago. I trust you have had opportunity to review its contents."

The men gave her affirmative nods.

"To briefly review the document—I state that my reasons for stepping down are personal, and certainly not due to any weakness in QIL's financial status. In truth, the company's financial health has never been better. Kingsley Forrester has just completed the acquisition of three more brickyards. Our canning operations in Monterey are expanding due to better and more efficient equipment. We've recently hired a London-based investment counselor who will soon open an office there to handle the huge volume of British investors. The loans division is healthy—both in the private and public sectors. It continues to expand even though most of our loans now require collateral.

"No, gentlemen, it's important for you to know my resignation is not due to financial failure of any kind."

There were murmurs of approval.

"Neither is it due to the unfortunate situation with my cousin Winston Carlisle-Jones, and the matter we discussed at length during our last board meeting. As you have heard, my cousin escaped from prison some weeks ago.

"I realize that Winny's connection to me could be a potential embarrassment to QIL, for all those reasons we've discussed before.

"I want to give you the opportunity to leave QIL if you think it prudent. We currently have the assets—including my personal resources—to buy back your shares, giving you a percentage of profit, if you would like to resign your positions.

"It would mean the demise of QIL as we know it, but you have the choice to walk away with a profit or to stay and take part in QIL's future growth.

"So gentlemen, subject to your approval, I would like to introduce my choice for QIL's new president, Kingsley Forrester."

There were more nods of approval. Molly smiled at Kingsley.

"One more word before I leave, gentlemen." She leaned forward intently, looking into their faces. "I've had the privilege of walking into a world that most women never see. I planted a small seed from which a company grew. I tended it and watched it grow, somewhat like a garden." She smiled, remembering how she'd told Zach the same thing so long ago. "Thank you for standing by me while together we watched QIL's growth and expansion.

"I've placed my personal resources at QIL's disposal, giving Kingsley power of attorney on my behalf. Until I return, gentlemen, I bid you farewell."

She smiled as they began to applaud. Suddenly they stood, still clapping.

Molly nodded her thanks, then shook hands with each. At her desk, she picked up her wide-brimmed straw hat and placed it on her head, attaching it securely with the long hat pin. She walked to the window for a last look out at the bay. She whispered a prayer and swallowed hard. It was time to leave.

After a moment, she left the room, closing the door behind her.

She gave a teary-eyed Victoria Parrott a quick hug, shook Jimmy Green's hand, then moved briskly to the elevator, not turning to look back.

Moments later, she found her seat on the trolley. The little bell jingled as it rattled along the tracks to the waterfront and the boarding terminal for the *Prince Edward*.

37

ZACH LEANED AGAINST THE SPLIT-WOOD FENCE that circled the corral, watching Jeremiah saddle a young Appaloosa.

"You're sure you feel up to this?" Jeremiah asked, looking worried.

Zach nodded. "I'll be fine." He winced as he tried to put his weight on his right leg. He'd nearly lost it from infection weeks earlier, and it still caused him pain. He smiled at Jeremiah. "Besides, I'll be riding, not walking."

The older man chuckled. "In all my picked-up-and-put-together, I've never seen a man so all-fired determined to be someplace other than where he was. I think you'd be willin' to walk to that little gal you tol' me about, if you had to."

"I believe you're right." Zach grinned. As usual, he enjoyed Jeremiah's odd way of stringing words together. "But luckily, your Appaloosa will keep me from it."

Jeremiah walked the gentle horse through the gate, and Zach limped over and patted its neck.

"I don't know how I can thank you for all you've done," he said. "You brought me back among the living."

The man shook his head. "I don't claim any credit. It was the old fisherman who brought you that done it. How he made it here in that storm, I'll never know. Sure beats all." He shook his head slowly.

Zach agreed, though he'd been unconscious during the journey. The last he knew until waking in Jeremiah's one-room shack, he'd been clinging to a pitifully small piece of broken hull. He'd felt himself slip into the dark water. Then he'd waited, suspended below the ocean's surface, for death to claim him. He remembered having no fear.

Then a hand, iron-strong and powerful, reached for his and pulled him into that small rowboat. Before he slipped into unconsciousness, Zach saw the old man's kind face and heard his words that Devon, too, was going to be all right. It didn't occur to him until much later to wonder how the fisherman knew. Zach still wondered if he'd dreamed it, though he couldn't explain the strange assurance he felt that Devon was safe.

Zach planted his foot into the stirrup, then swung his wounded leg over the Appaloosa's saddle. He winced in pain.

"You all right, son?" Jeremiah's face wore the lines of worry. "You should stay here another week. That infection could return. You aren't properly healed, yet."

"I'll be fine," Zach assured him again.

"I've packed enough bread and salt pork to last you. They're tucked inside the saddlebags."

"I'll send you payment for the horse as soon as I get to Monterey."

"You don't worry about that, now. But I would appreciate knowin' you made it safe and sound. You let me know, hear?"

"I'll do it, Jeremiah." Zach grinned down at him. "Better than that, if all goes according to plan I'll be sending an invitation to my wedding."

Jeremiah cocked his head sideways, squinting against the

sun. "That must be some pretty little gal who's got you high-tailin' it up to see her like there's no tomorrow."

"She is indeed, Jeremiah."

"God bless you, son," Jeremiah said with a nod. "You be careful now."

Zach nodded, and nudged the horse's flanks. Moments later, he had set out across the inland foothills to the nearest road leading north. And he settled back into the saddle, relishing the warmth of the sun after being so long indoors.

Molly strode from the *Prince Edward* boarding terminal to the dock, awaiting the tender that would take her to the ship.

A short distance away, near a coil of rope, a newspaper boy called out the headlines. To pass the time, she walked over and bought a paper, tucking it under her arm. A bay wind kicked up, slicing through her with its chill. She shivered and reached up to hold her hat, its silk cabbage roses fluttering in the breeze.

A three-masted schooner glided by, and she remembered the *Molly Quinn*, her joy when she had seen it the first time, her delight when Zach had pointed out its name.

Suddenly, she wondered what would happen to the vessel and his fishing business. Frowning, she realized she should have contacted Jam. And what about the seacliff house? It would stand empty, a silent monument to the love that would have filled it.

Molly drew in a deep breath, wondering if she was wrong to leave. Was she running away from her pain instead of facing it?

For the first time, she considered what Zach might want her

to do. He loved Monterey, the *Molly Quinn,* and the open sea. He'd built the house in the meadow by the cliffs for her. She thought of the precious things it held.

She sighed, looking out into the bay. Then boarding began and she took her place in line, valise in hand.

Zach's leg pained him, and he could see the bleeding had started again. It was nearing midday, and he was surprised at how quickly he had tired. He spotted a small stream ahead and halted the Appaloosa, then, with a grimace, slid from the saddle.

He rewrapped his wound, then drank his fill of the sweet water. After munching on the meal that Jeremiah had packed, he laid back under the shade of a live oak and rested, his hat pulled low over his eyes.

Soon his eyes closed in sleep. He woke a few hours later, slightly disoriented. He drank his fill again from the nearby stream. Refreshed, he remounted and started on his way again, hoping to reach Carmel by dark. He planned to stay with Devon, then rise before sunup for the short ride to the sea cliff.

Again, he wondered if Devon would be there.

Or if he'd dreamed about the old man who'd saved them both.

Molly settled into her stateroom, placing the newspaper on a bedside table. A portion of the headline faced up, and she looked at it curiously. THREE-YEAR ANNIVERSARY OF GREAT—She unfolded the paper to read the rest—SAN FRANCISCO QUAKE: TOMORROW, APRIL 18.

She opened her eyes wide. Tomorrow was the day that she

and Zach had promised to meet. Her heart sank. At dawn, she would be here on the *Prince Edward*, leaving the bay for the open sea, and eventually, for England.

"Oh, Zach," she whispered, drawing in a shaky breath. "My beloved..."

She walked to the porthole and peered out, seeing only a small patch of sky. Then she paced the small cabin, picked up the news article again, then set it down.

She reached up to unpin her hat, then, arms in midair, set her lips in a straight line and left the hat on her head.

Suddenly she knew.

She couldn't, wouldn't leave now. Or perhaps ever.

Molly snatched up the valise and hurried from her cabin, to quickly get passage back to shore.

An hour later, Molly boarded the train for Salinas. By sundown, she caught the last Del Cortés Special into Monterey. After hiring a horse-drawn carriage equipped with lanterns, she headed to the seacliff house. She stopped at the general store for a few food items and supplies, loaded them, then started on her way.

Dusk was beginning to fall when Molly urged the horse onto the road leading from Monterey. She followed Lighthouse Road around Point Piños.

The lighthouse torch glowed through the gathering darkness. She halted the horse and looked up. The *Hope,* she whispered, feeling strangely comforted before flicking the reins and riding on toward the forested hills beyond Pacific Grove.

Zach reached Carmel-by-the-Sea just as the moon was rising. He tied the Appaloosa to a small manzanita tree near Mary

Rose's cottage and limped to her front door. He waited not only for Mary Rose, but to see if Devon would be with her. He'd felt so certain that his friend had been rescued. But what if he'd been wrong? He didn't want to consider it.

He knocked, then listened as he heard someone approach the door. Seconds later, it swung open.

There was a stunned silence.

"Zach?" Mary Rose whispered, as if unable to believe her eyes. She dried her hands on her long apron. "Zach!" She gave a small cry, covering her mouth in amazement.

"What?" Devon came round the corner, then stopped abruptly when he saw Zach. For a moment, he couldn't speak, as he stared at the man standing before him.

Zach laughed softly. "It's me, honestly—not an apparition."

Then he reached out for his friends, and everyone started talking at once. There was hugging and laughing and crying before Zach finally was brought in the house. Before he would answer their questions about his rescue, though, Zach asked about Molly.

Mary Rose and Devon exchanged a glance, then Mary Rose reached for his hand. "Oh, Zach...," she said sadly. "Molly's leaving for England. She booked passage on the *Prince Edward*."

Zach drew in a sharp breath. "When does she leave?"

"Tomorrow morning."

He had to look away, unable to disguise his anguish. "From San Francisco?"

"Yes. She, we all thought that you..." Mary Rose couldn't finish.

"I understand," Zach said, but his heart wasn't in it. And now, he felt so desperately weary. The ride, the disappointment, had taken its toll.

Devon and Mary Rose seemed to sense his fatigue, and after a warm supper, Devon led him up the path through Mary Rose's garden and across the small bridge to the studio.

Before they bunked down, Zach asked one last question of his friend. "Have you set a new wedding date?"

Devon grinned. "Three weeks from now. That will give you just enough time to recover. We wouldn't do it without you, friend."

"In the mission?"

"No. We've decided on a garden wedding. It will be in Mary Rose's garden."

Zach smiled. "I can't think of anything more fitting," he said, as he headed to the small guest quarters off the main studio. He crawled into bed, noticing that every muscle and bone in his body ached, especially his heart.

He turned over, pulling the covers over his shoulders. Just before he fell asleep, an idea entered his mind, and he sat up in the dark to consider it.

Instead of heading to the house in the morning, he would ride straight to Monterey, gather the crew of the *Molly Quinn*, and sail toward San Francisco.

The little schooner would easily intercept the *Prince Edward*. And Molly would be in his arms before the passing of a fortnight. He could have Molly back in time for Devon and Mary Rose's wedding.

Perhaps it could be a double wedding!

That certainly was an idea worth his consideration, he thought happily as he laid his head back on the pillow and fell asleep.

Molly let herself into the house, hurrying to light a lamp to dispel the lonely darkness. She carried in the boxes of food, stored them in the pantry just off the kitchen, and climbed the stairs to the second floor, to the large room where the paintings hung.

She placed the lamp on a table, then set a few logs in the fireplace of the great room. Above the fireplace, *The Jeweled Dawn* seemed to take on a light of its own as the bright flames beneath it cast a flickering glow across the room.

Molly settled onto a small sofa and looked up at the oil. When she'd stayed here after the news of Zach's disappearance, she hadn't wanted to go out to the cliffs alone. But tomorrow she would walk there, to honor Zach's memory and their promise.

It had been a long day. Too weary to return to the kitchen to fix herself even a small dinner, Molly fell asleep on the couch, curled up with Zach's old and worn coat pulled over her.

She slept soundly, waking only once to the music of the waves in the distance. Nearby, the hooting of an owl and the chirping of crickets lulled her back to sleep.

Zach woke long before dawn. He rose without disturbing Devon, then washed and dressed and headed down the path to where the Appaloosa waited in a small field. He was glad that Devon had groomed, fed, and watered the horse the night before.

He buckled the saddle, then swung his leg over, noticing that his pain had lessened. Nudging the horse onto the main road through Carmel, he wound upward into the forest of pines on the hill between the small seaside town and his property on the cliffs.

A pale gray light was just coloring the eastern sky when Zach neared the turnoff. In his hurry to get to Monterey and set sail on the *Molly Quinn,* he rode past, pressing his heels in the horse's flanks.

He'd ridden a few miles north when he slowed the Appaloosa. For a long moment, he watched the sea reflect the changing light of the sky above it, and he couldn't let go of the thought, the prayer, the hope, that Molly—at this very moment—might be looking through her porthole at the same sight, holding their love in her heart.

Then he glanced down the road leading to the sea cliffs. Perhaps he should go back.

After all, it was the day, the very dawn, of their promise.

For a moment, he watched the changing sea, then he nudged the Appaloosa in the flanks.

It was still dark when Molly woke. She slipped into a day dress for her walk through the meadow to the cliffs. Shivering, she pulled on a long wrap, hugging it close as she stepped from the house.

The pale light of dawn was beginning to spread across the sky, and the day promised to be clear and beautiful, with a few spring birds already lifting their voices in song. A light breeze carried the scent of wildflowers toward her. Without knowing why, Molly's spirits lifted, and she sighed, momentarily forgetting her sadness.

She walked briskly to the cliffs, and by the time she stood overlooking the ocean, the sky had turned a dusky silver-rose and was rapidly changing to blue.

A few gulls circled, and here and there on the rocky shore below the cliffs, seals barked at the coming sun. Molly shaded her eyes, looking for sea otters, as she often did when on the beach.

Then, suddenly, Molly thought she heard the pounding of horse's hooves coming up the hillside road toward the meadow. She turned, but saw nothing. Thinking it was her imagination, she turned back to the ocean.

Then a horse whinnied behind her, and she looked again. This time there was no mistaking. A rider was approaching from across the meadow.

He came closer, and Molly thought her knees might give way beneath her. It was Zach!

But, no, it couldn't be!

Zach was dead. Devon saw it happen.

She held her breath as the rider drew nearer. Then, as the sun began to rise, it touched his face. And she knew. He rode closer, his gaze locked on hers. His expression brought quick tears to her eyes as she saw his pure, deep, abiding love—as if shining from some inner light—brighter than dawn's sunlight.

"Zach!" she cried, running toward him.

Zach halted the Appaloosa, but she'd reached him before he'd dismounted. He slid from the saddle and gathered her into his arms.

"Oh, Molly," he cried, holding her close. "My precious Molly."

She flung her arms around him, burying her face in his neck. They held each other without speaking.

"I don't want to ask how...or why...or anything yet," she whispered hoarsely. "I just want to feel your arms around me."

He held her even more tightly. "Oh, my beloved...," he breathed. "I want nothing more than to know I'm not dreaming...that you're really here, really in my arms. All these weeks..."

Then he leaned back, looking into her eyes. "Molly, I never want to be without you again."

Molly regarded the beloved man before her. It had taken almost losing him to convince her that this was where she belonged. For the rest of her life. She looked back at the house behind them. They would fill it with love and laughter and, someday, their babies' sweet voices and pattering footsteps.

God would build their family with those precious jewels of love and joy she'd read about in Isaiah...stones of turquoise, foundations of sapphires, battlements of rubies, gates of sparkling jewels, and walls of precious stones.

"I've come home, Zach," she finally whispered. "I'm home at last...and I won't leave again."

He cupped her face in his hands and touched his lips to hers, at first tenderly, then with deep passion. "I love you, Molly Quinn," he said finally, his voice husky.

"You are my life, my love." She felt tears again fill her eyes. "How I love you, Zach."

Then, tilting her head, she smiled into his eyes. "But I have a question, Mr. MacAlister."

He arched a brow. "Does it have to do with becoming Mrs. MacAlister?"

She laughed softly. "How did you know?"

"I just had a feeling." He kissed her again, this time on the tip of her nose. "And to answer your question, the sooner the better."

He cradled her with his arm, and they turned to watch the

rising sun slant across the ocean. A spattering of sunlight spread across the rippling water, looking exactly, Molly thought, like a million precious jewels.

EPILOGUE

Carmel-by-the-Sea
June 1, 1909

AS THE GUESTS TOOK THEIR PLACES in the garden, Molly waited inside the back door of Mary Rose's little cottage. She was dressed in her wedding gown, shipped the week before by train from the San Francisco seamstress.

Mary Rose, dressed in an exquisitely simple wedding gown that she had made herself, rounded the corner to wait with Molly. Smiling, she stepped up to adjust the crown of silk roses attached to Molly's veil, then turned for Molly's help with her own.

"You look absolutely radiant," Mary Rose said, grabbing Molly's hands when she turned around again.

Molly smiled, thinking exactly the same thing about her friend. "Your dress is perfect," she sighed. "You look beautiful." Mary Rose had lifted her normally unruly thicket of curls into a stylish twist at the back of her head. Her veil was attached at the crown with fresh flowers from her garden.

"Isn't it a wonder to think about all that God has brought about in our lives, Molly?" Mary Rose looked thoughtful.

Molly gave Mary Rose a quick hug. "I think of the way God used you and Devon to bring us all together .." Molly's voice broke off. "And I am in awe," she finally said. "He was working it all out before any of us knew anything about it."

Mary Rose nodded, smiling. "And the best is yet to come, Molly. Isn't it a joy to think about what he's got in store for us all!"

Molly knew that she was referring to the changes in all their lives. The attention Devon's painting received at the Opera House Gala auction had boosted his sales. His income had increased enough to allow him to follow his dream of studying abroad with some of the world's greatest masters.

Just last week, he and Mary Rose announced that Devon had been accepted for a year's study at the Paris Institute of Art. The family was scheduled to sail for Europe by the end of the month. Molly was going to miss Mary Rose desperately, though she knew it was the opportunity of a lifetime for them all.

And Molly and Zach were about to embark on a new business venture. Zach had come to her with a partnership plan for their businesses, and Molly—stunned with amazement and joy—agreed on all counts. They put their plan into immediate action: Zach began shopping for a small fleet of boats. Molly, having sold her majority interest in QIL, began negotiating for another cannery. They would run the new company together, combining the best of what they knew of both businesses.

When Molly reminded Zach that he'd once told her he would never give up sailing his own ship to own a fleet, he merely kissed her on the nose, arched a brow, and said, "That was before I considered what I'd be missing if I stayed out to sea too long."

Molly's reverie was interrupted when Jesse tore around the corner, dressed in his finest clothes, complete with his first pair of long pants. "I'm ready!" he announced, grabbing Mary Rose's hand. "When do we go?"